HEGEL'S HERMENEUTICS

HEGEL'S HERMENEUTICS

 PAUL REDDING

CORNELL UNIVERSITY PRESS ITHACA AND LONDON

First published 1996 by Cornell University Press.

Printed in the United States of America

⊚ The paper in this book meets the minimum requirements
of the American National Standard for Information Sciences—
Permanence of Paper for Printed Library Materials, ANSI Z39.48-1984.

Library of Congress Cataloging-in-Publication Data

Redding, Paul, b. 1948
    Hegel's hermeneutics / Paul Redding.
        p.   cm.
    Includes bibliographical references and index.
    ISBN 0-8014-3180-8
    1. Hegel, Georg Wilhelm Friedrich, 1770–1831—Contributions in
hermeneutics. 2. Hermeneutics. I. Title.
B2949.H35R43   1996   95-25886

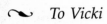 *To Vicki*

Contents

Preface

AT THE END OF the nineteenth century Hegel was an important presence in English-speaking philosophy, but the analytic revolution, spreading outward from breakthroughs in logic at the beginning of the twentieth century, appeared to consign him to history. Nevertheless, pockets of interest in Hegel survived, often in areas of philosophy in which social, political, or historical issues predominated. Thus Charles Taylor, in the final chapter of his 1975 work *Hegel*—a work that itself was to play an important role in widening such interest—could question why Hegel had continued to be relevant despite the fact that his systematic philosophical synthesis was "quite dead" and no longer a "live option." No one, Taylor asserted, believed Hegel's "central ontological thesis." Twenty years later, however, Taylor's presupposition about the death of Hegel's synthesis is not so obvious.

Since 1975, an increasing number of works have appeared in English which treat Hegel not simply as a rich source of insights about the nature of social life but also as providing an actual option for philosophy more broadly considered. To talk about a Hegel "revival" here might not be exaggerated, but it would be misleading, because the recent philosophical re-evaluation of Hegel has had little to do with any reanimation of earlier Hegelian verities and more to do with a reinterpretation of what Hegel's philosophy was all about.

The general philosophical ambience of the late twentieth-century English-speaking world has probably been important here. Like other revolutions, the "analytic revolution" looks rather different in retrospect.

First, like revolutions in general when they become a part of the past, it has necessarily lost much of its revolutionary look. Thus, the degree to which the work of Russell, for example, was bound up with and indebted to the perspective of his idealist teachers is now becoming evident. And, as is also common with revolutions, the actual outcome has appeared to many to have fallen short of earlier expectations. Thus apostate analysts, such as Richard Rorty, can reflect a broader if not so radically deflationary stance among analytic philosophers about the possibilities of analytic philosophy and philosophy in general.

But it has not simply been this "downside" of postrevolutionary analytic philosophy that has created an ambience for a reassessment of Hegel. One might see many of the developments in analytic philosophy in the last part of the twentieth century as leading to the sorts of issues its idealist pre-decessors were concerned with. Thus debates over "realism" and "anti-realism" lead naturally back to Kant, while the post-Wittgensteinian attention to the links between understanding, language, and social practice tend to point toward similar issues in Hegel's work. In general, such changes in the analytic scene have allowed some degree of rapprochement, not only with its idealist past, but also with contemporary Continental European philosophy, which itself has enjoyed comparatively greater continuity with its Hegelian past.

The interpretations of Hegel to which I refer cover a broad and complex range of approaches but tend to converge around a rejection of the kind of summary characterization of Hegel's "logico-ontology" offered by Taylor: "that the universe is posited by a Spirit whose essence is rational necessity" (Hegel, 538). The belief that the universe was "posited by a Spirit whose essence is rational necessity" is readily identifiable as "metaphysical" in the sense criticized by Kant as resulting from taking theoretical concepts beyond the limits of their proper usage. Accordingly, any interpretations of Hegel's work which deny that Hegel meant anything so metaphysical are commonly described as "nonmetaphysical"; understandably, such interpretations tend to see Hegel as a philosopher existing on *our* side of Kantian critical philosophy.

This, very broadly, is the framework within which I sketch an approach to Hegel's philosophy. Hegel is understood as a post-Kantian "Copernican" philosopher who, by appropriating and transforming ideas found in hermeneutics, another post-Kantian thread within German culture, was able to extend Kant's philosophical revolution. But although this book involves an interpretative reconstruction of central aspects of Hegel's philosophy, it is not meant to be primarily historical.

Somewhere along the road from first becoming interested in Hegel when I was a student to later attempting, in teaching and writing, to articulate and convey to others what I saw in Hegel's texts as worthy of their interest, I realized that one might actually relate to Hegel's philosophy as a "live option." And so this book is both an account of a general philosophical approach to the world that I find in Hegel's works and an attempt to present it in such a way that those works might be considered by others to contain a general philosophical landscape worth exploring and even possibly habitable.

I THANK A NUMBER OF PEOPLE for help and encouragement along the way. When I was a student, I was introduced to both Hegel and the traditions of idealism and hermeneutics by György Márkus at the University of Sydney. His was a dazzling introduction, and it provided me with the enthusiasm necessary to sustain the effort of trying to come to grips with Hegel's texts. In the years since, George has been very generous in his willingness to discuss seriously and sympathetically an approach to Hegel which clearly was diverging from his own. I have also gained much from conversations with others in the Sydney area, but, in particular, conversations with Ross Poole and Lizabeth During have helped me find my way around Hegel. More recently, Rick Benitez and Stephen Buckle have provided invaluable insights into the philosophical landscape, both ancient and modern, within which Hegel journeyed. Amir Ahmadi was a great help in preparing the manuscript, as was Peter Cook with the task of compiling an index.

During a short visit to the United States in 1992–93, I enjoyed profitable discussions on Hegel with Frederick Neuhouser and Kenneth Westphal in Boston, and attendance at a biannual meeting of the Hegel Society of America gave me the opportunity to learn from the greatest number of Hegelians I had ever encountered in one place. In Boston again, Peter McCormick offered very helpful advice and support. Work on this book was assisted by a University of Sydney Research Grant received in 1992. Lawrence Stepelevich, editor of the *Owl of Minerva: The Journal of the Hegel Society of America*, kindly gave permission to use material from two articles previously published there in volumes 22 (Spring 1991) and 26 (Fall 1994).

I would also like to thank the staff at Cornell University Press, in particular my editor, Roger Haydon, and manuscript editor, Teresa Jesionowski. Their professionalism, enthusiasm, support, and good humor have been greatly appreciated. Two anonymous readers for the press were enormously helpful in pointing out errors, opacities, misunderstandings, and hazards in the original manuscript. Here I was fortunate to receive the sort of feedback that allows one to appreciate how thinking is an essentially intersubjective activity.

Trying to do philosophy has its own peculiar hazards. Anyone who has read Hegel has learned about the danger of becoming entrapped within a necessary but limited aspect of thought which he refers to as *der Verstand*—the abstract understanding. If I have started to comprehend what might be actually at stake in this trap, this has largely been due to the influence of Vicki Varvaressos. From the example of her engagement with the world, I think I may have begun to get an inkling of the richness of its aspects—aspects which would have otherwise remained in some invisible beyond of my horizons.

PAUL REDDING

Sydney, Australia

Abbreviations

THE FOLLOWING ABBREVIATIONS have been used to refer to Hegel's works. In general I have given the page or paragraph number to the listed English translation, followed by the volume and page number from the German *Werke in zwanzig Bänden*. Where the German and English texts share numbered paragraphs, I have given the paragraph number only. On occasion I have modified the translation either in the interest of unification or to bring into clearer focus a dimension of the meaning of the text relevant for the point being made. In the latter case I have supplied the relevant original German word or phrase.

CJI   "The Critical Journal of Philosophy: Introduction: On the Essence of Philosophical Criticism Generally, and Its Relationship to the Present State of Philosophy in Particular." In *Between Kant and Hegel*, edited by George di Giovanni and H. S. Harris. Albany: State University of New York Press, 1985.

D   *The Difference between Fichte's and Schelling's System of Philosophy.* Translated by H. S. Harris and Walter Cerf. Albany: State University of New York Press, 1977.

EL   *The Encyclopedia Logic: Part 1 of the Encyclopaedia of Philosophical Sciences.* Translated by T. F. Geraets, W. A. Suchting, and H. S. Harris. Indianapolis: Hackett, 1991.

EPM   *Hegel's Philosophy of Mind: Being Part Three of the Encyclopaedia of Philosophical Sciences.* Translated by William Wallace. Oxford: Clarendon Press, 1971.

EPN   *Philosophy of Nature (Part Three of the Encyclopaedia of Philosophical Sciences)*. Translated by Michael John Perry. 3 vols. London: George Allen and Unwin, 1970.

ETW   *Early Theological Writings*. Translated by T. M. Knox. Chicago: University of Chicago Press, 1948.

PR   *Elements of the Philosophy of Right*. Edited by Allen W. Wood. Translated by H. B. Nisbet. Cambridge: Cambridge University Press, 1991.

PS   *Hegel's Phenomenology of Spirit*. Translated by A. V. Miller. Oxford: Oxford University Press, 1977.

RSP   "Relation of Skepticism to Philosophy, Exposition of Its Different Modifications, and Comparison to the Latest Form with the Ancient One." Translated by H. S. Harris. In *Between Kant and Hegel*, edited by George di Giovanni and H. S. Harris. Albany: State University of New York Press, 1985.

SEL   *System of Ethical Life*. In *Hegel's System of Ethical Life and First Philosophy of Spirit*, edited and translated by H. S. Harris and T. M. Knox. Albany: State University of New York Press, 1979.

SL   *Hegel's Science of Logic*. Translated by A. V. Miller. London: George Allen and Unwin, 1969.

SS   *System der Sittlichkeit*. In *Schriften zur Politik und Rechtsphilosophie*, edited by Georg Lasson. Hamburg: F. Meiner Verlag, 1967.

W   *Werke in zwanzig Bänden*. Edited by Eva Moldenhauer and Karl Markus Michel. Frankfurt am Main: Suhrkamp Verlag, 1969.

HEGEL'S HERMENEUTICS

INTRODUCTION

Hegel, Hermeneutics, and the
Copernican Revolution in Philosophy

THE BASIC THESIS advanced in this book is a simple one. Adding to the recent "revisionist" reassessments of the philosophy of Hegel, I interpret his achievement in terms of his ability to continue the unfinished revolutionary modernization of ancient philosophical thought initiated by Kant. Kant started the "Copernican" revolution converting ancient into modern philosophy but encountered a major obstacle because he lacked a way of thinking of intentional human subjects objectively. Hegel overcame this obstacle and advanced this project of transformation because he was able to borrow from an emerging style of thinking about such subjects—hermeneutics. Putting hermeneutic ideas together with Kant's Copernican philosophy, transcendental idealism, he was able to extend Kant's project of a modern postmetaphysical philosophy, a philosophy that stands in relation to the dogmatic metaphysics of its antecedents in a way analogous to that in which the modern scientific Copernican cosmology stood to its ancient geocentric precursor.[1]

[1] I use the term "metaphysical" here more or less as shorthand for the type of metaphysics Kant criticized as dogmatic. This is essentially how Hegel uses "metaphysics" when discussing "The First Position of Thought with Respect to Objectivity" at the start of the *Encyclopaedia Logic* (*EL*, §§26–36). One could with equal justification talk about Hegel's own metaphysics, with the understanding that he had freed metaphysics from its earlier dogmatic and "substantialist" forms. Here, I follow Klaus Hartmann in referring to Hegel's "ontology" rather than "metaphysics." See, for example, his "On Taking the Transcendental Turn," *Review of Metaphysics* 20 (1966): 223–49, and "Hegel: A Non-Metaphysical View," in *Hegel: A Collection of Critical Essays*, ed. Alasdair MacIntyre (Notre Dame: University of Notre Dame Press, 1976). As we will see, Hegel's ontology belongs more to the realm of hermeneutic or logico-semantic concerns than traditional "metaphysical" ones.

This simple thesis will almost surely strike some readers as simple-minded. Of the attempts to reclaim Hegel for philosophy, mine will surely look doomed from the start, for it attempts to annex what appear to be two contradictory approaches. In one, Hegel is seen as bringing the ancient philosophical project up to date; in the other, he is regarded as a hermeneutic philosopher *avant la lettre*.

Taken independently, the first of these two readings is worrisome enough. Although the view that Hegel actually achieved a modern and scientific—*wissenschaftlich*—philosophy essentially follows his own assessment of his work, any advantage accruing from this is surely overwhelmed by the congruent disadvantage—its sheer unbelievability. Even if one grants the intelligibility of the idea of some type of "absolute knowledge," the idea that Hegel had achieved it in the early nineteenth century could surely not be taken seriously. But even if such worries were held to one side, how could this view square with the idea that Hegel's work is "nonmetaphysical" in the way that twentieth-century hermeneutic philosophy intends to be? Isn't it the case that, despite its many internal sectarian differences, hermeneutic philosophy is a fundamentally *deflationary* movement with respect to the aspirations of the traditional philosophical impulse? One thinks here of the later Heidegger and of Hans-Georg Gadamer with their stress on the idea of thought as always grounded within historically given and linguistically articulated horizons, that is, that reasoning itself always rests on or works within something that is fundamentally *not* rational and so not to be assessed or evaluated *as* such. If one claims Hegel for *this* tradition, seemingly more "postmodern" than modern, then surely one contradicts the picture of Hegel as the modern achiever of something for which the ancients unsuccessfully struggled.[2]

How these two pictures of Hegel are not fundamentally incompatible is something I try to show in this book. Were the idea to be judged as massively misguided, I would of course prefer that this judgment came at its end rather than being made on the basis of its first few paragraphs; so let me say a few further words in defense of the mere idea of this thesis, before I start to fill it out.

One easy, popular, and very inadequate response to the charge that these two views of Hegel cannot be reconciled might go as follows: the triumph of rational thought applied generally (philosophically) and not just particularly (scientifically) consists precisely in the recognition that there *is* no scientific or quasi-scientific knowledge of "the general," or of

[2] Richard Rorty in his widely read *Philosophy and the Mirror of Nature* (Princeton: Princeton University Press, 1979) portrayed modern hermeneutics in this essentially deflationary way. See especially chapters 7 and 8.

"things in general," that is, things taken as a whole. The triumph is to *see through* the illusions that motivated the philosophic aspiration in the first place. Philosophy's final achievement is its self-annihilation.

This dialectical move, as unsatisfying as it is easy to state, does indeed reflect something of the shadow of Hegel's approach, but does not partake of its spirit. If we were to think of ancient philosophy as involved in a struggle with "unreason," let us say the mimicking of reason in sophism, then this move sounds like philosophy's capitulation. What this reply *does* capture, it seems to me, is the fact that philosophical reasoning can double back on itself and critically reflect on and so transform its own initial aspirations and presuppositions—that is, that philosophy is fundamentally self-reinterpreting. And because Hegelian philosophy involves the transformation of ancient philosophy's basic concepts, it cannot be thought of as representing some final triumph of that philosophy over its rival. But this "postmodern" move captures this type of self-reinterpretation too much from the point of view of the original opponents of philosophy, and so sees it as amounting to the collapse of the initial project. In contrast, Hegel's response to the failures of the traditional philosophical project was to reinterpret this project, and the war that it was waging, from the viewpoint of philosophy or reason itself and its real achievements. And to be able to conceive this combination of identity and difference of viewpoints required for the new interpretation of philosophy to count as an instance of philosophy was, on my interpretation, the core of Hegel's achievement.

This may not be much more satisfying that the "easy" dialectical reply first mentioned, but it is offered in the hope that its satisfies just enough to prevent too premature an assessment of the basic readings and arguments of this book. And with respect to this most general question as to how we should understand the nature of Hegel's philosophical advance, this strategy of the "just good enough," that is, of saying just enough to keep the reader from dismissing the thesis out of hand, will, I must admit, play a more general role in my account. Although it would seem appropriate to address head-on this issue of what philosophy could mean after Hegel, I am not going to do this to any great extent. For the most part the conception of what modernizing the ancient philosophical project would be like is left at the level of, at best, partially worked-out suggestions. What the bulk of the book is concerned with is an attempt to fill out, at a more prosaic level, my simple thesis—that of Hegel's successful continuation of the "Copernican" turn initiated by Kant's critical philosophy and the role of hermeneutic thought in this continuation. But in order to render even *this* intelligible in a provisional way, this sketch must still be filled in still a little more.

Kant and the Beginnings of Philosophical Copernicanism

Kant, in what may have been little more than a throwaway line, referred to his own critical philosophical method, as achieving a Copernican revolution in philosophy.[3] With this he was, of course, making an analogy between his role in philosophy and that of Copernicus in the transformation of the ancient cosmological world-picture into the modern one, the event which is usually taken as epochal in the creation of modern science. But Kant was also doing more than this. He was alluding to an analogy between the way that the positions of the sun and earth are reversed in the Copernican cosmological transformation and the way that the positions of knowing subject and known object are reversed in his own transcendental idealism. But, as Bertrand Russell complained, surely there seems something inappropriate about this metaphor—Kant should have "spoken of a 'Ptolemaic counter-revolution', since he put man back at the center from which Copernicus had dethroned him."[4] Russell's criticisms are illuminating because they exemplify a very particular and contestable interpretation of the nature of "Copernicanism," both scientific and philosophical, an interpretation against which a more adequate understanding of the significance of Kant's (and Hegel's) Copernicanism might be brought out.

Russell's charge had, in fact, been anticipated and responded to by the more sympathetic A. C. Ewing. "Just as Copernicus taught that the movement round the earth which men had ascribed to the sun was only an appearance due to our own movement," stated Ewing, "so Kant taught that space and time which men had ascribed to reality were only appearances due to ourselves. The parallel is therefore correct. Kant would, like Copernicus, say that this view was not more anthropocentric than that of his predecessors but less so, since it no longer, like their views, attributed to independent reality what belonged to men."[5] Ewing's defense of Kant here suggests that the *true* Copernican is the one who can, like Copernicus himself, escape the anthropocentrism of immediate experience by acknowledging it and reflecting on it. In fact, the difference between Russell and Ewing reflects very different understandings of what is at issue in the actual "Copernicanism" of the early modern scientific revolution and by implication in that of any philosophy that styles itself on it. As it is the understanding of Copernicanism implicit in Ewing's rather than Russell's

---

[3] Immanuel Kant, *Critique of Pure Reason*, trans. Norman Kemp Smith (New York: Macmillan, 1929), preface to the second edition, Bxv–xvii.
[4] Bertrand Russell, *Human Knowledge* (New York: Simon and Schuster, 1948), 9.
[5] A. C. Ewing, *A Short Commentary on Kant's "Critique of Pure Reason"* (Chicago: University of Chicago Press, 1938), 16. See also H. E. Matthews, "Strawson on Transcendental Idealism," *Philosophical Quarterly* 19 (1969): 204–20.

comments that is relevant for the understanding of Hegel developed here, it will be necessary to say a little more concerning this notion as relevant to both science and philosophy.

Scientific Copernicanism: The Problematization of Viewpoint and the Redescription of Experience

In contrast to earlier crudely empiricist concepts of the origins of modern science as resulting from a simple reawakening of interest in the observable world, more recent historians of science have placed greater importance on the theoretical interpretation of that experience. In its struggle with the classical Aristotelian cosmos, modern physics, it is argued, rather than emerging from experience of the world, was in many ways in apparent conflict with it. The emerging modern science had to employ abstract theoretical concepts in its problematization of experience.[6] The experience provided merely by "careful" and "unprejudiced" observation was itself no basis upon which the edifices of the modern sciences could be constructed.

One aspect of this problematization involved the "Copernican move." In this move some particular, previously unproblematic, experiential content is reinterpreted as revealing an only apparent rather than real state of affairs. The Copernican move does this by postulating the existence of particular *unexperienced* conditions of experience and then points to those conditions as themselves contributing to the nature of that experience. For the pre-Copernicans, experience demonstrated the daily passage of the sun around the earth. But this experience was brought into question by Copernicus: Might it not be the case that rather than us it is the sun that is at rest, while we observe it from the surface of a diurnally rotating earth? Would it not appear to such an observer, unable to observe his own motion, that the sun still passed across the heavens on its diurnal journey? In the Copernican thought experiment, the earlier real movement of the sun has now become merely apparent, as has the observer's earlier repose.

This Copernican move problematizes and denaturalizes immediate experience and, in directing attention to a variety of possible conditions, relativizes it. The "naive" observer is now assigned some definite place in the world, a place that *conditions* the way the rest of the world is experienced from it. As experiencing the world from a particular place in it, that

[6] Achieving somewhat classic status in this regard are Alexandre Koyré, *From the Closed World to the Infinite Universe* (New York: Harper, 1958), Thomas Kuhn, *The Copernican Revolution* (Cambridge, Mass.: Harvard University Press, 1957) and *The Structure of Scientific Revolutions* (Chicago: University of Chicago Press, 1970), and Hans Blumenberg, *The Genesis of the Copernican World*, trans. Robert M. Wallace (Cambridge, Mass.: MIT Press, 1987).

observer is now understood as having observed from a particular "point of view" or "perspective," and that which had been experienced from that point of view is now interpreted as somehow relative to it.[7]

Since the work of Karl Popper, Thomas Kuhn, and others, many have come to accept the idea that naive experience, as "theory laden," can never provide science with a certain and unrevisable foundation.[8] But the dynamics of what I have dubbed the Copernican move is probably brought out in more general terms in the accounts of the movements of *objective* thought put forward by Thomas Nagel and Bernard Williams.[9] In their accounts, objective beliefs or views are achieved via the reflective critique of more "subjective" ones. But here subjectivity is understood in a particular way: it is understood in terms of the idea of the *particularity* of the conditions under which the belief is formed, an idea expressed by the metaphor of the conditions under which one "views" the world—one's "perspective." Thus for Nagel, "A view or form of thought is more objective than another if it relies less on the specifics of the individual's makeup and position in the world, or on the character of the particular type of creature he is."[10] This means that "to acquire a more objective understanding of some aspect of life or the world, we step back from our initial view of it and form a new conception which has that view and its relation to the world as its object. In other words, we place ourselves in the world that is to be understood. The old view then comes to be regarded as an appearance, more subjective than the new view, and correctable or confirmable by reference to it."[11]

This Copernican approach gives a different gloss to the notion of "subjective" to that which it commonly carries in post-Cartesian philosophy. We should not think of subjective beliefs and conceptions, says Williams, as "totally unrelated to reality": a subjective conception is not illusory; it simply has features that are relative to a subject or a viewpoint.[12] The

---

[7] Here the thought experiment employing the analogy of the perception of motion by an observer located on a moving boat, an analogy used by both Copernicus and Galileo, is crucial.

[8] See, for example, Karl Popper, *Conjectures and Refutations* (London: Routledge and Kegan Paul, 1969) for a classic example of the nonfoundationalist approach. Indeed, as in the case of Thomas Kuhn, the historical study of Copernicus's revolution in astronomy provided a powerful impetus for the challenge to earlier empiricist and foundationalist accounts of science.

[9] Thomas Nagel, *The View from Nowhere* (New York: Oxford University Press, 1986), and Bernard Williams, *Descartes: The Project of Pure Inquiry* (Harmondsworth: Penguin, 1978) and *Ethics and the Limits of Philosophy* (London: Fontana, 1985).

[10] Nagel, *The View from Nowhere*, 5.

[11] Ibid., 4.

[12] Williams, *Descartes*, 241. This seems to be Williams's way of separating his view from phenomenalism or "representationalism."

tendency to think of subjective appearance as unrelated to reality is perhaps a result of thinking of the distinction between subjective and objective as itself absolute, but, as Nagel points out, this distinction is really "a matter of degree."[13]

Understood in this way, Copernicanism expresses an attitude to knowledge which is anti-empiricist and, more generally, anti-foundationalist. While not wishing to leave the realm of experience to ground its knowledge claims, it does not assume that any experienced content will provide a secure and unrevisable *foundation* for knowledge. What we experience is partly bound up with the *conditions* under which we relate to that which is experienced. We can theorize about *these* just as much as we can theorize about the *things* we experience, and so our theorizing in this former sphere might lead us to redescribe or reinterpret the "content" of our experience. Experience and theory interpenetrate: as each can provide a reason for the revision of the other, neither can play the role of ultimate foundation *of* the other. Theoretical change may lead us to redescribe our experiences just as new experiences may lead us to new theories.

Copernican Philosophy and the Post-Kantian Trajectory

Such an approach to the nature of scientific knowledge has, as is well recognized, a certain continuity with Kantian philosophy. Philosophers who have urged pictures somewhat like the one I am suggesting—for example, Charles Sanders Peirce, Wilfrid Sellars, Karl Popper, Jürgen Habermas, Hilary Putnam, Bernard Williams—all share in the opposition to simple empiricism by conceiving of experience as having aspects contributed by the knower. But all share approaches to knowledge *not* immediately obvious in Kant. Thus such thinkers usually stress the necessary *intersubjective* dimension of science: as we are finite beings with corrigible experience, we should therefore respond by countering the *particularity* of our experience and opening it to the correction of others.[14] But in contrast to this "corrigibilist" or "nonfoundationalist" approach, Kant himself thought that the "determinate" judgments of his contemporary science provided *certain* knowledge of the world.

---

[13] Nagel, *The View from Nowhere*, 5.
[14] See, for example: C. S. Peirce, "The Fixation of Belief," in *The Essential Peirce: Selected Philosophical Writings*, vol. 1, ed. Nathan Houser and Christian Kloesel (Bloomington: Indiana University Press, 1992); Popper, *Conjectures and Refutations*; Jürgen Habermas, "What Is Universal Pragmatics?" in *Communication and the Evolution of Society*, trans. Thomas McCarthy (Boston: Beacon Press, 1979); and Williams, *Descartes*. A central feature of a view of science such as this is that it provides a place for practice of the experimental control and manipulation of the conditions of experience.

When we look at Kant's writings, however, we find elements of the type of approach which stresses communicability and intersubjectivity. Kant typically fills out the idea of the objectivity of knowledge by appealing to those aspects of the *form* of experience which, as universal and necessary, characterize the experience of objects per se, thereby overcoming the particularity of the actual intuitive content which "fills out," as it were, the experience of any particular empirical subject. Thus, behind actual, psychological subjects there stands a formal generic structure common to all rational beings, the "transcendental subject of apperception."[15]

But there are places where Kant appeals to an approach to objectivity more like that found in Nagel and Williams by construing it as an *intersubjective* achievement. We find a clear example of this approach in the *Prolegomena to Any Future Metaphysics*, in which Kant distinguishes between what he calls judgments of perception (*Wahrnehmen*) and judgments of experience (*Erfahren*). In a judgment of perception, a subject attributes to an object qualities that are relative to the "subjective," that is, *particular*, conditions of its apprehension. Kant's examples are: "The room is warm, sugar sweet, and wormwood bitter."[16] One can validly say these things because they can be grounded in an actual perception. But one cannot say them with the expectation that "any other person shall always find it as I now do." Thus this validity is "subjective."

But the objective judgments of science are not like this. For those judgments: "What experience teaches me under certain circumstances, it must always teach me and everybody; and its validity is not limited to the subject nor to its state at a particular time. . . . I desire therefore that I and everybody else would always necessarily connect the same perceptions under the same conditions" (*PFM*, §19). For Kant, of course, this objectivity cannot be put down to the fact that such scientific judgments mirror the world as it is "in-itself." Rather: "The objective validity of the judgment of experience signifies nothing else than its necessary universal validity" (*PFM*, §18).

There are, therefore, two types of judging, one in which I "merely compare perceptions and connect them in a consciousness of my own state" and another in which I "connect them in consciousness in general" (*PFM*, §20). This "connecting" within "consciousness in general" suggests a *com-*

15 In a way somewhat analogous to this, Thomas Nagel talks of the "objective self" as a "part of the point of view of an ordinary person" and whose "objectivity is developed to different degrees in different persons and at different stages of life and civilization" (Nagel, *The View from Nowhere*, 63). Unlike Kant, Nagel does not think that this essential nature can be discovered a priori (61).

16 Immanuel Kant, *Prolegomena to Any Future Metaphysics*, trans. Lewis White Beck (Indianapolis: Bobbs-Merrill, 1950), §19. Further references will be given in the text referenced as *PFM*.

municative connecting. In cases of objective judgment, my particular judgment can be thought of as inserted into a social discourse within which it
can enter into logical relations with the judgments of other, differently
located subjects. The distinction between subjectively and objectively valid
judgments thus suggests that I may speak on behalf of two different au-
thorities. On the one hand, I may speak merely on behalf of myself (or
perhaps other similarly located judges) and, on the other, on behalf of the
entire community of finite but rational subjects.

A further suggestion of this intersubjective, communicative reading is
found in parts of the *Critique of Pure Reason*, despite its generally more
individualistic "Cartesian" framework. Thus, in the section "Transcendental Doctrine of Method" concerning "Opining, Knowing, and Believing,"
Kant distinguishes that way of holding a belief, "conviction"
(*Überzeugung*), in which the belief is justified by the fact that "the judgment
is valid for everyone provided he is only in the possession of reason," from
that of mere "persuasion" (*Überredung*), which "has its ground only in the
special character of the subject." In persuasion, a judgment is regarded by
a subject as objective despite the fact that it is only subjectively or "pri-
vately" valid, having its grounds solely in the individual subject. The
"holding to be true" (*Fürwahrhalten*) of such a judgment, Kant tells us,
cannot be "communicated" because no common ground can be appealed
to in order to bring about the requisite agreement (*Einstimmung*) of other
subjects. Such a communicative agreement forms a criterion for objectivity,
or more precisely, for the elimination of merely subjectively valid
representations:

> The touchstone whereby we decide whether our holding a thing to be true
> is conviction or mere persuasion is therefore external, namely, the possi-
> bility of communicating it and of finding it to be valid for all human
> reason. . . .
> So long, therefore, as the subject views the judgment merely as an
> appearance of his mind, persuasion cannot be subjectively distinguished
> from conviction. The experiment, however, whereby we test upon the
> understanding of others whether those grounds of the judgment which
> are valid for us have the same effect on the reason of others as on our own,
> is a means, although only a subjective means, not indeed of producing
> conviction, but of detecting any merely private validity in the judgment,
> that is, anything in it which is mere persuasion.[17]

Here, the securing of intersubjective validation for a judgment is clearly
put forward as a "subjective" alternative for the determination of objec-

---

[17] Kant, *Critique of Pure Reason*, A821/B849.

tivity to the more typical "objective" means, that of determining it in terms of the necessity and universality of those intuitions and concepts synthesized in the judgment. But it is in the third Critique, the *Critique of Judgment*, in the discussion of a further type of judgment—the "reflective" judgments proper to *aesthetics*—that the role of intersubjectivity comes to the fore.[18]

Reflective judgments are such that the synthesis of intuitions and concepts involved cannot be grounded, as can "determinative" judgments of science, in any determinate objective principle. I can never justify my judgment that *this* landscape, say, is beautiful by appealing to some general rule to which landscapes must conform if they are to be beautiful. Nevertheless, a *type* of objectivity is still possible here, the type that distinguishes true aesthetic judgments of beauty from those that deem things merely agreeable. Here Kant refers aesthetic taste to a kind of a "common sense," a *sensus communis*—a sense analogous to "a sense of truth, a sense of decency, of justice, etc." (*CJ*, §40). Common sense is the *ground* of the rational communicability of aesthetic judgments: it is a "power to judge that in reflecting takes account (a priori), in our thought, of everyone else's way of presenting [something], in order *as it were* to compare our own judgment with human reason in general and thus escape the illusion that arises from the ease of mistaking subjective and private conditions for objective ones, an illusion that would have a prejudicial influence on the judgment" (*CJ*, §40).[19]

Kant lists three maxims to elucidate the principles of common sense: "(1) to think for oneself; (2) to think from the standpoint of everyone else; and (3) to think always consistently." The second of these concerns the *broadening* of thinking in which a person "overrides the private subjective conditions of his judgment, into which so many others are locked, as it were, and reflects on his own judgment from a *universal standpoint* (which he can determine only by transferring himself to the standpoint of others)" (*CJ*, §40). This idea of "transferring [oneself] to the standpoint of others" had, by the 1790s come into prominence in German intellectual circles with J. G. Herder's notion of *"Einfühlung"*—"feeling into" or "empathy"—a notion taken up by the later hermeneutic tradition and offered as a peculiar

---

[18] Kant, Immanuel, *Critique of Judgment*, trans. Werner S. Pulhar (Indianapolis: Hackett, 1987). Further references will be given in the text referenced as *CJ*.

[19] As Rudolf Makkreel has recently emphasized, Kant also attributes a more general epistemological role to *sensus communis*, it being the basis of the universal communicability of *all* judgments. Makkreel argues that the notion of *sensus communis* answers problems implicit in the *Critique of Pure Reason* and essentially comes to play the role of a transcendental condition of Kant's critical epistemology. Rudolf A. Makkreel, *Imagination and Interpretation in Kant: The Hermeneutical Import of the "Critique of Judgment"* (Chicago: University of Chicago Press, 1990), chap. 8.

epistemological principle for the "human sciences." But as Rudolf Mak-kreel notes, despite this movement toward hermeneutics, Kant himself did not differentiate the "natural" from the "human" sciences.[20] In order to develop the notion of *sensus communis,* it would seem that Kant would have needed some concept of what it is to recognize the standpoint of another subject, but, as the advocates of hermeneutics were later to argue, from the viewpoint of the epistemology of the natural sciences, this is an entirely mysterious task.

Copernican Philosophy and Hermeneutics

It would seem that post-Kantian Copernican philosophy needed an ap-proach to the nature of the knowing subject that Kant lacked, an approach that *hermeneutics* might supply. By bringing together the issues of Coperni-can science and intersubjectivity, I hope that the general drift of the thought behind this claim has come at least partly into focus. The basic idea is this: in order *for* one to be open to the claims of another's experi-ence, another who is thought of as experiencing the world from within a set of conditions which are partially different from one's own, one must be able to conceive of that other both as an intentional subject for whom there is a world (or alternatively, conceive what the world is like from that other point of view) and also *as* an embodied and located "thing" within the world and subject to its conditions. But in his thinking about the subject, Kant seems still too "Cartesian" to do justice to this conception of others.

For Descartes, of course, the person was divided into two substances, a mind and a body, the former accounting for intentional life, the latter for intraworldly existence. Hypotheses about the pineal gland notwithstand-ing, Descartes had great difficulty in accounting for relations between body and mind. But it is not as if, in Descartes's conception, the body and mind were indifferent to each other. Epistemologically, the existence and effect of the body was very significant, but it was so in a predominantly *negative* way. Philosophy was faced with the task of freeing the mind from the effects of its contingent embodiment, a task translated into that of getting one's ideas "clear and distinct."

In comparison, by making human knowledge essentially dependent on the contribution of a passively received intuitive content and in ruling out the applicability of any ideal of experience freed from it by criticizing the idea of "intellectual intuition," Kant moved toward a conception in which the body and its situatedness had a more positive epistemological signifi-cance. Nevertheless, there still appears to be no way within Kant's philoso-

---

[20] Makkreel, *Imagination and Interpretation in Kant,* 166.

phy that one could really think of another person as *both* existing bodily within the world with the rest of its objects *and* making claims about that world as an epistemic subject. Qua object in the world, the other person is to be understood within the framework of the natural sciences, that is, as some sort of determined mechanism, and within such a naturalistically scientific conception of others the implicit *communicative* understanding of transcendental subjectivity could never be developed.

This naturalistic "scientific image" of human beings does not characterize how we for the most part think of each other in everyday life.[21] There we nonreflectively relate to other persons as somehow both embodied and enminded, and we somehow just allow these aspects to hang together in a rough and ready way. But here "folk psychology" seems in conflict with the sort of scientific view of the world we have inherited from the seventeenth century, despite the elaborations of and revolutions within this view.

It is not surprising, therefore, that since the seventeenth century there had developed a diversity of dissenting opinions anxious to maintain the more "humanistic" conceptions of everyday life and make them resistant to the naturalistic scientific critique.[22] In chapters 1 and 2 I sketch some of the background against which emerged that conception of "objective subjectivity" that I am here interested in, the hermeneutic conception of subjectivity. The humanistic discipline of hermeneutics emerged, of course, within a realm where the advantages of such a conception of others is obvious: developing from the self-reflection of practitioners of *textual exegesis and interpretation,* its milieu was precisely that of textually mediated communicative intersubjectivity. But, I argue, it could only emerge given the development of a theological background quite different from the one presupposed by the Descartes-Kant trajectory: this was the immanentist or pantheistic tradition. By the early nineteenth century, hermeneutics had become linked to those disciplines that took as their particular objects the existence and actions of human beings. And then, from the late nineteenth century on, more systematic efforts were made to fashion hermeneutics into a distinct nonnaturalistic epistemological doctrine adequate to the methodological and logical peculiarity of the "human sciences."

I shall have more to say about both the character of this form of thought and the types of internal transformations and critiques it has undergone up to the present. For the moment, however, let us remain with the issue of

---

[21] For a clear account of the specificity of the "scientific image" and its distinctness from the our everyday conceptions see Wilfrid Sellars, "Philosophy and the Scientific Image of Man," in his *Science, Perception, and Reality* (London: Routledge and Kegan Paul, 1963).

[22] Cf. Stephen Toulmin's attempt to temper the modern scientific tradition with that stemming from Renaissance humanism in *Cosmopolis* (New York: Free Press, 1990).

its relation to Kantian idealism. I have mentioned the impasse encountered at the Kantian conception of subjectivity. This was, I will argue (in chapter 3), recognized clearly by Hegel to be one of the crucially weak points, if not *the* weak point, of Kantian transcendental idealism. In fact, such a criticism is articulated clearly in Hegel's first published philosophical work, *The Difference between Fichte's and Schelling's System of Philosophy,* where Hegel deals with it as a central problem in the work of Kant's successor, J. G. Fichte. Fichte had, Hegel thought, been partially successful in characterising the human subject as embodied, that is, as a "subject-object." But he had been able to do this only "subjectively" from the moral point of view; what was needed was an objective conception of the human subject-object to complement his subjective one.

In this work Hegel believed that such a category was provided by his colleague F. W. J. Schelling, a philosopher who had up to that time been a follower of Fichte in his attempt to complete Kantianism. Schelling had, however, started to follow a path that seemed the antithesis of Kantian critical philosophy when he had attempted to revive the sorts of speculative metaphysics, especially speculative philosophies of nature, characteristic of earlier times. To many on this side of these bizarre decades that followed Kant in German philosophy, Schelling's turn has been seen as the sure way to that type of retrograde *uncritical* or dogmatic philosophy of which Hegel is commonly accused. In my interpretation, Schelling provided just what Hegel needed in order to break with the remnants of dogmatic metaphysics within Kantian philosophy. It was on the basis of his early Schellingian critique of Fichte that Hegel was able to elaborate a coherent account of objective subjectivity that allowed him to pursue the Copernican turn much more fully than Kant or Fichte had been able to.[23] Central to this was his development in the *Phenomenology of Spirit* of a concept that had been used by Fichte, the concept of "recognition" or "acknowledgment" (*Anerkennung*) of the other *as* a subject. For Fichte this had been a predominantly *practical* notion, but Hegel added an epistemic twist. One's recognition of another's intentionality will remain indeterminate and empty as long as it does not include an understanding of the content or object of the other's intention. And such understanding is internally linked to a certain kind of understanding of oneself as an intentional being with one's own intentional objects. This recognitive theory at the heart of the *Phenomenology of Spirit* is examined in chapters 4 to 6.

It is at this juncture that I might start to invoke some lateral support for my thesis as more and more attention has come to be focused on the

---

[23] H. S. Harris has argued for the crucial and lasting influence of Schelling's philosophy on Hegel's development in *Night Thoughts (Jena 1801–1806)* (Oxford: Clarendon, 1983).

significance of Hegel's theory of recognition. Scholars such as Ludwig Siep in Germany and Robert Williams in the United States have stressed the systematic role played by the notion of recognition in Hegel's early philosophy as well as in that part of his system dealing with human social existence—the realm of "objective spirit."[24] By linking recognition to the hermeneutic understanding of objective intentional subjects, however, I claim an even larger role for the notion of recognition within Hegel's philosophy than is found in such works.

If one work has been privileged in the twentieth century for revealing the "good" side of Hegel, it has been the *Phenomenology of Spirit*. This remarkable work indeed seems to have presaged a certain direction in subsequent European philosophy, especially the antimetaphysical direction found in the hermeneuticist philosophies of Heidegger and Gadamer. Here Hegel opened up domains of human experience to philosophical treatment that made the models of subjectivity found in earlier philosophers seem mechanical and contrived, and linked such modes of experience and thought with historically changeable forms of social life. The *Phenomenology* was indeed a book pregnant with much later philosophy.

But this work led, both chronologically and structurally, into a work that is often taken as paradigmatic of the "bad" Hegel—Hegel the dogmatic, "ultrarationalist," "pan-logicist" metaphysician. This was the *Science of Logic*. In chapter 7, however, I argue for a view of the *Logic* as the true successor of the earlier work. On examination it reveals the same reliance on the centrality of the figure of recognition as does the *Phenomenology* and the earlier Jena period works from which it grew. But this figure is generalized and diffused as it is put to work, systematically reinterpreting central philosophical assumptions from within. Furthermore, on my reading, the *Logic* is not so much "about" recognition, not so much a theoretical representation of some act or relation which it wants to put at the center of a new philosophical approach; rather, it itself constitutes a type of recognitive performance that Hegel hopes to initiate between himself (as writer) and the reader of that work. It is, I argue, within this framework of an expanded, hermeneutic concept of recognition, that the *Logic* articulates its Copernican image of what philosophy can be in the modern world.

Urging such a reading of this work now allows me to appeal to some more contemporary work for support for my understanding of Hegel as a

---

[24] Cf. Ludwig Siep, *Anerkennung als Prinzip der praktischen Philosophie: Untersuchungen zu Hegels Jenaer Philosophie des Geistes* (Freiburg: Alber Verlag, 1979), and Robert R. Williams, *Recognition: Fichte and Hegel on the Other* (Albany: State University of New York Press, 1992). Also of importance here is the study by Jürgen Habermas, "Labor and Interaction: Remarks on Hegel's Jena *Philosophy of Mind*," in *Theory and Practice*, trans. John Viertel (Boston: Beacon Press, 1974).

genuinely postmetaphysical philosopher, one who considerably advanced Kant's Copernican turn. Since the early 1980s, several interpreters have attempted, in ways that show considerable overlap, to develop a revisionist reading of Hegel's logic and systematic philosophy. On their readings, Hegel was not trying to construct, on a basis of pure reason, some general account that the world must live up to. Nor was he making some wild ontological claim that the world is, at basis, really a type of large single intentional subject—an "absolute spirit." Rather, Hegel's continuity with Kant is stressed, and the *Logic* is regarded as an attempt to construct a comprehensive categorial structure that will harmonize the various types of knowledge claims about the world which have come to be part of our nature as modern subjects.[25]

Such a view of Hegel as "category theorist" might be seen as complementary to the "hermeneutic" reading of the logic that I develop here. In fact, venturing a stronger reading of the relation, it seems to me that the category-theoretical approach *needs* the type of complementation that I am suggesting to be fully coherent. To break with the older metaphysical reading of Hegel, the category theorists have had to argue for a reading of this categorial structure as one that articulates thought that is in some sense "without a thinking subject." And yet the question of *how* we should understand this idea is seldom explicitly addressed. Bringing in the hermeneutic view at this point allows us to start to articulate a coherent reply. The structure of recognition allows us to view intersubjectivity *dialogically*, and it is this dialogical and internal relation between thinking subjects that allows us to conceive of thought that, while requiring thinking subjects, is strictly without a ("monologically") thinking subject.

Another approach to Hegel's logic and system which has some overlap with the approach advanced here is that found in the work of Michael Theunissen.[26] Theunissen shares with the category-theoretical approach to the *Logic* a rejection of the traditional idea that Hegel's position on metaphysics is a retreat to a pre-Kantian dogmatic approach. The *Logic*, accord-

---

[25] A major figure here was Klaus Hartmann, who advocated an interpretation of Hegel's logic as a "category theory." See above footnote 1. Other nonmetaphysical interpretations that, to varying degrees, take their bearings from Hartmann include Terry Pinkard, *Hegel's Dialectic: The Explanation of Possibility* (Philadelphia: Temple University Press, 1988), and Alan White, *Absolute Knowledge: Hegel and the Problem of Metaphysics* (Athens: Ohio University Press, 1983). Robert Pippin, in his influential *Hegel's Idealism: The Satisfactions of Self-Consciousness* (New York: Cambridge University Press, 1989), stresses the post-Kantian dimensions of the Hegelian project. Besides providing a very useful bibliographical essay on the various recent approaches to Hegel, Stephen Houlgate, in *Freedom, Truth, and History: An Introduction to Hegel's Philosophy* (London: Routledge, 1991), puts forward an interesting nonmetaphysical reading of Hegel.
[26] His central work in this regard is: Michael Theunissen, *Sein und Schein: Die kritische Funktion der Hegelschen Logik* (Frankfurt am Main: Suhrkamp Verlag, 1980).

ing to his reading, is critical of the project of dogmatic metaphysics as a search for some ultimate underlying substratum of the world. Focusing on the last of the three books of Hegel's *Logic,* Theunissen sees Hegel's theory as basically a theological one, the Christian concept of love providing the concept of a relation that challenges the model of relationality between things implicit in traditional philosophy, a model on which relations are conceived of as external and hence "indifferent" to their terms but which implicitly construe them as structures within which one term *dominates* another. But while agreeing that there are important links here between Hegel's logical and theological views, I believe that Theunissen's reading obscures the continuity between Hegel's logic and ontology and that of the Aristotelian philosophy that he is trying to modernize. The communicative relations thematized in book 3 of the *Logic* not only capture something about relations within a religious community; they also crucially capture for Hegel something about the pragmatic relations between speakers required for there to exist adequate *logical* relations between their thoughts. And as the conceptual thought of philosophy for Hegel represents a more encompassing form of thought than the essentially allegorical thought of religion, we should see his logic as explaining his theology rather than vice-versa. We might then think of book 3 as an attempt to schematize a philosophical pragmatics of philosophical reason itself.[27]

Focusing on the relations between the post-Kantian and hermeneutic dimensions of Hegel's logic and system allows one to raise the question of the *epistemological* consequences of his philosophical position and his relation to contemporary hermeneuticism. The "double action" of recognition is in essence Hegel's answer to the puzzle set by Fichte concerning the nature of self-constituting subjectivity. Recognition is not an act that is simply the act *of* a pre-existing subject. In being an act that constitutes the other in a determinate way, and in being by necessity reciprocal, it is an act that simultaneously *constitutes* the agent as such. Furthermore, it constitutes this agent, or subject, in a determinate way, with the sorts of

---

[27] In their most recent works, both Robert Pippin (*Modernism as a Philosophical Problem: On the Dissatisfactions of European High Culture* [Cambridge, Mass.: Blackwell, 1991]) and Terry Pinkard (*Hegel's "Phenomenology": The Sociality of Reason* [Cambridge: Cambridge University Press, 1994]) emphasize the situatedness of Hegel's philosophical project within the cultural framework of modern Western Europe. From such a point of view, the aspiration to philosophy is linked to the affirmation of a particular type of self-identity—the modern one of being a member of a community that can appeal to no *external* source of justifications for its beliefs and practices. One might see such a reading as providing a complementary direction to the one adopted here in that ultimately what is at stake in Hegelian philosophy is centrally linked to the affirmation or "acknowledgment" of a certain type of social identity adequate to the existence of the intentional dynamics of "thought" itself.

properties—epistemic and ethical competences, for example—that particular subjects have.

The role of recognition in its various forms in the constitution of knowing and acting subjects is seen most clearly in the *Realphilosophie* of Hegel's encyclopaedic system, in particular in the philosophy of objective spirit developed most fully in the *Philosophy of Right*. There in his treatment of the social institutions of modern life, the family, civil society, and the state, Hegel sketches the sorts of epistemic and ethical competences that are found within these realms. It is this work that gives Hegel's account of the finite epistemic and practical subject something of the feel of the more historicist approach that predominates in the hermeneutic tradition. Here Hegel plays the hermeneuts on their home ground.

It is not surprising, then, that many interpreters, isolating Hegel's *Philosophy of Right* from the system, are comfortable with it as a genuine contribution to social, political, and ethical philosophy, areas in which some form of hermeneutic thought has become most accepted.[28] But it is precisely the systematic *links* between this work and the *Logic* that allow Hegel to negotiate many of the traps that lie in wait for the more historicist approaches to philosophy that have come into existence since the nineteenth century.[29] It is the hermeneutic reading of the *Logic* which allows us to understand the systematic connections between it and the *Philosophy of Right* and to appreciate Hegel's profound relevance for many of the most recent debates found in social and moral philosophy. In chapters 8 through 12 of this book I attempt to sketch out, in a preliminary way, these sorts of connections between Hegel's theory of spirit, his nonmetaphysical logic, and his social and moral thought. By bringing Hegel's logical considerations onto the hermeneuts' home ground, we can understand more clearly how Hegel thinks of modern science and its relation to everyday knowledge as well as to philosophy. It also enables us to understand how as a culture we are related to, but different from, that culture from which many of our central ideas sprung, that of ancient Greece. And in allowing us to understand this, it allows us to understand how Hegel might have conceived of his own philosophical program as a type of inheritance of a past philosophy which, in attempting to be true to the spirit of that philosophy, transforms it from within.

[28] See, for example, Allen Wood in *Hegel's Ethical Thought* (Cambridge: Cambridge University Press, 1990) for an appreciation of Hegel as practical philosopher intent on splitting this aspect off from his systematic thought.

[29] Vittorio Hösle, in *Hegels System*, 2 vols. (Hamburg: Meiner Verlag, 1987), pursues the relation between the *Logic* and the philosophy of objective spirit in Hegel's system, raising the question of whether the former can be read as an intersubjective logic. But Hösle's presupposed opposition between "subjective" and "intersubjective" logics is one which, I believe, does not hold for Hegel's philosophy.

CHAPTER 1

Science, Theology, and the Subject in Modern Philosophy

LIKE MOST HISTORICAL FIGURES who have had the role of founder cast retrospectively upon them, René Descartes has come to assume an almost mythic status within the history of modern philosophy. The words *cogito, ergo sum,* recognizable in circles well beyond those of the philosophically literate, stand as a symbol for the peculiar significance that the multifaceted theme of subjectivity has had in modern thinking and reflection. I start the story of the genesis of Hegel's philosophical innovation and achievement at this conventional place in the history of philosophical thought, but confine the discussion to a few issues that bear directly on the subject. These center on the way Descartes attempted to make sense of that bizarre and puzzling product of early modern cognition—the new science.

I have earlier suggested that it was the problematization of the world as experienced in a pretheoretical or everyday way that was characteristic of the birth of modern science. Against the new and developing criteria for knowledge, the finitude of the embodied and located self and the associated perspectivity of its experience and immediate knowledge were grasped as a source of error. In contrast to the immediacy and perspectivity of perceptual knowledge stood the goal of aperspectival certainty for which one could struggle in the methodical application of reason.

Descartes captured the idea of such a rationalized view of the world, a view of the world liberated from the contingencies and conditions of embodiment, with that of the view of the world achieved by a mind unencumbered by embodiment and the perspectivity that goes with it. His conception of objective knowledge was indeed the prototype for what is now commonly discussed as the "God's-eye view" conception of knowledge. The knowledge for which we strive in science is the sort of knowledge that an actually disembodied mind has immediately—the view a transcendent God gazing at the world not from "somewhere" within it, but, as it were, from a Nagelian "nowhere." Such an idea of the knowledge natural to a transcendent God stood as a measure of the limitedness of our own immediate knowledge and a goal to which we could aspire via the self-discipline of *method*.[1]

Descartes's Response to Perspectivity:
Divine and Scientific Knowledge

In his *Meditations on First Philosophy* Descartes used the method of radical doubt to strip away those layers of prereflective opinion to reach what he believed to be the undoubtable nucleus of certain knowledge—his own certainty of his existence as a thinking thing.[2] This was not, of course, sufficient to re-establish the existence of the external world that had earlier been put in doubt. For this it was first necessary to establish the *existence* of a nondeceiving God. However, when the external world eventually was secured, now at the level of certainty rather than prereflective opinion, it had undergone a radical transformation. The new world was that which had been established from an examination of the ideas of perception in terms of their clarity and distinctness; and it was a world bereft of many of the qualities, the "secondary qualities" of sounds, colors, smells, and so on, which the perceiver had experienced as real prior to reflection.[3]

Why should the mind have been deceived into believing that these qualities belonged to the world itself? For Descartes there was certainly nothing essential about the mind that led it to fool itself in this way: it could *conceive* of the world without the use of secondary qualities, as it did, for example, in mathematically-based science. But while the understanding could think of things in this way, other nonessential aspects of the mind's operations—sensation and imagination—seemed tied to these deceptive secondary qualities. And while the understanding was the

---

[1] The theological dimension of Descartes's epistemology is brought out nicely by Edward Craig, *The Mind of God and the Works of Man* (Oxford: Clarendon, 1987), chap. 1. See also Karsten Harries, "Descartes, Perspective, and the Angelic Eye," *Yale French Studies* 49 (1973): 28–42.

[2] In *The Philosophical Writings of Descartes*, trans. John Cottingham, Robert Stoothoff, and Dugald Murdoch, vol. 2 (Cambridge: Cambridge University Press, 1984).

[3] Descartes, *Meditations on First Philosophy*, Sixth Meditation.

proper operation of the mind operating, as it were, *as* mind, sensation and imagination seemed linked to the fact that in us humans the mind was connected to the body.[4]

We can see, therefore, the importance for Descartes of the traditional theistic Christian idea of a transcendent and omniscient God. Beyond its role in re-establishing the existence of the external world per se, it was central in the establishment of the *nature* of that world. Reconstructed in its stripped-down version as a world of primary qualities, the new world was the known correlate of a particular kind of knowing mind, one transcendent to the world within which minds are otherwise embodied, the world known. We humans do not, of course, exist in this way, but as linked to a body. Thus we have to struggle for a knowledge of the world as it actually is. God, however, is such a mind. His knowledge of the world defines the goal of our struggle.[5]

Few now would accept Descartes's ontological argument for the existence of God, but buried in the third meditation is a powerful argument for the necessity of the *idea* of God; and this argument does have a counterpart in much modern philosophy. Having established with certainty the existence of the *cogito*, Descartes scans his mind for other ideas having equal clarity and distinctness. Ideas of material objects, other persons, and so on,

---

[4] The Copernican quality of this move to use the primary/secondary quality distinction to separate what is essential to the mind's activity from that which results from its merely contingent embodiedness emerges clearly when we juxtapose Galileo's use of it to a more typically Copernican move.

In *Dialogue concerning the Two Chief World Systems*, Galileo employs the well known "boat analogy" to bring out the mediating role the conditions of experience have for its content. If one is on a moving boat, and fixes one's gaze on the yard sail, does it appear to move? The point is made that the perception of motion is relative to the real relation between the perceiver and the perceived. By making the analogy to our perception of the sun, our initial experience of its movement and our rest is problematized. Galileo, *Dialogue concerning the Two Chief World Systems*, trans. Stillman Drake (Berkeley: University of California Press, 1967), 449 ff.

But in *The Assayer*, in his postulation of the distinction between primary and secondary qualities, Galileo questions the content of experience in terms of its *internal* rather than external conditions. Our experiences of tastes, sounds, and odors are likened to the titillation we experience when a feather is passed over the edges of the nostrils: such experiences are merely effects produced in us by objects impinging upon our receptive organs. Like the titillation, these "qualities" are located *in us* rather than in *the things themselves*. Galileo, "The Assayer," reprinted in *Philosophy of Science*, ed. Arthur Danto and Sidney Morgenbesser (Cleveland: Meridian Books, 1960), 28.

[5] Purified of the confusion introduced by sense and imagination, the clear and distinct idea of the wax is as a mode of extension freed from the bodily based characteristic "feels" of immediately perceived secondary qualities. This sounds as if in the effort to think the world in terms of the modification of extension—that is, in terms of mathematizable physics—we are aspiring to "perceive" the world in the way that God does.

he argues, might have originated in his own mind. As a finite substance, however, his mind could not have given rise to the idea of an infinite substance—God. Crucially, he argues that his conception of the infinite could *not* have come about by a *negation* of the idea of himself as finite. That is, to conceive of oneself as epistemically finite *presupposes* an existing idea of the infinite against which the finitude could be judged. "For how could I understand that I doubted or desired—that is, lacked something—and that I was not wholly perfect, unless there were in me some idea of a more perfect being which enabled me to recognize my own defects by comparison?"[6]

Descartes, of course, went on to link the necessity of the idea of God to that of that God's existence. But detached from its second step, the first idea has survived in the arguments of those realist philosophers who, combating what they see as perspectival relativism, have argued that the very idea that a knowledge claim is perspectival presupposes some norm or ideal of knowledge which is necessarily nonperspectival.

This idea, seen as appropriately freed from various unwanted aspects of Descartes's view, is essentially carried forward in Bernard Williams's well-known "absolute conception" of reality: "In using these notions, we are implying that there can be a conception of reality corrected for the special situation or other peculiarity of various observers, and that line of thought leads eventually to a conception of the world as it is independently of the peculiarities of any observers. That, surely, must be identical with a conception which, if we are not idealists, we need: a conception of the world as it is independently of all observers."[7] Williams's reference to idealism seems clearly directed at Kant because it is Kant who classically rejected the move made here from the universalizability of a conception—its independence from the peculiarity of any observer—to the world "in itself"—the world as it is "anyhow," independent of *all* observers.

Like Descartes, Kant attempted to characterize the finitude of the particular human mind by placing it in relation to the idea of one not so limited. But here, as we shall see, Kant specifically invoked a nontheological "infinite." And it seems to be precisely Kant's attempt to get away from some of the overtly theological aspects of Descartes's philosophy that led him to refuse the step taken by Williams and so to embrace a form of "idealism"—"transcendental idealism"—and reject the kind of realism—"transcendental realism"—common to both Descartes and Williams.

[6] *The Philosophical Writings of Descartes*, 2:31.
[7] Bernard Williams, *Descartes: The Project of Pure Inquiry* (Harmondsworth: Penguin, 1978), 241.

The Ambiguity of Kant's Response to Perspectivity:
Non-Theocentric Epistemology and Theocentric Ontology

Descartes's use of the idea of an aperspectival God's-eye view opposing the perspectival knowledge of the senses served two different but related purposes: first, it provided the idea of an *infinite* against which the finitude of the individual embodied mind in its immediate perceptual knowledge could be affirmed; second, it provided an interpretation of the *objectivity* of science in its distance from the realm of everyday belief. Both ideas could serve the cause of the new science in its opposition to the Aristotelianism of the premodern epoch. Negatively, the finite and perspectival nature of sense experience had to be affirmed to allow for its theoretically guided critique. Positively, since the new science did not account for immediate experience in the way the previous Aristotelian view had done, some new interpretation of the *type* of claims that it made was needed.

Kant's important move was to deny the latter equation of objectivity with divine intuition of the world from some aperspectival position transcendent to it. Such a fundamentally anti-theocentric move had, however, a complex effect on the first function of the God's-eye view. On the one hand, it allowed, as I will argue, for the idea of a nontheological "infinite" against which the finitude of any individual subject's cognitive claims could be measured. On the other, it reintroduced the theocentric conception of knowledge as a means of negatively characterizing the nature of that objective knowledge of which humans are capable.

In contrast to that of Descartes, Kant's epistemology turned on the idea that the human mind is essentially embodied. This is evident in the Kantian rejection of the possibility of "intellectual intuition." Because it is a condition of our knowledge that we are causally affected by the world in a way that provides us with the intuitive content of our experiences, we must rule out the goal of achieving a position transcendent to the world from which we could theoretically know it "in itself" in a way unconditioned by it. In Kant's terminology, we can never know "noumena," we only know things qua "phenomena," that is, things in relation to ourselves as knowing subjects.

And yet, despite our incapacity for intellectual intuition, we are still capable of scientific objectivity; and so some new interpretation of this notion other than the realist's notion of correspondence to the "in-itself" was needed. Kant's self-proclaimed Copernicanism becomes apparent in the new interpretation he supplies: objectivity is now dealt with not in terms of the mind's correspondence to an independent external object but rather in terms of the notion of objective *validity*. Although individual finite judging subjects cannot achieve a cognitive grasp of the world from a position entirely freed from its conditioning (the freedom characteristic of intellectual intuition), nevertheless, they can, as we have seen, escape the particularity of those specific conditions of experience separating each of them from all other rational, finite subjects.

As I have suggested, Kant provides two ways of thinking about the elimination of perspectival particularity in cognition: first, by the appeal to the universal and necessary formal conditions of experience *as such*, that is, to the structure of the "transcendental subject of apperception," and, second, by appeal to the *communicative* separation of "objective" from merely "subjective" validity. It is the latter conception that, so I have suggested, is at the origin of the nonfoundationalist epistemologies of Peirce, Sellars, Popper, Habermas, and Williams. Nevertheless, Kant still seems to have been forced back into the theocentric paradigm in his attempts to negatively characterize the objectivity humanly achievable. Knowledge of the world "in itself," the world of noumena, is dealt with as something we finite knowers are denied. As such, it must be a perfectly *coherent* notion, and so the God's eye-view idea of knowledge appears to be reintroduced at a "meta-level." We can put this in another way by saying that for Kant the noumenon is *thinkable* but *not knowable;* that is, one can have present to one's mind a concept of the thing-in-itself, but a concept that can do no work in articulating knowledge. Such a concept is an "idea" which regulates our cognition but which can play no constitutive role there. But with this thought of an intelligible but unknowable realm of the "in-itself," Kant's philosophy becomes a type of skepticism, a transcendental skepticism.

We might say, then, that with his idea of the thinkable but non-knowable supersensible noumenon, Kant had overlaid his non-theocentric *epistemology* with a theocentric *ontology,* or (translating this into a more recent idiom) with a theocentric (or "metaphysically realist") *semantics*—a semantics in which representations ("ideas") can refer to noumena despite the fact that nothing meaningful can be said about them.[8] Expressing this point in this latter way, we might see that the problem for the Kantian "idea" is much the same as that facing contemporary realist semantics, to which Hilary Putnam alludes when he asks the question of *how* such representations could possibly refer.[9] With respect to Kantian *concepts*, we can answer this question in ways that have come to be conventional—we

[8] Identifying "ontology" and "semantics" in this way is, I believe, justified in the context of a discussion of Hegel. Hegel identifies *ontology* and *logic*, and by the latter, as we will see in a later chapter, he includes the sorts of issues which are now treated under the domain of "semantics."

[9] See Hilary Putnam, *Reason, Truth, and History* (Cambridge: Cambridge University Press, 1981), chaps. 1 and 2.

might say that the concept has a use in the formation of true or false statements about the world. But Kantian *ideas* have no equivalent application: nothing intelligible can be said of their objects, and they cannot participate in true or false statements about these objects.[10] If they *do* refer, then they must do so in virtue of some "metaphysical glue" that attaches them to their noumenal objects independently of anything that is done with them. If we picture thought as structured by concepts, then we get an intelligible picture of how we finite humans can think. But to the extent that we could even have "ideas," that is, thoughts which, bypassing phenomena, can directly refer to noumena, then we seem to be capable of truly mysterious god-like capacities.[11]

One thing that we find in common between the forms of post-Kantianism found in hermeneutic thought on the one hand and Hegel on the other is an attempt to go beyond such remnants of theocentrism in Kant—those operating at a semantic or ontological level. And it is significant here that both hermeneutic thought and Hegel's philosophy emerged against a background of a type of heterodox religious thought that challenged the very idea of God implicit in the theocentric picture—the culture of pantheism. And so before resuming the story, we will take a short detour and consider briefly two theologically heterodox thinkers who were to have an effect on the transformations of German idealism between Kant and Hegel. They are the fifteenth-century Catholic cardinal Nicholas of Cusa and the seventeenth-century heterodox Jew, Benedict de Spinoza.

The Immanentist Tradition 1: Nicholas of Cusa

In histories of the scientific revolution of the early modern period it is now common to deal with the new science as not only having pitted itself against the geocentrism of Aristotelianism but also against the broader metaphysical structure of which this geocentrism was a part. Here the new

[10] For what I have described as the communicative post-Kantian position, the notion of truth is then cashed out with the use of the notion of "warranted assertability," thus avoiding the issue of "correspondence" to the world "in itself." This is in the spirit of the Kantian understanding of objectivity in terms of the notion of "objective validity."
[11] Transferred into the schemata of the communicative post-Kantian paradigm, this problem emerges as the problem of the conception of an ideal *telos* of our processes of rational communication—an idea that Peirce formulated with his notion of the "final consensus" of all rational communication—in which we finally reach Williams's "absolute conception of reality." As with the Kantian distinction between ideas and concepts, or noumena and phenomena, the idea of an ultimate distinction between some "final" definitive conception and actual and consensually achieved conceptions of the world seems to rest on a conception of a kind of knowing which is entirely unrestricted by conditionedness and finitude—the sort of knowing that a God as traditionally conceived *would* have, were there such a thing.

reflective and critical Copernican point of view is contrasted with the old unreflective and anthropocentric Aristotelianism. Recently, however, a different light has been shed on this history by focusing on continuities between certain heterodox elements of earlier Christian culture and the new science.[12] In particular, the fifteenth-century cardinal Nicholas of Cusa (also known as Nicolaus Cusanus) has been pointed to as a thinker who opposed the dominant geocentric view of the universe, even employing the thought experiment of the "boat analogy" found later in Copernicus and Galileo.[13]

To point to Cusanus's "Copernicanism" here is not to attempt to push back the origins of the modern scientific revolution to the fifteenth century. The heliocentric model after all dates back to Aristarchus of Samos. What was crucial from the scientific point of view was Copernicus's use of the heliocentric model in the solution of empirically generated problems internal to astronomy. In contrast, the context of Nicholas's claims was not really a scientific one. Rather than being motivated by internal problems of astronomy, Nicholas's criticism of geocentrism appears to have been motivated by more general metaphysical and theological considerations about the nature of the infinite as such. Thus, rather than being linked to empirically generated problems it operated at a conceptual level, bringing into question the very notion of any "center" to an infinite whole.

As the notion of a center is conceptually linked to that of a periphery, Nicholas' rejection of a cosmological center was also directed against the "Parmenidean" idea that an infinite can be bounded and thus known in terms of some determinate conception. For Nicholas the cosmos is infinite and acentric: its center is nowhere and everywhere (*OLI*, 2.11). And it is the critique of the idea of ever being situated at a "center" that can be applied to the epistemological correlates of Aristotelian geocentrism.

The Aristotelian unreflectively assumes the epistemological privilege of being located at the best place from which the cosmos can be known—its center. But for Nicholas the correct understanding of our location within the infinite must be based on the idea that there is no privileged location. The point that centers *our* view of the infinite universe is just one of an infinite number of points within the universe from which the rest of it can be viewed. We must thus understand that all views, including our own, are partial and perspectival. We must become learned about our ignorance.

[12] See especially Hans Blumenberg, *The Genesis of the Copernican World*, trans. Robert M. Wallace (Cambridge, Mass.: MIT Press, 1987).
[13] Nicholas of Cusa, *Of Learned Ignorance*, trans. Fr. Germain Heron (London: Routledge and Kegan Paul, 1954), bk. 2, chap. 12. Further references will be given in the text and cited as *OLI* followed by book number and chapter number. On Galileo's use of the boat analogy, see footnote 4 of this chapter.

We might thus see in Nicholas's thought an early form of another possible response to the Copernican issue of the perspectivity of experience. While this reflective grasp of the perspectivity of experience may constitute the same skeptical starting point concerning the givenness of experience as that found in Descartes and Williams, Nicholas's critique of the Parmenidean idea of the bounded infinite whole points in a different direction.

As we have seen, when considered in the context of the dynamics of post-Copernican science, the idea that all experience is perspectival seems to lead to the idea of a particular type of relation possible between different perspectives—the subsumption of the more particular and local, hence the more "subjective," under the more general, the more "objective." Thinking along these lines, we tend to think of different perspectives as related along a "vertical" axis moving from subjective to objective: at any point, a perspective will be conceived in a type of "meta" relation to the perspective below it.

But this is not the image of perspectives in relation to each other conjured up by Nicholas of Cusa's approach. His critique is not made in the context of a criticism of some actual account of the world, the hidden localness of which he discloses by the postulation of a more objective account. Rather, his opponent is the dogmatist who tacitly assumes that his or her own perspective is privileged. The aim here is to bring readers to the somewhat skeptical reflective awareness of the relativity of their own views, regardless of the content of those views. The image of the plurality of relative "centers" from which the world is viewed conjures up an image of perspectives all partially disclosing the world in their own ways and related to each other, as it were, more "horizontally" than "vertically."

And so Cusanus's argument, essentially directed to the virtue of toleration, focuses on the way in which different views on some matter might rationally coexist once the relativity of their claims has become appreciated. Perhaps the prototype of this sort of coexistence of differing "views" is to be found in Heraclitus's doctrine of the "unity of opposites." The road up is indeed the road down.[14] The single road is grasped as going up a mountain from the point of view of one traveler and going down from the point of view of another going in the opposite direction. Notions like "up" and "down" are, in an acentric universe such as that proposed by Nicholas, *relative:* they belong, along with "I" and "you," "here" and "there" and so on, to the group of subject-relative "indexicals." Differing perspec-

[14] G. S. Kirk, J. E. Raven, M. Schofield, eds., *The Presocratic Philosophers: A Critical History with a Selection of Texts,* 2d ed. (Cambridge: Cambridge University Press, 1983), 188.

tival views can, like indexical assertions in general, coexist without it being necessary that one eliminate the other.

The consideration of perspectives as related in this "horizontal" way is linked to another difference that differentiates Cusanus's thought from the type of thought found in Williams. The image of perspectives as related in a hierarchical or vertical way leads Williams to the idea of some all-inclusive and absolutely objective view that, in contrast to Kant, he identifies with a view of how the world is "anyhow"—in more traditional terms, a view of how the world is "in itself."

For Cusanus it is clear that, regardless of how issues to do with relative objectivity or subjectivity might be treated, there could be no view of the universe which was *ultimately* or *simply* objective—no "God's-eye view" or "absolute" view. This follows from his anti-Parmenideanism. For him there are no boundaries, and so there can be no "outside" of the infinite cosmological whole from which it could be viewed or known. There can be no "place" for any transcendent God, and, in keeping with this, Nicholas stands in the Neoplatonist tradition of Christian thought which veers toward an immanentist pantheism. The world, rather than being something separate from God and created by him, is the "emanation" or "explication" or "contraction" of God; the world, in a certain sense, is God, or an aspect of God.[15]

The absence of any "place" from which a God's-eye view of the whole of creation could be had tends to rule out the intelligibility of any determinate or discursive knowledge of the whole: "[D]iscursive reason gives names only to those things which are susceptible of 'more' or 'less'; when confronted with the greatest possible or the smallest possible, it is unable to find a name for it." And yet there is a *type* of intelligibility possible which grasps this whole as a unity: "[T]he absolute maximum is beyond our comprehension yet intelligible, able to be named whilst remaining ineffable" (*OLI*, 1.5).

It is within a symbolic or analogical form of thought that we are able to grasp the unity of the whole (*OLI*, 1.11). Cusanus draws on mathematical conceptions of the infinite, for example, to serve as a vehicle for analogical conceptions of the infinity of God or the universe. But the oneness of the

---

15 With the loss of the idea of a transcendent God such a conception cannot countenance anything like the epistemological idea or ideal of a "God's-eye view"—that image of a determinate knowledge of the whole necessary for the modern "realist" view of science. Whatever the grounds for criticism of any perspectival, experientially based knowledge claim, it could not be criticized simply in terms of a theoretical knowledge considered to correspond to the world "in itself." Even the appeal to the ideal of such a knowledge could not find a place here.

absolute One cannot be identified with *numerical* unity because the simple number "one" applies to things that are countable and hence finite.[16]

The relation between this absolute, prenumerical unity and the unity possessed by the enumerable finite things of the world is akin to that between a Platonic form and its finite copies. It is only in virtue of the mind's grasp of the absolute unity that there can be a process of enumeration of the finite. But of course such a "form" doesn't belong to a supersensible realm *beyond* the finite—it simply *is* the totality of the finite considered *as* a unity.[17] This has the implication that a finite thing is an image in which the primordial unity itself is indirectly brought into view: "A creature is not a positively distinct reality that receives the image of the infinite form; it is merely the image and nothing more, and in different creatures we see accidentally different images of that form." Every creature receives the infinite form in a "finite fashion"; it is a "finite-infinity" (*OLI*, 2.2).

Thus Nicholas rejects the "God's-eye view" conception of knowledge but retains some idea of an intelligible thought about the whole. But the ideas that make up the stuff of such thought have a peculiar logic indeed, and it is the concept of such a logic which will play a crucial role in the development of Hegelian thought. For Nicholas, if one conceives of God or the universe as the "absolute maximum," one will grasp that, as this idea falls outside of discursive reason with its countable more or less, such an absolute maximum will coincide with the "absolute minimum." That is, in thought about the One, opposites will *coincide*.

The Immanentist Tradition 2: Spinoza

We might then glimpse in Cusanus's heterodox ideas an alternative to the rather orthodox theological framework within which the scientific revolution was later appropriated within the Enlightenment.[18] But although the ideas of Nicholas of Cusa did not initiate any particular school of thought, there does, in fact, appear to have been something of a continuous countertradition of loosely related pantheistic ideas circulating within early mod-

[16] "Being capable of being added to, number can by no means be the simple minimum or maximum; unity cannot, therefore, be a number, though as minimum it is the principle of all number. Therefore absolute unity, where no duality is possible, is the absolute maximum of God himself. By the fact that it is unity as the absolute perfection, it excludes the possibility of the existence of another such being because it is all that it can be. It cannot therefore, be a number" (*OLI*, 1.5).

[17] The absolute is beyond perception in the sense that the whole to which one belongs cannot be perceived. In which direction could one possibly look to perceive the whole *as such*?

[18] We might even perhaps see it as a precursor to those contemporary forms of antirealist critiques of the "God's-eye view" conception of knowledge.

ern European culture with distinct epistemological, ethical, and political implications.[19] And whatever the early history of such ideas, pantheism was indeed to play a central role in the romantic background to German idealism.

While the ground for their reception within German culture was possibly prepared by the writings of the Third Earl of Shaftesbury, it was the irruption into German cultural life of the philosophy of Spinoza which provided a systematic challenge to the philosophical implications of theological orthodoxy within Enlightenment thought. In the 1750s Lessing and Mendelsohn and from the 1760s, Herder, had been influenced in some ways by Spinozism.[20] But it was Jacobi's revelation of Lessing's Spinozism in the mid 1780s that made Spinoza's pantheism, or "atheism" as it was considered, a public issue.[21]

As in the case of Nicholas, Spinoza's pantheism provided the framework for a systematic immanentist critique of the philosophical correlates of orthodox ideas of a transcendent deity. Rather than there being, as in Descartes, two substances of mind and extension, for Spinoza, the ideational order of mind and the extended, causal order of nature were the same substance (God or nature) grasped in terms of two different attributes.[22] In Descartes the idea of a transcendent God's mind could play the role of an epistemic ideal and measure of the limitedness of the finite mind because it was necessarily contained within the finite mind as an innate idea. In Spinoza's system, however, rather than the idea of an infinite mind being necessarily contained within the actual finite mind, the finite mind itself was conceived of as existing within or as a "mode" of an infinite one—its partiality defining its limitedness.

Qua mind, each finite subject consisted of a network of ideas belonging to a region of the total ideational network making up "substance" understood as divine mind, just as qua body, each consisted of a region of the total extended network of nature. We might see Spinoza's philosophy as having its own version of the Copernican strategy, but one operating with

---

[19] See Margaret C. Jacob, *The Radical Enlightenment: Pantheists, Freemasons, and Republicans* (London: Allen and Unwin, 1981).

[20] Cf. David Bell, *Spinoza in Germany from 1670 to the Age of Goethe* (London: Institute of Germanic Studies, University of London, 1984), and Frederick C. Beiser, *The Fate of Reason: German Philosophy from Kant to Fichte* (Cambridge, Mass.: Harvard University Press, 1987).

[21] In 1785 Jacobi published a tract *Über die Lehre des Spinoza* with which he meant to attack rationalism by showing how it led to Spinoza's fatalism and "atheism." Appended to this work were extracts from a work of the sixteenth-century pantheist Giordano Bruno, *De la Causa*, in which Bruno had himself reproduced in a summary way key arguments of Cusanus's *On Learned Ignorance* concerning the identity of the absolute maxima and minima.

[22] Or, as Henry Allison has put it, the two attributes can be understood as "different perspectives from which [substance] can be viewed." *Benedict de Spinoza: An Introduction* (New Haven: Yale University Press, 1987), 49–50.

different ontological assumptions from the post-Cartesian orthodoxy, and having different consequences.

For Spinoza as for Descartes, perceptual knowledge was limited by the particular contribution of the body. But, lacking Descartes's representationalist conception of perception as well as his dualist ontology, Spinoza's epistemology here seems closer to the type of approach found in Williams and Nagel. Perceptual knowledge is perspectival: it expresses particular states and relations of the knower's body. But given Spinoza's immanentist ontology, there could be no question of an ideal escape from embodiment per se. The escape from perspectivity would have to be interpreted in a way other than via recourse to the image of the view onto the world of some transcendent deity.

In Spinoza's system it is the *local* nature of perceptual knowledge, its centeredness in the perceiver's body, that is relevant to the Cartesian issue of the clarity and distinctness of ideas. Consider my complex perceptual idea of an external body—for example, the pen I am holding. This complex idea (visual, tactile, proprioceptive, and so on) will be that which, from my own first person point of view, that is, from my own particular region of the divine ideational order, corresponds to the complex modifications induced in my body by the pen itself: "The human mind does not perceive any external body as actually existing, except through the ideas of the affections of its own body."[23]

It is the *centering* role of my body which is relevant here in the epistemic inadequacy of my perceptual idea of the pen. First, my body, as it were, centers the pen on only one object out of the totality of that relational network within which it exists in the acentrically extended realm of nature. In contrast, a truly adequate idea of the pen would be that which was placed in the *totality* of ideational relations corresponding to the totality of the causal relations into which the pen, in its history, has been, is, and will be inserted. But my mind knows little of this totality. All it has to go on is the record left by the pen in the modifications of *my* body. There is a lot pertaining to the pen left out of my idea.

But my idea is perspectival in a further way: my perceptual idea expresses *more* than the pen because it expresses the nature of my particular body as well: "The idea of any mode in which the human body is affected by external bodies must involve the nature of the human body and at the same time the nature of the external body" (*E*, 2.16). Spinoza focuses on the complexity of the body as affected by the object. Today we might spell this

---

[23] Spinoza, *Ethics*, pt. 2, prop. 26, in *A Spinoza Reader, The "Ethics" and Other Works*, ed. and trans. Edwin Curley (Princeton: Princeton University Press, 1994). Henceforth, references will be included in the text and cited as *E* followed by the number of part and proposition.

out in terms of the complex and particular neurophysiological structures affected in perception. If I had a different physiological makeup, my perceptual "ideas" might be very different. And yet, as Spinoza points out, although the makeup of my body enters into the nature of my idea of the object, "[t]he human mind does not involve an adequate knowledge of the parts composing the human body" (E, 2.24; cf. 2.27). I do not need to know about neurophysiology in order to see, feel, hear, and so on, but without this knowledge, how could I appreciate the degree and nature of my contribution to the idea of the pen? And so I enter into my idea of the pen not only, as it were, negatively, as an excluder of its relations to things other than me, but also positively, as the contributing center of its relations to me. And so: "The ideas of the affections of the human body, insofar as they are related only to the human mind, are not clear and distinct, but confused" (E, 2.28).

For Spinoza, such ideas do not have the somewhat skeptical consequences that they had for Nicholas of Cusa. Knowledge can aspire to a non-indexical and non-perspectival telos; a comprehensive and systematic knowledge of the whole, "the intellectual love of God" stands as the goal of the sort of reflective overcoming of perspectivism achievable in scientific thought. But this knowledge aimed at cannot be thought of as the epistemic possession of a type of infinite conscious subject. The movement toward objectivity is rather a type of progressive breaking down of the distinction between self and the world. For Spinoza, the anthropomorphisms of those personalist theologies that view God as a type of infinite being but like ourselves, a human writ large, are superstitious and naive.

Hegel, Leibniz, and the Limits of Spinozistic Pantheism

Writing in 1833, half a century after the outbreak of the "pantheism dispute," Heinrich Heine could describe pantheism as the "open secret" of his contemporary German culture.[24] Like many others of his generation, Hegel was heir to the influence of "immanentists" such as Cusanus and Spinoza, and his philosophy was to develop in ways that appropriated this form of thought while maintaining a critical distance from it, a distance created by the Kantian critical philosophy.

In Hegel's case, Spinozistic and Cusan elements, reflected through the speculative thought of Schelling, would play a crucial role in his development from around 1800 up until the publication of his first major work, the

[24] "No one says it, but everybody knows it: pantheism is the open secret of Germany." Heinrich Heine, Religion and Philosophy in Germany, trans. John Snodgrass (Boston: Beacon Press, 1959), 79.

Phenomenology of Spirit, in 1807. But there he would record his distance from any such monistic conception of the absolute with his famous comparison of it to a "night in which all cows are black" (*PS,* §16; *W,* 3:22). As I will argue, he was to break with such a monistic metaphysics by transforming it from within with an innovative *hermeneutic* reading of Schelling's own "identity philosophy." But to get a fore-conception of what will be at issue here, it may be useful to look briefly to Hegel's own mature understanding of what he saw as the limits of Spinozism as presented in the *Science of Logic,* and in particular, at his brief comments concerning the way the Leibnizian, perspectival conception of the monad offered a way beyond those limits.[25]

In his interpretation of Spinozism at the end of book 2 of the *Logic,* Hegel reiterates the point expressed in the *Phenomenology* with the metaphor of the absolute as the "night in which all cows are black." "The substance of this system," he asserts, "is *one* substance, one indivisible totality; there is no determinateness that is not contained and dissolved *'angelöst'* in this absolute" (*SL,* 536; *W,* 6:195). And, as in the *Phenomenology,* he points to the radically eliminative consequences this had for the role of the subject within Spinozism, and links all this to Spinoza's restriction of thought to the level of "external reflection."[26]

With this latter point, Hegel alludes to the formality of Spinoza's "geometric" method in which the system is supposedly deduced from the starting point of the definition of substance as self-grounding, or *"causa sui."* But this "externality," or "formality," of method, Hegel seems to think, is in contradiction with the intended immanentism of Spinoza's philosophy: despite his conception of a unitary absolute substance to which thought is immanent, Spinoza still implicitly appeals to a form of thought which is dichotomously opposed to any conceivable form of thought found *within* substance.

Within substance we find only the thinking of human subjects conceived as "finite modes" of substance, and such a perspectival form of thought is

[25] Here I make no claims to evaluate either the accuracy of Hegel's own interpretation of Spinoza or the adequacy of his criticisms. For a synoptic reconstruction and evaluation of Hegel's critique from a Spinozist point of view see Yirmiyahu Yovel, *Spinoza and Other Heretics: The Adventures of Immanence* (Princeton: Princeton University Press, 1989), chap. 2.
[26] One of the standard objections that Hegel brings against other philosophers is that they exhibit a *formal* conception of reason, a conception articulated at the level of the form of thought only. As the one form of reason is applied to whatever subject matter is at hand, form is thus external or "indifferent" to content. On this view, therefore, reasoning will be seen as a matter of moving between truths, of which some will be able to be established in their independence *as* truths. It will therefore have a pre-Copernican or Aristotelian flavor: as a process of moving in a linear fashion from some already established truth to some new truth, reasoning will seek some initial point of certainty in which a chain of truth-preserving inference can be grounded.

dichotomously opposed to the aperspectivism of thought sub speciae aeternitatis. But Hegel now appeals to the Leibnizian monad as a way beyond this dichotomy: "The lack of reflection-into-itself, from which both the Spinozistic exposition of the absolute and the emanation theory suffer, is made good in the notion of the Leibnizian monad" (*SL*, 539; *W*, 6:198).

Here Hegel is appealing to Leibniz's conception of the monad as containing the absolute within itself as reflected from a particular perspective, or "point de vue." For Leibniz " every individual substance expresses the whole universe in its own manner" and " is like an entire world and like a mirror of God, or indeed of the whole world it portrays, each one in its own fashion; almost as the same city is variously represented according to the various situations of him who is regarding it."[27] For Hegel, the individual substance or monad is "one, a negative reflected into itself [ein *Eins, ein in sich reflektiertes Negatives*]; . . . the totality of the content of the world" but also something particular and determinate such that "the determinateness falls in the particular content and the way and manner of its manifestation" (*SL*, 539; *W*, 6:198). Thus there is between Spinoza and Leibniz a subtle but crucial change of focus in how the perspectivity of cognition is understood: whereas Spinoza thinks of the perspectivity of the finite mode entirely *negatively*, as something merely limiting the achievement of the "view from nowhere," Leibniz understands it positively as well, as the way in which a particular monad reflects "the absolute."

Leibniz's move, however, comes only at a cost to Spinoza's immanentism. Monads are "windowless," but there must be a general harmony between the differently perspectival monads themselves, and so Leibniz appeals to a transcendent creator: "[S]ince limited entities exist only as related to other limited entities, yet the monad is at the same time a self-enclosed absolute, the *harmony* of these limitations, that is, the relation of the monads to one another, falls outside them and is likewise pre-established by another being" (*SL*, 539; *W*, 6:199).[28] Nevertheless, it would seem clear that any way beyond the impasse of Spinozism would, on the one hand, have to be true to the Leibnizian *positive* conception of the perspectivism of cognition and, on the other, be able to account for the harmony between perspectival subjects without appeal to some transcendent intentional creator responsible for that harmony. The monads will

---

[27] Gottfried Leibniz, *Discourse on Metaphysics*, §IX, in Leibniz, *Discourse on Metaphysics / Correspondence with Arnauld / Monadology*, trans. George R. Montgomery (La Salle: Open Court, 1973). See also *Monadology*, §57.

[28] For Leibniz, Hegel writes, "the concepts concerning the distinction between the various finite monads and their relation to their absolute do not originate out of this being [that is, the monad] itself, or not in an absolute manner, but are the product of ratiocinative, dogmatic reflection and therefore have not achieved an inner coherence" (*SL*, 540).

have to be conceived in such a way that rather than being simply externally determined as harmonizing, they somehow collectively achieve a
harmony among themself. Such a way beyond both Spinoza and Leibniz
Hegel saw as the task of his own philosophy. And in attempting this he
could draw on the way that hermeneutic thinkers had developed the
Leibnizian notion of the "point of view."

CHAPTER 2

The Pathways of
Hermeneutic Philosophy

IF PANTHEISM WAS, as Heine had claimed, the "open secret" of Germany in the first third of the nineteenth century, then, as Hans-Georg Gadamer has pointed out, this was particularly true of German hermeneutic-historical thought.[1] We can easily see how a presupposed pantheist, or immanentist, framework might have been congenial to the originators of hermeneutics. Hermeneutic thought, originally concerned with the interpretation of ancient texts, came to be applied to the understanding of other societies. It was meant to capture what it was like to live *within* some other, distant society, to understand the world and act in it from the point of view characteristic of that society. It was this capacity to project oneself into some point of view onto the world different from one's own that Herder described as *Einfühlung*—"empathy."

Pantheism and Hermeneutics

In the mid-eighteenth century, Johann Chladenius, a German clergyman with an interest in history, had already sketched out the basis for a distinct ontology for the social world. In contrast to the merely physical events of nature were the "moral" events brought about by the voluntary actions of intelligent human beings: "The things which happen in the world are of both a physical and a moral nature. The former refers to changes of body

[1] Hans-Georg Gadamer, *Truth and Method*, 2d rev. ed., translation revised by Joel Weinsheimer and Donald G. Marshall (New York: Crossroad, 1992), 209–12.

and is generally perceived by the senses; whereas the latter happens through human will and understanding."[2]

Chladenius's way of distinguishing these realms anticipated the distinction, popularized in our time by analytic philosophers such as Elizabeth Anscombe and John Searle, between "brute" and "institutional" facts.[3] The Chladenean moral realm is a realm of institutions made up of "offices, titles, rights, grievances, privileges, and all such things which are created and abolished again through man's volition" (*HR*, 64). Associated with this ontological peculiarity is the peculiar epistemological status of knowledge of this realm: while the events of the physical world can be known through the senses, those of the moral realm require *reason*.[4] Such a distinction was to mature in the nineteenth century into that between the causal *explanation* (*Erklären*), on the one hand, and hermeneutic *understanding* (*Verstehen*), on the other. The notion of some particular event having a *meaning* for its agents—as "counting as" something—is the crucial idea here. For the hermeneutic social thinkers who followed on from Chladenius, just as for Searle, these relations of meaning were conventional—"rule governed"—rather than natural or causal: they hold only in virtue of the fact that they are understood by subjects *as* so holding.[5]

Chladenius also brought to bear the Leibnizian notion of "perspective" or "viewpoint" (*Sehepunkt*) to express the idea of some determinate set of epistemological conditions influencing interpretation: "We shall designate the term viewpoint to refer to those conditions governed by our mind, body, and entire person which make or cause us to conceive of something in one way or another" (*HR*, 66).[6]

The metaphor of viewpoint, while based on the idea of one's field of

---

[2] From Johann Chladenius, *Introduction to the Correct Interpretation of Reasonable Discourses and Writings* (1742), trans. Carrie Asman-Schneider in *The Hermeneutics Reader*, ed. Kurt Mueller-Vollmer (Oxford: Blackwell, 1986), 64. Further references will be given in the text and cited as *HR* followed by page number.

[3] Cf. John Searle, *Speech Acts* (Cambridge: Cambridge University Press, 1969), 50–53.

[4] "The things which happen in the world are of both a physical and moral nature. The former refers to changes of body and is generally perceived by the senses; whereas the latter happens through human will and understanding. . . . These moral things . . . must be perceived through reason" (*HR*, 64).

Similarly, Searle sees the facts of the institutional/moral realm as grasped only against a background understanding of the institutions involved. For institutional facts, the "physical events and raw feels only count as such events given certain other conditions and against a background of certain kinds of institutions." *Speech Acts*, p. 51.

[5] "These 'institutions' are systems of constitutive rules. Every institutional fact is underlain by a (system of) rule(s) of the form 'X counts as Y in context C'." Searle, *Speech Acts*, 51–52.

[6] Chladenius, like many after him, attributes the origin of the "viewpoint" concept to Leibniz. Leibniz himself, however, was well aware of the work of Cusanus, and so the hermeneutic idea of point of view may indeed have Cusan origins.

vision from a *spatial* location, was easily extended to include the institutional or "moral" conditions of experience as well.[7] Thus he notes, "A
rebellion is perceived one way by a loyal subject, a rebel perceives it
another way, a foreigner or a person from court will perceive it still another
way" (*HR*, 66). That is, within the "moral" or institutional realm,
differences in perspective will encompass differences concerning what
things, persons, and events are to "count as." The forces of person A may
be routed, but this only counts as a "rebellion" if A were the legitimate
occupier of a particular institutionally defined role, say the "king."[8] Later
in the century, Edmund Burke would famously criticize that revolutionary
philosophy which sought to strip human life of its "decent drapery . . . the
superadded ideas, furnished from the moral imagination"—that is, those
conventional rules determining what Heidegger has called the "hermeneutic as-structure" of the world.[9] Within such a "mechanical" philosophy, "a king is but a man; a queen is but a woman. . . . Regicide, and
parricide, and sacrilege, are but fictions of superstition. . . . The murder of
a king, or a queen, or a bishop, or a father, are only common homicide."[10]

In Germany, toward the end of the eighteenth century such ideas of a
distinct type of social substance were integrated with pantheism in the
social thought initiated by J. G. Herder.[11] For the traditional pantheist, the
world as a whole embodied a type of mind—the mind of God. But the new
conception of the social realm, with its idea that the concepts in terms of
which things were understood were actually *objectified* in the patterns and
institutions of social life, gave the idea of a "mind-like" objective world a
new meaning.[12] Such connotations of social reality as a type of mind-like

[7] Chladenius introduced the idea of knowledge from a viewpoint in a literal way to draw
attention to the perspectivity of all historical accounts. Three differently positioned spectators
observe a battle, one near the right flank, the second near the left, and the third from some
distance behind. The first and the second will have different accounts as each "will claim to
have perceived certain happenings that the other person will not concede to have witnessed
but will hold instead to something imagined. For the small changes and turns of a throng of
soldiers appear quite differently from a distance than from up close" (*HR*, 66).
[8] Here, abstracting from particularity to generality—describing the event as, say, the killing
of a man—will clearly not solve the disagreement, as in these cases disagreement is not over
the brute fact, the event itself, but its interpretation in terms of the background institutional
order; it is over that which Chladenius refers to as the *concept* of the event.
[9] Martin Heidegger, *Being and Time*, trans. John Macquarrie and Edward Robinson (Oxford:
Blackwell, 1967), 200–201. Hereafter abbreviated *BT*.
[10] Edmund Burke, *Reflections on the Revolution in France* (Harmondsworth: Penguin, 1969),
171.
[11] On the interweaving of Herder's pantheism and the philosophy of mind behind his approach to history, see Frederick C. Beiser, *The Fate of Reason: German Philosophy from Kant to
Fichte* (Cambridge, Mass.: Harvard University Press, 1987).
[12] Furthermore, such historically actual communities could be seen as having the sort of
primordial and irreducible individuality of the Neoplatonic "one"—each having its own

substance were embraced in the notion, popularized by Herder, of the distinctive *spirit* (*Geist*) embodied by any particular community.

In *Another Philosophy of History* (*Auch eine Philosophie der Geschichte*) (1774) and then in *Ideas towards the Philosophy of the History of Mankind* (*Ideen zur Philosophie der Geschichte der Menschheit*) (1784–91) Herder sketched his conception of the social historical world in terms that would be taken up by the romantic German historians of the following century. Although it wasn't until 1787, after the outbreak of the "pantheism dispute," that Herder produced an explicit account of his own vitalistically modified pantheist position in *God: Some Conversations* (*Gott, Einige Gespräche*), the general flavor of pantheism was implicit in the anti-dualism of the earlier works.[13]

The notions of spirit and viewpoint emerging in such developments in the late eighteenth century would provide a framework for a distinctive hermeneutic epistemology. For Herder, to interpret the events of a society different from one's own, one had to project oneself imaginatively *into* its spirit or viewpoint. Significantly, as has been noted by Frederick Beiser, Herder's notion of empathy was first developed in a discussion of the nature of *literary criticism* and only then generalized to historical understanding: "Just as a critic must judge a work according to the purpose of the author, so the historian must understand an action according to the intention of the agent. He must know not only the causes of the action (the conditions that make it necessary according to natural laws), but also the reasons for it (the values and beliefs that justify it in the eyes of the agent himself). No less than the critic, then, the historian must sympathize with the agent and identify with the language, customs, and values of his culture."[14] Indeed, such a process of projection or "divination" came to be seen as the aim of the developing philological sciences.[15] It was on the

unique "spirit" or "*Geist*," as the historian Leopold von Ranke later expressed it, each being a "thought of God." Furthermore, the pantheistic image of a loss or absorption of the particular self into the divine whole provided a convenient image for the nature of the *objectivity* of the knowledge here sought. Ranke, in reflecting on the goal of historiographical objectivity, equated it with the achievement of a type of self-extinction on the part of the historian.

[13] Andrew Weeks traces some of the links between Herder and the German mystical tradition in *German Mysticism: From Hildegard of Bingen to Ludwig Wittgenstein* (Albany: State University of New York Press, 1993).

[14] Beiser, *The Fate of Reason*, 142. The notion of "sympathy" had become popular in the aesthetic context in the early eighteenth century in an attempt to account for the effects of dramatic representation on an audience. See David Marshall, *The Surprising Effects of Sympathy* (Chicago: University of Chicago Press, 1988).

[15] Friedrich Schleiermacher, for example, claimed that there were two separate aspects involved in understanding the words of another: on the one hand, the necessary understanding of the grammar of the language shared, and, on the other, the principle of psychological "divination." See, for example, F. D. E. Schleiermacher, *Hermeneutics: The Handwritten Manu-*

basis of an interpretative immersion in some culture's products, importantly its linguistic texts, that one achieved this projection. In contrast to the cold "objectivizing" rationality of the Enlightenment, this type of empathy with, or "feeling into," the other culture required the mobilization of capacities that the rationalist tradition had vilified because of their tie to embodiment and particularity: the capacities of imagination and feeling.[16] That is, the type of knowledge aimed at here concerned that which Thomas Nagel has referred to as the "subjectivity" of a perspective, the "what it is like to be" the occupant of such a perspective or viewpoint.[17] The young Hegel later expressed this Herderian idea of empathy when he wrote in 1795–96: "We share in the interesting fate of unknown and even fictitious persons, we sorrow and rejoice with them; we feel in ourselves the injustice encountered by an Iroquois."[18]

This loosely woven fabric of ideas—that of a nonmechanistic, conventionalist social ontology allowing for the plurality of human life-forms, the extension of the idea of a perspective from a physical to a cultural notion that this social ontology allowed, the idea of a form of knowledge which captured the "subjectivity" of other perspectives, and the tendency to relativism—formed the philosophical cloth from which the broadly hermeneutic approaches to historical inquiry of the so-called German Historical School could be cut.[19] But this fabric could be held together only in virtue of developments opened up by a confluence of Kantian philosophy and the newly emerging discipline of *philology*, developments which gave new conceptions of the nature and conditions of subjectivity and which drew heavily on the implicit *communicative* treatment of subjectivity in Kant.

Romanticism, Language, and Subjectivity

The complexity of the romantic "philological" transformation of Kantian Copernicanism is clearly manifest in the attempts to "linguisticize" the structure of subjectivity, which followed hard upon the heels of Kant's

scripts, trans. James Duke and Jack Forstman (Missoula, Mont.: Scholars Press, 1977).

[16] Herder's direction to the historian was to "go into the age, into the region, into the whole of history, feel yourself into everything." Quoted from Johann Gottfried Herder, *Sämtliche Werke*, ed. B. Sulphan (Weidmann, Berlin, 1881–1913), 5:503, in Beiser, *The Fate of Reason*, 142.

[17] Again, the Cusan image of horizontally rather than vertically related perspectives seems the most appropriate and, not surprisingly, the "relativism" related to such an approach has never ceased to be a problem for this field of knowledge.

[18] G. W. F. Hegel, "The Positivity of the Christian Religion," in *ETW*, 78.

[19] For a synoptic presentation of the doctrines and development of this tradition, see G. G. Iggers, *The German Conception of History* (New York: Columbia University Press, 1968).

critical philosophy. In his critique of the empiricist wing of the post-Cartesian tradition, Kant had given the simple Cartesian subject an internal structure, an elaborate "architectonic" of necessary and universal structures of experience, judgment, and thought. As noted earlier, in Kant this merged into another, more communicative and intersubjective, interpretation of the subject's transcendental structure. Conceiving of the conceptual structures provided by the mind in its synthetic activity as *rules* for the formation of representations, Kant could appeal to *grammatical* rules as an analogy. "To search in our ordinary knowledge for the concepts which do not rest upon particular experience and yet occur in all knowledge from experience, of which they constitute as it were the mere form of connection, presupposes neither greater reflection nor deeper insight than to detect in a language the rules of the actual use of words generally and thus to collect elements for a grammar (in fact both inquiries are very closely related)" (*Prolegomena to any Future Metaphysics*, §39).

Kant was writing on the verge of an explosive interest in and development of the philological sciences, and it is not surprising that after this explosion Kantian oriented philological theorists such as Wilhelm von Humboldt and Friedrich Schleiermacher would take these "closely related" inquiries to be in fact identical. Thus Humboldt would describe language as "the formative organ of thought": intellectual activity and language are "one and inseparable from each other."[20] Similarly, Schleiermacher would assert: "Speaking is the medium for the communality of thought. . . . Indeed, a person thinks by means of speaking."[21]

But while philological thinkers would develop this idea, the equation of speech and thought and, behind them, the structures of transcendental consciousness and language, had already been asserted at the time of the appearance of Kant's first critique. In his unpublished review, "Metacritique of the Purism of Reason," J. G. Hamann had written that the "whole ability to think rests on language," which he described as "the first and last instrument and criterion of reason, with no other credentials but tradition and usage."[22] Hamann and the romantic philologists who came after him represent early examples of that transformation of Kantianism which substitutes for the Kantian universals of "consciousness in general" the com-

---

[20] William von Humboldt, *Werke in Fünf Bänden*, (Stuttgart: Cotta, 1960–1981), 3:426.
[21] Schleiermacher, *Hermeneutics*, 97.
[22] J. G. Hamann, "Metacritique of the Purism of Reason," translated in *J. G. Hamann, 1730–1788: A Study in Christian Existence, with Selections from His Writings*, by R. G. Smith (London: Collins, 1960), 216. For the importance of Hamann, see Hermann J. Cloeren, *Language and Thought: German Approaches to Analytic Philosophy in the Eighteenth and Nineteenth Centuries* (Berlin: de Gruyter, 1988), chap. 2.

munal structures of actual languages—a transformation resulting in what we might refer to as the "actual language paradigm."[23]

This philological transformation of the Kantian transcendental structure of subjectivity was precisely what was needed to render intelligible the type of ideas about social and historical existence found in Chladenius. The language of a community could be seen as a conceptual medium within which the social substance as well as its communal "point of view" received their shape. Such ideas as these began to be synthesized into coherent patterns of thought in the first decades of the nineteenth century to produce an intellectual paradigm so powerful that it is still one of the major frameworks of thought two hundred years later. Hermeneutic ideas such as these allowed Hegel to extend the Kantian project of developing a truly postmetaphysical philosophy.

Later Hermeneutics and Its View of Hegel

During the first years of the twentieth century, the German philosopher Wilhelm Dilthey came to believe that he had found in the discipline of hermeneutics the solution to a problem that had occupied him throughout his intellectual life—the epistemological problem of justifying an autonomous methodology for the human sciences.[24] *Autonomy* meant here, of course, autonomy from the positivist imposition of that mode of explanation which was thought to characterize the natural sciences. Dilthey sought in hermeneutics a philosophical defense of the de facto anti-naturalism that had marked the "historicist" tradition of nineteenth-century German historiography.[25]

[23] In this century an influential spokesperson for this point of view has been Ludwig Wittgenstein: "We are talking about the spatial and temporal phenomenon of language, not about some non-spatial, non-temporal phantasm. . . . But we talk about it as we do about the pieces in chess when we are stating the rules of the game, not describing their physical properties" (Ludwig Wittgenstein, *Philosophical Investigations,* trans. G. E. M. Anscombe [Oxford: Blackwell, 1953], §108). In the case of Hamann this was done with the same conservative intent that is found in the Burkean invocation of groundless tradition. To condemn the Enlightenment project of subjecting these traditions to the demands of reason Hamann used the idea that the traditionally given structures of one's mother tongue were presupposed by all use of reason.
[24] See especially the writings collected as "The Construction of the Historical World" in Wilhelm Dilthey, *Selected Writings* (hereafter abbreviated *SW*), ed. and trans. H. P. Rickman (Cambridge: Cambridge University Press, 1976).
[25] On the conceptual muddles surrounding the troublesome *"Historismus"* see D. E. Lee and R. Beck, "The Meaning of Historicism," *American Historical Review* 59 (1954): 568–77; Rolf Gruner, "Historism: Its Rise and Decline," *Clio* 8 (1978): 25–39; and C. G. Rand, "Two Meanings of Historicism in the Writings of Dilthey, Troeltsch, and Meinecke," *Journal of the History of*

The German Historical School, which had emerged from Herder's approach to history in the early nineteenth century, had come to oppose its empiricism to Hegel's philosophy, on the one hand, and naturalism, on the other.[26] While actually sharing much of the framework used by Hegel in his historical accounts, the historians stood, for the most part, in polemical opposition to his speculative, philosophical approach to history, and stressed instead a strongly empirical attitude: historiography should abandon all theoretical and philosophical preconceptions in its confrontation with the objects of its investigation. But despite this, it was opposed to any form of positivist imposition of the methods and explanatory procedures of the natural sciences, as advocated, for example, by Comte and Mill. For the Historical School, the goal of historical inquiry was the narrative "co-ordination" of particular events, not their "subordination" under general laws.[27] The Germans prized their sense of history, their "historical consciousness," with which they understood historical events and entities in their particularity and in terms of the unique spirit, or *Geist*, of the epochs which they expressed. To aim for a generalizing explanation by the subsumption of historical data under ahistorical laws was to be blind to the richness and variety of life and to the uniqueness of each particular historical age.[28]

Dilthey realized the degree to which Hegel, with his notion of "objective spirit," had systematized the assumptions about spirit unreflectively at work in the historians' approach, but shared their opposition to Hegelian metaphysics. Dilthey thus attempted to uncouple this concept from Hegel's thought by adopting a "life-philosophical" approach and interpreting objective spirit as a realm of expressions of the life processes of the community. This philosophical standpoint, "which makes into the foundation and criterion of everything something which essentially stands op-

---

Ideas 25 (1964): 503–18. Herbert Schnädelbach has a useful discussion of the various forms of the concept in *Philosophy in Germany, 1831–1933*, trans. Eric Matthews (Cambridge: Cambridge University Press, 1984), 34–40.

[26] For a synoptic presentation of the doctrines and development of the Historical School, see Iggers, *The German Conception of History*. See also Schnädelbach, *Philosophy in Germany*, 33–58.

[27] On the distinction between the co-ordinating texts of history and the subordinating texts of natural science see, for example, Jacob Burckhardt, *Force and Freedom: An Interpretation of History* (a translation of *Weltgeschichtliche Betrachtungen*), ed. James Hastings Nichols (New York: Meridian 1955). This debate has its twentieth-century equivalent in the response of "narrativists'" such as William H. Dray, W. B. Gallie, and Louis O. Mink to Carl G. Hempel's positivist approach to historical explanation in "The Function of General Laws in History," *Journal of Philosophy* 39 (1942): 35–48. For a survey of the forms of narrativist response see W. H. Dray, "On the Nature and Role of Narrative in Historiography," *History and Theory* 10 (1971): 153–71.

[28] It was Johann Gustav Droysen (1808–1884) who first clearly posited the dualism of *Verstehen* and *Erklären*.

posed to rationality, reason, concepts or the Idea—life as something irra-tional,"[29] had affinities with the earlier romantic movement and especially with Schelling's philosophy of nature. As expressions of "life," thought and its concepts could not be turned completely back onto this source to achieve a total conceptual comprehension of it: life was ultimately *unergründlich*—"unfathomable."

Such an approach, which construed the social realm as a realm of *expressive phenomena*, allowed Dilthey to generalize to the human sciences per se the type of methodology which had been developed explicitly for phi-lological hermeneutics by Friedrich Schleiermacher, a contemporary and antagonist of Hegel. Schleiermacher had appealed to a principle of psy-chological divination or empathy to account for the way a listener or reader could understand the expressions of another when they shared a common linguistic means of expression. For Dilthey, for living individuals to become determinate psychological subjects, they must take on the rule-governed structures of social interaction in a way analogous to the way they took on the grammatical rules of their language: they must "subject themselves to rules and set themselves purposes" implicit in those prac-tices in which they co-operate with others (*SW*, 196). Thus any human subject exists as a "bearer of" a historically particular system of social interaction and production, a system that could itself be considered an "ideal subject" (*SW*, 181). This in turn allowed Dilthey to ground that psychological commonality required for empathy: it was precisely the fact of sharing in some common form of life that allowed psychological sub-jects to "find themselves" in the expression of others. And just as we can come to understand the utterances of other language speakers by learning the explicit rules of their grammar, so too could we come to understand what it is like to live within other forms of human life by systematically understanding their systems of interaction. At the basis of all this was the idea that understanding others was ultimately underwritten by the fact that we were all participants in the universal of "life" itself.

A few decades later, however, Martin Heidegger, in *Being and Time* (1927), brought to the surface the contradiction lying dormant in Dilthey between his "life-philosophical" views and his need to secure "founda-tions" for objective knowledge.[30] If we are "always already" located within the "structures of significance" which guide experience and knowl-edge, then how can we hope to break out of the circle of unexamined presupposition and advance to objectivity? This question had been con-

---

[29] Schnädelbach, *Philosophy in Germany*, 141. Life-philosophy might be thought of as a type of derationalized pantheism that results when the more explicitly cognitive elements are re-moved from Spinoza's substance.

[30] Heidegger, *Being and Time*, 449–51.

fronted in nineteenth-century philology, which, although it had claimed to be a science, always proceeded from the philologists' understanding of their own language. And, Heidegger suggests, the same must also apply to historical knowledge: Historians must understand the past on the basis of their understanding of the present. How then could one achieve the rigor of science if one could never escape from a logically vicious circle? Surely "even in the opinion of the historian himself, it would admittedly be more ideal if the circle could be avoided and if there remained the hope of creating some time a historiology which would be as independent of the standpoint of the observer as our knowledge of Nature is supposed to be" (BT, 194).

But for Heidegger, concern about the "viciousness" of the circularity involved here was based on a *misunderstanding* about the nature of understanding itself: *"[I]f we see this circle as a vicious one and look out for ways of avoiding it, even if we just 'sense' it as an inevitable imperfection, then the act of understanding has been misunderstood from the ground up"* (BT, 194). One cannot avoid, even ideally, those very conditions that make knowledge—interpretation—possible in the first place. The norm of the avoidance of circularity involves a failure to recognize "the essential conditions under which it [interpretation] can be performed. What is decisive is not to get out of the circle but to come into it in the right way" (BT, 194).

It was Heidegger's problematization of Dilthey's hermeneutics that allowed Hans-Georg Gadamer in *Truth and Method* (1960) to return to the hermeneutic issues of the perspectivity of human knowledge and understanding the intentional states of others. Gadamer's achievement there was to flesh out Heidegger's suggestive ideas into a model of understanding which could give some sense to the idea that our interpretations, while based in the "fore-structures" of locatedness, could escape from being merely reflections or expressions of those structures. The fact that we occupy a standpoint within a "horizon" does not rule out the possibility of being open to other horizons; indeed it is a precondition of such openness.[31] In working out his model, Gadamer resumed the earlier hermeneutic theme of the central role played by language in the structuring of the world, but language was now considered not so much as medium of representation as that of the dialogical encounter of others.

Inquiring into the conditions of genuine communication, Gadamer focuses on those pertaining to the *addressee*—the sort of prior understanding that an addressee needs in order to learn that which is being told.

[31] Gadamer's use of the term *Horizont* plays on its uses in both Husserl's transcendental phenomenology (as the constitutive structures of objectivity) and Nietzsche's life-philosophy (in the sense of the finite locatedness of human existence). Gadamer, *Truth and Method*, 269–74. Further references will be cited as *TM* followed by page number.

Gadamer attempts to make this precondition explicit by saying that the addressee must be able to ask a question—that question answered in the telling (*TM*, 362–79). This seems to capture something about the "pragmatics" of telling: one typically tells another something on the assumption that the other *can* understand it and that he or she has some *interest* in learning it, that is, the other *could have asked* the question to which this is the reply. But Gadamer's point goes deeper than this. By giving pragmatic priority to the question, he now construes the proposition as an answer to a question posed rather than as a representation of some external and independent "fact." This move, akin to Kant's Copernican turn, allows Gadamer to circumvent the problem of the relation of the representation to any thing-in-itself. Rather, the issue now concerns the relation of the question to the perspectival "matter at hand" (*Sache*) which it *discloses*: "A question places what is questioned in a particular perspective. When a question arises, it breaks open the being of the object, as it were. . . . To ask a question means to bring into the open. The openness of what is in question consists in the fact that the answer is not settled" (*TM*, 362–63). The analogy to Kant here becomes striking when we note that Kant also had used the idea of the primacy of the directing question over its answer. In the preface to the second edition of *Critique of Pure Reason*, Kant tells us that reason, in order to be taught by nature, must approach it, "not . . . in the character of a pupil who listens to everything that the teacher chooses to say, but of an appointed judge who compels the witnesses to answer questions which he has himself formulated."[32] And yet there is a fundamental difference between Gadamer and Kant here. Whereas the Kantian concept of the primacy of the question is meant to bring out the active part played by reason as questions are *metaphorically* addressed to *nature*, which "answers back" in the content of experience, in Gadamer's account, the notion of the "question" maintains a much more *literal* sense. The question is always, at least implicitly, addressed to *another speaker*: it is a move in a *dialogue*. A three-sided relation is set up, consisting of addresser, addressee, and the "matter" disclosed in the discussion.

It might now be objected that this distinction is of little relevance as the possibility of dialogue presupposes that interlocutors, in speaking the same language, occupy the same horizon. But this is the point at which Gadamer's hermeneutic position departs from Kantianism. For Gadamer, the horizons from which two partners of a genuine dialogue speak *cannot* be thought of as identical. If a dialogue is a process that can be maintained between horizons marked by a degree of difference, then no *single* horizon can be thought of as enframing the dialogue itself or its matter.

[32] Kant, *Critique of Pure Reason*, 20.

The significance of the radical difference between interlocutors is brought out in Gadamer's analysis of the dialogical relation, in which he explores three possible modes of the practical relation of one subject to another within which the other is experienced and understood (*TM*, 358–62). In the first mode, I can construe the other as an *object*. In the second, the other is construed as another *person* whose intentions can be *fully grasped* as analogous to my own—that is, the way in which the other is conceived in Dilthey's notion of the hermeneutic "rediscovery of the I in the Thou."[33] But Gadamer contrasts this with a third form of construal of the other, the form proper to the communicative relationship of *genuine* dialogue, in which self and other share a common topic but from different perspectives or horizons.

The second mode of intersubjectivity is inadequate to real dialogue because here the relation of the I to the thou is really a "form of self-relatedness," lacks the immediacy of a genuine intersubjective relation, and is "reflective" (*TM*, 359). In such cases I take myself to be an "I" in the Cartesian sense of a *cogito* existing essentially independently of any worldly relation and in particular, independently of my relation to the thou with whom I enter into a relationship quite external to either of our identities. But from the dialogical point of view, this is a misconstrual of *what it is to be an "I"*. To be an "I" involves adopting an alienable role in dialogue, where the roles of "I" and "thou" mutually presuppose each other and change into each other as the interlocutors exchange speaking roles, an exchange without which the dialogue would be a monologue: "In human relations the important thing is . . . to experience the Thou truly as a Thou—i.e., not to overlook his claim but to let him really say something to us" (*TM*, 361).

It can now be seen why the interlocutors in a genuine dialogue cannot be conceived as speaking from identical horizons, as this would utilize the second model of intersubjectivity rather than the third. To assume that the horizon of the other is identical with my own is to collapse the "thou" into a mirror "I." Complete difference and complete identity of horizons must represent the limits where dialogue must cease. At one end of this continuum stretching between the absolutes of identity and difference, there would be loss of communicative contact as no topic of common concern could be found. At the other, dialogue becomes collective monologue with the "I" and the "thou" collapsing into a "we."

To thematize the irreducible dimension of difference between self and other in the dialogue is to hold open the possibility that intelligibility or agreement over how to proceed in the dialogue may break down due to a clash of criteria. Thus, for example, a question may meet the resistance of

33 Dilthey, *Selected Writings*, 208.

an answer unintelligible from the perspective of the questioner, indicating the presence of a different horizon. Or a question may be responded to with a second question that brings into focus and problematizes presuppositions—"prejudices"—implicit in the first. For Gadamer, as long as we struggle to *maintain* the dialogue, such resistance or opacity of the other is a productive phenomenon. It is the resistance of the other which forces bits and pieces of our horizon out into the open. This cannot happen directly but only in the context of a genuine shared concern over a necessarily underdetermined "matter." Nor can this process be total. It is always piecemeal and local. The hermeneutic experience of being forced back onto parts of one's horizon is the closest we can come to what has traditionally been conceived of as self-reflection and self-understanding.

For Gadamer, the dialogue plays the role of a model useful for thinking about the mode in which we are geared into the historical world of objective spirit. All expressive objectifications pass between the interlocutors in the dialogue of culture, mediating the process and allowing understanding to take place. If we experience objectifications inherited from the past as meaningful, it is because we are "always already" located in a prestructured horizon. The deepening of our understanding is achieved by being open, like a good conversationalist, to horizons other than our own, rather than by aiming at some neutral point *beyond* all horizons.

For the scientific hermeneutics that Dilthey tried to establish on the basis of the romantic nineteenth-century conception of understanding, the hermeneutic circle is a teleological one, ideally terminating in objective knowledge. It is a way of reaching an interpretation that is adequate to its object. But for Gadamer, the circular hermeneutic process is not a means to an end which, as such, anticipates its own termination in a "state" of total understanding. Rather, it is like a dialogue in which the difference of the other continually challenges the "claims" of one's own horizon and the criteria and assumptions which one prereflexively brings to the world. It is always an incomplete process of thematizing and reflecting on these claims, of considering other possibilities and alternatives. As engaging with the other in dialogue is a way of keeping our present horizon open, the important thing is not to terminate it, *even as an ideal,* but to keep it going. In this way, the "transcendence" I can achieve from my own horizon is always finite, to be pictured not in terms of any wholesale abandonment of it, but in the achievement of a *fusion* (*Verschmeltzung*) of my horizon with that of another—an agreement secured at an intersecting border and always against a background of difference (*TM,* 306).

DILTHEY HAD NOTED that nineteenth-century hermeneutic thought was indebted to Hegel. For his part, Gadamer strengthens the link between hermeneutics and Hegelian philosophy by enlisting Hegel into his own

Heideggerian critique of the epistemological assumptions behind the earlier hermeneutic-historical project. That project, originating in the work of Schleiermacher and coming to self-reflection in Dilthey's epistemological endeavors a century later, had seen the work of history as the reconstruction through empirical research of an objective representation of the past. But following Heidegger, Gadamer rejects such a goal and contrasts this mode of relation to the past with that advocated by Hegel. Whereas for Schleiermacher, the past was to be reconstructed for the present, for Hegel, it was to be integrated *into* the present: "Hegel states a definite truth, inasmuch as the essential nature of the historical spirit consists not in the restoration of the past but in *thoughtful mediation with contemporary life*" (*TM*, 168–69). From this angle, it would seem then that it is necessary for contemporary hermeneutics "to follow Hegel rather than Schleiermacher" (*TM*, 173).

But this does not mean that Gadamer simply wants to reinstate Hegelian philosophy, nor does it mean that he believes the tradition of historical hermeneutics was simply mistaken in its opposition to Hegel. Gadamer is in complete agreement with Dilthey's assertion against Hegel of the "need to preserve the consciousness of one's own finitude," and sees Hegel as celebrating the abandonment of such finitude in the attainment of the goal of "absolute knowledge." With this, Hegel had abandoned the wisdom encapsulated in Aeschylus's tragic dictum, "*pathei mathos*," "learning through suffering":

> This phrase does not mean only that we become wise through suffering and that our knowledge of things must first be corrected through deception and undeception. . . . Aeschylus means more than this. He refers to the reason why this is so. What a man has to learn through suffering is not this or that particular thing, but insight into the limitations of humanity, into the absoluteness of the barrier that separates man from the divine. It is ultimately a religious insight—the kind of insight that gave birth to Greek tragedy. (*TM*, 356–57)

While Gadamer applauds Hegel's conception of the self-correcting nature of experience (a conception that, as we will see, has clearly Copernican lineaments), he criticizes what he sees as Hegel's belief that experience is ultimately surpassed in conceptual knowledge—the "absolute knowledge" of philosophical science. In contrast, Aeschylean tragic wisdom has it that

> experience is experience of human finitude. The truly experienced person is one who has taken this to heart, who knows that he is master neither of

time nor the future. The experienced man knows that all foresight is limited and all plans uncertain. In him is realized the truth value of experience. If it is characteristic of every phase of the process of experience that the experienced person acquires a new openness to new experiences, this is certainly true of the idea of being perfectly experienced. It does not mean that experience has ceased and a higher form of knowledge is reached (Hegel), but that for the first time experience fully and truly is. In it all dogmatism, which proceeds from the soaring desires of the human heart, reaches an absolute barrier. Experience teaches us to acknowledge the real. (*TM*, 357)

Given Gadamer's desire for a type of hermeneutic Copernicanism without any final "view from nowhere," it is not surprising then that toward the end of *Truth and Method* he looks to Nicholas of Cusa for a model of hermeneutic thought (*TM*, 434–38).

In much of its detail, Gadamer's schematic reconstruction of hermeneutics indeed seems to follow Hegel. He acknowledges, for example, that the turn to dialogue that his own hermeneutics follows is already present in Hegel: "The dialectical progress of the *Phenomenology of Mind* is perhaps determined by nothing so much as by the problem of the recognition of the Thou" (*TM*, 343). But Hegel's philosophy is ultimately, he claims, based on a *monological* and so monopersectival, rather than a dialogical and multiperspectival, approach to knowledge and thought: "To elaborate the totality of the determinations of thought, which was the aim of Hegel's logic, is as it were the attempt to comprehend within the great monologue of modern 'method' the continuum of meaning that is realized in every particular instance of dialogue" (*TM*, 369). So Hegel the hermeneutic philosopher is usurped by Hegel the dogmatic metaphysician who relapses into a pre-Kantian mode of thought. In invoking this latter diagnosis of Hegel, Gadamer is invoking a time-honored view of his philosophy. But that it is time-honored is no guarantee that this view is an adequate one, and in the following chapters I attempt to show that indeed it is not so. The "hermeneutic" Hegel that Gadamer retrieves is far from hampered by such a dogmatic metaphysician. Hegel's hermeneutics is, rather, a "Copernican" hermeneutics.

CHAPTER 3

Hegel's Early Schellingianism

AT FIRST GLANCE Schelling's early philosophy seems to trace a bizarre path within the space of post-Kantian critical philosophy. Starting from Fichte's reworking of Kant's transcendental idealism, Schelling developed a form of nature philosophy, which progressively incorporated Spinozist and Neoplatonic elements. In terms of the Kantian critique of metaphysics, such "progress" seems precisely toward that type of philosophy which had been the object of the critical attack. Just as puzzling, however, is that Schelling then attempted to assert the "identity" of these two types of philosophical projects—the consciousness-based transcendental idealism of Kant and Fichte and the "objective" philosophy of nature—by unifying them as parts of his own "identity philosophy."[1] In the light of the Neoplatonic elements absorbed into his philosophy of nature we might see, however, how the Kantian-Fichtean exploration of transcendental subjectivity could have been regarded as structurally similar to Schelling's attempt to develop a parallel exploration of the objective world in the philosophy of nature.

[1] While Schelling's earliest works such as "On the Possibility of a Form of Philosophy in General" (1794) and "On the Ego as Principle of Philosophy" (1795) were straightforwardly Fichtean, his early sketches of *Naturphilosophie* in the Introduction to the first edition of *Ideas for a Philosophy of Nature* and "On the World Soul" were more attempts to extend Fichtean philosophy into this metaphysical area of largely Spinozist inspiration. With *Presentation of My System of Philosophy* (1801) and *Bruno; or, On the Natural and the Divine Principle of Things* (1802) he moved into his increasing Neoplatonic "identity philosophy" and further from Fichte. The first explicit acknowledgment of Schelling's break with Fichte came not from Schelling but from Hegel in *The Difference between Fichte's and Schelling's System of Philosophy* (1801).

From Fichte to Schelling's Identity Philosophy

In the early 1790s Fichte had emerged on the German intellectual scene to be regarded by many as the true continuer of Kant's Copernican revolution. The nature of Fichte's relation to Kant is complex and controversial; here I can merely allude to what, from the perspective of Hegel's philosophy, are a few of its most significant dimensions. Certain problems with the approach of Kant's first *Critique* had been obvious from the earliest days of its reception—most notorious among these being the apparently contradictory roles attributed to noumena. On the one hand, noumena were supposed to be unknowable; on the other, they seemed to be given a causal role in the account of experience as being responsible for its passively acquired "intuitive" content.[2] But from Fichte's perspective, other problems loomed just as large—the schism between theoretical and practical philosophy, a schism that seemed to rupture the unity of reason itself, and the accompanying lack of systematicity within the Kantian edifice.

Fichte's reworking of Kant was meant to be faithful to the critical spirit of his Copernicanism but was to proceed by way of a different presentation: "I have long asserted, and repeat once more, that my system is nothing other than the Kantian; this means that it contains the same view of things, but is in method quite independent of the Kantian presentation."[3] This new presentation was to start from a consideration of the nature of a key, but relatively unexplored, aspect of the Kantian edifice, the transcendental subject of apperception. With this notion Kant had claimed that the knowing subject's relation to known objects was dependent on a certain relation of that subject *to itself*—that "consciousness" was dependent on "self-consciousness." But the nature of this self-relation was far from clear.

An investigation of the nature of this primordial self-relation, the "I = I," would be Fichte's starting point, but to understand how this might provide a way forward, we must locate it against the importance placed by Fichte on Kant's project of the transcendental deduction of the categories. Such a deduction was indeed the way to establish a truly systematic and scientific approach to philosophy which did justice to the unity of reason, but Kant's own *actual* deduction was considered to be marred by his uncritical acceptance of the framework of Aristotelian logic. A genuine deduction could not be grounded in anything beyond some given certainty, and so emerged

---

2 F. H. Jacobi first outlined the problem, which has come to be known as that of "double affection." F. H. Jacobi, *David Hume über den Glauben, oder Idealismus und Realismus*, Beilage, *Über den transzendentalen Idealismus*, in *Werke*, ed. Friedrich Roth and Friedrich Kloppen (Darmstadt: Wissenschaftliche Buchgesellschaft, 1968), 2: 291–310.

3 J. G. Fichte, "First Introduction to the Science of Knowledge," in *Science of Knowledge*, ed. and trans. Peter Heath and John Lachs (Cambridge: Cambridge University Press, 1982), 4.

Fichte's own method as formulated and reformulated in the project of the *Science of Knowledge* (*Wissenschaftslehre*), as a critical reworking of the transcendental deduction of the first *Critique* grounded in certain self-evident truths about the I.[4]

It will be recalled that Cusanus's philosophical method proceeded from the idea of a primordial prenumerical unity that was thought as both the totality of all things qua unity, an absolute maximum, and at the same time the absolute minimum, the form of all forms of the diverse beings of the "contracted" universe. However, when viewed in terms of its *form*, the Kantian transcendental unity of apperception or Fichtean "*Ich*" ("I") could be regarded as analogous to that Cusan unity presupposed by the plurality of the contracted objective world. As the "I" is necessary for there to be a (phenomenal) world of determinate diverse objects, it could not simply have the type of unity which characterized those objects—the everyday countable "unity within plurality" of particular things in their relations of identity and difference. Like Cusanus's Neoplatonic One, the "I" must be regarded as in some sense *coextensive* with the world rather than a part of it: its unity is a precondition of that coherent diversity of singular things found within the objective world.

In fact this quasi-Neoplatonic character of the transcendental subject is intensified in Fichte's development of idealism, given his abandonment of what he saw as the unacceptable dualism of noumena and phenomena and his attempt to seek the unity of the categories in the dynamics of the primordial unity of the self-positing "I." With its Fichtean development, transcendental idealism would seem to have become ripe for such a Neoplatonic reinterpretation, one that could address some of its internal problems at the same time as initiate a rapprochement between critical philosophy and the burgeoning pantheism of German high culture.

Hegel's Schellingian Critique of Fichte

In his first published philosophical work, *The Difference between Fichte's and Schelling's System of Philosophy* (1801), Hegel provided a concise summary of what, from a Schellingian position, appeared as the strengths and short-

---

[4] In this I have followed the understanding of Fichte as having in mind the transcendental subject of the first *Critique* as the starting point of his deduction. While this seems true of the 1794 version of the *Wissenschaftslehre*, problems with this starting point seem to have pushed Fichte in the direction of conceiving of this starting point in terms of *moral* subjectivity. For a clear discussion of this change of starting points between the 1794 and 1797 versions, see Frederick Neuhouser, *Fichte's Theory of Subjectivity* (Cambridge: Cambridge University Press, 1990), chap. 2.

comings of Fichte's philosophy. Up to this point, Schelling had been seen *as* a Fichtean, but here Schelling's philosophy is presented as going beyond structural problems inherent in the *Wissenschaftslehre*, making him the genuine inheritor of the critical philosophy. Significantly, Hegel's title refers to the difference between the *system* of Fichte and Schelling; in certain respects Hegel saw these philosophies themselves as identical. More precisely, they were identical in terms of their content or principle, the Kantian "transcendental principle" of the identity of subject and object, the true content of all philosophy. By interpreting Kant's "transcendental principle" in this way, Hegel was pointing to Fichte's understanding of the transcendental subject as a self-identical "I" presupposed by the existence of a coherent empirical world as such.[5] Where Schelling surpassed Fichte, however, was in his ability to give an adequate account of the nature of this identity of subject and object.

Hegel's criticism of Fichte centers on the idea that while the transcendental identity of subject and object is the principle of Fichte's philosophy, this identity is not *displayed* (*aufgezeigt*) or *constructed* (*konstruiert*) in his system (*D*, 122, 126; *W*, 1:56, 61).[6] Rather, the unity of subject and object is only "postulated" (*postuliert*). Its realization is incomplete and never more than "subjective": the unity of subject and object appears only as a "subjective Subject-Object." What is lacking in Fichte's deduction and found in Schelling's is a complementary "objective Subject-Object" that can be set beside its subjective equivalent in such a way that both are demonstrated as united in an absolute that is "higher than the subject" (*D*, 82; *W*, 2:12). Although this "absolute" was still conceived as "reason," it could no longer be thought of as some kind of reasoning *I*, no longer as an "absolute I."[7]

This subjective one-sidedness of Fichte's system is, Hegel claims, connected with the fact that Fichte, like Kant, "surrenders Reason [*die Vernunft*] to the intellect [*der Verstand*] and passes over into the chain of finite [acts and objects] of consciousness from which it never reconstructs itself again as identity and true infinity" (*D*, 81; *W*, 2:11). Fichte has "equated Reason with pure consciousness and raised Reason as apprehended in a

5 It appears that Hegel's critique was directed to Fichte's 1794 text.
6 This characteristic of Fichte's exemplifies a common tendency that Hegel comments on in the preface to the first edition of the *Science of Logic*: "In its first manifestation, such [a new philosophical] idea usually displays a fanatical hostility toward the entrenched systematization of the older principle; usually too, it is fearful of losing itself in the ramifications of the particular and again it shuns the labour required for a scientific elaboration of the new principle and in its need for such, it grasps to begin with at an empty formalism. The challenge to elaborate and systematize the material now becomes all the more pressing" (*SL*, 27; *W*, 5:15–16).
7 Here the more Spinozist flavor of Hegel's and Schelling's position is apparent.

finite shape to the status of principle" (*D*, 82; *W*, 2:12). This has implications for the way the categories are developed from the starting point of the speculative principle I = I.

As recent interpreters of Fichte have stressed, this principle was not meant to make some metaphysical claim about the necessary existence of some absolute world-creating mind: such "precritical" metaphysics is far from Fichte's post-Kantian starting point.[8] As outlined above, it was meant to say something about the nature of Kant's transcendental subject as a condition of any manifest empirical world of coherent and stable entities. For Dieter Henrich, Fichte's "original insight" concerns the critique of traditional ways of conceiving of self-consciousness in which the self's knowledge of itself is conceived on the model of its knowledge of any other *thing*.[9] Fichte's point, however, is that the I should not be considered a thing at all. It rather "is" an *act*, in Fichte's neologism, a *Tathandlung*.[10] Concomitantly, the self's knowledge of itself should not be thought of along the lines of its knowledge of other things; it should not be thought of in terms of what Kant refers to as *Vorstellungen*—representations.

Hegel's charge that Fichte surrenders reason to the intellect amounts to the charge that despite his critique of the representationalist conception of self-consciousness, he does not succeed in freeing his account from this conception. In line with the framework of the abstract understanding, Fichte takes his basic principles—the three basic principles of identity of the I with itself, its opposing to the posited object of consciousness (the non-I), and the synthesis of these acts of identity and opposing—as *propositions*. That is, they are understood on the model of a consciousness's understanding of objects. Thus, in construing his starting point as a series of propositions, and thereby construing the form of the knowledge involved in self-consciousness along the lines of representation, Fichte has fallen back into the notion of the I as a type of self-positing *thing* rather than as a self-positing *activity*.

This criticism of other philosophical positions as not leaving the realm of "the understanding" would become a standard part of the Hegelian approach. Its associations here, however, are significant as they align the Schelling-Hegel critique of Fichte with central aspects of hermeneutic thought. First, the framework of *Verstand* is bound up with the founda-

---

[8] For example, Robert Pippin in *Hegel's Idealism: The Satisfactions of Self-Consciousness* (New York: Cambridge University Press, 1989), chap. 3, "Fichte's Contribution"; and Neuhouser, *Fichte's Theory of Subjectivity*, chap. 1.

[9] Dieter Henrich, "Fichte's Original Insight," trans. David R. Lachterman in *Contemporary German Philosophy*, Vol. 1, 1982, ed. Darrel E. Christensen et al. (University Park: Pennsylvania State University Press, 1982).

[10] The analogy here is with the word for *fact*—*Tatsache*. The thing-like connotations of "*Sache*" being eliminated with the use of the word for *act*, "*Handlung*."

tionalist pretensions of Fichte's system and its linear and formal conception of thought. Fichte wished to derive his categories in a type of logical movement that proceeds from a set of basic propositions that can be known with certainty. Significantly Hegel criticizes Fichte's deduction by appealing to a criterion of completeness that Fichte had himself specified in "Concerning the Concept of the *Wissenschaftslehre*"—the circular principle that "the very principle from which we began is at the same time our final result."[11] According to Hegel, "The result of the system does not return to its beginning" (D, 132; W, 2:68).[12] How Fichte's espousal of such circularity sits with the apparently foundational and linear conception of his method has been the subject of recent scholarly debate of which we will keep well clear.[13] What is relevant here, however, is how the issue of the necessary circularity is picked up by Hegel, because *his* way of understanding it will go in the anti-foundational direction now commonly identified with Heidegger's perspectival idea of the "hermeneutic circle" within which thought is always situated and moves.

The formality and incompleteness of Fichte's system are linked to another significant shortcoming: its inability to produce what Hegel refers to as an "objective Subject-Object." Although it is hard to say *exactly* what such an "objective Subject-Object" is meant to amount to, we might say that in general terms for Hegel the difficulty with Fichte's approach is that he has no way of conceiving of an "embodied-mind" from an external, third person point of view. That is, within the categories of Fichte's deduction there is no way to treat human beings in an *epistemologically hermeneutic way*, that is, to conceptualize them in such a way that one can recognize them as intentional subjects with points of view, and not as mere things.[14]

---

[11] J. G. Fichte, "Concerning the Concept of the *Wissenschaftslehre*" in *Fichte: Early Philosophical Writings*, trans. and ed. Daniel Breazeale (Ithaca: Cornell University Press, 1988), 117.

[12] Cf. "Thus the end of the system is untrue to the beginning, the result is untrue to the principle" (D, 138; W, 2:75).

[13] Tom Rockmore has argued that Fichte *himself* in the *Wissenschaftslehre* breaks with the foundationalist project and institutes a "circular" and "nonfoundational" approach to philosophical demonstration. See, for example: "Fichtean Epistemology and Contemporary Philosophy," *Idealistic Studies* 19 (1988): 156–68; *Hegel's Circular Epistemology* (Bloomington: Indiana University Press, 1986); and "Antifoundationalism, Circularity, and the Spirit of Fichte," in *Fichte: Historical Contexts/Contemporary Controversies*, ed. Daniel Breazeale and Tom Rockmore (Atlantic Highlands: Humanities Press, 1994), 96–112. But see also the articles by Breazeale and Perrinjaquet in the same volume which question Rockmore's interpretation. Hegel's charge that, for the 1794 *Wissenschaftslehre* at least, Fichte's method is basically meant to be that of *linear deduction* from a *certain* starting point is supported by most current interpretations. Thus, for example, Neuhouser notes: "Fichte's basic position is a familiar one to post-Cartesian philosophers: If philosophy is to provide us with genuine knowledge, then it must begin from a first principle that possesses absolute certainty in itself and independently of the system that is to follow from it." *Fichte's Theory of Subjectivity*, 42.

[14] In the light of Hegel's charge, the following comments on Fichte's idea that the subject

Early on in the essay Hegel makes this point in a variety of rather abstract ways:

> The objective I does not become identical with the subjective I; they remain absolutely opposed to one another. I does not find itself in its appearance, or in its positing [*Ich findet sich nicht in seiner Erscheinung oder in seinen Setzen*]; it must annul its appearance in order to find itself as I. The essence of the I and its positing do not coincide: *I does not become objective to itself.* (D, 122–23; W, 2:56)[15]

It is in the context of Hegel's latter discussion of the application of Fichte's philosophy to the social realm, however, that the idea that this lack is a *hermeneutic* one becomes most apparent.

The problem first emerges in the Fichtean approach to nature. That the rational being must "make unto itself a sphere for its freedom" into which it posits itself "exclusively" means that everything beyond that rational being, that is, the "objective" realm of nature, will be posited in an antithetical light. That is, it will be construed as a totally lifeless and mindless realm—a realm totally lacking freedom, a realm of things to be used by the rational subject in the pursuit of its own freedom (D, 142–43; W, 2:80).

Such a lifeless determinacy, the determinacy of the mechanical Newtonian universe, had characterized the knowable objective realm for Kant. But, of course, for Kant, other human beings could not be *treated* as lifeless, intentionless mechanisms. The moral self had to treat others as free and rational beings, "ends in themselves" rather than means to its own ends. This meant that a radical gap had emerged between the way in which others are presented *objectively* to consciousness and how they are regarded from a "practical" point of view. For Hegel, Fichte too had become caught in this dichotomy between these two unbridgeable conceptions of others.

---

exists *only* for itself are significant: "[I]t ceases to exist in the absence of its own self-awareness and can exist, *qua* subject, only for itself, never for another conscious subject" (Neuhouser, *Fichte's Theory of Subjectivity*, 112). The impossibility of an intentional subject appearing to a third person perspective is what I mean by the lack of a hermeneutic dimension in Fichte's thought.

[15] Hegel purposefully skews the grammar in these passages by using the first person pronoun with the third person conjugation of the verb—for example with "*Ich findet sich (nicht),*" (literally "I finds itself (not)"), rather than either grammatical alternative, "*Das Ich findet sich,*" "the I finds itself," or "*Ich finde mich,*" "I find myself." This would seem to signal a concern to stress the internal unity between subjective and objective aspects of a subject which is so central to his approach. Here and elsewhere I have modified the translation by using "I" rather than "Ego" for *Ich.*

Any rational being is doubled [*ist ein gedoppeltes*] for any other : (a) it is a free, rational being; (b) it is modifiable matter, something that can be treated as a mere thing. This separation is absolute and once it has, in all its unnaturalness, been made basic, there is no longer the possibility of a pure mutual connection in which the original identity could present and recognize itself [*sich darstellte und erkennte*]. (*D*, 144; *W*, 2:81; translation modified)

In short, there could be no categorial structures within Fichte's system adequate to any sort of hermeneutic recognition of an objective other as another rational being. This was a major shortcoming of both the theoretical and practical sides of Fichte's system. One could only conceive of another in an objective presentation, as a "mere" object, not as a "Subject-Object." The only Subject-Object to find a place in Fichte's system was that of the moral self, the subject who aimed to objectify its moral subjectivity in action. As a consequence of this inability to characterize others as Subject-Objects, the only form of description that would be available for society was one that construed it in mechanical rather than hermeneutic terms: "But that State as conceived by the intellect [*Verstandesstaat*] is not an organization at all, but a machine; and the people is not the organic body of a communal and rich life, but an atomistic, life-impoverished multitude. The elements of this multitude are absolutely opposed substances, on the one hand the rational beings as a lot of [atomic] points, and on the other hand a lot of material beings modifiable in various ways by Reason, i.e., by intellect, the form in which Reason is here present" (*D*, 148–49; *W*, 2:87). We can assume that within Schelling's and Hegel's social thought this lack of a hermeneutic dimension is meant to be rectified. But this rectification cannot be mere emendation: it will have to follow from the correct systematic development of the transcendental principle of the unity of subject and object. It is here that the "Neoplatonic" cast of Schellingian thought would become apparent.

The Coincidence, or "Indifference," of Opposites in Schelling's "Constructed Line"

As Hegel asserts in the *Difference* essay, for Schelling the existence of the subjective Subject-Object is matched by that of an objective Subject-Object in such a way that both are "united in something higher than the subject" (*D*, 82; *W*, 2:12). This "something higher" is "the absolute," and the "indifferent" unification of the two Subject-Objects in it is what is meant by the "identity of opposites." It is thus that Schelling retrieves the Cusan notion of the *coincidentia oppositorum*, a move that would form the basis of his reply to the Kantian interdiction against pursuing theoretical knowledge beyond the realm of the finite.[16] And yet for Schelling this was a progression *beyond* Kant and Fichte; it allowed what we might think of as a "post-Kantian" treatment of typically "pre-Kantian" metaphysical concerns.[17]

In his work of 1801, *Exposition of My System of Philosophy*, Schelling had attempted to capture the unity of those opposites that Hegel labels the subjective and objective Subject-Objects in terms of a schema called the "constructed line." In section 45 of that work, Schelling asserts that neither subjectivity nor objectivity can be posited separately in themselves but only as predominating aspects of the one and the same absolute, or, as he has it in section 46, in terms of that which predominates (*überwiegt*) of the "opposed directions" of the absolute conceived "under the image of a single line."

In this schema, clearly meant to replace the three initial principles of Fichte's *Wissenschaftslehre*, the line representing the self-identical absolute $(A = A)$, can be seen as running between two poles. Regarded as stretching from left to right, the absolute will be regarded in terms of the dominance of subjectivity, designated by the term "A," and from right to left, in terms of the dominance of objectivity, "B." The predominance of one over the other is indicated by a "+" sign. Thus the whole structure can be analyzed into three elements, the two "poles" $(\overset{+}{A} = B$ and $A = \overset{+}{B})$ and the "indifference point" midway between them $(A = A)$.[18]

---

[16] Extracts from Giordano Bruno, *De la Causa*, which reproduced key arguments of Cusanus's *On Learned Ignorance* concerning the identity of the absolute maxima and minima were appended to Jacobi's *Über die Lehre des Spinoza*. This seems to be the transmission route for the Cusan conception of *coincidentia oppositorum* into German Idealism, becoming the principle of the "indifference" of identity and difference in Schelling's absolute idealism. Cf. Klaus Düsing, "Absolute Identität und Formen der Endlichkeit: Interpretationen zu Schellings und Hegels erster absoluter Metaphysik," in *Schellings und Hegels erste absolute Metaphysik (1801–1802)* ed. Klaus Düsing (Köln: Jürgen Dinter, 1988), 114, 151.

For Schelling, in "the Absolute" considered as a unity, mind and matter, subjectivity and objectivity, must coexist as "indifferent"; and yet the mind seems compelled to grasp these as incompatible opposites rather than as identical. This difference, argued Schelling, is really the result of a type of perspectival illusion: it is only when thought from the point of view of a limited, finite consciousness that such differences become unbridgeable. When the Absolute is considered from its own standpoint, the objective and subjective realms are seen to coexist in a way that recalls Spinoza's coexistence of mind and extension as two attributes of a single substance.

[17] Michael Vater appropriately refers to Schelling's project of identity philosophy as an attempt to do "Kantian metaphysics" in his introduction to F. W. J. Schelling, *Bruno; or, On the Natural and the Divine Principle of Things*, trans. Michael G. Vater (Albany: State University of New York Press, 1984), 73.

[18] Schelling's *"Indifferenz"* is a neologism meant to convey the idea of the non-difference (coincidence) of opposites. It should not be confused with the sense conveyed by the English "indifference" which is standardly translated by *"Gleichgültigkeit"* ("like-valid-ness").

$$\frac{\overset{+}{A} = B \hspace{6cm} A = \overset{+}{B}}{A = A}$$

What should be kept in mind here is the significance of the fact that the poles of the line are *not* designated subjectivity and objectivity (A and B) respectively. They are *both* labeled A = B and differentiated by which term *predominates* over the other. That is, rather than representing the dichotomy of subject and object per se, the poles represent the subjective and objective "Subject-Objects" of the *Difference* essay.[19] Thus, the line cannot be thought of as stretching between and joining two *pre-existing* poles, as both poles are thought of in terms of different aspects of a unity (a Subject-Object). Rather, it is as if the line itself, with its necessary double directionality, is primary (it is the absolute), and the poles really serve to indicate the existence of these two opposed *directions within* or *aspects of* the line.

The Cusan flavor of this diagram is thus apparent. It is wrong to think of the line as being "in space": as it is the absolute, there can be no points "outside" it—it *is* the "space" being considered. And parallel to the coincidence of center and periphery within the Cusan absolute, here poles and "indifference point" (the point on the line midway between the poles) coincide such that each pole can be considered as present *in every point of the line*: "What counts of the whole line, counts also of each single part of the same in the infinite. . . . so is each point of the line indifference point, pole, and this or the opposed pole" (§46 addition).

Although such schematizations of the structure of the absolute throughout Schelling's works of this period are shifting and elusive, the general outline of his thought is clear enough. Different forms of human intentionality give different bearings of the same "absolute." For example, the empirical discoveries of natural science could be explained, that is, could have their *possibility* demonstrated, in terms of the type of metaphysical scheme represented here. Such a naturalistic perspective onto the absolute was to be had from the pole in which objectivity predominated over subjectivity—A = $\overset{+}{B}$. But science did not exhaust the knowledge of the absolute, and so, when the perspective of the opposite pole was adopted,

---

[19] Within the framework of this schema, Hegel's critique of the Fichtean conception of the absolute amounts to the claim that it lacks the pole A = $\overset{+}{B}$. In this description of the unity of the subjective and objective Subject-Objects in *Differenz* Hegel clearly has the schema of the "constructed line" in mind: "[T]he system of subjectivity also contains the objective, and the system of objectivity contains the subjective. Nature is an immanent ideality just as intelligence is an immanent reality. The two poles of cognition and being are present in each, so that each has also the point of indifference in itself; but in one system the ideal pole prevails [*ist . . . überwiegend*], in the other the real pole" (*D*, 166; *W*, 2:107).

the resulting philosophical science was the Fichtean science of transcendental idealism.

The constructed line schematizes a structure Schelling also describes as one of "potences" (or "powers" or "levels")—*Potenzen*—an idea that can be traced back to the Plotinian *hypostases*.[20] Schelling himself attributed the notion of "potence" to his contemporary Karl Eschenmayer; the senses of the term importantly include the mathematical sense of exponential "power."[21] However , as in the case of the coincidence of opposites, the influence of Nicholas of Cusa transmitted via Bruno is crucial here, inasmuch as Nicholas had coined the term *possest* to capture the idea of a self-actualizing potency that eludes the dichotomy of potential and actual.[22]

The analysis of nature into levels or potences follows from the "triune" ontology that is consequent on Cusanus's concept of *coincidentia oppositorum*. In *On Learned Ignorance* Cusanus had argued that "unity," or "essence," and "entity," or "existence," are "convertible," that is, that the absolute maximum, the primordial unity, must, in some sense, simultaneously *be* that totality of contracted "unity in plurality," the created world. It is this which gives a strongly pantheist flavor to his system—the equation of God and nature: "It is clear then how we arrive at the truth on the Providence of God and similar subjects from the foregoing considerations, which show us the Maximum as a Being, to whom nothing stands in opposition, because all beings, in whatsoever way they be, are in Him and He in them."[23] For Cusanus, this relation between "creator" and "creature" was captured anthropomorphically in the Christian idea of the relation between divine Father and Son in the Trinity. The father symbolizes the primordial "unity," the incarnate son—the Word made flesh, the created world generated out of this unity—the plurality of diverse and mortal or finite creatures.[24] In turn, the Holy Spirit represents the *unity* of these first two terms. Given the identity of the *absolute maxima* with the *absolute*

---

[20] Cf. Plotinus, *The Enneads,* trans. Stephen MacKenna (London: Faber and Faber, 1969).

[21] Cf., H. S. Harris, "Hegel's System of Ethical Life: An Interpretation," in *Hegel's System of Ethical Life and First Philosophy of Spirit,* ed. and trans. T. M. Knox and H. S. Harris (Albany: State University of New York Press, 1979), 15.

[22] Douglas W. Stott, in his translator's introduction to Schelling's *The Philosophy of Art,* ed. and trans. Douglas W. Stott (Minneapolis: University of Minnesota Press, 1989), traces the term to Cusa via Bruno, but to the Latin *"potentia"* (p. xxxv). However, it would seem that the relevant Cusan term is his neologistic *"possest."* On Cusa's use of *"possest"* see Peter J. Casarella, "Nicholas of Cusa and the Power of the Possible," *American Catholic Philosophical Quarterly* 64 (1990): 7–34.

[23] Nicholas of Cusa, *Of Learned Ignorance,* translated by Fr. Germain Heron (London: Routledge and Regan Paul, 1954), 50–51

[24] Importantly, Cusa's scheme here is anti-Aristotelian. There is no sense of the created world consisting of form imposed *upon* a receptive matter.

minima, this triune structure of unity, entity, and relation must be somehow reflected in each object in the "contracted" world. Each finite object is, in some sense, an image of the unity itself, an image of God, just as each point on Schelling's line represents the whole.[25]

The Perspectival Character of Potences

In *Ideas for a Philosophy of Nature,* Schelling also refers to the potences as "ideas" or "monads" and, taking up the latter equation, allows us to understand better exactly what Schelling is getting at with the notion of the potence.[26] As we have seen, Leibniz had envisaged his "substantial forms" or "monads" as expressing, in a way proportional to the degree of their perfection, the totality of the universe to which they belonged. That is, the monad provides a particular point of view or perspective onto the totality of which it is a reduced expression. Such a perspectival character can be seen as already implicit within the "constructed line," which must be viewed running between opposing poles from which the same absolute is viewed such that each view is the inversion of the other. This perspectival schema is continued in Schelling's elaborations of the potences. In *Philosophy of Art,* Schelling stresses that we should not think of the absolute as actually passing over into other beings by means of division or separation. Rather, since the one being is indivisible, "diversity among things is only possible to the extent that this indivisible whole is posited under various determinations. I call these determinations potences."[27] That is, the world is divided into some structure of potences *only* inasmuch as it is viewed under particular "ideal determinations"—we might say, from particular

---

[25] Hegel had originally believed that religious thought alone could capture this type of unity whereas Schelling believed that it had its highest comprehension in *art.* Later, however, Hegel came to the view that such unity was able to be conceptually thought within philosophical science.

[26] F. W. J. Schelling, *Ideas for a Philosophy of Nature as Introduction to the Study of This Science,* trans. Errol E. Harris and Peter Heath, with an introduction by Robert Stern (Cambridge: Cambridge University Press, 1988), 48. "Idea" is here meant, of course, in a Platonic, nonsubjective, sense. But without the transcendent separation of the ideal and real realms the ideas are *worldly* in a way they are not for Plato. This makes them something like Aristotelian forms, but with the difference that form and matter can no longer be thought dichotomously. The form or soul of a thing is not imposed onto an indifferent passive matter (an indifferent potential). Form and matter are rather indifferently unified in the idea or potence, as they had been in Cusanus's *possest,* the etymology of his neologism suggesting the unity of possibility and actuality, that is, matter and form.

[27] Schelling, *The Philosophy of Art,* 14.

epistemic conditions or perspectives.[28] And just as for Cusanus the whole cannot be a thing, so for Schelling, the absolute itself *cannot* be a potence.

And so something like the Cusan and Leibnizian forms of pluralism emerges in Schelling. The different potences are correlated with different points of view onto the same absolute, from different points within it. Thus, it is noted that when observing nature, history or art, for example, our objects should not be seen as distinct things or ontologically distinct realms. Rather, in all these contexts we are observing the same absolute under some particular set of ideal determinations found within it. "If one could remove these [potences] and view the *pure essence,* as it were, completely exposed, the same essence would truly be found in each."[29]

And so any apparent "realism" of the philosophical mapping of nature in terms of potences should not mislead us into missing the implicit Kantian dimension of Schelling's thought here. Potences are "real" inasmuch as they imply the existence of structures of ideal determinations from which they will appear as real to some form of cognizing subjects who themselves have to be thought of as within this structure. With these simultaneously real and ideal dimensions of the potences we can appreciate why the production of sensitive and eventually *conscious* life is a necessary part of the unfolding of the absolute within nature. Correlative to any particular structure of real or natural potences, there must be some kind of perspectivally conscious being for whom these are present as such and within whom they are idealized.

We might now finally start to see how Schelling could have considered himself a postcritical philosopher and the unifier of Fichtean transcendental idealism and the philosophy of nature. Fichte's transcendental idealism, adopting the perspective of the predominance of subjectivity ($\overset{+}{A} = B$), generates the structure of the world, the non-I, from out of the logical conditions of subjectivity. Philosophy of nature, on the other hand, locating itself at the opposite pole of the constructed line, follows the unfolding of the structure of the real world through its inorganic and organic articulations, ultimately reaching the position of an emergent conscious *Ich* (I) as the necessary end product of nature. That is, each starting from its own unique point ends up with a content that is the starting point of the other. As Hegel puts it, "[I]n one science cognition is matter and being is form,

---

[28] This would seem to mark an important difference between the Schellingian account of the world in terms of potences and the earlier vitalistic approach of Herder with its notion of *Kräfte*—"powers," in the more usual sense of the term. Kant had criticized Herder's concept as "metaphysical." (See Frederick C. Beiser, *The Fate of Reason: German Philosophy from Kant to Fichte* [Cambridge, Mass.: Harvard University Press, 1987], 146–53). But Schelling's potences are not "naively realistic" in this sense.

[29] Schelling, *The Philosophy of Art,* 14.

while in the other being is matter and cognition is form" (*D*, 169; *W*, 2:110).[30] For Schelling and Hegel, Fichte's sin was to fail to understand that in taking the transcendental realm of ideation as fundamental, he had chosen only one aspect of the absolute, had viewed it from *one* perspective.[31]

The question of the right and wrong ways to think of the relations between opposed philosophical viewpoints is broached again in the introduction, apparently written mostly by Hegel, to Schelling's and Hegel's *The Critical Journal of Philosophy* of 1801. There Hegel starts with the Schellingian notion that there is a single "idea" of philosophy because "the truth of reason is but one": that is, that which is truly thought by philosophy is always the same—it is the "absolute." This means that genuine philosophical doctrines will always have a single content, but will express that content in forms that reflect the particular finite conditions under which those doctrines had been articulated. That activity which was to be practiced in the journal, philosophical *criticism*, had the task of separating out such a content from the finite forms in which it will have found itself expressed: it must "interpret the way and the degree in which [the idea of philosophy] emerges free and clear, and the range within which it has been elaborated into a scientific system of philosophy" (CJI, 277; *W*, 2:174). To do this, it must itself reject any "one-sided point of view [*einseitigen Gesichtspunkt*] as valid *against others* that are likewise one-sided"; otherwise it will be no more than "partisan polemic" (CJI, 285; *W*, 2:186; emphasis added).

Concerning how criticism is to achieve this, however, there is offered only the slightest hint in the introduction—but it is a tantalizing one. Schelling's position was that the unity of the "indifference point" was captured in an aesthetic act of "transcendental intuition," but Hegel himself was to become increasingly critical of any such notion of "intellectual" or "transcendental" intuition. Here Hegel talks, in a Schellingian way, of the need to recognize "the idea" of philosophy in opposing philosophical standpoints (supposing that they *are* genuinely philosophical). Where "the

---

[30] H. S. Harris captures this sense of the inversion of form in the opposition when he notes: "The *reality* of the opposition appears here as a reversal of categorial values. From the point of view of transcendental philosophy the objective aspects of experience are empirical or accidental facts; but from the point of view of natural philosophy the subject aspects are epiphenomenal or accidental forms." Introduction to the *Difference* essay, 46.

[31] Cf. Schelling, *Ideas for a Philosophy of Nature*, 51. In the Introduction to *The Critical Journal of Philosophy*, vol. 1 no. 1 (apparently authored primarily by Hegel despite the fact that Schelling was the principal editor), the ideal relationship between antithetical metaphysical views is described in terms of the relationship of reciprocal recognition (CJI, p. 276). See also the introductory essay by H. S. Harris, "Skepticism, Dogmatism, and Speculation in the Critical Journal," in *Between Kant and Hegel*, ed. George di Giovanni and H. S. Harris (Albany: State University of New York Press, 1985), 253–54.

idea is lacking," what will appear to the critic will be "only two subjectivities in opposition," and there will be no common content perceived. But Hegel *also* contrasts the dichotomous opposition between standpoints with the situation in which there is "reciprocal recognition" between them. Here Hegel has apparently shifted from the requirement that the *critic* recognize (in some form of Schellingian intuition) the absolute in each philosophical standpoint, to the requirement that those located *at* each standpoint recognize *the other* as reflecting the same absolute that they themselves grasp, but from a standpoint different from their own.

But *more* than this would seem to be implied in that the recognition must be *reciprocal*—it would seem that this all could take place only if the other standpoint adopted the same attitude toward us! Here, however, in what is, apparently, the first usage of a notion that will come to play a central role in Hegel's philosophy—that of "reciprocal recognition" (*gegenseitige Anerkennen*)—we are given little indication as to how this might be spelled out. And yet for the moment it would seem that it had provided Hegel with a distinctive way of understanding the Schellingian constructed line. The achievement of a coincidence between two otherwise opposing perspectives on the absolute must involve each perspective's coming to recognize itself in the other—coming to see the other as the same as itself, albeit, in an inverse or roundabout form.

We might crudely list some of the aspects of the philosophical position of the early Schelling crucial for understanding Hegel's development. First there were those critical epistemological consequences of pantheist ontology: the rejection of *dualism* and the claim of the essentially embodied and hence perspectival character of consciousness; the critique of Kantian *Verstand* as grounded in such a perspectivally limited consciousness; and the critique of any "theistic" support for the concept of knowledge found in scientific or transcendental realism with its notion of an extra-worldly God's-eye view. Next we might list the positive uses of the Neoplatonic form of pantheist ontology: the use of the *coincidentia oppositorum*, or "identity of identity and difference," and the extension of this into the idea of those perspectival potences that provide the appropriate level for philosophical analysis of the world.

These were the constituents of that framework from within which Hegel was to work out his own distinctive philosophical method and system in the years leading up to the construction of his great early work, the *Phenomenology of Spirit*. But in these years Hegel would also move away from aspects of Schelling's philosophy, importantly his notion of intellectual intuition. And as we have seen hinted in his introduction to the *Critical Journal*, the notion of *recognition* (*Anerkennen*) would come to play the major role here. We can see further indications of this later development, however, already in Hegel's 1802–3 manuscript, *System der Sittlichkeit* (*System of Ethical Life*). We know that at this time Hegel still saw his position as essentially belonging to Schelling's identity philosophy, and yet Hegel's text shows clear anticipations of what was to emerge as the distinctive position of his *Phenomenology*.[32]

Recognition and the Constructed Line: Hegel's Early Analysis of Ethical Life

Congruent with the project of mapping ethical life along the lines of Schelling's potence theory, Hegel proceeds from his own formulation of the constructed line in which "concept" and "intuition" play the role of A (subject) and B (object) respectively. Hegel's formula is now that of the unity of concept and intuition in the "Idea." Thus the guiding thought for an analysis of the ethical order will be that "[k]nowledge of the Idea of the absolute ethical order [*Sittlichkeit*] depends entirely on the establishment of perfect adequacy between intuition and concept" (*SEL*, 99–100; *SS*, 415). Accordingly, Hegel's procedure will be to look at structures of ethical life which can be schematized in terms of a constructed line, the poles of which are ideal determinations in which concept "subsumes" intuition and vice-versa.

To get our bearings with Hegel here we might situate his construction against the background of the type of construction in terms of potences found in Schelling's own writings. In his *Ideas for a Philosophy of Nature*, Schelling used the potence structure to try to schematize nature as *living* rather than mechanical.[33] For example, we can map the world this way into three potences. First, the universe can be thought of as a simple *plurality of objects*, but then, this requires the existence of a second potence, a set of general unifying laws of mechanics, to comprehend their movement. And yet, thought in *this* way, it is as if the laws belong to some alien realm beyond the objects themselves. But if we look at a living *organism*, the third potence, we see an instance of a body which is moved in a regular manner from *within* rather than from without. We thus now have a triune structure in which the organism represents (like the Holy Spirit between

[32] Hegel's text was apparently used as a basis for his lectures. It had, however, evidently been prepared for publication as part of a single systematic work only to be abandoned before completion. We can see it as an attempt to apply Schellingian identity philosophy to moral and political science. Structurally the text was to find its place within the system as the *third* of four parts—logic, natural philosophy, social philosophy, philosophy of religion—a structure in which can be recognized the Cusan/Schellingian quadratic structure of Absolute unity followed by its development through the three exponential powers.
[33] Schelling, *Ideas for a Philosophy of Nature*, 50–51.

the God the Father and the Son) the point of "indifference" unifying the other two opposed levels. Schelling thus refers to the organism as a "perfect mirror-image of the absolute in Nature and for Nature."[34] It is a perfect mirror-image of nature as a unity because it is, as a type of self-organizing being, that which contains its concept, i.e., its soul, within it, just as nature, conceived as absolute, itself must. Moreover, it is a mirror image of the whole *for* nature because it can, as sensate, mirror or represent nature within it.

The organism is itself capable of being understood in terms of the opposed poles of body and soul with the principle of their indifference, the unity of body and soul. In such a schema we cannot think of body and soul as different *substances* joined together *in* the organism; it is triune whole, not a composite one. Once this progressive unfolding of the absolute has reached this level of the sentient organism, we can see how the ideational realm will emerge. The organism, via the primitive representational capacities of its soul in sensation, starts to transform the real into the ideal, such a process reaching its zenith in humans, where reason, the capacity for philosophical thought *about the absolute itself*, completes the process of the idealization of the absolute subsequent to its unfolding within the real: "[H]ere, where the embodiment of the infinite into the finite reaches the point of absolute indifferencing, it immediately resolves itself again into its opposite and therewith into the *aether* of absolute ideality, so that with the perfectly real image of the absolute in the real world, the most perfect organism, the completely *ideal* image, also immediately enters, as reason."[35]

Humans, with their rational souls, are able to reunify within the order of ideation—that "*aether* of absolute ideality"—all that which sensory intuition had presented to them as diverse. Facing two ways into both the natural and ideational realms, humans thus stand at the indifference point between the realms charted by the philosophical sciences of natural philosophy and transcendental idealism. Hegel expresses the Schellingian point in the following way: "The point of transition, the middle term [*das Mittlere*] through which identity constructing itself as nature passes over to identity constructing itself as intelligence, is the internalization of the light of nature, the lightning stroke of the ideal upon the real, as Schelling calls it, its self-constitution as point. This point is Reason, the turning point [*Wendepunkt*] of both sciences [i.e., of the real and the ideal—philosophy of nature and transcendental idealism]" (*D*, 170; *W*, 2:111).

It is this type of progressive mapping or "construction" in terms of the

---

[34] Ibid., 51.
[35] Ibid.

triune potence structures that Hegel applies to the *ethical* realm in *System of Ethical Life* with his schema of unities of concept and intuition. The Kantian terminology here is significant. Such a terminology is applicable because potences are structures of "ideal determination": like Kantian transcendental structures, they are simultaneously both structures of *standpoints* from which objects are grasped (the conditions of experience and knowledge) and general structures of the objects as experienced and known from those standpoints. Also, that intuition and concept are always present together agrees, of course, with the Kantian doctrine that "neither concepts without intuition . . . nor intuitions without concepts, can yield knowledge."[36] Furthermore, the distinction between judgments in which intuition subsumes concept and those in which concept subsumes intuition can be seen to reflect Kant's distinction in the *Prolegomena* between judgments of perception and judgments of experience, or his distinction in the *Critique of Judgement* between "reflective" and "determinative" judgments. Thus, for example, in judgments of perception, the intuited "feel" of the perception predominates (I *feel* that "the room is warm") while in the latter the universalized conceptual judgment ("air is elastic") will outweigh how things *appear* to me.[37]

Hegel commences his mapping of the ethical landscape at the level of *feeling*—a starting point consistent with the fact that this section of the manuscript was to follow systematically that of philosophy of nature where the unfolding of the potences would have ended, presumably, with the sentient organism. But the "feelings" involved in this section, while overlapping with those attributable to animals, are essentially human ones: they are feelings with a recognizable *intentional structure*.

As recent interpreters of such mental states as "emotions" have stressed, the analyses must combine "subjective" and "objective" aspects (feeling *and* concepts) in order to account for the fact that we typically identify such feelings in terms of the *objects* toward which they are directed. It is this aspect of human "feelings" that Hegel is able to capture with his idea that here "concept" is present but "subsumed" by intuition. Thus, hunger (the feeling with which Hegel starts) presents itself *as* a feeling, but as one directed to a definite (and so conceptually determined) type of (intentional) object—food.

Hunger naturally leads to consumption and the annihilation of the ob-

---

[36] Kant, *Critique of Pure Reason*, A50/B74.
[37] One major difference from the Kantian position is clear, however. Kant's universalism implies that the validity of cognitive judgments will always outweigh the other two: the truth of the phenomenal world is simply given in Newtonian science. But for Hegel, both intuitively dominant and conceptually dominant perspectives will be unified in the indifference point of the third element of the triune structure.

ject, but another possible outcome coincides with the *inversion* of the relation of concept and intuition: the feeling might motivate productive work, an act that *defers* satisfaction but *transforms* its object. *Now* the intentional structure is such that *intuition* is subsumed under the *concept* as gratification of the feeling is deferred and the intuited object is understood under the concept of that *which it is to be* (*SEL*, 106–7; *SS*, 420–21). And it can no longer be this *singular* thing that is the object of this intentional state because *this* thing is transformed in the work. Furthermore, the endurance of the object at the natural level is mirrored by its endurance at the *ideal* level. It gains a more permanent place in an ideational *aether* as a concept that directs the bodily intentional activity.

We need not concern ourselves with the detail of the rather baroque structures that Hegel unfolds: what is significant for us is how this analysis leads to the theme of recognition. After a brief discussion of the structure of possession as the outcome of labor, Hegel considers the application of labor to different types of objects: plants, animals, and humans. By the last of these shapes of activity and object he means, of course, education— *Bildung* (*SEL*, 108–09; *SS*, 422–25).

This series of objects of labor has itself, as is expected, the triune structure of the potence, the laboring consciousnesses involved providing, as it were, the points of view in terms of which the potence is structured. The plant has no individual significance because the labor here is directed toward the inorganic conditions of the plant's existence—the earth in which it grows: "Labor can have little or nothing of the specific life of the plant" (*SEL*, 108; *SS*, 423). And so here concept (directed at the universal) outweighs intuition. In contrast, labor on the *animal* (its domestication) is directed toward the *particular* animal itself, and so "the concept of the living thing [is] subsumed under intuition" (*SEL*, 108; *SS*, 423). As we might anticipate, the potence structure of labor on the human being, education, and its product, "intelligence" (the intelligent human being as such) represents the "absolute identity" of the first two structures, the identity of the two reciprocal subsumptions, repeating Schelling's triunity of inorganic, organic, and rational life.

We must remember that the potence is a level of ideal determination, that is, it exists as *real* only inasmuch as it simultaneously exists *for* a cognizing or representing consciousness. Hegel answers the implicit question of the point of view *for which* man exists as man when he states that "[m]an is a potence, universality, for his other, but so is his other for him" (*SEL*, 109; *SS*, 424; translation modified). That is, the *point of view* from which an intelligence is recognized as such is that of *another* intelligent being of the same kind, a result anticipating the role accorded to recognition in the *Phenomenology of Spirit*.

Within the Schellingian theory, the rational human organism represents the point of absolute indifference between the realms of ideation and extension, and it is at this point that Hegel's theory of recognition emerges. Here, the other has to have an ideal determination as an object and yet be an object that is also a *subject:* "The ideal determination of the other is objective, but in such a way that this objectivity is immediately posited as subjective . . . ; for if something is to be a potence for another, it must not be pure universality and indifference in a *relation* to it; it must be posited for itself or a universal truly and absolutely—and the intelligence is this in the highest degree" (*SEL,* 110; *SS,* 425; translation modified).

Intelligence only exists for intelligence, and so what now follows is an analysis of *this* potence structure in terms of possible ways in which one rational human can exist *as such* for another.[38] Again Hegel starts with the form of practical consciousness of feeling, but now it is sexual desire, a human desire directed at another particular human, which is relevant. And just as hunger had its outcome in that action which continues the existence of the individual organism, sexual feeling leads to the perpetuation of the species in the child. All this of course must be matched by its inverse structure in which intuition is subsumed by the concept, and *this* structure instantiates human relations mediated by the *tool.* The tool mediates not some *particular* working activity (*this* subject working on *this* thing) but a *generalizable* activity: it is a "persistent norm of labor." Thus: "Anyone can make a similar tool and work with it" (*SEL,* 113; *SS,* 428). Thus here too we are dealing with *recognizable* intelligent activity because the tool allows the transmission of a goal-directed activity by *copying.*

There must be a third unity that is the identity of the "child" and the "tool" (which respectively represent unity [intuition] and separation [concept]), a third that must possess both the uniqueness of the child *and* the

---

[38] In his work of 1800, *System of Transcendental Idealism,* Schelling had argued that paradoxes surrounding the principle of the intelligence's self-generation could only be solved by the existence of a type of predetermined harmony existing between the self-constituting act of that intelligence and an act of *another* intelligence:

> In a word, this act must not be the direct ground of a producing in the intelligence, but again, conversely, the intelligence must not be a direct ground of the action, and likewise the *presentation* of such an act in the intelligence, as an act independent of it, and the *act itself,* outside it, must coexist, as though the one were determined by the other.
> Such a relationship is conceivable only through a pre-established *harmony.* . . .
> But such a harmony is conceivable only between subjects of equal reality, and hence this act must have proceeded from a subject endowed with just the same reality as the intelligence itself." (160–61)

From this Schelling derived the principle: "The act of the self-determination, or the free action of the intelligence upon itself, can be explained only by the determinate action of an intelligence external to it" (161).

ideality of the concept. This third is "*speech*, the tool of reason, the child of intelligent beings" (*SEL*, 114; *SS*, 429).

Speech is the "middle term" of intelligence recognizing intelligence, which is itself absolute ideality. Thus we must not think of speech here as an "accident" of an intelligent subject. As a potence, intelligence only exists inasmuch as it is recognized, and speech is the medium, the middle term, of this recognition. It has real and ideal aspects: intuitive presentation and conceptual meaning; both are essential. Without meaning there would be nothing to recognize *in* the speech; without intuitive presentation, nothing *in* which meaning could be recognized. But its bodily form is well suited to the ideational *aether* in that it is "infinitely vanishing . . . a light and ethereal body which passes away as it is formed" (*SEL*, 113; *SS*, 429). When Hegel says of speech that its "reality is completely absorbed into its ideality" (*SEL*, 114; *SS*, 429), we might take this to mean that the entire effect of speech is achieved *only* in virtue of its being recognized as containing intelligence or meaning. Without this recognition, how could this momentary, minor fluctuation of the air have *any* significance?

As a totality, speech itself has three potences. In the first, it is exemplified by gesture, mien, or "their totality in glance of the eye." The "shifting ideal play" in such forms of expression achieves no permanent place in the ideal order because it operates at an unconscious level, expressing feeling and being responded to in kind. When intuition is subsumed under concept in the next potence, what results is that which Hegel refers to as the "formal concept of speech." The text here is far from clear, but what Hegel seems to be alluding to is speech as it is commonly conceived in philosophy. Here speech "expresses nothing but the reference to the subject and the object, between which it is the ideal middle term; but this linkage is made clear by a subjective thinking outside the object" (*SEL*, 114; *SS*, 430). It would seem that this is speech in which the spoken sign is thought of as standing *for* a thing, the bond being held in virtue of a unifying act of the single subject. Such a "monological" character of this level of speech is further suggested by his reference to this kind of speech as a "corporeal sign" with the "ideality of the tool" (*SEL*, 115; *SS*, 431). As a tool is applied *to* an object, this "corporeal sign" is directed to its object, that to which it refers. This monological character is thrown into relief when compared to the third level of speech—"sounding speech" or "resounding speech" (*tönende Rede*)—which unites the two earlier potences.

How should we think of the semantics of "sounding speech" if it has a potence structure different from that of formal speech? Hegel does not say much concerning what type of speech we might see as exemplary here. We can, however, still gain a few clues as to what he has in mind. While in formal speech the emphasis was on the objectivity and corporeality of the sign, here the use of the present participle *tönende*, or "sounding," suggests the *event* or *performance*-like aspect of the speech act—a *speaking* that cannot be conceptualized simply as the production of an objective sign by a speaker.[39] And given that it is the speech itself that is "sounding," perhaps the suggestion is that of an act without an underlying preformed agent, an act such as that found in Fichtean "positing."

Furthermore, it would seem that sounding speech is not speech used instrumentally like a tool, as this would belong to the second potence. To get someone to do something by speaking to them is to use them like a tool: it is primarily to *use* their intelligence rather than to address them *as* an intelligence. However, sounding speech "is the middle term of intelligences; it is logos, their rational bond" (*SEL*, 115; *SS*, 431). This suggestion that sounding speech is essentially *dialogical* in contrast to the monological character of formal speech is reinforced in the idea that while the *recognition* involved in formal speech is "dumb" (*stumme*), that involved in sounding speech is *absolute*. Presumably the recognition of sounding speech is manifested in *further* speech rather than in something other than speech, such as action. But here these are all only hints, and the relevance of this model will not become clear until we can see how all these aspects are eventually fitted together in Hegel's later work. And we will see them reappear, not only in Hegel's *Phenomenology*, but also in his logic and his system.

[39] Here the translators of the English edition do not capture the peculiarity of Hegel's phrase with their "spoken word."

CHAPTER 4

The Revolutionary Philosophical Form
of Hegel's *Phenomenology of Spirit*

IN THE PREFACE to the *Phenomenology of Spirit*, Hegel invokes the Schellingian ideational *aether*, stating that philosophical science will require
"that self-consciousness should have raised itself into this *Aether* in order
to be able to live—and [actually] to live—with Science and in Science" (*PS*,
§26; *W*, 3:29).[1] Indeed, this will be the task of the *Phenomenology* itself—to
map the progress to the realm of this *aether* of science of a consciousness
initially mired in the immediacy of sense. Thus the terminus of the *Phenomenology* will coincide with the starting point of philosophical science
per se, the *Science of Logic*, a point of "*pure* self-recognition in absolute
otherness" (*PS*, §26; *W*, 3:29).

This all sounds as if the striving for philosophical knowledge will demand the complete abandonment of one's singularly embodied and located subjective viewpoint and the attainment of some "absolute point of
view" or "view from nowhere," which is also the absolute's, that is, God's,
viewpoint. Kierkegaard later summed up such an interpretation of Hegel
when he declared that for Hegel philosophy aimed at a cognitive state in
which "being an individual man is a thing that has been abolished," a state
in which the speculative philosopher "confuses himself with humanity at

---

[1] Here Hegel repeats his earlier Schellingian sounding characterisation of the spiritual
"*aether*" as the "pure self-recognition in absolute otherness . . . the ground and soil of Science
or knowledge in general." (*PS*, §26; *W*, 3:29). As in the 1803/4 sketch of his systematic
philosophy of spirit, it is the relation between a singular, subjective consciousness and consciousness in general which is at issue.

large; whereby he becomes something infinitely great, and at the same time nothing at all."[2]

This is not Hegel's view, however. A Kierkegaardian reading of the preface depends on understanding Hegel as unilaterally affirming the viewpoint of "Science" over against an antithetical viewpoint of "consciousness"—but such is not the case. It is true that the standpoint of consciousness within which the conscious subject knows "objects in their antithesis to itself, and itself in antithesis to them" counts as the very opposite or "other" of science and as involving a *loss* of spirit. But, conversely, consciousness has its own, somewhat Kierkegaardian, complaint against science, because science appears for consciousness as a "remote beyond in which it no longer possesses itself." Thus: "Each of these two aspects [of self-conscious spirit] appears to the other as the *inversion* of the truth [*das Verkehrte der Wahrheit*]" (*PS*, §26; *W*, 3:30; emphasis added).

The counterclaim of the individual consciousness against science cannot be simply denied: consciousness is aware of its "right" to be shown the "ladder" to the standpoint of science, a right based on its "absolute independence," which it is conscious of possessing "in every phase of his knowledge." The singularity of a knowing subject cannot be eclipsed because the individual is, for each phase of knowledge, "the absolute form"—the "immediate certainty" of itself or "unconditioned being."[3] Philosophy must aspire to the *aether* of science, but science itself must "show *that* and *how* this element [of self-certainty] belongs to it" (*PS*, §26; *W*, 3:30).

A little further on we find more evidence against the Kierkegaardian reading of Hegel. In ancient times the stress in science was on the elevation of the individual consciousness to universality, but in modern times the task has become more that of "freeing determinate thoughts from their

---

2 Søren Kierkegaard, *Concluding Unscientific Postscript*, trans. David F. Swenson and Walter Lowrie (Princeton: Princeton University Press, 1941), 112–13.

3 Such "immediate certainty" here should not be confused with that of the Cartesian variety. In terms of the distinction between "form" and "content," the self-certain Cartesian consciousness is certain of itself as its essential *content* and its certainty is a form of *determinate knowledge*. But neither should we, however, interpret this in Kantian terms in which the transcendental ego *is* essentially "form" of a distinct and indifferent content rather than "content" itself. Like Fichte, Hegel is describing a *real* ego here, not just a formal one.

Hegel's "absolute form" here is more akin to Cusa's "form of forms." From this perspective form and content are thought of as different and yet identical, as in the Cusan doctrine of the unity of opposites, rather than as dichotomously opposed as within both Aristotelianism and Kantianism. Furthermore, like Cusa's *imago dei*, this self is a "finite-infinity" and so not a mere determinate thing, amenable to the representations of discursive reason. Cusa had thought that such unity could only be made present to the mind in a type of indirect, analogical and apparently contradictory form of thought. As we will see, this idea also seems operative in Hegel, for whom the self is presented to itself in a fundamentally *hermeneutical* and analogical way: it recognizes itself, but in an "inverted" form, within the expressions of another.

fixity so as to give actuality to the universal, and impart to it spiritual life," and *this* is achieved "when the pure certainty of self abstracts from itself— *not by leaving itself out, or setting itself aside*, but by giving up the *fixity* of its self-positing" (PS, §33; W, 3:37; emphasis added). For Spinoza it may have been the case that abstracting from the self meant "leaving oneself out" or "setting oneself aside" so as to reach some selfless "view from nowhere." For Hegel, however, abstraction from self means something different; it involves the giving up of that "fixity" of one's initial self-conception rather than one's singular self-certainty per se.

Philosophy and Everyday Consciousness in Hegel's Essay on Skepticism

The issue of the relation between everyday consciousness and philosophy is one that had been addressed by Hegel in his earlier Jena writings. In line with the aspirations for philosophy he shared with Schelling, Hegel attacked those who had wanted to limit philosophy to the standpoint of finite, everyday consciousness.[4] As is clear from Hegel's long essay "The Relation of Skepticism to Philosophy," however, it was not the standpoint of common sense per se that was the problem so much as the *dogmatic* adherence to it.[5]

In this essay, directed against the skeptical philosophy of his contemporary G. E. Schultze, Hegel was concerned to bring out the difference between *ancient* skepticism and post-Cartesian varieties of skepticism such as Schultze's. Ancient skepticism was not directed *against* philosophical knowledge, as is its modern counterpart, but rather against the dogmatism of "ordinary common sense" or "ordinary consciousness," a dogmatism that "holds fast to the given, the fact, the finite . . . , and sticks to it as certain, as secure, as eternal" (RSP, 332; W, 2:240). In fact, it would seem that common sense can be held nondogmatically—this is the attitude of common sense that ancient skepticism addresses and engages with in its efforts to free it from dogmatism by demonstrating to it "the instability of this kind of certainty, in a way which is at the same time *close to ordinary consciousness*" (RSP, 332; W, 2:240; emphasis added).[6]

---

[4] This is most obvious in his attack on the approach of W. T. Krug, who, influenced by the Scottish "commonsense" school of Reid, gave a foundational role to the standpoint of common sense. It is also clear in the concern expressed in the introduction to the *Critical Journal* to differentiate genuinely speculative philosophies from those "unphilosophies" that are mired in finite everyday consciousness.

[5] For a thorough treatment of this essay and of the general relevance of ancient skepticism for Hegel see Michael N. Forster, *Hegel and Skepticism* (Cambridge, Mass.: Harvard University Press, 1989), esp. chap. 1.

[6] Rather than the problem being located in common consciousness itself, it is located in certain dogmatically held assumptions *about* that consciousness.

Post-Cartesian skepticism is very different in its relation to common sense. Hegel's claim is that this skepticism is held as a conclusion derived from an initial *dogmatic* assumption about consciousness: namely, that in consciousness there is something known with certainty—the "facts of consciousness." Here it would seem that the type of skepticism Hegel is attacking is a kind that is based on the representationalist conception of consciousness such as is found in Descartes, the idea that consciousness is *directly aware* of its own contents (ideas or representations) and *only* directly aware of those contents. On the basis of this assumption, the skeptic now raises the question as to how the mind can know anything *beyond* its representations, and concludes that it cannot.

It is to counter this dogmatic starting point that Hegel appeals both to ancient skepticism *and* to common sense itself: "[W]e ought to refer the most recent skepticism, with its certainty of the facts of consciousness, above all things, to this ancient skepticism . . . *or to common sense itself,* which is very well aware [or recognizes, "*erkennt*"] that all the actual facts of its consciousness, and even this finite consciousness itself, passes away, and that there is no certainty therein" (RSP, 332; W, 2:240–41; emphasis added). Thus ancient skepticism can appeal to a type of skepticism already implicit in common consciousness itself; but again, this skepticism is very different from that at which modern skepticism arrives. The skepticism of the modern skeptic involves an inferential annihilation of the possibility of knowledge of anything beyond the self: it starts with the certainty of the facts of consciousness and ends with the conclusion that "that certainty is nothing." In contrast, common sense, when it expresses its skeptical core, says something *positive*—it "expresses itself thus: 'Everything *is* transient'" (RSP, 332; W, 2:241).

HEGEL'S BRIEF REFLECTIONS on the phenomenological method in the Preface follow and cohere with a passage in which he explicitly criticizes Spinoza's equating the goal of objectivity with the loss of the singularity and subjectivity of everyday consciousness. Spinoza's philosophy, claims Hegel, had "shocked the age in which it was proclaimed" because it submerged self-consciousness in substance rather than preserved it.[7] In con-

---

[7] Now, in a sense this, of course, is not what shocked German intellectuals in the 1780s when the Spinozist controversy erupted. What shocked them was the apparent *atheism* of this philosophy: judged against the conventional theist assumptions of a transcendent and anthropomorphic God, Spinoza's substance looked anything but divine. Thus Hegel here reinterprets this shock, displacing it from the religious terrain to one that seems both philosophical and political. What is shocking about Spinozism is that, in expelling individual subjectivity from substance, it denies the *right* of each individual to maintain its absolute singularity while existing within the medium of a universal mind.

trast, Hegel's view is that "everything turns on grasping and expressing the True, not only as *Substance,* but equally as *Subject"* (*PS,* §17; *W,* 3:23).

This passages is commonly interpreted in such a way that Hegel is seen as positing a type of divine "supermind," a cosmic intentional subject akin to the omniscient Christian God but who, in contrast, somehow actualizes himself *through* his own creatures, attaining his own perfect and infinite self-consciousness through their individually imperfect and finite cognitive capacities.[8] On such a view, Hegel has ended up with a type of (probably incoherent) amalgam of Spinozist pantheism and a traditional personalist and transcendent theism. But the idea of "grasping and expressing the True, not only as *Substance* but equally as *Subject"* can, like the idea of the *verkehrte* standpoints of consciousness and science, suggest Hegel's continuing use of the Schellingian "constructed line."

Later in the Preface the image of the "constructed line" clearly stands out in Hegel's contrast of philosophical demonstration with that of mathematics (the model of philosophical demonstration accepted by Spinoza). Philosophical thought, Hegel claims, unites the process in which the *"determinate existence* [*Dasein*] of a thing comes about *as* determinate existence" with that "in which its *essence* or inner nature comes to be": "The movement is the twofold [*gedoppelte*] process and the genesis of the whole, in such wise that each side simultaneously posits the other, and each therefore has both perspectives [*Ansichten*] within it; together they thus constitute the whole by dissolving themselves, and by making themselves into its moments" (*PS,* §42; *W,* 3:43). The question to be asked is: Can Hegel make something of such early Schellingian figures? Can he conceive of the "spiritual" relations existing among individual finite consciousnesses in a conceptually coherent way that rejects the recourse to "dogmatic" metaphysical ideas, such as the idea that we must all be parts of some divine supermind?

It is my contention here that much of Hegel's intellectual labor is directed toward achieving just that, and that in this project he is far more successful than is generally acknowledged. To see how such an end might be achieved, we must see how his theory of spirit is developed in chapter 4 of the *Phenomenology,* a theory centered on the hermeneutic idea of a two-way recognition between conscious subjects permitted by the communicative and inverting "Word." Before moving toward this, however, it is necessary to say a few preliminary words concerning that which enframes the whole project of the *Phenomenology:* "consciousness."

In the *Phenomenology* Hegel commonly uses "consciousness" as a type of

---

[8] See, for example, Charles Taylor, *Hegel* (Cambridge: Cambridge University Press, 1975), 87–90.

shorthand expression for "a conscious subject." There are other occasions, however, when the term is used more abstractly and, like Kant's "consciousness in general," as a "mass" rather than a "count" noun.[9] Thus, Hegel also writes of consciousness itself as a type of *aether,* or "element," an *aether within which* a conscious subject is related to its objects, a relatedness he characterizes variously as a "disparity" (*Ungleichheit*) or as "the negative."[10] In this latter sense, "consciousness" presupposes but does not coincide with any "conscious subject"; rather, the conscious subject is one of the poles of consciousness. Such an idea of consciousness as a *relationship* between a subject and a disparate object looks forward to the more modern concept of "intentionality."[11]

A third, *dynamic* way of talking about consciousness tends to subsume both of these senses, however. Thus in paragraph 82 of the Introduction, Hegel describes consciousness in terms of its double action of *distinguishing itself from* and *relating itself to* something—its object: "[A]nd the determinate aspect of this *relating,* or of the *being* of something for a consciousness, is *knowing.*" This dynamic conception recalls Fichte's account of "the I" as that which *posits* its object and thereby *posits itself* as determinately related to that object.

Like the Kantian idea of a subject's "constituting" activity, the Fichtean subject's "positing" was thought of as an act in which objects came to have a determinate existence for the knower. But the idea of objects as having a *thinkable* existence beyond their determinately knowable one was rejected as a breach of Kant's own injunction against applying concepts to "things in themselves." Thus, as self-positing, the subject could not be thought of

---

[9] As the term implies, "count" nouns (for example, "book," "cat") name discrete, countable things (books, cats) whereas "mass" nouns ("water," "sand" etc.) designate the sort of "stuff" that we *take as* continuous and that we parcel out in terms of *amounts.*

[10] In the *Phenomenology* section of part 3 of the *Encyclopaedia of the Philosophical Sciences,* Hegel talks about consciousness and *Ich* in a way that brings out the double meaning I am trying to capture here. The *Ich,* he tells us, is both "one side of the relationship and the whole relationship" (*EPM,* §413).

[11] It is this sense of consciousness as an *aether* of relationships that allows Hegel to find a certain structural homology between consciousness and what he terms "spirit" and, what is initially even more puzzling, between consciousness and the "the concept," a homology that is essential for understanding how phenomenology can be the starting point of philosophical science. It would seem that the point being made is that spirit too should be thought of as a type of "space" of relationships between disparate, or *ungleich,* elements—subjects and objects—and that an examination of the relations of consciousness will show the dependence of its relations and processes on this more broadly ranging and complex set of relations and processes. In an analogous way, and at an even greater level of abstraction, Hegel's notion of "the concept" signifies the *logical* space, or *aether,* within which concepts or "thought determinations" are related to each other. Without this understanding, such formulations as consciousness being the "immediate determinate existence [*Dasein*] of spirit" (*PS,* §36; *W,* 3:38) might mislead us to picture spirit as a god-like conscious being.

as *any kind of object* which existed independently *of* its own knowledge of itself. As self-consciousness, it did not "represent" itself but *posited* itself, and this act of positing had to be one in which the subject was somehow brought *into existence*. But this did not necessarily mean that the Fichtean subject was a type of self-creating thing. It meant that it was not a type of "thing" or "substance" at all. Rather than some kind of thing or a fact— *Tatsache*, the subject was a *Tathandlung*, an *action* for which there was no pre-existing *agent*.[12] For Hegel as well, and analogous to the noncoincidence of consciousness qua subject and relational *aether*, we should be wary of understanding the "distinguishing" and "relating" "acts" of consciousness as acts of an underlying single "conscious subject." As we will see, these are "acts" that can only be performed in the context of the like acting of *other* conscious subjects.

The "doubleness" of the distinguishing and relating here is meant to capture something of the double relation to an object that exists in one's knowledge of it. As in Kant, beyond the sense of the thing *as known*, there must be another sense of the thing as it is independent of its relation to the knowing subject. "In consciousness one thing exists *for* another . . . ; at the same time, this other is to consciousness not merely *for it*, but is also outside of this relationship, or exists *in itself*: the moment of truth" (*PS*, §84; *W*, 3:77).[13] Elsewhere, Hegel captures this doubleness of consciousness with the idea that the objects or actions of consciousness have a certain ambiguity or "double-sensedness" (*Doppelsinnigkeit*)[14] (*PS*, §178; *W*, 3:142).

Like Fichte, Hegel rejected any interpretation of the doubleness of the objects of consciousness which involved the metaphysical opposing of thinkable noumenon to knowable phenomenon. However, Hegel's innovation hangs on the idea that the doubleness of any intentional object is derived from the fact that besides one's own subjective intending of an object one can always in principle also recognize the same object as the object of some other subject's—that is, some other "objective Subject-Object's"—intending. Individual consciousness is doubled because to be a

---

12 While opening up a new conception of subjectivity as activity rather than substance, Fichte seems to have failed to attain any final satisfactory articulation of this conception. His accounts changed significantly between his various versions of the *Wissenschaftslehre* from 1794 onward as he constantly attempted to fine-tune his basic idea of the self-positing subject. Dieter Henrich has charted these changes through subtly different key formulae for the self-positing subject in "Fichte's Original Insight," trans. David R. Lachterman in *Contemporary German Philosophy*, Vol. 1, 1982, ed. Darrel E. Christensen et al. (University Park: Pennsylvania State University Press, 1982).

13 Cf. Paul Weiss's claim that "[t]o know is to acknowledge a real being as the counterpart of a judged articulation of it; it is to confront the judgment of a being with the being the judgment purports to be about." "Cosmic Necessities," *Review of Metaphysics* 4 (1951): 368.

14 Hegel also talks of the *"gedoppelte Bedeutung"* of the act of self-consciousness (*PS*, §182; *W*, 3:146).

consciousness, that consciousness must *already* be involved in relations with other consciousnesses, relations in which each is able hermeneutically to understand the contents of the other's intentional states. What has been said of Donald Davidson might equally be said of Hegel: "The basic idea is that one cannot recognize that one's beliefs constitute a subjective point of view on something objective, except insofar as one also recognizes other subjective points of view. Hence self-conscious believers must also be self-conscious communicators, i.e., interpreters of others."[15]

We might regard the schema of the "constructed line" as amounting to a hint of how the relation of these subjective viewpoints is to be conceived. We certainly cannot regard it as a *representation* of "how things are" in some general sense because this would be to cast ourselves outside the schema into the role of a transcendent viewer regarding a bounded whole from the outside. Schelling's solution is, like that of Cusanus, an essentially metaphorical one, and Hegel's demand is that it should be a fully conceptualized one. The task of thinking this through will, in fact, be the task of Hegel's entire oeuvre, but the key to this will be the recognitive theory of spirit found in the main text of the *Phenomenology*, and it is to this that I now turn.

The Phenomenological Drama and Its Audience

As is well known, the main text of the *Phenomenology* weaves together two different layers or levels of discourse, layers or levels aligned with two clearly separated points of view. The most obvious and striking of these is a type of "dramatic narrative" depicting the progress and setbacks of a character who has embarked on a quest.[16] This character is "consciousness" (in the sense of naturally conscious subject), and the quest is the achievement of the standpoint of philosophical science.[17] In this narrative, consciousness moves within and between configurations or "shapes" of theoretical and practical consciousness (in the sense of *aether*, or "element")—sense-certainty, perception, understanding, self-certainty, and so on—which we may think of as relatively coherent or unified theoretical and practical perspectives within which consciousness relates it-

---

[15] Carole Rovane, "The Metaphysics of Interpretation" in *Essays on Truth and Interpretation,* ed. Ernest Lapore (Oxford: Blackwell, 1986), 423.

[16] The importance of the dramatic structure of the *Phenomenology* was emphasized by Kenley Dove in his influential article "Hegel's Phenomenological Method," in *New Studies in Hegel's Philosophy,* ed. Warren Steinkraus (New York: Holt, Rinehart & Winston, 1971), while Joseph Flay has stressed the "quest" structure of this work in *Hegel's Quest for Certainty* (Albany: State University of New York Press, 1984).

[17] For reasons already touched on (see note 7 above), I think that it is misleading to describe the protagonist of this drama as something called *spirit.*

self to an intentional world. Movement within and between these shapes is triggered by the fact of this character's apparently unavoidable tendency to become entangled in webs of contradictions. These contradictions, rather than being mere mishaps that befall our character, seem to result from clashes between aspects of the "shape" that such a natural consciousness has assumed at that time and some other aspect of its existence. Like the heroes of tragic drama, there is something *within* this hero, some flaw, or hamartia, which brings about such crises.[18]

But not all the news here is bad. While these crises are responsible for the demise of particular shapes of consciousness, they are also responsible for the birth of new ones, as they provide the occasions for consciousness's reflective consideration of the old shape. Within each of these crises, consciousness learns something about itself that it did not know before, abandons what now appear to be the illusions that it once held, moves to a new outlook onto and orientation toward the world, and starts afresh. The "Copernican" aspects of this reflective disinvestment of a perspective are clear enough. But in addition to this, we might again draw a parallel with ancient tragedy: for consciousness, the problems within which it entangles itself form the occasion for a type of anagnorisis, the self-recognition opened up to the hero by the reversal of their fortune.

In watching a drama unfold on a stage or in the pages of a novel or narrative history, those of us in the audience typically have to "forget" our own existence as audience—that is, forget ourselves *as* sitting in the theater or our rooms, as gazing at *actors* or hearing *words*—in order to become absorbed in the drama, to participate imaginatively in *its* world. But not all dramatic or novelistic forms allow us to remain unequivocally absorbed in this way, and the *Phenomenology* itself shares in an antimimetic impulse.[19] In between the sections of dramatic depiction there are sections in which, speaking now in his own voice, Hegel addresses us *as* an audience, discussing what "we" can see and know of consciousness's progress and problems. We might think of Hegel as standing at a lectern to the side of the stage, pointing out to us aspects of the action, highlighting features we may have otherwise missed, directing our attention. But as speaking as a representative voice of the "phenomenological we," Hegel is clearly purporting to be on our, the audience's, side of the proscenium. He, no more

[18] Cf. Elliot L. Jurist, "Hegel's Concept of Recognition," *The Owl of Minerva* 19 (1987): 5–22. Robert Williams also brings out the tragic dimension in Hegel's thought in *Recognition*, chaps. 9, 10.
[19] Plato is the forerunner to what has been described as the "antitheatrical prejudice." Jonas Barish, *The Antitheatrical Prejudice* (Berkeley: University of California Press, 1981). In books 2, 3, and 10 of *The Republic*, Plato develops his well-known critique of mimetic art. Kenley Dove compares Hegel's technique in the *Phenomenology* to the Brechtean *Verfremdungseffekt*. "Hegel's Phenomenological Method," 627.

than we, belongs to the world of the drama: he can neither intervene in the events unfolding there nor communicate with the protagonists.

This metadiscourse simply makes clear something that is implicit in all dramatic narrative: besides the points of view of the depicted protagonists themselves, the depiction itself is presented *to* a point of view. But unlike the points of view of depicted characters, this metaperspective is not, at least *apparently* is not, a particular one. Observing a character as situated within its world, we typically learn about the particular way in which that character observes and assesses what happens in the world. But this learning itself seems based on the premise that our view onto the depicted world is not hampered by the particularity that dogs the character. Rather, our, the audience's, perspective is a general one, providing a type of God's-eye view (or view from the gods) onto the action depicted.

Now the paradox about many twentieth-century dramatic and novelistic forms is that this presupposition concerning the nonparticularity of the view onto the action is itself brought into question; and, significantly, it tends to be these somewhat "skeptical" approaches that, critical of the presumed *realism* of the view onto the action, thematize the position of the "we."[20] The question of whether we might think of Hegel himself as ultimately putting forward this type of account is one to which we will have occasion to return; for the moment it is important to remain at the level of the acceptance of the difference between the generality of the audience's perspective and the particularity of that of the characters.

In fact, this separation between the objective gaze of the philosophical subject (here the "we") and the contextualized and particular outlooks of those forms of consciousness observed is central to the whole question of Hegel's phenomenological method. Just as the progress of an observed drama cannot be affected from the position of the audience, so neither is the progress of natural consciousness in the *Phenomenology* to be affected by the contributions of the phenomenological we. We are meant merely to contemplate the action without the "need to import criteria, or to make use of our own bright ideas and thoughts during the course of the inquiry" (*PS*, §84; *W*, 3:77). That we do not "need to import criteria" here is an aspect of the fact that we *understand* the actions of the character on stage, for to understand an action involves recognizing what it aims at, that is, recognizing what would count as success even if the action fails.

That we can recognize in the action the evaluative criteria for its own success testifies to the doubleness of the agent's own consciousness: im-

---

[20] Here we might contrast the radically antirealist motivations of the Russian formalist literary theorist in their championing of this device with those of Brecht. For a classic statement see Victor Shklovsky, "Art as Technique," in *Russian Formalist Criticism: Four Essays*, ed. L. T. Lemon and M. J. Reis (Lincoln: University of Nebraska Press, 1965).

plicit in that consciousness is an aspect that has a universality akin to our external view onto the action, an aspect able to provide the necessary corrective for the purely "subjective view." As these two aspects of the action, "the criterion and what is to be tested, are present in consciousness itself," that is, manifested in this conscious ego's actions, natural consciousness will itself be able to carry out its own assessment of its progress and so "all that is left for us to do is simply to look on" (PS, §85; W, 3:77).[21]

As with the question of the particularity or generality of the audience's perspective, we will have occasion to return to this issue of the spectatorial or contemplative image of the philosopher later on. Here it should be noted, however, how deeply involved with some form of hermeneutic concept of the philosophical method the Phenomenology is. Our ability to follow the progress of the character is dependent on our ability to empathize with his experience and ambition: we will, in the words of the younger Hegel, "share in the interesting fate" of this person, "sorrow and rejoice with" him; "feel in ourselves the injustice encountered" by him (ETW, 78). We simply cannot grasp the events that unfold if we completely refuse to participate in this way. That is, for the Phenomenology to make any sense at all, we must regard "consciousness" in its various forms to be at the apex of a recognizable human point of view that we can and do "take up." With Nagel we might say that there is something "that it is like to be" that natural consciousness in each of its various forms; we simply cannot regard the unfolding scene onstage as a representation of a merely impersonal and subjectless natural world.[22] But at the same time we retain the external point of view onto the character on stage. The doubleness of consciousness demanded of the dramatic persona of the Phenomenology is demanded of the spectator as well.

This said, however, we seem to encounter an immediate problem once the "drama" of the Phenomenology begins. In the first three chapters, the shapes of consciousness depicted by Hegel seem far from being shapes of natural consciousness, untainted by any external philosophical theorizing. Indeed, the series of sense-certainty, perception, and understanding often seems to read more as a depiction of philosophical theories about consciousness rather than of any possible natural consciousness. But the impression that it is theories which are at issue here might be seen partly as an inescapable effect of the phenomenological method itself. Given the dramatized presentation and the spectatorial conception of the "we," such forms of consciousness must display themselves for what they are and in

---

[21] We should see Hegel's concern with the Doppelsinnigkeit of contents of consciousness as his way of addressing the Kantian distinction between phenomena and noumena.

[22] The phenomenological method is as wedded to the participation of "subject" in "substance" as Spinoza's geometrical method is linked to subjectless objectivity.

looking for the means for such presentation we surely cannot go beyond Aristotle's conception of drama as the depiction of *actions and words*.[23] This point is expressed in Joseph Flay's claim that what begins the dialectics of sense-certainty "is a description of how knowledge or knowing would be described in this unreflective mode of experience, if that description were to be elicited from one in the attitude of sense-certainty."[24]

And so what we have at the start of the *Phenomenology* is a depiction of a living character, but one pared down to barely recognizable abstracted aspects of a life. It is this that gives the early drama a somewhat Beckettian flavor: we picture consciousness as alone onstage (perhaps as simply an almost disembodied pair of speaking lips) thinking aloud, trying to capture the certainty of the "this" and the "here"—those immediately presented sense contents that this attitude accepts as reality. Later the drama becomes rather more conventional; the scenery becomes more and more filled out; our protagonist interacts with others; eventually the stage is thronged, as whole forms of life and momentous historical events are depicted. But at first there is just this apparently isolated character, perhaps analogous to Descartes's famous depiction of himself alone in his room, determined to get where he is going under his own steam, freed from the interferences of opinions of others and of the world outside the room.

Sense-Certainty: Certainty of the "This"

Natural consciousness in these opening chapters of the *Phenomenology* appears philosophical because it must attempt to display its truth to us, that is, it must display to us that which it takes to be the "truth" of its own content. The overall progression here is from its taking as this truth that which is most immediately present to sense to that which is initially absent from it but reached by reasoning. This is the progression from sense-certainty through perception to understanding. At the end of these three "scenes" consciousness comes to recognize in a moment of "anagnoritic" insight something that we in the audience (with the help of Hegel) had been able to observe all along: while consciousness, in its various shapes, had taken itself as a passive *contemplator* of things "given," it had, in fact,

---

[23] As Dove remarks, here there can be no question of an "omniscient narrator" with "special access to the inner recess" of the consciousnesses of the depicted characters, and so the experience of consciousness must come to appearance in language and action in order to be observed. "Hegel's Phenomenological Method," 626.
[24] Flay, *Hegel's Quest for Certainty*, 29. This point is neatly linked by Flay to the role of the dramatist in *eliciting* this description. Hegel as playwright is assuming a role analogous to that of the Socratic questioner.

been actively involved all along in the *constitution* of those things. Once this "myth of the given" is dispelled, consciousness now becomes "self-consciousness," reinterprets the nature of his quest, and begins again. Interpreted as an implicit philosopher, consciousness, having now perceived its role in the constitution of its objects, has passed from being a phenomenalistic empiricist to become a type of Kantian or Fichtean idealist. And what was the dynamic of the movement through these forms to their final renunciation?

To get a glimpse of this we should look at the very start of the dialectical progression. Sense-certainty is a form of knowing subjectivity for which reality is that which is given to it in immediate sensory intuition: the immediate apprehension of "what is" is taken as the "richest" and "truest" knowledge (*PS*, §91; *W*, 3:82). But such knowledge is hardly "rich," for what is known of such "objects" is simply that they "are"—the application of general concepts to them would compromise the immediacy of their apprehension. And so they are picked out by demonstratives such as "this," "now," and "here." This stripped-down character even applies to the apprehending "I": in such knowledge "this I" knows "this object" and no more.

Or at least this is how things initially appear to the knowing subject with this attitude. It would seem that to have an epistemic *position* or *attitude* means to have this attitude articulated at some level in a *general* way. One does not simply have a belief in the being of "this" and "this" and "this": one has a general attitude to the whole *class* of "thises." As Hegel comments: "An actual sense-certainty is not merely this pure immediacy, but an *instance* [*Beispiel*] of it" (*PS*, §92; *W*, 3:83). Even these apparently simple intentional contexts are ambiguous or "double-sensed."

Hegel's task is to show that this truth will make itself apparent to such a consciousness through its own experience. It will come to learn that what it takes to be immediately presented singulars are, in truth, "universals." The attempt to do this takes Hegel into the convoluted realm of the logic of demonstratives and indexical expressions in general. Let us examine just one instance.

No case of sense-certainty, it is argued, is simple. As forms of consciousness, all involve at least the poles of subject and object. It may thus be asked which pole is the truth or the essence of the knowledge. It would seem then that we might find within sense-certainty the variants of "realism" and "idealism," the former affirming the independent reality of the objects, the latter, that of the subjects. First, taking his example from time, Hegel directs a question to the realists as to the identity of this object : "What is Now?" Any attempt to answer this will invoke some *non-indexical* time specification as in "Now is night." But if this is meant to specify something essential or true, then it should have the "eternal" nature of non-context-sensitive thoughts or utterances. And yet, of course, it does *not*: tomorrow morning the thought "Now is night" will be *false*. The "now" preserves itself in time in such a sentence (the sentence is still intelligible the next day) but not as a term that designates this or that particular time: it is, rather, "preserved" as a *universal,* for "now" can designate *any* time—it simply designates *the time of the saying.* Each singular now or this is also an instance of a pragmatic universal, is "a now" or "a this."[25]

As pragmatic universals, such indexical expressions as "this" and "now" designate via elements of the context within which they are used, and so are in some sense *speaker-centered.* Hegel interprets this realization as bringing about a reversal from the "realist" position to the "idealist" one—the essential thing about the specification of the singular object is not the object itself but *the subject* who specifies it: " 'Now' is day because I see it; 'Here' is a tree for the same reason" (*PS,* §101; *W,* 3:86). But the same dialectic sets to work here as well, for it is not *me* who is at the center of this relation but *whoever it is that speaks* and so *says* "I." Again, it is the *universal* and not the singular that has shown itself to be essential here.[26]

The dialectic goes through further stages, but we have so far seen enough to note some crucial points. First, it is with his idea that consciousness must *say* what the nature of its object is, that Hegel, in these opening pages of the body of the *Phenomenology,* appears to invoke the communicative paradigm: a claim to truth must in principle be communicable to another point of view in order to separate rational conviction from mere persuasion; and so a content of consciousness must be *specifiable* to another. (A parallel move at the start of Hegel's *Logic* where the attempt to specify pure "being" as a *thought* rather than a sense content encounters similar problems.) As we have seen, sense-certainty's problem consists in the fact that it can only say what it means in *indexical* terms such as "this," "here," "now"—terms that *change* their particular meaning on each occasion of their saying. How *could* one, with such terms, communicate to another that singularity one *meant* at a particular moment? One might

[25] As Willem A. deVries points out, in the later *Phenomenology* of the *Encyclopaedia* (*EPM,* §418) Hegel abandons his earlier use of spatial and temporal indicies, assigning them to intuiton and hence "sensation" (*Empfindung*) rather than sensuous *consciousness* (*sinnliche Bewusstsein*). *Hegel's Theory of Mental Activity: An Introduction to Theoretical Spirit* (Ithaca: Cornell University Press, 1988), 88. The question of this change in Hegel's thought is linked to the vexed one of the change of the relationship between the *Phenomenology* and the system with the intrasystemic location of the later *Phenomenology.*
[26] Willem deVries makes the point that "I" has a "two-part sense" for Hegel which allows reference to individuals, contrary to the popular understanding of Hegel. *Hegel's Theory of Mental Activity,* 89–99.

"mean" something singular with a demonstrative but such terms can function only because of their pragmatic universality. Sense-certainty's attempts to specify its object turns that object from something immediately accessible only to a unique consciousness into something conceivable "from a wholly universal point of view." From Hegel's choice of words here this is obviously no minor thing: language has the "*divine* nature of directly reversing [*verkehren*] the meaning of what is said, of making it into something else" (*PS*, §110; *W*, 3:92).

We have here a strong hint that language is intimately involved with the fact that an intentional content or object can have a double aspect or double significance: on the one hand, the immediate meaning it holds for the subject from the "first person" point of view and, on the other, an inversion of this, something accessible to an opposing point of view. Indeed, the double layering of the *Phenomenology*, so crucial because it allows us as readers both to see things from the point of view of consciousness *and* to see consciousness's activities from the outside, might itself be thought of as a result of the "divine" nature of its dramatic medium: language.

It is, of course, true that consciousness itself eventually comes to grasp the contradictions inherent in its claims and so an understanding of its own "pragmatics" could not be forever beyond it. But the difference between "our" ability to see these things and that of consciousness is that *it* can do this only in *recollection*. It has to have *already acted* (so that there is something to recollect) and then ceased acting and attained in memory a quasi-spectatorial position with respect to its own past self. Consciousness, in its moment of anagnorisis, is able to recognize that which had been observable to us all along, placed as we had been outside the scene of its practical involvement with the world and so having an objective perspective on it. But in this achievement sense-certainty has also transformed itself into a different shape.

Perception

In the course of recollection, consciousness in the shape of sense-certainty comes to see something that we could see all along—that what it took to be a singular "this" was in fact a "universal," and from this insight develops a new interpretation of its content: in *perception* (literally, "truth-taking"—*Wahrnehmen*) consciousness "takes what is present to it as a universal" (*PS*, §111; *W*, 3:93). That is, what is now apprehended by it in any individual act of perceiving is taken as an instance of something intrinsically able to be perceived universally.

With this shape of consciousness Hegel refers to the type of shareable "commonsense" apprehension of things in terms of their perceivable properties—the unproblematic perception of everyday life. In sense-certainty, the immediate but uncommunicable certainty of the simple first person perspective was thought of as the touchstone of truth. Here the situation is the reverse: the unanimity of different acts of perception is taken as unproblematic. Against this background, consciousness, in any single act of apprehension, becomes "aware of the possibility of deception" so that "if a dissimilarity makes itself felt in the course of this comparison, then this is not an untruth of the object . . . but an untruth in perceiving it" (*PS*, §116; *W*, 3:97).

And so in perception there comes to be made an implicit distinction between an underlying single substance, or substrate, and the properties that inhere in this substance—a distinction that we might think of being made explicit in Descartes's reflections on the piece of wax. It thus combines that first person perspective to which the sensuous properties are immediately apparent with a more "universal" point of view no longer conditioned by that first perspective, the particularity of which was responsible for the possibility of error.

Just as the unacknowledged presence of the universal in sense-certainty constituted its weak point, we might expect that the unacknowledged presence of intuited singularity will constitute an analogous weak point for the claims of perception to be an adequate form of knowledge. And this in fact turns out to be the case. Both of those distinguished aspects of the perceived thing—the plurality of the diverse properties which it has and the underlying self-identical substrate indifferent to these properties—are necessary: while we must be able conceptually to separate the thing *from* its immediately intuited properties, these properties nevertheless always enter into its "determination." Without them, the thing could be no more than subjectively "meant."

The difficulty here is that perception has no real way of uniting these two contradictory aspects of the perceived thing (singular and universal, intuitive content and conceptual form) apart from a bland and self-contradictory conjunction: the thing is the underlying imperceptible substance—a self-identical "for-self"—but the properties remain the only way of determining that thing—properties that are "for another." In practice the perceiving subject in its dealing with such objects simply swings erratically and unknowingly between these contradictory poles, taking each, at different times, as the thing's essence or truth (*PS*, §122; *W*, 3:101). As long as there is consensus about the thing, the intuited properties are taken as determinate of the thing. Where agreement with others breaks down, that which is immediately intuited is taken as mere error to be corrected by the judgment of others. And as consciousness is, in the process of acting, still *unaware* of its activity, so it is unaware that its activity *is* erratic and inconsistent.

Again, Hegel comments on what is observable *to us* as spectators of this activity. Perceiving consciousness is *not* simply the passive receiver of the given, as it claims. For one thing, it is *active*, as it shows in its dealings with the possibility of its own error. Thus it can come to recognize, correct, and so transcend the occasions of its own "untruth"—we might think, for example, of Descartes learning not to trust his perception of the shape of towers at a distance. And having so acted, it is now able to become aware of this activity. Thus, the "behaviour [*Verhalten*] of consciousness . . . is thus so constituted that consciousness no longer merely perceives, but is also conscious of its reflection into itself, and separates this from simple apprehension proper" (*PS*, §118; *W*, 3:99).

"Der Verstand" as the Understanding of the Natural Sciences

Perceptual consciousness has corrected the idiosyncrasies of its own individual experience against the "commonsense" judgments of its community. But as we have seen, this degree of self-correcting "truth taking," characteristic of the Aristotelian epistemology, would be inadequate to the reflective demands of modern science. From the Copernican standpoint of scientific thought, the common perceptions of everyday life can themselves be construed as locally perspectival and so correctable against some ideal rather than actual consensus of self-correcting rational inquirers. It is this type of difference between common perceptual knowledge and science that is marked in Hegel's distinction between perception and the "understanding" (*der Verstand*) discussed in chapter 3 of the *Phenomenology*, a distinction that essentially repeats the Kantian distinction between the localness of judgments of perception and the universality of judgments of experience.

Paradoxically, in its critique of common sense we might see science as involving a reassertion of the claims of the singular and idiosyncratic experience that had been unilaterally "subsumed" by the common within perception. Thus the single experimental result, for example, may make the claim to be true against the weight of everyday, common experience. But the particular experience only does so insofar as it claims to represent a "higher" nonactual universality—one that stands over the merely given *generality* of common judgement.[27] And characteristically, in contrast to

---

[27] And so with the advance from sense-certainty through perception to *Verstand* we can thus see that for Hegel, the relation between subjective and objective is, as it is for Thomas Nagel,

the judgments of science, those of everyday perception will now seem to be "subjective" and as colored by the characteristic "feel" of an immediate interaction with the world.

Such a claim to universality of the particular scientific experience can be purchased, of course, only in virtue of its reflexivity: rather than merely accept what is apparent to it, understanding must continually reflect on and theorize the conditions under which it has been shaped. Thus it will be achieved by an extension of that "outward movement" involved in the first correction of sense-certainty by the communal consensus and so might be seen as a continuation or radicalization of the Copernican move inherent in that initial necessary correction. In this ability to surpass and reflectively to correct the apparent, it now grasps the "truth" of its own content as a hidden "inner"—something necessarily located *beyond* the reach of the senses and attainable only by thought. That loose alliance of sensuously present properties and substantial core found in the object of *perception,* an alliance based on the commonness existing among perceiving subjects, has here become unstuck, and in his sketch of *Verstand* Hegel moves through various possible configurations of the relation between a posited suprasensuous truth and its sensuous appearance.

First, the understanding is described as interpreting what is sensuously present to it as the *expression* of some hidden underlying force within the thing. Here Hegel probably has in mind the "forces," *Kräfte,* postulated by Herder in his vitalistic natural philosophy.[28] But this form of consciousness does not differ greatly from the structure of perception, and structural problems similar to those besetting perception appear here as well. While force is conceived as the independent inner essence, it can only have a determinate form in terms of its (inessential) expression. Force must therefore be grasped as opposing and made determinate by something equally essential—*another force.* The understanding now conceives a configuration of opposed forces, a "play of forces" as the truth behind the sensuously given world.

We are now getting well away from the relatively simple subject/object dichotomy initially presupposed by consciousness. This opposing of hid-

---

relative. In relation to sense-certainty, perception is objective, whereas in relation to understanding it is subjective. Or, to put it in more Hegelian terms, in relation to the judgments of sense certainty, those of perception are universal whereas in relation to the understanding they will be particular.

[28] See Terry Pinkard, *Hegel's "Phenomenology": The Sociality of Reason* (Cambridge: Cambridge University Press, 1994), 36. But I do not think that Hegel considers Schelling's natural philosophy, being one aspect of identity philosophy, as prey to the same sorts of problems. Thus my understanding of what is at issue both here and in the following section on the "inverted world" differs somewhat from Pinkard's account, in which Hegel is portrayed as more critical of Schelling.

den, inner forces brings about a significant *desubstantialization* of the factors involved. In their opposition, forces

> do not exist as extremes which retain for themselves something fixed and substantial, transmitting to one another in their middle term and in their contact a merely external property; on the contrary, what they are, they are, only in this middle term and in this contact. . . . They have thus, in fact, no substances of their own which might support and maintain them. The *Notion* of Force rather preserves itself as the *essence* in its very *actuality;* Force, as *actual,* exists simply and solely in its *expression. (PS,* §141; *W,* 3:114–15)

In perception, the sensory realm had been articulated in terms of the relatively simple concepts of properties of discrete objects. As the realm of the "play of Forces," however, it is now construed as a *"totality* of show" or a *"movement of appearance"* within which or through which the understanding perceives an inner *truth (PS,* §143; *W,* 3:116). No longer construed in terms of relatively substantial notions such as that of force, this truth is understood rather in terms of an abstract *law* governing an entire phenomenal realm—"the *simple element in the play of Force itself' (PS,* §148; *W,* 3:120).

That Hegel has in mind here the post-Copernican mathematized physical sciences becomes explicit in his discussion of the reductionist program of Newtonian physics in which a single general law, the law of gravity, is posited as the "truth" of a plurality of more particular laws. The example helps us understand what Hegel is referring to in these abstract descriptions. In Newtonian physics the sensory realm as a whole has become conceived in terms of those mathematical relations holding between abstract measurable parameters of the sensory world, parameters such as space, time, and mass. In this way qualities are drained from the Newtonian world, as they had been reduced to the entirely subjective status of "secondary qualities": the world is no longer made up of discrete propertied objects with their characteristic "feels." Here "manifest" and "scientific" images of the world have pulled well apart and are opposed to each other as error and truth.[29]

In the discussion of understanding, at least from that point in which reality is conceived as the play of forces, it is clear that any simple subject/ object model of cognition has been surpassed. Rather than our knowledge being about a substantial object, it is about an abstract law. Nevertheless, there is still something analogous between the perceived object and the

---

[29] Wilfrid Sellars, "Philosophy and the Scientific Image of Man," in *Science, Perception, and Reality* (London: Routledge and Kegan Paul, 1963).

conceived law. The law is just as much in need of determination from the realm of inessential appearance (that is, from the "*totality* of show" or "movement of appearances") as the substantial object was from its accidental properties. What Hegel is pointing to here is a contradiction inherent within scientific realism between its actual activity and its assumptions about reality. It wants to establish its own abstract version of reality in place of that provided in shared perception. To do this it construes the perceptual world as erroneous, something to be negated by the new scientific account. But the scientific account, in order to have any content, still stands in need of an input from this merely "apparent" world, so it cannot be conceived as its simple negation.[30]

Hegel's point is that here, as in perception, the immediately intuited cannot simply be eliminated from our account of the world: even within the realm of science, concepts without intuitions are empty. To point to contradictions here, however, is not to embark on a criticism of science as a form of knowledge; it is rather to criticize what we know as "*scientism*"— the philosophical belief that empirical science, as (potentially) giving us a unified account of the world (as it is "in itself" or "anyhow"), is able ultimately to subsume all nonscientific knowledge. But as in the other cases, Hegel wants this critique to emerge from scientific consciousness itself.

Hegel's reflection on the dream of the ultimate scientific explanation of the universe in a single comprehensive law (some final "theory of everything") leads into his difficult but important discussion of the "inverted world." Much is opaque here, but there are enough relatively clear patches in the discussion to allow us to attempt to reconstruct some of the main ideas involved.

In many ways, the scientific understanding still naively conceives of itself as a form of perception. It grasps its own operations as a type of higher-level seeing, a seeing directed at supersensible rather than sensible entities, some inner world *behind* appearances. And these supersensible abstract entities it takes as *genuine* reality against which the manifest world is *only* an appearance. But the idea that the understanding will ever reach some *final, comprehensive* knowledge in this way will, Hegel thinks, always be undermined. An abstract physical law might be posited as the "truth" of appearance, but it "does not fill out the world of appearance. In this the law is present, but is not the entire presence of appearance" (*PS*, §150; *W*, 3:121). That is, it can never explain the *entirety* of appearance.

---

[30] We are reminded here of the tendency of scientific realism to discount the reality of those "appearances" out of which its own theoretical account developed. Hegel deals with this in book 2 of the *Logic*.

Hegel's main line of thought throughout this section seems to be the following. Sciences typically progress by *unifying* explanations. To use Hegel's example, in the breakthrough in early modern physics, the work of Galileo and Newton resulted in a *single* science of mechanics which could explain types of phenomena that had previously been explained separately—the movement of falling bodies, on the one hand, and the movement of the planets, on the other. It is this ability to move to *reductively* unifying explanations that leads to the idea of the existence of a single, final, all-encompassing explanation. "The understanding imagines that in this unification it has found a universal law which expresses universal reality *as such.*" But taking the theory of gravity at the heart of classical mechanics as an example of such a final explanation, Hegel insists: "The unification of all laws in *universal attraction* expresses no other content than just the *mere concept of law itself*" (PS, §150; W, 3:121).[31]

Let us look at the two parts of this claim. First, why does Hegel think that the process of explanatory reduction, if it progressed to a final single law, would be *empty,* resulting in no explanation at all? Here Hegel insists that any single law needs *other laws* in order to be made "determinate." This is a suggestion made earlier with respect to explanation in terms of the postulation of some single inner *force (Kraft),* and as his point is more apparent *there* let us try to fill out that argument first.

There Hegel's point seemed to be the following. In order to identify that inner force deemed responsible for some phenomenon, we need to be able to refer to a *particular context* in which the force can be manifest. For example, in order to identify the force of gravity we need a situation in which we can demonstrate its action—thus I might release a rock that I have been holding and let gravity do its work, let it "manifest" itself. The idea is that such a demonstration requires *another force*—here, that which is manifest in my *initial* supporting the rock *against* the force of gravity. This is a particular form of a general claim that Hegel uses recurrently, the Spinozist claim that "all determination is negation," that is, that all particular things are identified in terms of contrasts to *other* things. Here, the claim is that the manifestation of something "inner" requires, as it were, a background *against which* it can be manifest, a background *in which it is not manifest.* And to this is added the idea that the only kind of thing which could prevent a force from being manifest is another force.

The supporter of the idea of the final "theory of everything" might suggest, of course, that *all* motion, including that involved in my holding or dropping rocks, will *eventually* be explained in terms of gravity, or some more fundamental successor force. Hegel's reply would be that we could

---

[31] I have translated *Begriff* as "concept" rather than "Notion" throughout.

then have no way of *identifying* such a force because we could have no background against which it could be made manifest.[32]

We are meant, I take it, to transfer something like *this* idea over to the project of conceiving a final *law* that would explain everything. We might say that in order to *explain* in terms of a particular law, we need access to situations in which we could *identify* the law at work. For example, we would need to refer to something like the doing of an experiment or the making of measurements, such that we could gain access to those parameters whose relations the law captured—open up a phenomenal realm, as it were, in which the law was expressed. But would then the activity of this opening up itself be explainable in terms of the law? To assume that it could be so explained would seem to put us in a position analogous to that of the person who claimed that the activity manifesting a force could be explained in terms of that single force. It would be to subsume under the law a realm for which we had deprived ourselves the opportunity of identifying the relevant law. It would seem that the manifestation of *anything*, even something as abstract as a regularity, requires a background of its not being manifested.

This seems to be the underlying reasoning behind the claim that any final law must be empty, but what does Hegel mean by the *second* part of the claim that "the unification of all laws in *universal attraction* expresses no other content than just the *mere Notion of law itself*"—an idea he further paraphrases with the idea that such a unified law "asserts that *everything has a constant difference in relation to other things* [*beständigen Unterschied zu Anderem*]"? (*PS*, §150; *W*, 3:121).

What Hegel seems to be getting at here is that to postulate the existence of a law, regardless of its content, is to postulate the existence of *some* regularity or constancy of relation among the parameters involved, regardless of the *nature* of that regularity. To return again to Hegel's example of falling bodies—to explain this in terms of Newton's laws is to postulate some precise relation that holds between the "moments" of the motion— "the time elapsed and the *space* traversed," namely that these moments are related "as root and square" (*PS*, §152; *W*, 3:123). But abstracting from the *actual* relations involved, we might say that to postulate a law per se is to claim that *some* constant relation holds here: it is to assert that the world is law-like, that the "truth" of change is some underlying constancy. To claim *this* is to assert the *notion* of law, and it is an assertion at the heart of every

---

[32] If this is the essence of Hegel's argument, then it is really an application of the basic criticism of Herder's attempts to explain the world in terms of such *Kräfte*. It is directed to the *conditions* of experience—here the conditions of experience of any force—and argues that the postulation of such ultimate forces goes *beyond* such limits.

explanation that appeals to a law, regardless of the actual content of that law.

But the law *has* a content only because there *is* change or difference within the realm of appearance—here movement within space and time—which can be measured. That is, the world that the law "explains," the world of appearance, *must* contain change for the law to have a content, but as is asserted in the *concept* of law, that which is at the truth of that change (the law itself) is something *inert, changeless, and stable*. Therefore any law which is *present* in appearance, as the aspect of constancy in the change, will not be "the entire presence of appearance," as it will not include the dimension of *change itself*.[33]

Such is the background to Hegel's puzzling account of the "inverted world" into which the discussion crosses. Hegel had used the term in his introduction to *The Critical Journal of Philosophy* in 1801 in referring to the relation of the world of philosophy to that of ordinary common sense,[34] and as we have seen above, in the Preface to the *Phenomenology* consciousness and science are described as appearing to each other as the "inversion of the truth" (*PS*, §26; *W*, 3:30). There is clearly *some* continuity with these earlier usages in that the "inverted world" is about a relation between viewpoints such that each grasps the other as getting things upside-down or back-to-front. But the account here goes in directions not hinted at earlier.[35]

We have seen how the understanding has turned Platonistic in the *Phenomenology* and has postulated an inert and stable realm of laws behind the flux of appearance, a "supersensible world" present in the enduring fixed

[33] Similar claims regarding the "flow" of consciousness and directed against analyses that fail to capture this temporal element recur in psychological accounts of consciousness. William James made the classic claim in *Principles of Psychology*, and the same point has been repeated by Israel Rosenfield: "[C]onsciousness has a temporal flow, a continuity over time. . . . [A] sense of consciousness comes precisely from the *flow* of perceptions . . . from the dynamic but constant relation to them as governed by one unique personal perspective throughout a conscious life; this *dynamic* sense of consciousness eludes the neuroscientist's analyses." *The Strange, Familiar, and Forgotten: An Anatomy of Consciousness*" (New York: Alfred A. Knopf, 1992), 6.

[34] "[I]n its relation to common sense the world of philosophy is in and for itself an inverted world" (*CJI*, 283).

[35] As Pinkard points out, the phrase had a well-established usage in German popular culture in Hegel's time—that of the designation of a "topsy-turvy" world in which normal events and relations are reversed (Pinkard, *Hegel's "Phenomenology,"* 42). This is clearly relevant, as is the connection noted by Gadamer, to satirical drama. (Hans-Georg Gadamer, "Hegel's 'Inverted World,' " in *Hegel's Dialectic: Five Hermeneutical Studies*, trans. P. Christopher Smith (New Haven: Yale University Press, 1976), 48–49). Nevertheless, it does not seem to me that this indicates that Hegel's whole discussion here is a type of *reductio ad absurdum*, as Pinkard seems to suggest. A *reductio* demonstrates that we started with incompatible premises but itself lacks any positive outcome. In contrast, the section on the inverted world has a very significant outcome in that it gives rise to the concept of infinity.

relationships within appearance. But it is not the entire presence of appearance because it is unable to do justice to the *reality* of change and transience within appearance.[36] Thus the understanding will eventually give rise to another conception of the supersensible or "inner" world which is the inverse of that. Rather than posit the supersensible world as a realm of stable, self-identical unities, it will posit it as made up of elements that are essentially unstable and self-transforming. The logic of this transition is far from clear, but it is somehow bound up with the inherent failure of the "first" supersensible world as an explanatory device and its inability to acknowledge the *reality* of change on which it relied to supply its laws with content. But in all its efforts here, the understanding *itself* manifests change in its constant "to and fro" movement between its assertion of unity (unifying laws or forces at the center of things), on the one hand, and diversity (the changes within phenomena required to give the laws content), on the other. In *asserting* timeless unities as the reality of things, it undermines its ability to consider change and diversity real; in *appealing to* the change and diversity needed to give its laws content, it contradicts its criterion or *concept* of reality. The understanding cannot achieve its purpose of reaching the ultimate unifying account of the world because this is, given its own assumptions, a conceptual impossibility. It therefore, comes to understand its own activity as directionless—*pure* change or flux rather than movement toward a fixed goal.

And so while originally the understanding had focused on what was *stable* in appearance and had tried to express this in its postulated laws, with its experience of its own ceaseless movement, it has the *converse* aspect of appearance thrust before it—that of *pure* change. "But since the *concept, qua* concept of the Understanding, is the same as the *inner being* of things, this change becomes for the understanding the law of the inner world." That is, instead of modeling its inner world on that *stability* it perceived within appearance, as it had done, it now models it on that *transience* within appearance to which it originally failed to do justice but which has subsequently forced itself upon it. It now has a new law "whose content is the opposite of what was previously called law, viz., difference which remains constantly selfsame; for this new law expresses rather that *like* becomes *unlike* and *unlike* becomes *like*" (PS, §156; W, 3:127).[37] And so

---

[36] As we have seen from his discussion in the *Skepticism* essay, for Hegel, common sense is only too aware of this dimension of change.

[37] That is, because of the contradictions within the scientistic view, the advocate of scientism has been led to a position that appeals to a conception of reality much like that of consciousness's original starting point—sense-certainty. The movement through the first three chapters has "come full circle." We are not, however, simply back where we were at the start of the book. First of all, at the start we phenomenological observers simply accepted the existence on

the original supersensible world of the understanding is now faced with a world that is its "inversion." "With this, the inner world is completed as appearance. For the first supersensible world was only the *immediate* raising of the perceived world into the universal element; it had its necessary counterpart in this perceived world which still retained *for itself the principle of change and alteration.* The first kingdom of laws lacked that principle, but obtains it as an inverted world" (*PS*, §157; *W*, 3:128).

We have now seen a number of examples of this "inverted" structure existing between two "worlds" or "worldviews" to make us suspect that again we are going to encounter yet another example of the schema of the "constructed line." And indeed we do. Hegel stresses that it is only when looked at *superficially* that "the inverted world is the opposite [*Gegenteil*] of the first in the sense that it has the latter outside of it and repels that world from itself as an inverted *actual world.* . . . [S]uch antitheses of inner and outer, of appearance and the supersensible, as of two different kinds of actuality, we no longer find here" (*PS*, §159; *W*, 3:129). That is, neither of these worldviews is something that is conceivable as separate from and independent of the other—each *is* an inversion of the other. For example, the first worldview can no longer be thought of independently of the second because the second contains that "principle of change and alteration" which the first needed and lacked. We have to think of these opposing worlds in such a unity, and understanding itself will have to come to grasp this, because such a structure provides the basis for a more adequate explanation of the nature of each than did either separately. For example, the "Platonic" view of the timeless essence has now found (in its inverted opposite) the resources for thinking of the nature of change which had earlier been lacking. No longer is the world of Heraclitean flux a "mere" appearance hiding a changeless reality, it is now an aspect *of* reality which is revealed *from* another point of view—one analogous to, but an inversion of, the Platonic view itself that reveals timeless laws.

This understanding of the relation between the two worlds is available to *us* (the phenomenological observers), but it is not necessarily how the proponents of these worldviews themselves will immediately regard their

---

the stage of the "character" sense-certainty. That is, the existence of this basic form of cognition was accepted as an *unexplained given.* Now, however, we see this as a type of consciousness which is likely to be produced *under certain conditions,* for example, as a type of *reaction* to the failure of scientistic claims about the truth of the world. Sense-certainty has been recontextualized from being a lonely Beckettian speculator about the nature of truth to a consciousness locked into an argument with another, a disputant whose claims we can understand as responses to an opposing view. Thus the one-sidedness of the views of this character is no longer interpreted as resulting from the simplicity of a starting point; it is a one-sidedness which results from argumentative opposition within a communicative relationship.

situations. They may still accept the differences between "appearance" and "reality," "outer" and "inner," and so on, thinking that their opponents get the *real* relation upside-down. But then they will be stuck with the contradictions that flow from *accepting* these rigid distinctions. However, "from the representation [*Vorstellung*] of the inversion . . . we must eliminate the sensuous idea of fixing the differences in a different sustaining element" (the elements of appearance and reality) because we can appreciate the greater explanatory power allowed by the idea that they are both different points of view onto the one reality (*PS*, §160; *W*, 3:130; translation modified). And if the understanding wants to get beyond its contradictions, it will have to free itself from these fixed antitheses as well.

And so we have reached Hegel's earlier Schellingian schematization of the "absolute." This structure of an "inner difference" between the two inverted worldviews that each "contain the other within it," the reciprocally inverted poles of the "constructed line," Hegel here calls "infinity" or the "absolute unrest of pure self-movement" (*PS*, §163; *W*, 3:133). In chapter 4 he will name it "spirit," and as in the earlier Jena writings, he will claim that what is at its heart is the "reciprocal recognition" by each of the poles of itself in the other.

There are hints of this already, but what *has* been developed is at least the idea of the necessarily contextualized nature of the self which *explains*. At this stage, however, this is still only apparent for *us*, the phenomenological we. Here Hegel describes the structure from each of its poles thus: "I distinguish myself from myself, and in doing so I am directly aware that what is distinguished from myself is not different [from me]. I, the self-same being, repel myself from myself; but what is posited as distinct from me, or as unlike [*ungleich*] me, is immediately, in being so distinguished, not a distinction for me" (*PS*, §164; *W*, 3:134–35).[38] This sounds as though the consciousness involved has not yet understood that it is necessarily embedded in a social relationship but that it believes that it generates its own relationships by virtue of its own individual activity. That "blindness" toward aspects of the situation an agent is within and to aspects of its own activity, a blindness we might see as parallel to that of the Copernican observer toward its own conditions of experience, continues even when consciousness has, at the end of chapter 3, found itself as one pole of an

---

[38] These still *sound like* the "movements" of a single Cartesian "I" (although it is difficult to envisage what we as phenomenological viewers could possibly be *observing* here). But we should remember that the loss of substance suffered by understanding's "object" has also eviscerated the understanding *subject* as well. It can surely be no Cartesian thinking "thing"— a form of self-understanding tied to the now abandoned fixed distinction of "inner" and "outer." Rather, the ego is now quite "Fichtean"—an *activity* or *process* rather than a thing or a substance. Moreover, it is Fichtean in the more specific sense of a "self-dividing" process (although the nature of the dividenda will be for Hegel very different).

inverted world. Although the tragic recognition of anagnorisis has occurred at the end of chapter 3, and consciousness has become reborn as
self-consciousness, it still does not understand its own place in things
correctly, in particular its necessary contextualization within an inverting
identity with another. Hegel's point is crucial:

> It is true that consciousness of an 'other', of an object in general, is itself
> necessarily *self-consciousness,* a reflectedness-into-self, consciousness of
> itself in its otherness. The *necessary advance* from the previous shapes of
> consciousness for which their truth was a Thing, an 'other' than them-
> selves, expresses just this, that not only is consciousness of a thing possi-
> ble only for a self-consciousness, but that self-consciousness alone is the
> truth of those shapes. But it is only *for us* that this truth exists, not yet for
> consciousness. But self-consciousness has at first become [simply] *for it-
> self,* not yet *as a unity* with consciousness in general. (*PS,* §164; *W,* 3:135)

Our character as self-consciousness is still as blind to itself as it was as
consciousness. *Then* it believed itself to be a passive receiver of what was
truly given. *Now* it sees itself as a refuser and an annihilator of the given,
and as *unilaterally* responsible for the positing of objects; it does not see
itself as existing within the greater "space" of "consciousness in general," a
space to which belong, *by necessity,* other consciousnesses. It will take the
first steps along the path to learning this in "act" four of the drama. And
this will not only involve great upheavals in self-consciousness's own
conception of its own existence; it will in fact, start to involve great upheavals in the self-conception of ourselves, the audience as well. Brecht
was not the first to be aware of the peculiar type of self-forgetting that
threatened the audience of a drama.

CHAPTER 5

Hegel's Recognitive Theory
of Spirit

THE FORM OF INTENTIONALITY with which the development of conscious-ness ended is that with which the "self-consciousness" of chapter 4 starts. It is a form of consciousness/self-consciousness in which the I's immediate knowledge of itself is taken as *foundational* and as providing a criterion for the assessment of the reality of all *other* phenomenal contents. That is, it is essentially the form of self-consciousness which bases itself on the cer-tainty of the "I = I," the starting point for Fichte's deduction of the catego-ries in the 1794 *Wissenschaftslehre*. Like Fichtean self-consciousness, that which Hegel calls "self-certainty" is fundamentally *practical*—it is a form of *striving*, or, as Hegel puts it, it is "*Desire* in general" (Begierde *überhaupt*) (*PS*, §167; *W*, 3:139).[1]

With the presentation of the inverted world, we phenomenological ob-servers have already grasped something of the complex intersubjective conditions necessary for the constitution of such a Fichtean intentionality. This will be elaborated in chapter 4 of the *Phenomenology* as the theory of spirit (*Geist*), a circular intersubjective structure within which each of two egos can recognize itself within the other's recognition of it. But we can now also start to see the difficulty that will face the ability of the imme-diately self-conscious ego to achieve this point of view.

---

[1] It can be objected that Hegel is not concerned with *philosophical* conceptions of subjectivity until later in the *Phenomenology*, such as when he explicitly examines the nature of idealism at the end of chapter 5, "Reason." However, the shape of "self-consciousness" that he is examin-ing at the commencement of chapter 4, the shape that starts from the idea of the *immediate* self-identity of I = I, is essentially the shape that the Fichtean account, in Hegel's view, presup-poses. In this sense it is an indirect examination of Fichte's philosophy.

The ability to recognize the self in the other clearly includes a hermeneutic dimension: one must be able to recognize the other as an objective but intentional being, a being who is *in* one's world but in it as a being like oneself with recognizable beliefs and desires *about* that world. That is, one has to recognize the other not only as a being within one's perspectivally disclosed world but also as at the apex of another world-disclosing perspective. But, if Hegel is right about Fichte, then a major weakness of the Fichtean schema, linked to its reduction of reason to scientific consciousness (*Verstand*), is its inability to develop categorial forms adequate to such "objective Subject-Objects." In fact it is this inability that is at the root of the Fichtean ego's more general inability to recognize the ultimate reality of anything *other* than itself.

Within the *Phenomenology*, the achievement that will transcend the limitations of the Fichtean immediately self-conscious ego will be that of the recognition of another subject like itself. Here an objection will be immediately raised, however. Was it not Fichte *himself* who, in his theory of rights, first introduced this notion of intersubjective recognition as a solution to the problem of "the other"?

The nature of Fichte's account of intersubjective recognition, its relation to his general philosophical program of the *Wissenschaftslehre*, and, indeed, its relation to Hegel's own recognitive theory of spirit—all are issues that have attracted considerable recent attention and are far too complex to receive any adequate assessment here.[2] In touching on Fichte's approach here, I will be guided by the question of the relevance of the charge that Hegel raises in the *Difference* essay—the charge that Fichte lacks any objective Subject-Object—for his theory of intersubjective recognition. Even if this charge were to prove to be unfounded, consideration of it nevertheless provides us with some idea of what Hegel understood to be the requirements of a successful theory of intersubjectivity.

---

[2] The problematic question is how Fichte's deduction of intersubjectivity in the *Grundlage des Naturrechts* is meant to relate to that of the *Wissenschaftslehre*. If the *Wissenschaftslehre* is taken as *foundational*, then the intersubjectivity that emerges in Fichte's theory of rights is somehow subordinate to the absolute ego. This is the interpretation offered by Ludwig Siep, in *Anerkennung als Prinzip der praktischen Philosophie: Untersuchungen zu Hegels Jenaer Philosophie des Geistes* (Freiburg: Alber Verlag, 1979). On the other hand, for the "French School" (Philonenko, Ferry, Renaut) intersubjectivity is already implicit in the *Wissenschaftslehre*. See, for example, Alexis Philonenko, *La liberté humaine dans la philosophie de Fichte* (Paris: Vrin, 1966) and *L'oeuvre de Fichte* (Paris: Vrin, 1984); Luc Ferry, *Political Philosophy 1: Rights—The New Quarrel between the Ancients and the Moderns*, trans. Franklin Philip (Chicago: University of Chicago Press, 1990); and Alain Renaut, *Le systèm du droit: Philosophie et droit dans la pensée de Fichte* (Paris: Presses universitaires de France, 1986). Useful discussions of these issues can be found in Robert Williams, *Recognition: Fichte and Hegel on the Other* (Albany: State University of New York Press, 1992), and Edith Düsing, *Intersubjectivität und Selbstbewusstsein* (Köln: Dinter Verlag, 1986).

Fichte's Concept of Recognition

We might refer the role of recognition in Fichte's philosophy back to that problem which follows from his linked abandonings of the Kantian "thing-in-itself" and of the passivity of the Kantian ego in its reception of the intuitive content of its experience—the problem of somehow limiting the apparently infinite world-shaping power of the ego. In the 1794 *Wissenschaftslehre*, Fichte faced this problem with the claim that the absolute ego in its activity experiences a check (*Anstoss*) to that activity from without.[3] This idea has parallels to, but important differences from, the Kantian idea that cognition involves a necessary passive dimension. For Kant the received intuitive *content* limits the "spontaneous" activity of the understanding which contributes the *form* of experience, but such a conception faced the problem of "double affection."[4] In contrast, for Fichte both the form *and* the content of experience ultimately derive from the subject: only on being reflected back to the subject on the encounter of the "check" are these products experienced as deriving from some external object. Nevertheless, the idea of the check retains enough of the Kantian idea of the subject's dependence on an independent non-self to put it in apparent contradiction with Fichte's first principle of the absolute independence of the subject. Fichte's strategy here was to accept the contradiction as unsolvable at a theoretical level and seek its resolution within practical reason. *Theoretically* the ego will never free itself from the experience of its conditionedness on an independent objective world, but *practically* it can strive in its moral actions to make the objective world conform to its own moral will, that is, to make the "is" into what "ought to be." The absolute independence of the I is no longer so much a reality as a *demand*.

This move subordinates theoretical reason to practical reason. While the conception of the ego's activities as limited or determined from without threatens to lapse back into dogmatism-objectivism, the ego *can* nevertheless be thought of as determined or required to actively limit or determine itself. Thus the check "would not set bounds to the activity of the self; but would give it the task of setting bounds to itself" (*SK*, 189).

It is in relation to this idea of a *demand* being placed on the ego to limit itself that the Fichtean notions of intersubjectivity and recognition come into play. In his *Grundlage des Naturrechts* of 1796 (translated as *The Science*

---

[3] J. G. Fichte, *The Science of Knowledge*, ed. Peter Heath and John Lachs (Cambridge: Cambridge University Press), 189–95. Further references will be given in the text with the citation *SK* followed by the page number.

[4] See F. H. Jacobi, *David Hume Über den Glauben, oder Idealismus und Realismus, Beilage, Über den transzendentalen Idealismus,* in *Werke,* ed. Friedrich Roth and Friedrich Kloppen (Darmstadt: Wissenschaftliche Buchgesellschaft, 1968), 2:291–310, for the first outline of the problem subsequently known as "double affection." See also chapter 3 above, at footnote 2.

of Rights) Fichte gave himself the task of deriving the conception of *right* as itself a "necessary condition of self-consciousness."[5] This derivation hangs on the demonstration that intersubjectivity constitutes a transcendental condition of self-consciousness, that "a rational being can not self-consciously posit itself as such, without positing itself as an *individual*, or as one of many rational beings, which many it assumes outside of it by assuming itself" (*SR*, 17).

In part 1 of that work, "The Deduction of the Conception of Rights," Fichte works his way toward the issue of intersubjectivity from a restatement of the contradiction between the absolute independence of the *Ich* and the *Anstoss* principle. The rational subject cannot perceive and comprehend an object without ascribing to itself the powers of determination, but it cannot do this without conceiving of an independent object toward which the act of determination is directed. If it assumed that it also determined *this* object, then another underlying object would have to be presupposed, and so on, ad infinitum. The only way out of this regress is to conceive of this object as having no independent substratum, that is, "that the causality of the subject is itself the perceived and comprehended object" (*SR*, 51). The contradiction involved in thinking this and the way beyond it essentially repeat the plan of the *Wissenschaftslehre*: "The activity of the subject is therefore by this synthesis required to be both checked and absolutely free. How is this contradiction possible? It is possible . . . when we think *the subject as being determined to determine* itself; or when we think a requirement addressed to the subject to resolve on manifesting its causality" (*SR*, 52). This "object" from whence the requirement comes must be given in sensation but "can be comprehended only as a requirement addressed to the I to act" (*SR*, 52).

This is an incredibly fertile suggestion by Fichte and one in which we can recognize much that is of contemporary philosophical interest in the issue of intersubjectivity and "otherness." The "object" required to halt the regress is, of course, another subject—but not conceived as any particular kind of *thing* but rather as an *act*, an act of *address* to the ego. It is this act of address which "recognizes" the (first) ego as a free and rational being and which demands of it that it respond in kind, that is, that it recognize the addresser in turn as a free and rational subject. This is why the subject can recognize *itself* within this sensuously given phenomenon: it recognizes itself as the *addressee* of the act that is directed toward it. Furthermore, it recognizes itself as free and rational because this is surely a "pragmatic"

---

[5] This work of Fichte's was translated by A. E. Kroeger as *The Science of Rights* (Philadelphia: Lippincott, 1869). References to this work will be given in the text with the citation *SR* followed by page number.

presupposition of such a demand. We might say that for a speech act to count as a "demand" the addressee must be capable of the sort of behavior demanded, here the behavior of limiting its own freedom of action so as not to impinge on the freedom of the demander.

We might recall here the Fichtean conception of the subject as act without any pre-existing agent. It is not that the act of *either* subject is the act of some substantial pre-existing agent. Just as it is a condition of the existence of the subject as an intentional being that it be *addressed* by another subject with its demands, so too is that other subject only a subject if *it* is addressed in turn. Thus the recognitive address must be reciprocal: "No free being can recognize the other as such, unless both mutually thus recognize each other; and no one can treat the other as a free being, unless both mutually thus treat each other" (*SR*, 67). But although Fichte's treatment certainly points in productive directions, we might re-pose the question of Hegel's basic criticism: Is Fichte by these means really able to conceive of an "objective Subject-Object" necessary to overcome the "subjective" one-sidedness of his attempt to complete Kantian idealism?

Although it is beyond the scope of this work to pursue this exegetical question, we might gain some sense of how the question could be approached by focusing on the notion of *Anerkennung* on which this aspect of Fichte's work turns. Like the English verbs "recognize" and "acknowledge," *anerkennen* has a *performative* dimension: to acknowledge another in some particular way is to acknowledge the *validity* of some implicit claim and thereby bind one's actions in relevant ways. Thus, if I acknowledge some person's greater expertise or knowledge in certain matters, I will in future, all other things being equal, defer to that person's judgments in such matters.[6] But the word *anerkennen* is also closely connected with its cognates *kennen* and *erkennen*, which have predominantly *epistemic* senses (*kennen*—to have direct knowledge of or to be familiar or acquainted with; *erkennen*—to know or recognize something). (As the English word "recognize" spans both of these dimensions, to avoid confusion I will henceforth use "acknowledge" and "acknowledgment" to convey the *performative* dimension of *anerkennen* and "recognize" and "recognition" to convey the latter *epistemic* dimension of the word. Where neither dimension is dominant I will use "recognize" and "recognition.")

A little reflection reveals that these performative and epistemic issues are actually interwoven in quite complex ways. One does not acknowledge another *simpliciter:* one acknowledges another *as* (an expert, the

---

[6] The implied dimension of *validity* here is caught by the semantic proximity of *anerkennen* to *"gelten lassen"* (to accept) in which the term *"gelten"* (to be valid) is etymologically derived from the noun for *gold*.

prime minister, honest, . . .). That is, performative acknowledgment is itself bound up with hermeneutic issues concerning the recognition of another *as* a certain kind of subject.[7] And conversely, given that *knowing* itself involves a form of "validity claim," that of *truth*, it is bound up in complex ways with acknowledgment as an act.

Thus we might see the concepts of *anerkennen* and *Anerkennung* as standing at the center of a complex semantic field, stretching "performatively" in one direction and "epistemically" or "hermeneutically" in another. I have argued that we can understand Hegel's claim, in the *Difference* essay, that Fichte is unable to find a place in the objective world for an "objective Subject-Object" as equivalent to the claim that Fichte lacks the resources for any *hermeneutic* understanding of other subjects. As one might expect from the priority he generally gives to the practical over the theoretical, Fichte's use of the term seems to be predominantly *performative*, but, as we have seen, any performative "acknowledgment" must surely have some sort of epistemic connections.

For Fichte, the predominant context of its use is in the recognition of human "rights," and it is implicit in acknowledging a person as the bearer of *rights* that one is *recognizing* him or her *as* the type of being capable of having rights—a being with "free will." Thus we might re-pose the question of Hegel's charge: Is Fichte able to cash out his notion of rights in concrete ways that involve the acknowledgment/recognition of others *as* willing subjects? Hegel's answer, which will emerge in his own account of rights in his later *Elements of the Philosophy of Right*, is again negative. As we will later see (in chapter 8), for Hegel, any adequate recognition of another's rights must include an understanding of *what* it is that the other indeed wills. Merely to acknowledge another as a bearer of rights *as such*, is to limit oneself to a formal, and merely "immediate" conception of the will. In brief, for Hegel, this immediate determination of the will will be able to be filled out with content only with the mediation that comes from the action of *Anerkennung* as *he* understands it. But this is to leap ahead: for the moment we must look to the context within the *Phenomenology* where Hegel's own distinctive use of *anerkennen* emerges.

The Emergence of Recognition
from the Processes of Life

In the bewildering opening paragraphs to chapter 4, "The Truth of Self-Certainty," Hegel attempts to show how a living (desiring and striving) subject is the immediate form of the "new shape of knowing, the knowing

---

[7] Again, the German *gelten* sheds light on these issues—*gelten als*, meaning "to count as," or "be taken for," is a notion at the heart of hermeneutic thought.

of itself" (PS, §167; W, 3:138) which emerged from chapter 3—that form of Fichtean self-consciousness immediately aware of its self-identity.[8] We observers are (presumably) meant to see how that "inverted" relationship between a timeless essence and an essence of self-transforming flux (earlier taken as essences of *objects* but now providing models for rival essences of consciousness itself) is instantiated by a desiring subject immersed in the processes of life. Hegel's idea seems to be the following. Qua self-conscious subject, a living being construes the objects of its appetites as *mere* means for its continuation. That is, for itself, *it* is the only enduring reality that it strives to perpetuate, all its "objects" that stand over against it are but transient "shapes" with no enduring reality. As we were reminded earlier, animals "do not just stand idly in front of sensuous things as if these possessed intrinsic being, but, despairing of their reality, and completely assured of their nothingness, they fall to without ceremony and eat them up" (PS, §109; W, 3:91).

The failure of this form of subjectivity to recognize the independence of the world is apparent to us as viewers because *we* see the larger context to which such beings belong; but it will only become apparent for this type of subject itself as it is drawn into the processes constituting the living realm to which it belongs.[9] The main lesson it will have to learn is that what is

---

[8] Indeed *formally* the intentional structure of desire seems to provide an excellent model for the Kantian combination of "empirical realism" and "transcendental idealism." At one level we think of a desiring consciousness realistically. When a subject perceives an object as desirable, there is no question that the object is something objectively "other"—an independently existing thing. But when we consider the fact that the desiring consciousness becomes, in the desire, centered on and filled by its object to the exclusion of other aspects of the world, and when we inquire into the conditions of this fact, we become aware that the desired object has been picked out by criteria belonging to the desiring subject itself. Viewed at this transcendental or "meta" level, the independent object is something that seems merely to fill a logical space *constituted* by the self.

We also see how a form of consciousness is contextualized within a structure of self-consciousness. While a desire aims at something different from the self, reflection reveals that this object is not the ultimate terminus of the intention—not the ultimate *objective* of the desire. Beyond the food at which hunger aims, stands the continued life *of the desiring agent*. We interpret *life itself* as the true object or meaning—the "truth"—of hunger; and the "practical inference" derived from a desiring consciousness helps reproduce this living self.

[9] A little reflection on the internal structure of such a form of practical intentionality quickly reveals its inadequacy as a model of intentionality as such, or, in Hegel's terms, of self-consciousness internally mediated by consciousness. Consider the nature of what we might recognize as a *purely* practical intention—that of a "hungering" subject, say—a predatory animal absorbed in the hunt, an infant's relation to the breast, or perhaps even a human adult driven to desperation by starvation. From the point of view of such a subject we might say that an object will *only* count in terms of its capacity to satisfy that hunger. As object it is marked by a type of negativity: it exists *only in order to be consumed*. Beyond its ability to fulfill that desire, an object "counts as nothing."

Such an extreme form of intentionality in which the significance of the object is totally determined within the framework of the practical intention might be thought of as *solipsistic* in a peculiarly "hermeneutic" sense—hermeneutic because it concerns the determination of

other has an equal claim to reality and endurance as itself, and, congruently, that its own "otherness" or objectivity is equiprimordial with its subjectivity, and that *it* is as transient as its objects.[10] And *this* lesson will be linked to learning the necessary role of another pole of consciousnesses in the constitution both of itself and its objects. Further, it will achieve this insight somewhat "naturalistically" as a result of its involvements within the processes of life.[11]

Hegel's question is going to be: What are the conditions within which a practical subject can achieve the necessary doubled perspective on its object? And the answer is going to be provided within that section of the *Phenomenology* which has probably become the most well known part of his writings. Hegel will attempt to show that in order for the structure of self-consciousness to exist, its internal and mediating form of consciousness must take for its "object" nothing less than another self-consciousness.[12] This is the structure exemplified in the famous "struggle of recognition" which ends in the primitive political form of life of master and slave. It is in this section that the linked concepts of recognition and spirit emerge. Despite its familiarity, however, this section is commonly misunderstood; and it is misunderstood in such a way that the hermeneutic character of Hegel's theory of spirit is missed. As it is crucial for under-

---

what the object is to *count as*. While this purely practical intentional subject construes the world as if it were simply designed to satisfy its desires, *we* (phenomenological observers) have got a different perspective on the situation—we can see a wholly different relation between subject and world, a relation that stems from the fact that the subject *belongs to* or *is part of* the world itself. From our point of view, what the purely practical subject lacks is a sense of how its object can be *both* something to satisfy its intention *and* something more—as Hegel expresses it in the introduction, how the object can have a "doubled meaning" (*gedoppelte Bedeutung*) or possess "double-sensedness" (*Doppelsinnigkeit*).

[10] Conversely, immediate self-consciousness will learn that the other can be a "subject" for it only to the extent that it is *also* an "object" for it. This is what the Fichtean account of recognition does not recognize given its understanding of the other as a pure "act" or "claim" directed to the self.

[11] By invoking the model of natural desire as a way of understanding something about the Fichtean moral subject, Hegel here signals a criticism of transcendental idealism which is fundamental to his overall relation to that philosophy. There is, of course, a world of difference between the form of practical intention recognizable in an animal and that exhibited in moral action. However, to the extent that an intention is thought of as *purely* practical, such a difference, for Hegel, is eclipsed by the structural similarity. Like a "natural" intention, a moral intention can also become hermeneutically solipsistic. This will happen when the world itself has its significance reduced to that of providing a context for the performance of a moral action.

[12] The "solution" to the problem of solipsism here will be something that the intentional subject will be led to in virtue of the fact that it is led into a new context by its own attempt to satisfy its original practical intention. This is a recurrent figure in Hegel's accounts of intentionality: the effort to realize an intention will lead a subject into a situation where it attains a new perspective on that initial intention.

standing how the concept of spirit develops in chapter 4 and, in particular, for understanding the relation of spirit to life, we must examine closely what is exactly at issue in Hegel's use of the Schellingian concept of life.

In the first three chapters of the *Phenomenology* Hegel had started from a consideration of the presentation of bare singulars to consciousness, and had been carried by the phenomenological method to the dynamics of the understanding and the structure of the inverted world. In this we got a presentiment of the idea that to be adequate to its own implicit internal structure, a form of consciousness had to exist within a relation to an inverted opposite.

From within the earlier "potence" framework it had been the living organism that had formed a unifying third within this triune structure, and this movement is repeated here. In mechanical thought we think of the laws of the movement as an externally imposed form on separate matter, but in thought of the *living* world we grasp the particular beings as *self-moving*, and so form and content now come together. It is this which gives the organic realm its "holistic" character, the particular living being existing within relations to other living beings.

Starting from the concept of life as a universal element or sphere, Hegel attempts to incorporate those assumptions that form part of our "everyday" understanding of life: that to live one has to eat and that only living matter is edible; that living beings are born of other living beings and can in turn give birth to others; that the lives of individual organisms ultimately and necessarily terminate in death; and so on.

But as universal element, life can be thought of neither as some ultimate self-subsistent unitary *substance* nor simply as an "abstract" property shared by particular living beings. Qua "substance" it exists only as divided up and dispersed into separate living "shapes": beyond the plurality of individual living organisms there is no other *thing*. But qua living, these organisms cannot be conceptualized entirely atomistically because their individual lives are *necessarily* tied up in concrete relationships with the lives of others such as those from which they were born, those on which they feed, and so on. To understand a living being *as* a living being demands then some type of dynamic "holistic" approach to the living realm.

Within this realm, the type of movement exhibited by the elements seems to have both centrifugal and centripetal dimensions. All organisms strive to maintain their own particular existence but do this in ways that involve the annihilation of particularity. Thus one feeds on another, breaking down the separation between it and that other in the very act of maintaining itself as distinct. And so, while viewed from one direction, the living process looks to be about the maintenance of particular identities *in* their separation; viewed from another, it seems equally to be about the collapse of this separation. Hegel's wording here recalls the relationship between unity and unfolded plurality in Neoplatonic thought: "Thus the simple substance of Life is the splitting-up of itself into shapes and at the same time the dissolution of these existent differences; and the dissolution of the splitting-up is just as much a splitting up and a forming of members" (*PS*, §171; *W*, 3:142).

But two points are worth noting here if we are not to miss the direction of Hegel's thinking. That a single process can be characterized in contradictory ways as simultaneously a "splitting-up" and a "forming" follows from the fact that we can look at it from two different and opposed points of view. For example, the process of one organism feeding on another is formative from the point of view of the first organism and dissolutive from the (inverted) point of view of the second. And that we can talk of "point of view" here is surely crucially tied to the fact that the entities under discussion *are* living.[13] And second, Hegel's "Neoplatonic" schema allows him to agree with a roughly "holistic" view of the organic world while rejecting a common assumption to which holism commonly leads: the assumption that as the life of each separate individual organism derives from a place within a system, the *system itself* can be thought of as a type of *giant single living organism*. From the collective point of view of those organisms that at a particular time are being split up, the biological process as a whole will look like one in which individual differences between shapes of life are themselves being dissolved. But from the collective point of view of those organisms being formed in these very processes, these same processes are about the formation of separate and individual shapes of life. And so: "The simple substance of Life is the splitting-up of itself into shapes and at the same time the dissolution of these existent differences." That is, the whole living process cannot be thought of as a single living organism as there is no single point of view which reflects, as it were, the interests of the whole. Just as the absolute analyzed in terms of potences was not itself a potence, "life" itself is not a living thing and so has no "viewpoint" of its own.[14]

---

[13] Cf. Daniel Dennett: "When an entity arrives on the scene capable of behaviour that staves off, however primitively, its own dissolution and decomposition, it brings with it into the world its 'good.' That is to say it creates a point of view from which the world's events can be roughly partitioned into the favourable, the unfavourable, and the neutral." *Elbow Room: The Varieties of Free Will Worth Wanting* (Oxford: Clarendon Press, 1984), 23.

[14] In contrast to Hegel, the idea that the totality can itself be thought of as some kind of living individual is an assumption not uncommonly encountered in modern holistic approaches to the biosphere, such as the Gaia hypothesis. Cf. James Lovelock, *Gaia: A New Look at Life on Earth* (Oxford: Oxford University Press, 1987).

Importantly this point puts Hegel at variance with the Spinozistic form of holism upon

Thus for Hegel, life is a system within which we can recognize opposed practical points of views which are located within the system and which project onto those processes constitutive of the system. This is a structure that will become familiar in our explorations of spirit. There will be, however, a crucial difference between systems of life and spirit: the *purely* natural desiring subject, embedded in the relations of living nature, incorporates the "perspectives" of others only in the sense of *actually* incorporating those others *themselves* (and hence annihilating their "points of view"). Within the system of *spirit*, however, individuals, as they can "idealize" others—that is, know them *as* intentional beings—can *ideally* incorporate the viewpoints of those others into their *own* points of view. This will be how the doubly structured intentionality of true self-consciousness will be attained.

This difference, however, should not lead us abstractly to place the realms of life and spirit in opposition. It is against the background of the struggles for life into which naturally desiring subjects may be led that Hegel presents *another* type of struggle which will have an outcome unobserved in the rest of nature. We are invited to think of a struggle between two desiring beings brought into conflict simply *by* their desires.[15] Here the fact that each stands as an obstacle to the other's satisfactions means that a new desire appears as a means to the fulfillment of the first—the desire to eliminate the opponent.

This new desire, taking as its object another intentional being, has created the conditions for a new level of intentional complexity. The struggle into which these subjects have been drawn has presented each with an intentional "object" within whose activity each can recognize its own intentions for that object. That is, each can recognize that the annihilation each means for the other is simultaneously meant for itself. Thus each now has the opportunity to grasp the "doubled meaning" of the process in which they are involved. Furthermore, the attainment of this insight will be linked to another: since its own *life* is for each the ultimate object of the struggle, it may be worth forsaking the immediate object of the struggle, some particular life-enhancing desired thing, in order not to succumb to the annihilation threatened. Thus capitulation and the acceptance of servi-

---

which Schelling had drawn. In the *Ethics* in a discussion of "compound bodies" in which an individual at one level may itself be composed of parts which themselves are considered as individual bodies, Spinoza notes that we may proceed up a hierarchy of individuals of greater and greater complexity: "We may easily proceed thus to infinity, and conceive the whole of nature as one individual, whose parts, that is, all bodies, vary in infinite ways, without any change in the individual as a whole" (*E*, 2.13, lemma VII, note).

[15] My reading here is at variance with the popular Kojèvean account concerning the origins of the struggle in a primordial "desire for recognition." This is an issue I address in the following chapter.

tude and, with that, the institutionalization of a political relation, becomes a possible outcome, an outcome achieved not now in the act of killing but in the sign or *word* of submission, a word with which the slave will henceforth acknowledge the master's power over him and which will cement the form of their relationship.

Anerkennung, Spirit, and the Hermeneuticization of Kant

The crucial concept that marks off this piece of nature, this "potence" structure, from the rest of the natural world is that of *Anerkennung*—recognition or acknowledgment. This is a concept that will have largely unacknowledged resonances throughout Hegel's systemic works, and it is important to appreciate the complexity of this notion as it appears even here in this simplified model. In contrast to Fichte's use of the concept, Hegel's shows a complex integration of epistemic and performative aspects.

First there is a clear *epistemic* dimension to recognition, and this dimension has a distinctly *hermeneutic* flavor. Hermeneutically, each subject *finds its own intentionality* in the other: each recognizes the other's intention toward itself because it recognizes its *own* intention to "kill the other" *in* the actions of the other. In this sense the term is continuous with the more straightforwardly epistemological *wieder erkennen*.[16] More specifically, in this hermeneutic recognition there is a dimension of the *Platonic* recognition of the universal in the particular. If X recognizes his own intention to kill Y as expressed in Y's actions toward him, it cannot be the case that it is simply Y's *particular* intention that is at issue, as Y's intention is to kill X. Rather it is the intention articulated at a higher level of generality. Rather than recognize the intention to kill "this" *particular* being, X recognizes the intention to kill *whoever* is Y's "other" and understands that he *himself* is that other just as Y is *his* other.[17]

But when we look further into this peculiar epistemic ability we find further layers of complexity. As we have seen above, exactly what *is* recognized in the other's behavior toward the self must be a generalized and shareable intention—the intention to kill not simply *this* singular thing (they both intend to kill different things) but that which is other or op-

---

[16] It is also the sense of "recognize" in which the phenomenological "we" can be said to have been able to recognize the intentions of consciousness throughout the drama or that one "intelligence" could be said to "recognize" another in the example of tool-using activity in the "System of Sittlichkeit."

[17] This should not be interpreted as if each were able to infer the intention in the other on the basis of its own *immediate* perception of this intention in the self, as this would revert to the epistemological position of *sense-certainty*.

posed to the self. Each combatant shares this same intention. But simultaneously the intentions of each protagonist could not be more opposed. From the *particular point of view* of each subject, the intentions are opposite: X is struggling to maintain *X's life;* Y is struggling to bring about *X's death.* And so here we might talk of shared or common intentional *content* with inverted or opposed *indexicality* or *subjectivity.* This contradictory structure of identity within opposition occurs because each *must* simultaneously maintain two points of view onto the situation: *one* indexically centered on his own particular desire (in which the other counts as the object of that desire) and *another* which escapes centering on the self by being reflected through the subjectivity of the other.[18] This will be the essence of Hegel's answer to the demand for the doubled (*gedoppelte*) character of consciousness and his way beyond the aporias of Fichte's development of Kant. It is by the intermediary of another, opposed consciousness that any one consciousness can get a double bearing onto objects, grasping them from its own particular point of view while simultaneously conceiving them as existing independently of this point of view.

Here again we encounter Hegel's own version of the Cusan "identity of opposites" or the Schellingian "indifference" of opposites in the constructed line. However, there is no question here of there being any *logical* contradiction involved: to recognize another's intention as the same and yet opposite or inverted is not like affirming both *p* and not-*p*. Rather, the "contradiction" works here at the level of the "indexicality," "subjectivity," or "point of view" from which the intentions are held, not at the level of any propositional *content:* it arises when an intention is common to subjects facing each other from *opposed points of view.* This is more the type of "contradiction" found in Heraclitus's famous assertion concerning the dual and inverted identity of the single road.

Thus the battle fleshes out those sorts of inverted identities schematized in Schelling's constructed line. Each combatant is a living "Subject-Object" able to recognize itself in an inverted form in that Subject-Object facing it.

---

[18] It is this complexity that is lost in the popular assumption that what is involved in Hegelian recognition is the same as that narcissistic form of identification of self in the other described by the psychoanalyst Jacques Lacan in his discussions of "the mirror phase" ("The Mirror Phase," in Jacques Lacan, *Écrits: A Selection* [London: Tavistock, 1977]). Schiller effectively circumscribed this narcissistic form of "*méconaissance*" when he spoke of the person who "never sees others in himself but only himself in others" (Friedrich Schiller, *On the Aesthetic Education of Man,* trans. E. M. Wilkinson and L. A. Willoughby [Oxford: Clarendon Press, 1967], 173). But the demand in Hegelian recognition here is that it involves a moment in which the self is grasped as *object* or other of the other's intention (I grasp the otherness of myself). Qua intentional subject of which I am the object the other is no thing—it is just the act directed toward me. If I *only* grasped the other qua subject as mirroring my intentionality, the Lacanian analysis might hold. Lacan's "mirror phase" seems largely to overlap with Gadamer's *second* form of intersubjectivity, while Hegelian recognition instantiates the third.

More specifically, from X's particular perspective, Y is presented as an objective Subject-Object, that is, an objective being with intentionality. Because X can see its own intentional desire reflected back to it in Y's action, it can grasp *itself* as the subject of that intention. But it can only recognize Y's behavior as intentional because that behavior is directed toward an *object*, and X itself *is* that object. So X's recognition of Y's behavior as intentional, a recognition that is a precondition for grasping its own subjectivity, also implies that X must grasp its own *objectivity*. It is thereby that each Subject-Object becomes self-conscious of itself *as* Subject-Object, or, to use the Cusan term, as a "finite-infinite."

But the *Anerkennung* structure cannot be thought of as an *essentially* epistemological one concerning the understanding of intention. *Anerkennung* is also *necessarily* an act in which this understanding of the other is *acted out*. In the sort of struggle alluded to, it is only in virtue of the fact that each acts out his understanding of the other in patterns of attack and defense that each presents *to the other* a phenomenal expression, an objectification, of his own recognitive understanding of the other as an intentional being. (This is a sense of recognition not present, at least so far, in the recognition performed by us readers, the phenomenological we.) This phenomenal expression is crucial because it is precisely in virtue of Y's performative acknowledgment of X that X can epistemically recognize itself in Y. Each recognizes himself not simply *in* the other but *in the recognition/acknowledgment of* the other—that is, in the other's *act*. Thus, as in Fichte's schema, the system here can only be understood as a circular whole and cannot be "assembled" out of pre-existing components. Not only is each combatant qua intentional being necessarily linked in a circular way to the other; but also the performative and hermeneutic dimensions of *Anerkennung* itself are circularly linked as mutually presupposing each other. It is only inasmuch as each antagonist is engaged in *active* struggle that hermeneutic recognition can occur and yet engagement in this peculiar type of struggle *depends on* the "hermeneutic" recognition of the other's intention.

But while *we* can "recognize recognition" in the struggle, it can be really no more than a heuristically helpful image of a truly recognitive structure. Within the context of the struggle these beings never leave the sphere of *life*. The objective other is "idealized" in that it is recognized as an intentional being, an "intelligence," and yet this idealization is momentary and tied to immediate intuition—unable to be fixed in the ideational *aether*. This fixity is only achieved when the recognition becomes expressed in something other than the fleeting patterns of combat, specifically, in the *word of submission*. In acknowledging the other as "master," the slave "posits" himself *as* slave and the other *as* master because he fixes his idealization of the other with this enduring and repeatable concept. Now the singular intuitions of self and other are "subsumed" by the concept. Both are given their places in a new configuration structured by the conceptual pair of master/slave, the conceptually clothed and articulated realm of a very basic but recognizable form of human social life.

Hegel's transformation of Fichte's schematization of self-consciousness has important consequences, as the fact that there are now necessarily *two* points of view and two "acts" involved overcomes the problem caused by the Fichtean rejection of Kantian noumena—the problem of understanding the *otherness* of the world to one's subjective bearing onto it. As the existence of another embodied and located subject is a precondition to the *achievement* of self-consciousness, the limits to the constituting power of a single subject's intention is provided for *without* the need for metaphysical recourse to the thing-in-itself or the *Anstoss*. Rather, the limits are now provided by *another intentional being*, within the world. The particular I is not contextualized within the act of a primordial omnipotent I, but rather within a "we":

> A self-consciousness exists *for a self-consciousness*. Only so is it in fact self-consciousness; for only in this way does the unity of itself in its otherness become explicit for it. . . . A self-consciousness, in being an object, is just as much 'I' as 'object'. With this, we already have before us the concept of *Spirit*. What still lies ahead for consciousness is the experience of what Spirit is—this absolute substance which is the unity of the different independent self-consciousnesses which, in their opposition, enjoy perfect freedom and independence: 'I' that is 'We' and 'We' that is 'I'. It is in self-consciousness, in the concept of Spirit, that consciousness first finds its turning-point [*Wendungspunkt*], where it leaves behind it the colourful show of the sensuous here-and-now and the nightlike void of the supersensible beyond, and steps out into the spiritual daylight of the present.
>
> Self-consciousness exists in and for itself when, and by the fact that, it so exists for another; that is, it exists only in being acknowledged. (*PS*, §§177–78; *W*, 3:144–45)

In short, what the structure of reciprocal recognition has done is to allow Hegel to hold onto the Fichtean idea that the subject is involved in its own creation with a type of act of self-positing. This act *is* the act of recognition. To employ Fichte's somewhat misleading image of the mirror, as a performative the recognitive act creates the conditions that allow the other to intuit itself in the "mirror" of the first's *act:* it creates the conditions for the other to *be* self-conscious. But in doing so, the first subject is simultaneously creating the mirror for its *own* self-apprehension: I can only (hermeneutically) recognize myself as a subject in the other because I simultaneously *acknowledge* the other *as* a subject. The problem of the self-mirroring mirror or the self-seeing eye is overcome by postulating a structure engaging two Subject-Objects in which each is simultaneously "mirror and eye."[19] And this act, at the same time, furnishes that "turning point" of nature into spirit, the Schellingian "lightning stroke of the ideal upon the real" that Hegel had discussed in the *Difference* essay.

Hegelian Philosophy as a Development of Postmetaphysical Kantianism

With Hegel's concept of the recognitively structured realm of spirit we can now start to appreciate the broad outlines of his transformation of Kantian idealism. The structure of self-consciousness with its abstract empirical and transcendental poles has now been replaced with a complex pattern of interactive recognition involving two conscious subjects, each able to achieve a distance between his "empirical" and "transcendental" self because of the mediating role played by the other. Thus the picture we get of spirit in this passage is that of a "circular" intersubjective structure within which two self-consciousnesses recognize both their identity or like-mindedness, their "we-ness," and their difference and opposition, their "I-ness." With the formula " 'I' that is 'We' and 'We' that is 'I' " Hegel seems to be trying to capture the fact that this circular structure can be captured abstractly *neither* atomistically nor holistically. Neither is it the case that the "We" results from the combination of independently conceivable "I"s, nor is it the case that the "I"s are merely derivative parts of a self-subsistent "We."[20] In a way parallel to that which was found in life, here the "whole,"

---

[19] Dieter Henrich gives an account of Fichte's changing metaphorics of "eye" and "mirror" in "Fichte's Original Insight," trans. David R. Lachterman in *Contemporary German Philosophy*, vol. 1, 1982 by Darrel E. Christensen et al. (University Park: Pennsylvania State University Press, 1982).

[20] Edith Düsing notes that while overcoming atomistic conceptions of the ego, Hegel "in no way relapsed into the type of socialization model popular today for the explanation of the genesis of personal identity, in which the particular determination of an action-competent, self-knowing individual results merely from experiences of interaction and processes of communication. . . . In Hegel's theory the completed formation of the I comes about neither within an autarchic and self-sufficient inner life within which it is trapped, nor purely passively through the crossing of intersubjective influences. Hegel does not accept that complex disposition of social interactions as a reality *sui generis*, rather indicates methodically and categorically the specific relation between the self-constitution of concrete existing subjective spirits on the one hand, and the constitution of intersubjectivity on the other." "Genesis des Selbstbewusstseins durch Anerkennung and Liebe," in *Hegels Theorie des subjektiven Geistes*, ed. Lothar Eley (Stuttgart-Bad Cannstatt: Frommann-Holzboog, 1990), 245.

spirit itself, is no existing *thing*, and crucially, no existing *conscious* thing with its *own* point of view. It only exists *insofar as* it is dispersed or split up into its "parts," those mutually recognizing self-consciousnesses. Just as the system of nature is not itself a living individual, neither is the system of spirit itself a spiritual individual. But equally, these independent self-consciousnesses cannot be considered in abstraction from that system of relations to which they belong. There are no "spiritual" (*geistig*) beings apart from their relation to one another within a spiritual *system*, that is, within spirit.

But we might, in fact, retrospectively see the seeds for this move in which the empirical I is contained not within the acts of an all-powerful transcendental subject but within this dialogical relation of "I"s within a "we" as implicitly present within the communicative reading of Kant himself. As we have seen, it is hardly difficult to appreciate what Kant was attempting to do with his "negative" concept of the noumenal. Once the notion of knowledge as involving the *active* contribution of the knower to the knowledge is introduced, the need to preserve the sense of the otherness or independence of the thing known becomes acute. Without the notion of the thing-in-itself, metaphysical idealism appeared to threaten as objects seemed predestined passively to match and fall in line with the constructions of a transcendental subject. For all its problems, the notion of the thing-in-itself provided the object of cognition with its requisite *Doppelsinnigkeit* of appearance and reality, holding onto the commonsense idea of the world just "as it is" independent of our knowledge of it.

It is precisely in order to hold onto this basic idea in a nonmetaphysical way that a number of recent Kant interpreters have denied that Kant in fact meant two different sorts of *thing* with the phenomena/noumena distinction and yet have *defended* his need to talk about some *an sich* considered in its independence of our knowledge of it. Gerhold Prauss, for example, has argued that Kant's various references to the thing-in-itself should not be read as referring to some sort of supersensible object. Rather, Kant's typical formulations suggest that he was trying to convey the idea that we could *consider* the things of our world in two ways: first, as objects of knowledge—as phenomena—and, second, as they are in themselves, independent of us and our knowledge. The *Ding an sich selbst*—thing-in-itself—is meant as the *Ding an sich selbst* betrachtet—the thing *considered* in itself. For Prauss this implies that the idea of a "thinkable" or "considerable" "thing-in-itself"—which, however, cannot be known—should be interpreted along different lines from the traditional skeptical way. Talk about noumena is not about unknowable supersensible entities: it is rather about ordinary things in their "otherness," as it were, *to* our knowledge. To consider the thing in the aspect of its otherness to our knowledge is to "acknowledge" it in the aspect *of* its independence. And such acknowledgment—*Anerkennung*—is a precondition of our actual ability to *know* it. An act of *Anerkennung* is a precondition of *Erkennung*, knowledge.[21]

A suggestion for a similar reading of Kant can be found, coming from a very different direction, in the work of Stanley Cavell. In the context of a Wittgenstein-inspired meditation on the nature of skepticism, Cavell contends that its "truth" is not that there is an unknowable supersensible world (as in the "transcendental skepticism" of the traditional Kant), but rather its truth resides in the idea that knowledge does not exhaust the ways in which the world presents itself to us. "[W]e think skepticism must mean that we cannot know the world exists, and hence that perhaps there isn't one. . . . Whereas what skepticism suggests is that since we cannot know the world exists, its presentness to us cannot be a function of knowing. The world is to be *accepted,* as the presentness of other minds is not to be known but acknowledged." But we tend to grasp this fact from the wrong angle, that is, in terms of the idea that there is something we *cannot do,* and so: "[T]his is why we take Kant to have said that there are things we cannot know; whereas what he said is that something cannot be known— *and* cannot coherently be doubted either, for example, that there is a world and that we are free."[22] Thus Cavell, like Prauss, suggests a reading of Kant which stresses the idea that among the conditions of knowledge there be a type of act of acknowledgment of the world as in some sense *other* than as it is given, or ever can be given, in knowledge.[23]

Regardless of the answer to the exegetical question of the degree to which this represents the letter of Kant's consistent position, it indeed does seem to capture the spirit of his more Copernican and "communicative" moments and serves to indicate the direction in which Hegel was to take the Copernican revolution. For the Copernican, at any stage in his or her knowing of the world, there must be the implicit recognition that this actual knowledge *is conditioned* in some perspectival way: one always knows the world from somewhere within it and subject to the localness of the conditions of knowing that this implies. Moreover, this primacy of acknowledgment must not be seen as a merely psychological point. If one starts, in an *anti-theistic* way, by rejecting the *idea* of a transcendent mind

---

21 Gerhold Prauss, *Kant und das Problem der Dinge an sich* (Bonn: Bouvier Verlag Herbert Grundman, 1974), 145–46.

22 Stanley Cavell, "The Avoidance of Love," in *Must We Mean What We Say? A Book of Essays* (Cambridge: Cambridge University Press, 1976), 324.

23 Cf. Wittgenstein, "Knowledge is in the end based on acceptance-recognition [*Anerkennung*]." *On Certainty* (Oxford: Blackwell, 1969), §378.

free from embodiment, then it would apply to *all* potential knowers, not just ourselves, and would be more like a logical precondition of knowing.

Cavell's Hegelian-sounding comments concerning the role of the acknowledgment of *other minds* are surely pertinent here. If communication with others is the road to the establishment of objectivity, then it would be circular to construe the presence to us *of those others* with whom we communicate as simply "objective." Like all things in the world, our communicative partners *can* be construed objectively as things to be known, but this must immediately compromise the normativity of their claims qua knowers. And so, given their role within the conditions of objectivity, they surely provide paradigms of those things whose "presentness to us cannot be a function of knowing." And along with this we must surely say that any conception of what it is to understand others will be misguided if it models itself on conceptions of what it is to know the world objectively. Such thoughts thus point in the direction of some kind of non-naturalistic or hermeneutic approaches to understanding others but also, further point toward more radical challenges to foundationalist or epistemologically based philosophy.

The radicalness of these moves which Hegel shares with the Kant of Prauss and Cavell can be brought into focus if we invoke Heidegger's characterization of the Western "onto-theological" tradition as the "metaphysics of presence," the tradition that has confused "being" with some kind of knowable thing able to be made present to the mind in knowledge. We might say that a fundamental strategy of this foundationalist thought has been to *acknowledge* as real *only* that which is known. In presupposing what Thomas Nagel has described as an "epistemological criterion of reality," it makes ontology a subsidiary of epistemology.[24]

That is, within such philosophy *knowledge* is regarded as the condition of acknowledgment: we acknowledge as existing only that of which we can be certain. But a philosophy that makes acknowledgment equiprimordial to knowing must be seen as challenging this metaphysics of presence. Such a philosophy will focus on "the word" addressed to another not as foundational but as central among the conditions within which knowledge can occur. We might say that for Hegel as much as for Gadamer, what the primacy of the word of acknowledgment means is that the other is present to us *not as a knowable object* but as someone *addressed*. But, as we have seen, it will be crucial for Hegel not simply to follow the Fichtean path and *negate* the idea of the other as knowable. Acknowledgment will always contain an interpretative dimension—the other is acknowledged *as* such and such.

---

[24] Nagel, *The View from Nowhere* (New York: Oxford University Press, 1986), 15.

But this recognition is not *simply* knowledge. The recognition of the other as such and such will be simultaneously an engagement with the other in a process in which all identities are open to reinterpretation because open to the possibly different "horizon" of the other's reply.

It is this challenge to foundationalism and the "epistemological criterion of reality" which Hegel promises to make good, and it is such a dialogical conception of intersubjectivity implicit in his recognitive theory of spirit which gives him the resources to fulfill this promise. This primacy given to communicative intersubjectivity allows him to draw on ideas from the hermeneutic tradition, a tradition that also challenged the primacy of cognition with the concept of recognition, but to avoid its implicit metaphysics.[25]

---

[25] Again we see a Neoplatonist dimension to Hegel's approach to spirit. Spirit cannot be thought of as a determinate thing knowable by discursive reason. As the necessary context for the existence of a conscious/self-conscious subject, it escapes the cognitive reach of that subject. It is known only under the form of an analogical, "contradictory" understanding. It is simultaneously a unity and a plurality, an I and a We.

CHAPTER 6

Figures of Recognition

THE THEME OF RECOGNITION in Hegel's *Phenomenology* is probably most familiar to readers via Alexandre Kojève's *Introduction to the Reading of Hegel*, the text of a set of influential lectures delivered in Paris in the 1930s.[1] Although in some circles Kojève's readable lectures have come to stand as the unproblematic account of Hegel's obscure and difficult text, as an interpretation of Hegel's account of recognition they are fatally flawed. The notion of recognition appears in different and contradictory ways in Kojève's account, imparting to it a circularity from which it cannot escape.[2]

In some places Kojève discusses the context of recognitive intersubjectivity as a necessary condition for self-consciousness (e.g., "human reality can be begotten and preserved only as 'recognized' reality"), and the struggle leading to the master/slave institution itself provides a simple model of a recognitive context ("it is only in and by such a fight that the human reality is begotten, formed, realized, and revealed to itself and to others").[3] Elsewhere, however, he discusses recognition as the *goal* of a

---

[1] Alexandre Kojève, *Introduction to the Reading of Hegel*, ed. Allan Bloom, trans. J. H. Nichols, Jr. (New York: Basic Books, 1969). Kojève's reading was crucial in shaping the "Hegel" which was first embraced in France in the 1940s and 1950s and then increasingly criticized since about the early 1960s. Kojève's Hegel has once again come into prominence with Francis Fukuyama's thesis on the end of cold war. See Francis Fukuyama, "The End of History?" *The National Interest* 16 (Summer 1989): 3–18, and *The End of History and the Last Man* (New York: Free Press, 1992).

[2] I have argued this at greater length in "Hermeneutic or Metaphysical Hegelianism? Kojève's Dilemma," *The Owl of Minerva* 22 (1991): 175–89.

[3] Kojève, *Introduction to the Reading of Hegel*, 9, 7–8. There is a systematic ambiguity in the

distinctive and essential human desire—the "desire for recognition."[4] The contradictory nature of these accounts is apparent in the circularity that dogs Kojève's account of the "first" or "original" struggle for recognition. Read as the most basic context within which recognition can occur, the struggle provides an initial *context* within which human intentionality can emerge. And yet for Kojève the struggle is itself motivated by a distinctly human motive—the desire for the "essentially nonvital" end of "pure prestige." That is, while the struggle is conceived as brought about by, *born from*, human desire—the desire for recognition—it is also seen as providing a necessary condition for the emergence or *birth of* the only sort of being capable of having that motive.

This type of contradiction within Kojève's account had been noted by Stanley Rosen, who pointed out that Kojève's purported *genetic* account of the creation of self-consciousness actually presupposes the prior existence of self-consciousnesses: "In order for me to 'recognize' myself in the visage of another self, I must first know myself, or be conscious of myself. So far as phenomenological experience goes, there can be no explanation at all of self-consciousness."[5] Therefore, according to Rosen, intersubjective recognition must be *secondary* to some more basic form, the religious form of self-recognition in God: "Hegel's meaning, which does not become clear until after we know the logic, is that I can recognize myself in the other because we are both instances of the self-consciousness of absolute spirit. The structure of my relations to the other is the externalized version of my 'relations' to myself. And these interior 'relations' are the expression of the absolute."[6] While Kojève's Heideggerian-Marxist approach to Hegel had

---

significance attributed to the struggle by Kojève. On the one hand, it is a context for reciprocal recognition. On the other, it demonstrates the existence of a being capable of risking its life for the nonbiological end of recognition. Thus the significant "and" in the sentence: "Now the human reality is created, is constituted, only in the fight for recognition and by the risk of life that it implies" (12).

[4] In "Introduction to the Reading of Kojève," Patrick Riley notes that for Kojève it is the desire for recognition that "explains everything." *Political Theory*, 9 (1981): 15.

[5] Stanley Rosen, *G. W. F. Hegel: An Introduction to the Science of Wisdom* (New Haven: Yale University Press, 1974), 158.

[6] Rosen, *G. W. F. Hegel*, 159. Rosen admits that his reading is not motivated by the *Phenomenology* but requires the *Logic*: "The most one could say is that Hegel is extremely unclear whether this 'intersubjective' process produces self-consciousness or whether it is a development of an already present, albeit generic, version of self-consciousness. My exposition of the logic contains reasons for assuming the latter of these alternatives. Certainly it is only in this manner, for which there is a secure Hegelian basis, that we can make sense out of the discussion in the *Phenomenology*. There is no doubt that for Hegel, contrary to Fichte and Schelling, the individual acquires self-consciousness in a stable way only in and through external experience. At no point does the Hegelian ego detach itself from external experience in order to return to itself by an act of intellectual intuition. Despite his great emphasis upon negative activity, Hegel never follows the *via negationis*. This is also evident from the fact that

originally seemed to hold out the promise of an interpretation which would avoid the old "metaphysical Hegel," it would seem that it presupposed it afterall.

But in fact the problem-ridden "anthropological" and "genetic" account of Kojève's rests on a questionable interpretation of Hegel's text. When we look at the *Phenomenology* itself there is little evidence supporting Kojève's essentialist and anthropological construal of the notion "desire for recognition" and the concomitant idea that the "first" struggle is generated from a specifically human and nonvital "desire for recognition." Kojève's key phrase, "desire for recognition," does not appear anywhere in the section on the struggle and its resolution, and when Kojève boldly asserts: "According to Hegel, Man is nothing but Desire for recognition," he quotes as evidence the very different Hegelian sentence *"der Mensch* ist *Anerkennen"*—"man *is* recognition."[7] Rather, what we find in Hegel is the struggle and its institutionalized outcome presented as structures of intersubjective recognition which allow the existence of that doubly structured consciousness essential for intentionality. Whereas the struggle itself cannot constitute a stable, enduring recognitive structure, the master-slave relation can: it represents a type of minimal institutionalized pattern of mutual recognition (and hence objectified spirit), albeit in an inadequate and self-contradicting form.

Since the late 1970s, however, there have emerged more sophisticated and exegetically accurate accounts of the role of recognition both in the *Phenomenology* and in Hegel's pre-phenomenological writings which challenge the picture of Hegel as either Kojèvean philosophical anthropologist or dogmatic pre-Kantian metaphysician. Thus, for example, in the work *Recognition: Fichte and Hegel on the Other*, Robert R. Williams has argued that an examination of the systematic role of this notion in the *Phenomenology* shows how Hegel cannot be reduced to a "metaphysical idealist" philosopher unable to acknowledge the irreducible "otherness" of the

---

self-consciousness is 'stabilized' only in the family, and thus in the state. But the externalizing and 'politicizing' dimensions of the stabilization of self-consciousness are in fact externalizations of the generic ego or Absolute Spirit. Interpreters like A. Kojève, who assimilate Hegel's logic into the *Phenomenology* or provide us with an 'anthropological' account of Hegel, *drop the generic ego or universal Spirit.* Thus Kojève, for example, is faced with the impossible task of generating finite self-consciousness from the struggle for recognition" (160–61).
[7] Kojève, *Introduction to the Reading of Hegel*, 192. Kojève construes the "desire for recognition" as a "desire for a desire" (5–7). Gadamer, however, has pointed out that, unlike the French *"désir,"* the German *"Begierde"* cannot really carry the construction "desire for desire," and on the basis of this questions Kojève's analysis of this section of the *Phenomenology*. See Hans-Georg Gadamer, "Hegel's Dialectic of Self-Consciousness" in *Hegel's Dialectic: Five Hermeneutical Studies*, trans. P. Christopher Smith (New Haven: Yale University Press, 1976), 62 n. 7.

world to thought.[8] Williams helps correct the tissue of misunderstandings which derives from the Kojèvean misreading. The *intersubjective* dimension of recognition, Williams contends, undermines the individualist Cartesian approach to subjectivity while at the same time not reducing individual intentional beings to mere moments of social structure. Furthermore, when we understand Hegel's spirit as constituted by intersubjective relations of recognition, we will see the error of equating spirit with any transcendental ego or the absolute ego, the error encouraging the view, such as is held by Gadamer and Rosen, that for Hegel intersubjective relations are ultimately subsumed within a "monological" relation to self which allows no alterity.[9] Williams approaches intersubjective recognition in terms of the complex intentional structures involved, and, using the Husserlian distinction between "eidetics" and "empirics," shows that the structure of recognition cannot be reduced to the intentionality of *desire*, as is implicitly assumed by both Kojève and those of Hegel's critics who see him as refusing alterity.[10] Nor should recognition be equated with that single instance focused on in the Kojèvean "struggle for recognition." If any instance of recognition is prototypical for Williams it is that of "love"—more prevalent in Hegel's earlier Jena writings than in the *Phenomenology*. Williams's "eidetics" allows him to examine systematically the other instances of recognition which appear throughout later chapters of the *Phenomenology*, especially the religious form of recognition instantiated in "forgiveness," and to attempt a reading of "absolute knowing" as other than a form of cognitive self-relation.

Given the focus of *Recognition* on the theme of otherness, Williams directs attention to passages in the *Phenomenology* where Hegel seems to be struggling to preserve otherness *within* recognition, that is, preserve the sense that the other cannot be *reduced to* the recognizer's interpretative concept. Thus, for example, in a key paragraph where he schematically describes the "doubled" action of recognition, Hegel declares that the recognizing self-consciousness "gives the other self-consciousness back to itself . . . and lets the other go free" (*PS*, §181; *W*, 3:146).[11] Williams notes the similarity of Hegel's *entlassen* (to "release" or "allow to be") to the term *Gelassenheit*, a notion used explicitly with the sense of "releasement" by the Christian mystic Meister Eckhart and more recently by Martin Heidegger.

---

[8] Robert R. Williams, *Recognition: Fichte and Hegel on the Other* (Albany: State University of New York Press, 1992). Williams draws on research on this topic going back over about two decades, particularly on Siep's important, *Anerkennung als Prinzip der praktischen Philosophie*.
[9] Williams, *Recognition*, 2–6. Williams's target in this work is not so much Gadamer as Hegel's French-speaking critics and especially Emmanuel Levinas.
[10] Williams, *Recognition*, 155.
[11] Williams importantly draws attention to Miller's grammatically possible but surely erroneous translation of this crucial paragraph. See *Recognition*, 155 and 167 n. 52.

Williams glosses *entlassen* here with "granting the other the freedom to recognize or to withhold recognition . . . the recognition that really counts is the recognition from the other that is not at the disposal of the self."[12]

Such an element of "releasement" or "letting be" is most clear in the complex structure of love and also recurs in Hegel's religious thought.[13] But from what we have seen from our analysis of the struggle, it would seem that even this context has its aspect of "releasement" as well. There the realization is forced upon the combatant that the world is not simply as it appears from its subjective point of view: first, the combatant includes itself as an object *in* the world and not just as a knowing subject *of* the world; next, it includes *its* other as more than a cognizable object, and even more than an intentional subject mirroring its own intentions. It has to recognize the other as an intentional subject for whom *it* is a direct object, and this is an intentionality it itself could never directly have. In fact, it would seem that if the element of releasement is a structural feature of acknowledgment per se, then indeed Hegel had described precisely that "third" form of intersubjectivity that Gadamer attributes to genuine dialogue. And if recognition turned out to be a basic structure of Hegel's philosophical thought, it would further seem that Gadamer is wrong in seeing intersubjectivity as eclipsed within Hegel's thought by those "lower grades" of intersubjectivity which do exclude alterity. These are themes to which I will return, but for the moment let us examine some of the different shapes of recognition as they appear throughout the *Phenomenology*.

Master and Slave

Within the struggle, as we have seen, each recognized itself in the other as simultaneously subject and object of a desiring consciousness, a "for-itself" as well as an "in-itself." In the institution of slavery, however, each protagonist now has a single role: the master occupies the role of a desiring "for-itself" and the slave that of object, an "in-itself" who has to renounce its own desiring subjectivity. As a model social institution based on recognition, master and slave instantiate a simplified hermeneutic social ontology. Their respective roles are indeed "fictions" in the sense that they exist only inasmuch as they are recognized. Stripped of this "clothing of the imagination," each is only a "man." Nevertheless, these roles are actual. Inasmuch as the master *is* treated as a master by him whom he treats as a

---

12 Williams, *Recognition*, 155.
13 In Stanley Cavell's writings on acknowledgment, noted above (chapter 5, note 22), this dimension of love is commonly at the focus of his attention.

slave, he *is* a master; and inasmuch as the slave is treated as a slave by him whom he treats as a master, he *is* a slave. Here the question "But, *despite* their common opinion, is the one *really* a master and the other *really* a slave?" has no application. There *can* be nothing more to being master or slave than this. And so, to understand this social configuration we cannot simply abstract away from those social categories within which it defines itself, because they are, as hermeneutic social thinkers have constantly reiterated, *constitutive* of that reality. But this is not to say that the participants themselves necessarily fully understand the nature of those categories.

Here, as with other forms of everyday consciousness seen so far, we *as audience* can see more of the structure of this situation than is immediately available to the protagonists in the situation. For each of the protagonists, the master is the "essential" self-consciousness, the only one who wills, the one who has achieved "independence." The slave has had to banish or repress his desires for particular things. But we in the audience recognize *embodied* consciousnesses only; and insofar as the master has become passive while the slave in his work for the master is *active*, it is in the *slave's* activity that we recognize the practical consciousness of one who "wills."

This recognition is not immediately available to the slave himself, however. While his actions are part of the objective world as it is manifest to us, they are not, at least immediately, part of the objective world as manifest to *him*. The slave will first have to encounter something in the world which displays his own agency in a parallel way, and this will be provided by the eventual *outcome* or *product* of his activity. Thus the categories of "mastery" and "slavery" are bound up in more complex ways than as were first apparent to those who instantiated these categories. Mastery can come to be seen in the actions of those who serve, while those served by others can come to be seen as slaves to their own desires.

Further, in focusing on this institution we should not be misled by its degree of apparent "organic unity." From one point of view, the master and slave function like a single natural organism: the slave is as a *part* of the master (like a "right-hand man") converting desires into action and results—"for what the bondsman does is really the action of the lord" (*PS*, §191; *W,* 3:152). Furthermore, the institution itself has to be thought holistically because the roles mutually presuppose each other: to be a master means to have a slave, just as to be a slave means to have a master. With such facts in mind we might appreciate the appeal to hermeneutic thinkers of organic theories of society with their stress on functional unity.

But of course the master needs the acknowledgment of *another* self-consciousness located at another point of view in order to be the master: the slave cannot be "part" of the master. Nor is there any "supraindividual

individual" of which the pair of self-consciousnesses are themselves mere parts. There are just the two of them in their particular relationship. There exists no single consciousness or point of view in which they merely share. As mutually presupposing but *differently* embodied and located self-consciousnesses, they are linked by recognition, a relation that maintains difference as essential; they are not submerged within some overarching supermind.

As there are here two finitely embodied and individuated minds, what this institution requires is a communicative mechanism to link its members. Within the struggle, the (future) slave had to be able to recognize the other's desires hermeneutically in order to *resist* them. Now, he has to recognize them in order to *act on them*. While in the struggle he could recognize them in those actions that aimed at their fulfillment, clearly this is not applicable here: the whole point of having a slave is to *avoid* the action that leads to the fulfillment of one's desires. So here desires must be able to be recognized by other means. Here it must be a matter of some form of symbolic representation, presumably the representations of the master's *speech*.[14]

The recognitive "spiritual" form of the communicative link here is crucial. In Spinozist substance, individual bodies are linked within social wholes in the same way that parts of the body are linked within individual bodies. Spinoza can use the notion "communicate" for relations at both levels because by this he simply means "have effects upon." But for Hegel two communicatively linked humans within a social whole cannot be adequately thought in such quasi-naturalistic terms because here any patterns of effectivity are mediated by acts of recognition: the production of a communicative effect presupposes the recognition by the hearer of the speaker's intention.[15] And for Hegel recognition carries that Diltheyan inflection of recognizing something of the self in that which is recognized. The slave can recognize his master's expressions of desire because he himself has experienced similar desires: he knows what it is like to have them, knows what sorts of things typically satisfy them, and so on. But this all makes the relation of servitude more complex than it first appears to its

---

[14] This relation between service, the nature of work, and the necessity for language is neatly summed up by Kojève: "The slave who works for the master represses his instincts in relation to an idea, a concept. And that is precisely what makes his activity a specifically *human* activity. By acting, he negates, he transforms the given nature, his nature; and he does so in relation to an idea, to what does not exist in the biological sense of the world, in relation to the idea of a master—i.e., to an essentially social, human, historical notion" (*Introduction to the Reading of Hegel*, 48).

[15] This point is made by J. M. Bernstein in "From Self-consciousness to Community: Act and Recognition in the Master-Slave Relationship," in *The State and Civil Society: Studies in Hegel's Political Philosophy*, ed. Z. A. Pelczynski (Cambridge: Cambridge University Press, 1984).

participants. That there are *two* points of view involved gives everything that goes on between them a double significance.

The master believes himself master because the slave acts on *his* desire. But we have seen earlier how an item of my sense-certainty cannot be put into language and remain straightforwardly *mine*. Thus the desire to which the slave subordinates himself cannot, strange as it may seem, be straightforwardly that of the master. The slave has to be able to recognize his desire in the expression and, even more important, has to be able to *make it his own* (we might say *acknowledge* it as his own) and have it direct *his* actions. While the master remains the mere passive recipient of a naturally given "intuition" of desire, the slave, through his active recognition of the master's expression, has recognized and acts upon a *conceptualized* desire. And by replacing his own *intuited* desire by that of the master, he "subsumes" intuition under concept.

That the potence structure of Hegel's Schellingian early writings is still present is manifest in the link between the slave's intentionality and the activity of *work*.

> Work . . . is desire held in check, fleetingness staved off; in other words, work forms and shapes the thing. The negative relation to the object becomes its *form* and something *permanent*, because it is precisely for the worker that the object has independence. This *negative* middle term or the formative *activity* is at the same time *the singularity* [*Einzelheit*] or pure being-for-self of consciousness which now, in the work outside of it, acquires an element of permanence. It is in this way, therefore, that consciousness, *qua* worker, comes to see in the independent being [of the object] its *own* independence. (*PS*, §195; *W*, 3:153–54)[16]

The serving consciousness can now, in the products of his activity, recognize something that was obvious to us onlookers all along: he can now see that *he is* the essential and independent side of the bifurcated self-consciousness, not the passive, dependent master, tied to his own intuited desires. The slave's servitude has become inverted into a type of mastery over the world through work. And because the master still essentially belongs to this world of nature, the slave has potentially achieved mastery over the master himself. We will not expect such servitude to last.

---

[16] Throughout I have followed the translators of *The Enclycopaedia Logic* by using "singular" to translate *Einzelne* and "singularity" to translate *Einzelheit*, and have modified other translations accordingly. See the discussion of this issue in *The Encyclopaedia Logic*, pp. xix–xx.

Penitent and Priest: Unhappy Consciousness

In his recognitive relation to the master, the slave achieved the dual consciousness required for the establishment of intentionality, that complex
point of view in which all things gain a double significance. However, he
did not himself become conscious of this fact. He thought he was merely
sacrificing his subjectivity to his master's wishes. A subsequent form of
self-consciousness, the "unhappy consciousness," is the first shape within
which self-consciousness potentially becomes aware of being this duality.
The slave saw his essence or will in the master, a particular sensuous
presence. In contrast, unhappy consciousness is a form of self-
consciousness that, mirroring the understanding as a form of consciousness, identifies its essence in an *absolute* master who is radically removed
from the sensuous world, a master who is, in contrast to the slave's, max-
imally *suprasensuous*.

The "unhappy consciousness" with which chapter 4 ends is a form of
religious consciousness for whom the eternal and unchangeable essence of
its own being, a *transcendent* God, stands in opposition to its own sensuous
and changeable particular existence. Hegel interprets a number of forms of
religious life as attempts to overcome this unbridgeable duality and
achieve unity with God. As unhappy consciousness always identifies its
particular self as the inessential antithesis of the unchangeable essence,
God, the religious quest takes the form of attempts to *free* the self from the
particularity of its own existence. The most extreme is perhaps the ascetic
who because of his embodied sensuous existence must internalize the
struggle, turn on himself, and treat himself as "the enemy" (*PS*, §209; *W*,
3:164).

As long as the two poles are in dichotomous opposition there can, of
course, be no resolution. It is recognition of self in an objective yet intentional other which is the key to the reconciliation of opposites: where the
other is conceived as an abstract supersensible self-consciousness there
can be no possibility of that. One can only recognize oneself in another
particularly embodied and so finite consciousness; thus the satisfaction
this form of self-consciousness craves can come about only via some intermediary who can somehow link sensuous and supersensible worlds, a
mediator who is himself a particular self-consciousness but who is seen as
the representative of God on earth—a priest. It is in subordinating itself to
the advice and counsel of the priest, who is regarded as having a direct
relation to God, that the unhappy consciousness can renounce its immediately given desires (*PS*, §§227–28; *W*, 3:174–75).

It is clear that the relation between priest and unhappy consciousness
here constitutes a recognitive relation formally similar to that between

master and slave. Like the slave, the unhappy consciousness must divest itself of its particular natural will, its action, and its enjoyment. It abases itself into a thing (*PS*, §229; *W*, 3:175–76) and has its actions determined by another, the priest. As in the master/slave dialectic, it appears to the participants as if agency comes from one side only: it is an absent God, who, speaking through the medium of his worldly representative, can direct the will of the penitent. But again the phenomenological "we" can see things in a better, more complete, light.

The unhappy consciousness sees its own role here as negative because it annihilates its own particular willing. But we see that this is one moment of the double action of *Anerkennung* and that the penitent's act must have *positive* as well as negative significance. The positive significance of the act inheres in its "positing of [its] will as the will of an 'other', and specifically of [its] will, not as a singular [*einzelnen*], but as a universal will." That is, the penitent acknowledges the normativity for it of the will of the other (God via the priest) *as* a universal will. Hegel says that the sacrifice of the unhappy consciousness actually "contained within itself the action of the other" (*PS*, §230; *W*, 3:176), that is, seemingly contained within itself its own redirection.

The slave renounced himself in the face of the master, a representative of the universality of death. But the unhappy consciousness renounced itself in the face of the priest, a representative of God; and the rule of God is different from the rule of death. In acknowledging God, unhappy consciousness affirms a universal will that is expressed in a *law,* a law which it affirms as governing its actions but which it has transgressed. But this law governs its relations not so much with the priest as with the other members of the religious community. There is a universality inherent in the act of unhappy consciousness, not because it makes contact with some universal and transcendent being, God, nor because it acknowledges a particular person (the person of the priest), but because it acknowledges, through the priest, an entire law-governed community.

But all this is still hidden from the unhappy consciousness. Like the slave, it believes that all the power resides in the other. But we can see how it now has access to an external point of view of its situation something akin to ours. In the recognition of the priest it can recognize itself from, as it were, a godly point of view. But it can recognize itself only in the words the priest addressed to it because the priest is like it, a human being. And because, as in the case of the slave, the penitent is the only one who actually *does* something, we can see how it might learn to perceive in its actions that which effects its reversal from guilt to innocence and might develop the view that the power of God actually resides *within itself* rather than in some transcendent world. This is an inference that our protagonist is going to make throughout the following lengthy chapters on Reason and Spirit which culminate in the shape of self-consciousness of "morality."

The Culmination of Objective Spirit in Morality

In the *Encyclopaedia Logic* Hegel talks of spirit as involving the "expansion" of cognition (*EL,* 20; *W,* 8:35), and what we see charted in the rest of the *Phenomenology* is the progressive expansion or development of patterns of theoretical and practical cognition together with that of the patterns of recognition within which they are able to function. Thus in the section "Reason" that follows that of "Self-Consciousness," the developing forms of intentionality per se are charted, each developing out of structural problems inherent in its predecessor, while in the following section, "Spirit," the focus is more on the context of historically actual patterns of recognitive intersubjectivity identified within the course of European history from the Greeks to Hegel's present.[17] Again, there is expansion here, involving both the widening of the intersubjective range of these recognitive patterns (a "universalizing" characteristic of modernity) and their "deepening," as these widened recognitive structures are in turn "reflected" within the viewpoints of the subjects involved. Both sections culminate in returns to the essentially Kantian problem of the reconciliation of transcendental (universal) and empirical (singular) poles of consciousness, but in the concluding part of "Spirit"—"Spirit that is certain of itself. Morality"—the emphasis is more on the presupposed intersubjective dimensions of this Kantian conception.

In the "moral view of the world," self-consciousness knows its objective *duty* to be the absolute essence of its action (*PS,* §599; *W,* 3:442). Construed in an individualistic Cartesian way, this project is doomed. The for-itself subject here believes that it can know the moral essence of its actions, its duty, in an immediate fashion, and as the objective realm of nature is, from this point of view, irrelevant to moral action, nature will be posited merely as indifferent. At the same time, however, nature, in the form of natural inclinations, is needed as a positive opponent against which morality can struggle and display its own reality.

Furthermore, as observers of the scene in which moral consciousness appears, we can see that it exists in a world that provides a context in which its actions unfold: for onlookers, actions are intelligible precisely

---

[17] For a synoptic account and defense of the structural transitions of the *Phenomenology* from the perspective of a nonmetaphysical reading see Robert Pippin, "You Can't Get There from Here: Transition Problems in Hegel's *Phenomenology of Spirit*" in *The Cambridge Companion to Hegel,* ed. Frederick C. Beiser (Cambridge: Cambridge University Press, 1993).

because of their intentionality, their directedness to particular elements present in the context within which they unfold. But although this is apparent to us, it is not immediately apparent to moral consciousness itself. For it, the world remains as something outside the realm of its thoughts and deliberations, as outside the reach of its action. In this way nature is left to itself as an autonomous, free presence: "a *Nature* whose laws like its actions belong to itself as a being which is indifferent to moral self-consciousness, just as the latter is indifferent to it" (*PS*, §599; *W*, 3:443). For us, that such a dichotomy of duty and nature rests on "such completely conflicting presuppositions" is obvious, but it only becomes obvious to this form of self-consciousness itself as a result of its ensnarement in contradiction.

We know that what is needed for moral consciousness to overcome such contradiction is for it to find itself in some form of recognitive relationship to another finite subject. As long as it sees itself as directed toward some nonworldly ideal and as long as the realm of duty is taken in dichotomous opposition to worldly reality, this will be impossible. It is thus an advance when a form of moral self-consciousness appears which believes the moral essence of its actions to exist within *itself*. This character believes that in its *conscientious* actions it is motivated by some inner pure moral certainty (*PS*, §632; *W*, 3:464). We now have a form of moral self-consciousness in which morality can present a human face to the world. We can also now imagine a form of spirit embodied in a community of mutually recognizing conscientious agents. But exploration of this idea shows the hope to be short-lived. We here have insuperable pragmatic problems associated with the communicative relations between those involved.

Recognition of "conscientiousness" demands that it has some form of phenomenal presentation, and when we ask what could count as such a phenomenal presentation, we quickly see that the action *itself* could not really suffice. *It* is something that has various worldly connections—preconditions, ramifications, and so on—of which the acting subject could never be fully aware. But the conscientious subject believes it acts on the pure, immediate, and complete grasp of its *duty*. This means that what could be recognized by others must be its *word*, its honest *espousal* of its felt conviction that it acts on duty: "[W]hat is valid for that self-consciousness is not the *action* as an *existence*, but the *conviction* [*Überzeugung*] that it is a duty; and this is made actual in language" (*PS*, §653; *W*, 3:479).

But again, as onlookers, we can see the problems here. Language is a medium in which that which is *only* available in some private, first person way could *never* be expressed as such. This was the lesson of sense certainty that has been repeated inexorably since. A communicative partner has to be able to recognize something of *himself* in the communicated representation. And so there is no way here for recognition or communication of such immediate pure *conviction* to take place. Despite its attempts at communicating its conviction, this agent is still an abstract "I" = "I," not one pole of the spiritual I/We. Here: "All life, all spiritual essentiality, has withdrawn into this self and has lost its difference from the *I* itself" (PS, §658; W, 3:483).

In place of any real dialogue all there can be is a battle of monological interpretations of the conscientious agent's motives for acting. In this struggle an actor, certain of the purity of its motives, faces a moral judge who, unable to find meaning in the verbal presentation of conviction, can *only* judge the actions themselves. But this judge is still tied to the dichotomous opposition of pure duty and worldly action, and so is a judge for whom *no* actions, because of their entanglement in the world, could *ever* instantiate pure duty: "For the consciousness which holds firmly to duty, the first consciousness counts as *evil* . . . and since . . . this first consciousness declares its action to be in conformity with itself, to be duty and conscientiousness, it is held by the universal consciousness to be *hypocrisy*" (PS, §660; W, 3:485).

But as we have seen much earlier, struggles have their own recognitive possibilities. The judge in its denouncing of its evil and hypocritical opponent is, of course, *also* acting, and in this judgmental action, is appealing to its *own* immediate certainty of what constitutes duty. And equally, because it is *as* unable as the first agent to make good in discourse the basis of its judgment, it too is caught in the first's dilemma. The judgment itself is "hypocrisy, because it passes off such judging, not as another manner of being wicked, but as the correct consciousness of the action, setting itself up in this unreality and conceit of knowing well and better above the deeds it discredits, and wanting its words without deeds to be taken for a superior kind of *reality*. By putting itself, then, in this way on the level with the doer on whom it passes judgement, it is recognized [*erkannt*] by the latter as the same as himself" (PS, §666; W, 3:489).[18]

As in the earlier life-and-death struggle, the hermeneutic insight here leads to a *new* communicative action: The first, acting consciousness, "beholding [*anschauend*] this identity and giving utterance to it, . . . confesses this to the other, and equally expects that the other, having in fact put himself on the same level, will also respond in words in which he will give

---

[18] "[T]hrough this judgement [the judging consciousness] places itself . . . *alongside* the first consciousness, and the latter, *through this likeness*, comes to see [*kommt . . . zur Anschauung*] its own self in this other consciousness" (PS, §664; W, 3:487).

utterance to this identity with him, and expects that this recognition will now exist in fact [*das anerkennende Dasein eintreten werde*]" (*PS*, §666; *W*, 3:489–90; translation modified).

In Hegel's narrative the "hard-hearted judge" at first does not reciprocate and maintains its "uncommunicative being-for-self." But the opportunity for this hermeneutic insight is, nevertheless, as available to the judge as it was to the other; and so, sooner or later, the judge "renounces the divisive thought . . . because it has in fact seen itself [*sich selbst . . . anschaut*] in the first" (*PS*, §670; *W*, 3:492). Thus in this context of mutual forgiveness and reconciliation we approach, from a different direction, a form of community akin to that approached in the resolution of the unhappy consciousness, and we are on the border of the absolute spirit of religious consciousness, "The word of reconciliation is the *objectively* existent Spirit, which beholds [*anschaut*] the pure knowledge of itself *qua universal* essence, in its opposite, in the pure knowledge of itself *qua* absolutely self-contained and exclusive *singularity* [*Einzelheit*]—a reciprocal recognition which is *absolute* spirit" (*PS*, §670; *W*, 3:493). "The reconciling *Yea*, in which the two 'I's let go [*ablassen*] their antithetical *existence*, is the *existence* of the 'I' which has expanded into a duality, and therein remains identical with itself, and, in its complete externalization and opposite, possesses the certainty of itself: it is God manifested in the midst of those who know themselves in the form of pure knowledge" (*PS*, §671; *W*, 3:494).

Religious Consciousness and Absolute Knowing

I have been arguing that the Hegelian notion of spirit is meant to refer not to some infinite individual conscious and self-conscious subject, that is, some form of traditional God, but rather to the form of recognitive intersubjectivity adequate to support the existence of fully conscious and self-conscious finite living subjects. This, of course, is not the traditional reading of this notion. Traditionally Hegel's "spirit," or, more exactly, "absolute spirit," is understood as referring precisely *to* such a divine subject—not the transcendent god of Christian theism, the God needed by the Cartesian finite mind, but rather a God which externalizes itself in the world of nature and human society and which, through the self-consciousness of members of that society, can itself become "self-conscious."

The final section of the *Phenomenology*, dealing as it does with religion and then absolute knowing, seems to provide overwhelming evidence for such a traditional reading. Does not the language even of the single sentence quoted above which marks the onset of the discussion of religion commit Hegel to some notion of an actual personalistic God having become incarnate in the religious community? Does it not imply that the We of the religious community is more than a structure in which finite individual I's reciprocally recognize each other in both their interdependency and separation and that it is in fact simultaneously the vehicle for another, higher-level, unified "I," a divine infinite self-knowing one? Furthermore, isn't it the case that this is needed to make sense of the very idea of "absolute knowing," the knowing that is this divine I's consciousness of its own self, a self-consciousness through the consciousness of that external reality into which it has expressed itself?

I have already noted Robert Williams's quite different approach to the religious dimension of Hegel's thought which thematizes precisely that element of recognition, its dimension of "releasement," which allows subjects to be reconciled by the "word of reconciliation" in such a way that their singularity is neither eclipsed nor absorbed into a single unified self-consciousness. For Williams this is the distinctive essence of Hegel's view of Christianity.[19] But how are we to understand the "much-debated question" of Hegel's personalizing discussion of God?[20] The first move in a nontheological reply to the traditional reading here is usually to remind the traditionalist that, for Hegel, religion is superseded by philosophy and that philosophy expresses *adequately* in terms of concepts what religion expresses less adequately in terms of images or pictures. This involves a traditional hermeneutic ploy in which it is argued that we must understand Hegel as speaking "metaphorically" when he talks of "God" or when he uses any other part of the vocabulary of religion. Religious discourse is for Hegel a *façon de parler*, which is not meant to be taken literally. But this is only a first move and really does not engage with the most important aspect of this whole issue.

It is commonly agreed that Hegel does not have a standard traditional Christian idea of a transcendent God. But this in itself introduces a great deal of free play in Hegel's texts: once one gets into the realm of *nonstandard* ideas of God, these concepts get so fuzzy that it is difficult to know just what someone is committing himself or herself to in speaking *of* God. What is crucial for us is how Hegel's talk of God, metaphorical or not, is relevant for the more detailed parts of his philosophy. It is for this reason that I want to shift the focus from God to God's "self-consciousness"—absolute

[19] Williams also discerns the essential "tragic" element of Hegel's religious thought, the very element that Gadamer sees as missing in Hegelian wisdom. Cf. Williams, *Recognition*, chap. 10.

[20] Although he is keen to deny the equation of Hegel's "spirit" with any form of transcendental or absolute ego, and although he sees Hegel as a critic of any "metaphysical theism," Williams in this work remains agnostic on the "much debated questions whether God is subject, and whether such 'subjectivity' is personal." Williams, *Recognition*, 226.

knowing. After attempting to establish something about this I will then return to the question of what the bearer of such a knowledge might be.

Toward the end of the section "Religion," at the very threshold of the goal of "absolute knowing," we find what is almost a replay of the unhappy consciousness episode, this time not in the context of a single consciousness but in terms of that which was earlier revealed as the truth of God's forgiving intervention into the world, the religious community. "Revealed religion" presents the Christian religious community as a community that has grasped in religious terms the necessity for a *particular* self-consciousness to mediate its relation to the absolute. For the unhappy consciousness this intermediary particular self-consciousness was the priest, but for the Christian community it is, of course, *Christ*. But this belief expressed, as it is, in the terms of the relation of a father to a son, is articulated in a picture language. There is something about the content here, something about the necessary mediating role played by particulars in one's relation to universals, that philosophy will have to understand *conceptually* rather than metaphorically or mythically. But for Hegel, these myth pictures are only a hair's breadth away from "absolute knowing," and the transition, when it comes, is swift and difficult to follow.

For us in the audience, this is surely the most demanding part of the presentation. So much hangs on what is happening on the stage, and yet there seems to be *so little* of it. Leaning forward in our chairs, we struggle to see how religious thought is somehow going to be converted into the absolute knowing of philosophy. We look anxiously over to Hegel at his lectern, but it is hard to follow what he means in his comments. We know that religious thought is stuck on the brink of absolute knowing because of its "picture thinking," which it somehow has to leave behind, rethinking its content in terms of the concept. But suddenly it seems all over. We are reviewing in a compressed summary all the scenes we have witnessed concerning the experience of consciousness; the standpoint of absolute knowing has somehow been achieved, and then it seems we are being given a preview of the logic and the rest of the system.

In reading these sections we must keep in mind what we have learned about recognition throughout the *Phenomenology*. At key points in the text, consciousness has undergone a form of anagorisis in a way that has turned it and the action around. I have suggested that, as in the theater, we can follow the experience of consciousness because we can recognitively put ourselves in the various points of view it assumes in its history. Surely then we must also be able to recognize something of ourselves in consciousness's own experiences of recollective anagnorisis? Might it be that there is something of this complex movement going on at the level of absolute knowing and that the review of the whole drama constitutes *our anagnorisis*? This, it seems to me, is something like what is supposed to happen here: there is meant to be some strong sense of recognition of the self on *our*, the readers', part. We must be careful here, however, as this can be interpreted in very different ways.

As we have stressed, the *Phenomenology* has been, up to this point, a text working at two distinct levels, the level of the experiences of consciousness in its various forms, and the level of the "phenomenological we" who watch on. However, as has been pointed out by a number of commentators, at this crucial part of the text, this structure seems to have changed. When consciousness achieves absolute knowing, something of the dual structure breaks down, as the phenomenological we no longer stands at some transcendental point *outside* the drama, able to observe aspects of the situation of which consciousness is unaware. This is because consciousness has *itself* now made it to philosophical knowledge: we are now somehow both located on the *same* level. We might ask how this has occurred and question further the location of this final "level." The most immediate answer to the question of how this distinction of levels is breached in absolute knowing is to invoke some much stronger sense of the "we's" recognition of the series of characters onstage than has so far been implied.

So far we have spoken of the recognition involved as akin to what goes on in a *fictional* drama where one's ability to recognize seems to hang on the dramatist's ability to represent widely shared strivings, dilemmas, and so on, within a particular fiction. Qua *particular* configuration of people and events, the fiction is not true to the facts, but, if successful, might be true in some other, more general sense—"true to life." But as directed to readers from the background of modern western European culture, the *Phenomenology* is surely *more* than this—not only is it meant to represent *real* rather than fictional episodes in the collective life of a community, that community is meant to be *our* community.

In some sense the *Phenomenology* has taught us to see ourselves not as self-sufficient atomic beings but as beings whose existence is, in a strong sense, dependent on belonging to the recognitive structure of a community. Moreover, throughout the *Phenomenology* we have seen the borders of this community—this "we" to which each of us as an "I" belongs—expand to encompass a greater and greater range of peoples, times, and places—all of those who count as part of our history. Is it not the case that what we have come to grasp in following the drama is that those on stage are not *just* other humans *like* us but that they *are* "us," our historical community that has come to claim some kind of universality? We are witnessing the drama of *ourselves*.

Following this line of thought, we might start to see the experience of reading the *Phenomenology* as undergoing a type of recollection. Of course in normal cases of remembering *I* am the one who had the original experience that can be recalled. But if I come to see my existence as part of the existence of a community, then the fact that it was not actually *me* who originally lived through the experience is no longer so important: it can be communicated to me through the language and culture uniting me to others. And if we start to think of the drama of the *Phenomenology* in this way *as* a type of collective recollection, then we might start to see how its two discursive levels might come together. In following its progression we have grasped the various parameters of the process of our self-constitution. We have become, in memory, fully self-conscious beings.

This line of thought, however, has surely simply taken us back to the standard reading of the *Phenomenology* which I have been at pains to contest, that is, the reading that construes the narrative as about the development of a single type of self-conscious megasubject for which we collectively provide the vehicle. If the *Phenomenology* is a type of collective recollection of that community which unites us, then why *not* describe this as about a process in which some kind of unitary thing embodied in this remembering "we" and its culture—spirit—comes both into existence and to self-consciousness? Is not this precisely what is meant by Hegel's peculiar theology?

But while this interpretation can seem convincing, on examination it is not. The best way to appreciate this fact is to refocus on the question of the "location" of this observing, now recollecting, "we." It is commonly asserted in the critical literature that the phenomenological we has somehow, since the start of the *Phenomenology*, always been situated at the level of absolute knowing.[21] Indeed this assumption has formed the basis of a criticism of the whole method: the progress of consciousness here, it can now be said, has been rigged from the start.[22] We were supposed to have merely watched the progression through forms of consciousness, self-consciousness, reason, and so on, without contribution. However, if we had always been located at absolute knowing, that is, if our view had always implicitly presupposed the ontology of Hegel's *Logic*, then the categorial structure of our thought would have surely constrained what we had observed and learned. (After all, Hegel was not just a member of the audience, *he also wrote the play!*)

If, however it *is* the case that "the we" has somehow been located at the

---

21 For example: "The reader who is to understand the various parts of the work must already dwell in the 'element of philosophy.' The 'We' that appears so often denotes not everyday men but philosophers." Herbert Marcuse, *Reason and Revolution: Hegel and the Rise of Social Theory* (Boston: Beacon Press, 1960).
22 This is essentially the view of Heidegger in *Hegel's Concept of Experience*, trans. K. R. Dove (New York: Harper and Row, 1971).

level of absolute knowing from the start, then this fact would seem to be radically out of step with the content of those lessons in which we had seen consciousness instructed throughout the drama. One lesson that had been repeated over and over concerned the inadequacy of assuming a spectatorial conception of knowledge. Another had been the inadequacy of the assumption that the *truth* of the world is located in some transcendent beyond. However, these seem to be precisely the sorts of assumptions presupposed by the "phenomenological we" throughout the drama.

Throughout the *Phenomenology* we as audience have viewed the progress of consciousness as a type of theatrical representation and have assumed throughout that the *truth* of that which consciousness was, at each of its stages, initially unaware because of its own contextualization within the world of the drama, *was,* nevertheless, directly and unproblematically manifest to *us.* That is, looking on from a viewpoint that, with respect to those *in* the drama, was located in a transcendent beyond, we had assumed that our conscious apprehension of the drama revealed its *true* meaning.

Moreover, the emergence of the *strong* sense of recognition in which we see the events onstage as a type of recollective representation of ourselves does not at all alter things. We might think that because we grasp that it is *ourselves* represented on the stage (now the stage of memory) then it is no longer the case that we as observers belong to a transcendent beyond to those onstage: "they" are just our earlier selves belonging to the same world as our present selves. But this does not help. We are watching from *our* present, and if it is the case that it is for an observing or remembering subject situated *here* that the truth of the past will be manifested, then, from the point of view of our *past* selves, our present selves might as well be in some otherworldly beyond. For Hegel, it is that which *cannot* appear to conscious subjects that counts as being transcendent; and while the *past* can appear to us in memory, the *future* has simply *no* way of appearing until it happens. (This seems linked to the fact that for Hegel there can be no philosophical presentation of the future—that is, no philosophical prediction.)

Furthermore, the assumption that the truth about the self is manifest in a type of spectatorial relation to one's past self is surely in contradiction with what we had learned explicitly from chapter 4 onward: that self-consciousness is achieved only when one self-consciousness recognizes or acknowledges itself in the recognition or acknowledgment of another. For while we had been *recognizing* something of ourselves in the actions and words of the characters in the drama, we certainly had not been in any sense *acknowledging* them, or they us. Rather, we had regarded their words and actions as representations—"*Vorstellungen*"—to be viewed from a third person perspective, rather than as expressions addressed to us as a second person "*you.*" (And so in this way spectatorial thought is akin to religious thought.) We could not *be present to,* and so could never be acknowledged or addressed by those "onstage," because, while they appeared to us, we had never appeared to them.[23] (We might recall the Brechtian "alienation-effect" here, utilized to break the type of realist assumptions that go with viewing a drama and the universality of the viewing position.)

Given Hegel's explicit views concerning the recognitive structure of spirit, it is therefore difficult to see how the final "standpoint" in which absolute knowing were to be achieved could be anything like that spectatorial one of the drama, or even of memory, if *its* operations were conceived on a dramatic model: neither could the "we" have occupied the standpoint of "absolute knowing" all along, nor could its viewpoint be the goal of consciousness's journey. But if it is not the case that in absolute knowing consciousness has finally achieved "our" point of view, may it not then be that something of the reverse movement has occurred? May it not be the case that in the final moment "we" have been in some way brought down to the level of those historical characters represented—that is, "brought down to earth" such that we grasp *ourselves* as always existing in worldly contexts that provide the conditions and limits of our theoretical and practical consciousness?

We might now start to see what could be at issue in seeing absolute knowing as involving *acknowledgment* and not just recognition. To *acknowledge* the history that we have just seen represented as *our* history (and conversely, to allow ourselves to be acknowledged by that historical recounting as being about us) is not just to come to the general insight that as thinkers we must inhabit particular worldly contexts: rather, it is to acknowledge that we can come to occupy a "universal" point of view *only* in virtue of the fact that we *are* members of that particular community of thought whose history we have seen represented.[24] We might again refer to the struggle as a simple model of recognition/acknowledgment. Each

---

[23] I take this notion from Stanley Cavell's discussions of recognition and acknowledgment and its modes in relation to the theatrical and cinematic experience. See especially *The World Viewed,* enl. ed. (Cambridge, Mass.: Harvard University Press, 1979).

[24] This theme of the role within absolute knowing of the acknowledgment of this history as one's own is expressed in Terry Pinkard's discussion in *Hegel's "Phenomenology": The Sociality of Reason* (Cambridge: Cambridge University Press, 1994), 267: "The *Phenomenology of Spirit* is thus the philosophical reflection on who we are in modern life. It is the explanation of how we came to be the people for whom 'absolute knowing'—that is, the human community's coming to a reflective non-metaphysical understanding—of what it must take as authoritative grounds for belief and action—is not *just* a possibility but something that essentially characterizes our self-understanding. History alone cannot tell us this."

combatant was able to gain a sense of himself as an intentional subject because each could recognize his own intention as that displayed by the other but could only recognize that intention inasmuch as he could recognize himself as the *object* to which that intention was directed. That is, knowing oneself as a subject required simultaneously knowing oneself as an object of another intentional subject.

Here, we see the same paradox that self-conscious subjectivity is achieved only in the *abandonment* of the project of coming to exist as a *pure* subject, unencumbered by worldly conditionedness. Gaining access to the transcendental level of the phenomenological "we" is achieved not by escaping the constraints of objectivity but by belonging to a certain *type* of objectivity—a type structured by certain normative patterns of intersubjectivity which are adequate to support its members as having existence as free, thinking agents. That is, it is achieved by acknowledging as normative, and by being acknowledged as a participant in, institutions adequate to the instantiation of the relation of reciprocal recognition needed for the existence and reproduction of free and thoughtful forms of life. And for Hegel, the institutional conditions for such forms of life have been achieved, at least in outline, in the modern Western world, understood as having developed and institutionalized certain ideas that had first appeared in ancient Greece.

The most developed form that these institutionalized relations have so far taken in the West's history has been that of the spiritual community of Christianity, the absolute religion, with its practice of mutual forgiveness. But while the members of this community implicitly instantiate this form of spirit, they themselves understand it, and the relation that each bears to it, according to the *Vorstellungen* of a representational consciousness. That is, the members see absolute spirit as something given, separate, and standing over against themselves, rather than as something in whose creation they each participate (*PS*, §785; *W*, 3:571). What needs to be added to this content is the *form* of self-conscious subjectivity, the type of self-consciousness seen developed in the moral self-consciousness which had so entranced Fichte and which understands its own *act* as reality. Absolute religion will become absolute *knowing* when it recognizes itself in the recognition of its abstractly self-conscious antithesis, an act which requires, of course, that this antithesis recognize itself in it. It would seem, then, that just as religious consciousness has to see the spirit with which it seeks reconciliation as brought about by its own act, the type of self-consciousness seen in morality has to grasp its own act not simply as a negation of the given, finite world which stands over against it, but also as involving some type of "forgiveness" or acceptance of that world. Because religious consciousness and moral self-consciousness come to understand themselves as mediated by the other, each is now raised out of its earlier one-sidedness: "Each for the other lets go of [*lässt . . . ab*] the independent determinateness with which it comes forth against it. . . . Through this movement of action, Spirit has come on the scene as a pure universality of knowing, which is self-consciousness, [and] as self-consciousness that is the simple unity of knowing" (PS, §796; W, 3:581; translation modified). "This last shape of Spririt—the Spirit which at the same time gives its complete and true content the form of the Self and thereby realizes its concept, just as it in this realization remains within its concept—this is absolute knowing" (PS, §798; W, 3:582; translation modified).

If something like this is close to Hegel's meaning, then absolute knowing can be nothing like the achievement of a body of *complete* or *final* knowledge, or some ultimate principles upon which such knowledge would be based.[25] Rather, absolute knowing would include within it the (tragic) insight that particular and determinate bodies of knowledge are *always* conditioned and so perspectival. It would include within it the explicit and self-conscious acknowledgment that the reflective, specta-torial relation to the self and the world was itself always only a "moment" of a fuller process of practical engagement with things and others in the world. This insight would not be the skeptical insight that we will forever be denied complete knowledge (although it can look like it) but would involve the shedding of the illusion of any ideal of "complete knowledge" itself—the achievement of some *permanent* spectatorial or *pure* subjectivity transcending all objective conditions.

This reading of the closing scenes of the *Phenomenology* depends on the "we" not having been located at the level of absolute knowing throughout the course of the text. Where, then, were we? One answer that might be given here is that the we, the readers of the *Phenomenology,* were "located" at the level of the dominant philosophical and cultural position of Hegel's time—transcendental idealism.[26] In fact, such a reading fits neatly with the type of recognition called for in absolute knowing on the reading offered here. The type of transcendental idealism resulting from Fichte's "comple-tion" of Kantianism was adequate only to the "subjective" subject-object,

---

[25] As is assumed, for example, by Kojève, for whom absolute knowing involves the achieve-ment of "*universally* and *eternally* valid knowledge," a knowledge of the "*totality* of existing being" (*Introduction to the Reading of Hegel,* 33, 31). In contrast, Pinkard, stressing the role of identification with the historical community of the West, sees absolute knowing as necessarily engaged and situated: "Modern Hegelian philosophy, understanding itself as engaged in such a historical practice, cannot therefore claim to go on *outside* of the rest of culture—as if philosophy looked at things from the purely impersonal standpoint, the 'standpoint of eter-nity,' uninfluenced by the life around it—but firmly *inside* it, part of it and its history, in a way similar to other ways in which that form of life has tried to reassure itself that it was on the right track." *Hegel's Phenomenology,* 266.
[26] I am indebted to George Markus for this suggestion.

but could not recognize any subject-object in its *objective* manifestation. But this is precisely what the "phenomenological we," which was itself a type of subjective subject-object, is asked to do in absolute knowing—it is asked to recognize or acknowledge *itself* as belonging to a concrete, objective historical community as one abstract moment of that community. But it is a crucial moment—a moment which allows that community to go beyond religion to philosophy.

The approach to absolute knowing sketched here differs from the traditional view for which the transition to absolute spirit introduces a new unitary and singular point of view—God's. Thus Charles Taylor, for example, speaks of the section on religion as from "the standpoint of *Geist*'s or the absolute's consciousness of itself."[27] Taylor makes the point, of course, that for Hegel mind is always embodied—so God must be incarnate, embodied in a living community. But to be embodied is to have a point of view, and if a community is to bear this singular "super" point of view, then presumably its internal differences must be somehow absorbed into a singular collective "we" without internal difference or opposition. But this would no longer be spirit, for it would have lost its internal recognitive structure.

Taking up the communicative post-Kantian reading of Hegel, I have argued that his explorations of spirit are motivated by finding conditions adequate for rational and free intentionality. Caught up in the recognitive relations of spirit, an individual subject can achieve that "double-sensedness" of its acts of knowing and willing which alone allows them to count as such acts. Throughout the *Phenomenology* we have seen the attempts of a variety of subjects, searching for some unitary essence either of their objects or themselves, to deny one or other of those aspects of themselves which appear in recognitive relations. That is, they attempt to deny either the "in-itself" aspect of their own existence or their "for-self-ness." These amounted to attempts to abstract the self from its constitutive recognitive relations, and they have led consistently to its collapse. The underlying reasons have been apparent to us, cognizant as we have been since chapter 4 of the necessary intersubjective structure of spirit.

The lessons here for us have counted as reminders that such attempts to secure a unitary "monological" account of the self or the world are doomed. They have been lessons in the structures necessary for knowing and willing per se. But the metaphysical reading of spirit introduces a new knowing and willing subject here *not so* constrained to these structures and thus seems to run against the grain of all those lessons. The alternative is the one I have been suggesting: that spirit names not a "super-subject" possessed of consciousness and self-consciousness in ways denied to us

[27] Charles Taylor, *Hegel* (Cambridge: Cambridge University Press, 1994), 197.

finite subjects but rather the structural conditions which have been developing in the European community and in which finite subjects themselves can come to be fully conscious and self-conscious. Let us recall Hegel's words in the paragraphs effecting the transition from morality to religion: the reconciling word is the objectively existing spirit "which beholds the pure knowledge of itself *qua* universal essence, in the pure knowledge of itself *qua* . . . singularity"; it is "the *existence* of the 'I' which has expanded into a duality, and therein remains identical with itself and . . . possesses the certainty of itself" (*PS,* §§670–71; *W,* 3:494). Christian theology has, of course long symbolized God as the "word"—but what can *Hegel* mean with this equation? We must remember that for Hegel a word is always double-sided—qua performative token, it is recognitively *addressed* to another; qua semantic concept, it is something under which anything other can be *representationally* subsumed. In my representational use of words, the world comes to exist as something for my understanding and so is brought under my power, but as performative address it "releases" the world from *my* exclusive grip by recognizing a source of its otherness to me, another viewpoint irreducible to my own.

To reach the standpoint of "absolute knowing" would then be to become a self-conscious "speaking I"—to become self-conscious in one's use of one's words. But words are about the world, and so this self-consciousness would effectively mean coming to understand the world in the light of this understanding of the dual nature of words. It would mean no more than this—it would not mean achieving a direct understanding and mastery of oneself as speaker and the world-constituting powers of one's words. But it would mean no less—to come to understand *this* would be to achieve a profound and transforming insight of the sort normally reached in the indirect *Vorstellungen* of religious thought (or at the level of feeling in art). Hegel may indeed have given language something of the powers we have traditionally given to gods, but this neither makes its users god-like, nor reduces them to being mere puppets of its external force—language is not like *that* sort of god.

Our Progress So Far

These features of spirit are, I believe, sufficiently discernible throughout the text of the *Phenomenology* to warrant a sympathetic reading of those passages where Hegel, in his personifying descriptions of spirit, seems most committed to the sort of view traditionally attributed to him. They might be added to the evidence accumulating from the work of sympathetic readers such as Robert Williams to suggest that the traditional reading of Hegel is far from secure. But is this enough?

It is my belief that the possibility of this reading must be taken further than the *Phenomenology of Spirit*. Unless Hegel's *system* itself can be shown to be compatible with such an understanding of him as a philosopher who, through the Copernican and hermeneutic aspects of his thought, was able to progress beyond Kant, the door will always be open for Gadamerian response: the response that despite the hermeneutic richness of Hegel's philosophy, it is ultimately defeated as a form of hermeneutic thought by the Aristotelian telos of "thought thinking itself," a telos which is explicit in the final chapter of the *Phenomenology* and which governs the overarching framework of the system.

As we will see, it is clear that the principle of recognition emerges once more in the third part of the system, the *Philosophy of Spirit*. But it is equally clear that if Hegel's *Logic* is not also investigated from this point of view, then we will be at a loss to explain how it can once again appear in that subsequent part of the system, given that it is meant to be *founded* on the *Logic*.

But we do not even have to invoke these reasons to require that we look at Hegel's *Logic*, as even the coherence of what we have seen so far, the role of recognition in the *Phenomenology*, requires a degree of engagement with the *Logic*. We can see this as exemplified in a difficulty that Williams has in accounting for the relations between different forms of recognition. In pointing to a weakness of Ludwig Siep's account of recognition as a "synthesis of love and strife [*Liebe und Kampf*]," Williams notes that "Hegel does not try to synthesize or reconcile love and strife, so much as to show that these are different types or shapes [*Gestalten*] of recognition."[28] But clearly this cannot be meant in any usual sense such that love and strife are as two "species" of the same "genus," as Williams goes on to describe strife or struggle as signifying "*Anerkennung* in the mode of failure (*Nichtanerkennen*), refusal, rejection. Conflict is one possible shape of intersubjective relation; it signifies the refusal of recognition."[29] Conflict may be a type of intersubjective relation, but how the *failure* of recognition can be a "type" or "shape" of recognition is far from clear. Nevertheless, it seems to me that Williams's basic insight here is correct—struggle is both a "negation" of and a type of recognition. But to understand how this could be so requires understanding something of Hegel's own logical alternatives to the categories of the "logic of *Verstand*." For all these reasons I now turn, albeit briefly, to Hegel's *Science of Logic*.

28 Williams, *Recognition*, 85.
29 Ibid., 87.

CHAPTER 7

The Logic of Recognition

IN DISCUSSING THE complex anatomy of *Anerkennung* structures in the *Phenomenology*, Hegel occasionally and unexpectedly invokes the terminology of Aristotelian logic. Thus he describes the complex triadic relationship between the "unhappy consciousness," its God, and the mediating minister as a syllogism (*ein Schluss*), in which the extreme terms of that consciousness and the "unchanging consciousness" of its God are united or closed with each other (*zusammengeschossen*) by means of a "middle term," the minister (*PS,* §227; *W,* 3:174–75). Here, the minister's action "mediates consciousness as such," allowing the unification of the unhappy consciousness's *singular* first person perspective with that *universal* point of view implicit in consciousness, thereby resolving its otherwise divided structure.

Although without using the word "syllogism," Hegel had earlier described the relations between master and slave in essentially the same way: "Each is for the other the middle term, through which each mediates itself with itself and unites [or closes, *zusammenschliest*] with itself" (*PS,* §184; *W,* 3:147).[1] Whereas the minister allows the extreme of the "unchanging consciousness" to appear for the singular unhappy consciousness, it is the universality of death, "the absolute Lord" that is made present to the slave in the shape of his particular political master (*PS,* §194; *W,* 3:153).[2]

---

[1] Significantly this sentence is immediately followed by what is perhaps Hegel's most explicit reference to the recognitive structure of spirit: "They *recognise* themselves as *mutually recognising* one another."

[2] "[T]his [servile] consciousness has been fearful, not of this or that particular thing, nor at this or that moment, but rather has feared for its entire essence; this is because it has experi-

Again it is the mediation of the particular "middle term" which allows the slave to overcome his own immediately given singularity, his determination by some fixed and given desire, and to take on universality—to adopt the stable and categorizable identity of an objective social role.

Hegel's syllogistic structure of singular–particular–universal refers to his own reinterpretation of Aristotelian logic, which he was later to make explicit in the third book of *Science of Logic*. A brief reading of this section of the *Logic* against the background of the theory of recognition may help both to throw further light on this notion at the heart of the earlier work and clarify the puzzling "logical" doctrines of the *later* work. But first let us very briefly put Hegel's treatment of the syllogism in the *Logic* in the context of that work as a whole.

The Project of the Science of Logic

Considered as an *aether* or *element* within which the ontologically "diverse" subject and object are related, consciousness is homologous to the logical space Hegel designates as "the concept"; and at the end of the *Phenomenology of Spirit*, the science of the experience of consciousness leads us into the starting point of the exploration of that conceptual space, the *Science of Logic*.[3] This latter work is divided into two sections, the first, the "Objective Logic," comprising two books, "The Doctrine of Being" and "The Doctrine of Essence," and the second, the "Subjective Logic," comprizing a single book, book 3, "The Doctrine of the Concept," that book within which the syllogism is explored. As the *Logic* is an investigation into the categorial structure of thought, its starting point will be the most immediate thought determination, that presupposed by all others: *being*, or *das Sein*.[4]

Given the homology between the structures of consciousness and the concept, it is not surprising that this logical start with "being" reveals parallels with the start of the *Phenomenology* in "sense-certainty." And just as the attempts to make that apparently immediate content of consciousness determinate gave rise to its dialectical development in further shapes

---

enced the fear of death, the absolute master" (*PS*, §194; *W*, 3:153; translation modified).

[3] For an account of Hegel's *Logic* which develops the nonmetaphysical "category theoretic" approach of Klaus Hartmann see Terry Pinkard, *Hegel's Dialectic: The Explanation of Possibility* (Philadelphia: Temple University Press, 1988). More recently, Pirmin Stekeler-Weithofer has approached Hegel's *Science of Logic* as a type of critical *semantic* theory in *Hegels analytische Philosophie: Die Wissenschaft der Logik als kritische Theorie der Bedeutung* (Paderborn: Ferdinand Schöningh, 1992).

[4] For my purposes here I have not differentiated between the presentation in the *Science of Logic*, and the "Lesser Logic" of the *Encyclopaedia of Philosophical Sciences* and have chosen examples from either according to convenience.

of consciousness, so too does the attempt to specify "being" give rise to a dialectical progression of different thought determinations.

As in the *Phenomenology*, the dialectic resulting from the attempt to specify the category of being here clearly rests upon the non-coincidence of subjective and non-communicable and objective and communicable aspects of this thought determination. When this thinker says or thinks "being," he or she "means" it as absolutely opposed to its contrary category, "*nothing*." However, "*Let those who insist that being and nothing are different tackle the problem of stating in what the difference consists* [anzugeben, worin er besteht]" (*SL*, 92; *W*, 5:95). The problem is, given the primitiveness of these categories, there is no *other* thought available to mark their differentiation—their difference can be "meant" but not "said." And so, from the objective point of view, which demands more than a subjectively intuited "meaning," the difference collapses: each thought "passes over" into the other.

Thus, like objects of consciousness, these thought determinations are "double-sensed" and contain an internal perspectival "contradiction" between the singular first person point of view and the communicable universal aspect. It is this contradiction that is the motor of the dialectical progression, driving the attempt to think these categories beyond such dichotomies as "being" and "nothing" to the positing of new determinations within which these contradictory poles will be contained, in this case, the thought "becoming."

I have argued elsewhere that Hegel's "being-logic" in fact describes the categorial structure of a type of pre-predicative thought which relies on analogy and metaphor to form its basic statements.[5] In contrast to the categorial structure of the "essence-logic" of book 2, being-logic lacks the conceptual resources to differentiate any underlying substrate from its properties. The closest it can come to predication is to (metaphorically) identify the different as in the "passing over" of its categories into their contraries.

As Robert Pippin has stressed, despite the fact that its particular categories (like "being" itself) can gain a content only *in virtue* of their contrasts to other categories, the categorial structure *itself* does not have the resources to *think* how this is possible. This type of thought always looks to the single thought determination *itself* as the "source" of its own determinacy and cannot grasp that the thought may be determinate *because* of its relation to something other than itself.[6] It *relies* on relations but cannot state them

[5] Paul Redding, "Hegel's Logic of Being and the Polarities of Presocratic Thought," *The Monist* 74 (1991): 438–56.
[6] Robert B. Pippin, *Hegel's Idealism: The Satisfactions of Self-Consciousness* (New York: Cambridge University Press, 1989), 196–200.

beyond the crude device of the "passing over." As a categorial structure, it is therefore incomplete.

It would seem then, that the problems of its first starting point in "being" could never be overcome conclusively within being-logic. "Being" is replaced by "becoming," which in turn is replaced by a further category, and so on. But, we might object, the concept of becoming itself retains a moment of immediate being which is "infected" by the same problems as its parent category. By "becoming" we presumably mean a concept in contrast to "enduring" but again, how could we "say" in what this difference consists? Ultimately this whole conceptual terrain will have to be remapped, and this remapping will take the form of the logic of essence.

The logic of essence is undoubtedly richer than that of being. Its "parent" categories are the pair "essence and appearance," and, here, attempts to reconcile the contradiction between the first-person subjective aspect of its thought determinations and the shareable "universal" aspect will locate the members of such contrary pairs on different ontological planes. The category "essence" is to capture that which is universal and true while that of "appearance" will capture the contextual and subjective. It is therefore not surprising that the framework of essence-logic is adequate to the "Copernican" movements of the positive sciences, and so here we find categorial pairs such as "ground and consequence" and "cause and effect." But again, like being-logic, essence-logic will be shown to be ultimately incomplete.[7] This time the incompleteness results from the fact that it has been built on the *negation* of the starting point of being-logic—the immediately given. For it, that which is immediately given is an appearance that must be *negated* in the process of reaching the underlying "essence." But if appearance counts as *nothing*, then it would seem that there is nothing for essence *to account for*.

The incompleteness of essence-logic is manifested in the shortcomings of those metaphysical schemas that appeal to an ultimate essence as the basis of that which appears in the phenomenal world—forms of metaphysics based on the idea of *substance*. And so we find throughout book 2 sketches of various forms of substance-metaphysics up to and including its most advanced and modern form—the philosophy of Spinoza. We have already seen something of Hegel's criticisms of Spinoza here: the criticism that all determination and individual subjectivity is ultimately "dissolved" within the monistic absolute; that of the formality of the geometric method; and that of the lack of "reflection" of the whole into individuals qua "finite modes." But Hegel also points to a circular form of reasoning within Spinoza's *Ethics*. In order to escape emptiness, the notion of sub-

---

7 Cf. ibid., chap. 9.

stance needs some further determination, a determination that it finds in the analysis of substance into the attributes of thought and extension. However, that substance has *these* attributes is for Spinoza not something that is true *sub speciae aeternitatis* but only true from the perspective of its finite modes—that is, ourselves. And yet the derivation of the finite modes is, in Spinoza's attempted linear geometrical method, *subsequent* to the derivation of attributes.

Metaphysical thought has to be liberated from the one-sided logic of essence with its category of substance: it must become articulated in the framework of book 3 of the *Logic,* the doctrine of the concept. Substance-thinking implicitly relies on the reality of the perspectival and subjective (and its cognate, "appearance") but cannot find a place for it. It is thus that book 3 starts off with the category of the subject, but now understood in a new way.

The metaphysical positions congruent with the conceptual structures of the concept-logic will be those *subsequent* to the Kantian revolution and its critique of dogmatic metaphysics. Subjectivity here, as in Fichte, is not to be understood as any kind of spiritual *substance.* Rather, it is identified with "the concept." Here the term means something like the space of "thought determinations" (or categories) that is carved out by a rigorous "deduction of categories"—a space mapped by a systematic unpacking of the conceptual structures involved in the activities of judging and inferring. It is thus that the dialectic of book 3 passes from "the subject" to *judgment* and then to the *syllogism.* Let us now rejoin the attempt to unravel the connection between the syllogism and the structure of recognition.

Hegel's Critique of Aristotle's Logic

First, let us glance at this peculiar schematism for the syllogism. Here Hegel follows Aristotle, by representing the syllogism as a linear array of three terms and by distinguishing the three "figures" by the position occupied by the "middle" term with respect to the major and minor extremes.

For Aristotle, the first figure, designated A B C, represents a pair of premises AB and BC such that the middle term B binds major and minor terms into the conclusion AC. In Aristotle's notation the two terms represent predicate and subject respectively in each of the three propositions involved; and the idea of one term being *predicated* of another is also described as that other "being in" the first "as in a whole" (*Pr. An.* 24b27).[8] (As we will see, this latter notion is crucial for understanding Aristotle's

[8] That is, if A is predicated of B then B is in A as in a whole.

idea of proof.) By the middle term, B, Aristotle tells us that he means that term "which is both itself in another and contains another in itself: in position also this comes in the middle" (*Pr. An.* 25b35)—we might say that it is the middle of the three terms in both *semantic* and *positional* or *syntactic* senses.

It is this coincidence of the two senses of "middle" which is crucial for the first figure, which is thought of as *perfect* (*Pr. An.* 25b32 and 26b29) because it "needs nothing other than what has been stated to make the necessity evident" (*Pr. An.* 24b23). It is the middle position of B between the containing A and the contained C which allows us to appreciate immediately that C is contained in A, or that A is predicated of C: "Whenever three terms are so related to one another that the last is in the middle as in a whole, and the middle is either in, or not in, the first as in a whole, the extremes must be related by a perfect deduction" (*Pr. An.* 25b32–35), or, in the complementary terminology: "If A is predicated of every B, and B of every C, A must necessarily be predicated of every C" (*Pr. An.* 25b38).

At this point Hegel's only substantive departure from Aristotle thus consists in identifying Aristotle's major, middle, and minor terms with universal, particular, and singular terms respectively.[9] While at first glance this seems hard to reconcile with Aristotle's syllogistic, on reflection Hegel's motivation seems clear. What Hegel seems to be getting at with the categories of universal, particular, and singular is an attempt to capture the relations of *semantic inclusiveness* between the A, B, and C of Aristotle's first figure.[10] We might think, for example, of the group of *all* Athenians as containing within it "as in a whole" a particular group of *some* Athenians, just as this latter group might contain within it some *single* Athenian, Socrates. On this reading, then, the relation between universal, particular, and singular would stand as a *model* of a relationship between such relations of inclusion regardless of whether their terms were *actually* universal, particular, and singular terms respectively.[11]

---

[9] Hegel also reverses the order of subject and predicate within the propositions and, with it, the Aristotelian ordering of major and minor premises. This results in his schematizing the first figure as S P U rather than U P S. As this change tends to obscure the obviousness of the validity of the first figure syllogism, a feature of Aristotle's syllogistic important in Hegel's argument, I have restored the Aristotelian ordering within Hegel's account.

[10] For example, Aristotle distinguishes between universal and particular predications or belongings (in the positive and the negative) rather than universal and particular "terms." Furthermore, despite the well-known mortality of Socrates, *singular* terms are rarely found within Aristotle's syllogisms.

[11] Furthermore, Hegel's use of this schematism might be defended on the basis that for Aristotle any syllogistic chain must, in the context of a demonstration, ultimately terminate in a judgment the predicate of which could not occupy the position of subject of a further judgment (*Posterior Analytics*, book 1). Such a term, it could be argued, would have to be a singular rather than a particular term.

We might now start to see how the syllogism so described might be regarded as homologous to the structure of recognition in, say, the relation of the penitent to the priest. Just as the middle term of the syllogism, the "particular" allows the "singular" term of the minor premiss to be united with the "universal" term of the major, so too does the middle of the recognitive structure, here the priest, who is, importantly, a *particular* person *like* the unhappy consciousness, allows the minor term, the unhappy consciousness himself, to overcome the singularity of his determination and achieve unification with the universal point of view, something which is rightly an aspect of consciousness itself but which the theocentric "unhappy consciousness" projects onto a separate and transcendent *God*.

But Hegel does not say that the mediated relation of recognition is *like* a syllogism; he says that it *is* a syllogism. But what could this possibly mean? How could a relationship between living and intentional beings be identified with a relationship between the terms of a logical inference? To start to answer this question we must turn to how Hegel *departs* from Aristotle's understanding of the syllogism and from the whole formal approach to logic to which it gave rise.

For Hegel, Aristotle's first figure is, predictably, not so much the "perfect" syllogistic form but simply its most "immediate" form—its immediate obviousness being akin to that of the truth of the forms of judgment found in unreflective "perception." In fact, the section on the syllogism in book 3 of the *Logic* is preceded by a discussion of judgments in which a central issue had been the "Copernican" demonstration that apparently immediate perceptual judgments could be equally understood as "mediated" by a hidden premiss. A perceptual judgment could be unpacked and shown to contain an internal inference, that is, to be an implicit syllogism: "[T]he syllogism," it was said, "is the truth of the judgment" (*SL*, 669; *W*, 6:359). We might now expect some sort of unpacking of the syllogistic structure which parallels that of the judgment in the preceding section. This would introduce "reflection" and "mediation" into the structure of the syllogism and, presumably, end in the genesis of some greater whole of which the various syllogistic forms were parts and which, on reflection, could be shown to be the "ground" for the original "formal" syllogisms, just as the formal syllogism emerged as the ground of the problematic, particular judgment. This indeed happens: the prototypical first figure syllogism of Aristotle passes through a series of further figures and ends in the "syllogism of reflection," and this in turn develops in a similar way into what Hegel calls the "syllogism of necessity." By the time we have reached this syllogism, the very conception of what a syllogism is has indeed undergone considerable reinterpretation. The suggestion I wish to broach here is that this "syllogism of necessity" which forms the ground of the earlier formal syllogisms should be thought of as a type of intersubjective practice embodying thought—a type of "syllogizing" as it were—and that *this* practice is by necessity intersubjective and recognitive. We might think of the syllogism, formally considered, as the logical schematization of the most developed form of recognition, that in which thinkers acknowledge others *as* thinkers. But the formalization can schematize this dynamic process precisely because the latter is the embodiment of these "syllogistic" relations—the "word" of the syllogism, as it were, made flesh.

The earlier dialectical development of the judgment had involved the construction of an order among different types of judgments. In the discussion of the syllogism Hegel proceeds in the same way by ordering the various syllogistic figures as a progression in which the constitutive judgments become progressively "mediated." This progression correlates with Aristotle's use of conversion rules to reduce the second and third figures to the first two moods of the perfect first. But in contrast to Aristotle's understanding of this as a *reduction,* Hegel reads it as involving a type of *generation* of the latter figures *from* the first.

The first figure (e.g., Barbara: A is predicated of all B, B is predicated of all C, therefore A is predicated of all C) instantiates the Hegelian U P S (universal, particular, singular) structure.[12] Predictably Hegel first treats the major and minor premises as immediate judgments. It is only the conclusion that is "mediated," having its extremes linked by the (now disappeared) middle term. But we know that the traditional view of the syllogism as ultimately grounded in immediately intuitable premises must be erroneous because "the syllogism is the truth of the judgment." It is not surprising then that Hegel links this criticism of the immediateness of the propositions to the demand that the premises of any syllogism themselves be demonstrated—"that *they likewise shall be presented as conclusions* [Schlusssätze]" (*SL,* 672; *W,* 6:362).

Aristotle had regarded such a conception as threatening an infinite regress. Thus in the *Posterior Analytics* (bk. 1, chap. 3) he affirmed his own view that the originative source of knowledge is immediate and nondemonstrated, and he criticized those who denied the possibility of nondemonstrative knowledge.[13] In contrast, Hegel accepts such an infinitizing

---

[12] As mentioned above, in order to preserve the parallel with Aristotle I have reversed the Hegelian ordering of the S P U structure. The direction of the order itself makes no difference to Hegel's argument.

[13] Aristotle discusses two views that oppose his own: "For the one party, supposing that one cannot understand in another way, claim that we are led back *ad infinitum.* . . . The other party agrees about understanding; for it, they say, occurs only through demonstration. But they argue that nothing prevents there being demonstration of everything; for it is possible for the demonstration to come about in a circle and reciprocally" (*Post. An.* 72b8 ff.). However, Aristotle goes on to argue that circular demonstration is empty, as all it can ultimately prove

of the syllogism and sees it as signifying "the sublation of the progression itself and the form which is already determined by it as defective [*mangelhaft*]. This form is that of mediation as U P S" (*SL,* 673; *W,* 6:363). That is, the development of the syllogism will reveal the "defectiveness" of the "perfect" first figure just as the reflective development of the judgment revealed the defectiveness of the immediate judgment of perception.

Hegel starts his development by taking as his "second" figure Aristotle's *third.* In the *Prior Analytics,* Aristotle describes this figure by way of the middle term: it is the term of which the other two (the major and minor terms) are predicated in the premisses, while positionally it "stands outside the extremes, and is last in position" (*Pr. An.* 28a12–15).[14] Hegel follows this account and using his own terminology designates this syllogism with the sequence U S P. We might think of this schema as an attempt to keep track of the relation of this figure to the first to which it reduces, conversion having resulted in reversing the order of minor and middle terms in the minor premiss.[15]

Exploiting the ambiguity of the middleness of the middle term, Hegel says of this syllogism that the *singular* term now plays the role of middle and so "mediates" the PU structure of the conclusion in the way that the particular played the mediating role in the first figure syllogism. Positionally, the singular term is, of course, now the "middle," but semantically, the middle is still the particular (which resumes the positional role of middle in the first figure to which the second reduces). That is, this expansion of the syllogism has resulted in a structure in which the two senses of middle *no longer coincide.*

Finally, for the third of his formal syllogisms Hegel takes Aristotle's second. Aristotle describes this in terms of the middle term, which is here predicated of both subjects and is "first in position."[16] Hegel's schematization again coincides, as he schematizes this syllogism as P U S. Again we can see that the conversion of this syllogism into the first will be achieved by conversion rules that reverse subject and predicate terms in the major premiss.[17]

---

are judgments like "if A is, A must be." For him, therefore, the lack of a finite terminus in tracing back a deductive chain can only have skeptical consequences.

[14] For example, in scholastic terminology, Darapti: A is predicated of all B; C is predicated of all B; therefore A is predicated of some C. Aristotle would write this A C B.

[15] For example, Darapti can be reduced to Darii in the first figure (A is predicated of all B; B is predicated of some C; therefore A is predicated of some C) by conversion of the minor premiss re-establishing the A B C (or U P S) order.

[16] For example, Cesare: B is predicated of no A; B is predicated of all C; therefore A is predicated of no C.

[17] For example, Cesare reduces to Celarent in the first figure (A is predicated of no B; B is predicated of all C; therefore A is predicated of no C).

Hegel describes this process, in which the singular and universal terms come to usurp the particular term in its role of "middle," thereby undermining the intuited basis of the syllogism's validity, as one in which the terms become progressively *formal*. Such a development subsequently terminates in a "fourth figure," the "mathematical" syllogism, in which all three terms are represented as universals because the *semantic* ordering of the three terms, that is, "the relationship of inherence or subsumption of the terms," has been completely lost (*SL*, 679; *W*, 6:371).[18]

It is this whittling away of immediacy within the premises in the elaboration of the syllogistic structure that is crucial for Hegel. Here he is drawing the consequences of an insight that emerged at the end of the section on the judgment, the Copernican insight that no simple judgment can stand as an atomic judgment independently of its relations to others: any premiss of any syllogism can *always* be construed as the conclusion of some other syllogism. Specifically, the premises of the perfect first figure are themselves able to be construed as the conclusions of syllogisms of the second and third figures. Therefore, neither judgments nor inferences can be found that can root the process of reasoning in some immediately intuited certainty. In place of a linear form of reasoning from well-grounded premises, thought will be faced with a circle—a "circle of reciprocal presupposing":

> In the first place, the syllogisms of [determinate] existence [*Schlüsse des Daseins*] all mutually *presuppose* one another and the extremes united in the conclusion are only genuinely and in and for themselves united in so far as they are *otherwise* united by an identity that has its ground elsewhere. . . . But this *presupposed* element of each of those mediations is not merely a *given immediacy* in general . . . but is itself a mediation, namely, for each of the two other syllogisms. Therefore what we truly have before

---

18 We are later given a concrete example of this type of development in Leibniz's "subjection of the syllogism to the calculus of combinations and permutations" and "the idea of a *characteristica universalis* of concepts—a language of symbols in which each concept would be represented as a relation proceeding from others or in its relation to others—as though in rational combinations . . . a content still retained the same determination *that it possesses when fixed in isolation*" (*SL*, 685; *W*, 6:379). Elsewhere Hegel elaborates on the problems of such *fixation* of concepts in logical notation when he comments on the efforts of Euler and others to represent conceptual relations algebraically or geometrically. Such a procedure, he claims, is based on a confusion between the relations between the signs themselves and that of what they signify—their concepts. One tries to represent, say, the relation between subsumption and inherence by some disposition of geometrical spaces. But thought determinations are "not inert entities like numbers and lines whose relation does not itself belong to them; they are living movements" (*SL*, 617; *W*, 6:294). It would seem that from Hegel's point of view, the same strictures would be directed to post-Fregean logic, despite its radical break with the syllogism.

us is not mediation based on a given immediacy, but mediation based on mediation. . . . The circle of reciprocal presupposing [*der Kreis des gegenseitigen Voraussetzens*] that these syllogisms unite to form with one another is the return of this act of presupposition into itself, which herein forms a totality, and thus the *other* to which each individual syllogism points is not placed through abstraction *outside* the circle but embraced *within* it. (*SL*, 680–81; *W*, 6:372–73)

What re-emerges here is another instance of an insight that we first saw at the end of chapter 3 of the *Phenomenology*—the insight that a truth arrived at by inference is not in any ultimate sense secondary to or derivative from immediate or noninferential truth—and here Hegel is applying this idea in such a way as to reinterpret what is typically seen as a threat to reasoning.

Aristotelian reasoning (and that advocated by Aristotle's post-Cartesian "foundationalist" successors) searches for an immediate starting point for knowledge and its rational development. Consequently, it takes as a threat to reason the discovery that each starting point is equally *mediated* in that it can be construed as the *conclusion* of an earlier implicit syllogism. Such a despairing discovery involves a negation of its premises: although it was originally believed that immediate starting points could be found, now it appears that all starting points are really mediated. But the "negation of the negation" of immediacy goes further: it brings into question the very distinction immediacy/mediation itself by questioning the *intelligibility* and not just the possibility of the absolutely "immediate." We should not think of "reasoning" without an absolute starting point as stretching back infinitely along a chain of presupposition of presupposition of presupposition: such an idea still rests on the image of some *absolute* distinction between a premiss and a conclusion. The traditional image of the linear infinite regress still depends on the intelligibility of that which it cannot achieve, an absolutely immediate starting point, and so its intelligibility collapses with that of its unreachable ideal.

The image of the circle of reason moves us one step closer to Hegel's way out of the dilemmas of "pre-Copernican" logic. This is, of course, the kind of circle that the Aristotelian fears, a circle in which the thinker tacitly presupposes something that he or she will conclude: the circle of reciprocal presupposition between premise and conclusion. But the problem is that the Aristotelian still understands this circle *formally*, and Hegel's reinterpretation of the circle of reciprocal presupposition is premised on the critique of this formal conception of thought. At this stage in Hegel's presentation, the consequences of this reinterpretation are still only hinted at, but let us try to draw out two of these hints so as to gain a sense of where the analysis is headed.

Among the number of readings of "other" in the last sentence of the passage just quoted, I take it that the "other to which the individual syllogism points" can, in line with the "formal" construal of thought here under question, be taken as referring to the *subject matter* to which the reasoning applies. This "other" is not to be placed outside of (conceived independently of) this circle but "embraced within it": the system of thought determinations is now "not to be regarded as an empty framework that can only be filled up from outside, by objects that are present on their own account" (*EL*, §192 addition)—the syllogism itself has now become "pregnant with content" (*SL*, 695; *W*, 6:391). Thus logic is no longer about the relationships between the forms of thoughts about *independently* existing contents: we might say that it concerns relations existing between things inasmuch as they *are* thought (rather than, say, merely perceived or imagined). Analogously, we might say that *the logical subject* must too be "embraced within" the circle: there is no position outside the circle of thinking for the subject to "think from"; no *thought* can originate outside this circle. That is, it is not as if we, situated inside such circles, can think about what is outside the circle *as having* some logical, that is thinkable, form. Thinking from within such an immanentist conception of thought we must now surely change the sense given to the very idea of what it is to be a "presupposition."

If we think of reasoning as necessarily starting from existing presuppositions, we might ask *from where, by whom* have these presuppositions—*Voraussetzungen*—been posited (*gesetzt*) prior to their reflective unearthing by the thinker, that is, prior to their emergence from an actual process of inferential reasoning. The thought that there simply *is* an infinity of presupposed "thoughts" that will enter into any bit of reasoning seems itself to presuppose a view of the world as already posited (*gesetzt*) prior to (*voraus*) *any* human cognitive involvement with it. It is as if the world has already been provided with thought determination that we in our collective thinking simply come to approximate or reflect. That is, it suggests a conception of the human activity of thinking as movement within an *already existing* conceptual space or *aether* whose pathways have already been mapped out. But, from Hegel's point of view, there is no transcendent "positor," there is no "outside" of the circle of thought.

This familiar Hegelian theme is here connected with another line of thought leading from this problematization of the dichotomy between the immediate and the mediate, or the presupposed (*vorausgesetzt*) and the posited (*gesetzt*). Hegel is searching for some conception of thought as a circle with no outside, the analogue of Fichte's absolute "self-positing subject," and, as we have seen, such a circle must be one in which that which is reciprocally presupposed is also reciprocally *posited*. But this is the characteristic of that "hermeneutic circle" within which, according to Heidegger and Gadamer, thought always moves. In its forward movement thought always moves on the basis of presuppositions—in Gadamer's terms, "prejudices"—but it can equally move in a retrograde manner and reflectively reinterpret, that is, "posit," those presuppositions in the light of the conclusions they have led to.[19] And such a circle is, I will suggest, one with which we are already familiar: Does not the notion of dynamic spirit as a structure of reciprocal recognition consist of such a *circle of reciprocal positings of presuppositions*?[20] This is the thread we must from here on follow in our brief excursion within Hegel's logic if we wish to explore the possibilities of a reading of it based on an essentially hermeneutic understanding of spirit.

The Concrete "Syllogism of Necessity"

As Hegel's exposition of the syllogism unfolds, the immediate syllogism of determinate existence develops through the syllogism of reflection and issues in the "syllogism of necessity" in which we see a return of the P U S structure of the third syllogistic form, the form which in the syllogism of existence resulted in the "circle of reciprocal presupposing." Whereas the

[19] Recently the idea that the process of retrospective recategorization is a central feature of thinking has been argued on neurobiological grounds by Gerald M. Edelman. See his *Bright Air, Brilliant Fire: On the Matter of the Mind* (New York: Basic Books, 1992).

[20] While Robert Williams seems to think that the notion of recognition is not present in Hegel's *Logic* (Robert R. Williams, *Recognition: Fichte and Hegel on the Other* [Albany: State University of New York Press, 1992], 279 n. 62), my thesis is that "syllogism" simply is the logical term for the structure of recognition. In response to the objection that this involves the unwarranted anticipation of a notion that, with regard to its place in Hegel's system, is only developed subsequent to the *Logic* in the *Philosophy of Spirit*, I briefly raise two points. First, in the opening pages of book 3 of the *Science of Logic*, Hegel comments on the parallel between the determinations of logic and spirit in this way: "[T]he pure determinations of being, essence and the concept constitute the ground plan and the inner simple framework of the forms of the spirit; spirit as *intuiting* and also as *sensuous consciousness* is in the form of immediate being; and similarly, spirit as *ideating* and as *perceiving* has risen from being to the stage of essence or reflection" (*SL*, 586; *W*, 6:257). This establishes a parallel between the objective logic and section A (chapters 1–3) of the *Phenomenology*, "Consciousness," and so we might expect that the parallel will continue to hold between the subjective logic and the *Phenomenology*, section B, "Self-consciousness," with its introduction of the recognitive theory of spirit. Second, in the addition to *EL* §187 Hegel notes that the three "'members' of philosophical science . . . the logical Idea, Nature, and Spirit," themselves form a "threefold syllogism" such that each "occupies the position both of an extreme and of the mediating middle." Even ignoring the difficult question of the relation of the *Phenomenology* to the system, we should not think of the movement of the *Logic* through philosophy of nature to philosophy of spirit as in any way like a *linear* derivation.

universal contained in the formal syllogism of existence was abstract, here it undergoes "reflection into essence" and becomes *concrete*.

In the case of the syllogism of existence we could be aided by Hegel's general approximation to Aristotelian logic. The power of logic as a formal enterprise has been weakened, however, by the demonstration that there can be no secure starting points for logical inference and that all inference is in some sense circular, as our *interest* in achieving certainty for our truth-preserving inferences will presumably be lessened by being denied certainty for any initial truth to be "preserved." But if logic is *not* a formal project, then what is it? What is it for a syllogism to be "concrete" and "pregnant with content" rather than abstract and formal?

From a modern point of view Hegel here seems to be in murky waters. The necessity involved in his syllogisms of necessity includes necessary *existence*, and so we enter the terrain of such traditionally metaphysical arguments as Anselm's ontological argument. Now the logical progression is from something "conceptual"—the syllogism as traditionally considered—to the existence of something *actual*, and the syllogism of necessity stands at the transition from section A of book 3, the subjective concept, to section B, "the object."[21] With this can we still hope to maintain our nondogmatic or hermeneutic interpretation of Hegel?

To pursue a positive answer here we might keep in mind that which had resulted from formal logic—the circle of reciprocal presupposition. With the idea of this circle Hegel essentially repeats at the level of logic his diagnosis and resolution of the now familiar problem of circularity.[22] The concrete and circular "syllogism of necessity" should, I have suggested, be understood as the concrete and pragmatic *recognitively circular* context within which finite thinking subjects necessarily exist. As such it is the circle within which the circularity of formal reasoning can be redeemed, a circle in which both the thinking subject and the thought object are included such that there can be no idea of some absolute place *outside* the circle, the place for any transcendent subject whose reasoning and knowledge can stand as an ideal against which all finite reason and knowledge is skeptically judged. In conceiving the self-negating circle of thought as the "hermeneutic circle," I have so far construed this, roughly after Heidegger, as a circular movement of thoughtful interpretation. But it is perhaps in the thought of Gadamer that we find the hermeneutic circle dealt with in more

[21] For Hegel the problem with Anselm's argument of course hangs on its acceptance of a thinglike conception of God. The unity of God is presupposed and assumed to be an "an sich" unity (*EL*, §193 add.).

[22] It would now seem that Spinoza's problem had nothing in particular to do with the actual concept of substance: rather circularity must dog any account that attempts to argue in a linear way from some absolute starting point.

Hegelian terms, because for Gadamer the hermeneutic circle is necessarily a *dialogical* circle: it is only in virtue of being situated within a communicative and recognitive circle with others that I *can be* a "thinking" being—i.e., a being capable of rational judgment and inference.[23]

By the time we reached the syllogism of necessity, the circle had already been thought through "subjectively" within the reflective syllogism's circle of presuppositions. But as something subjective it must equally be able to be thought "objectively" (from the "objective pole" of the constructed line, as it were) and so as an objective process embodied within an objective world. Thus what this anatomy of thought determinations must now do is retrace its movements, this time unfolding and mapping structures of objectivity adequate to the embodiment of that which has been shown subjectively. Let us reflect on what such structures of objectivity would have to be adequate to.

Presumably the objective structures and processes now explored will ultimately have to be able to *instantiate* the syllogistic processes of thought itself; otherwise this would have to be assigned to some unthinkable transcendent realm. That is, it would have to include intentional beings able to make judgments and communicate them to others and so on. It therefore looks as if we are eventually going to be on a terrain something like that of Schellingian nature philosophy in which emergent cognitive processes supervene on natural living systems. From what we have seen in the *Phenomenology*, it will be anticipated that such systems will be ones in which living beings are raised to the level of thinking subjectivity in virtue of the recognitively structured interactions in which they participate. In short, the form of objectivity being aimed at in this part of the exposition is going to have to be a form of communicative human life rich enough to support the most developed processes of cognition—we might say, a form of logical-life.

The Complex Structure of Objectivity

I have suggested that in this syllogism we get a glimpse of the type of content that this form is pregnant with—some type of living thought

---

[23] In Gadamer it is this ongoing dialogue between subjects about the *Sache* of their concerns which replaces the Kantian transcendental subject of apperception as the condition of cognition. This means that although the transcendental structure is understood as historically given and concrete it nevertheless must escape determinate conceptualization as some type of complex objective "thing" or structure. Thus Gadamer's thought here aligns with that of Hegel and Cusanus in their opposition to the type of thought found in Parmenides or Spinoza. From within a context that constitutes the conditions of one's thought and knowledge, one cannot form a coherent concept of that context.

taking place within the recognitive and communicative interactions between finite intentional beings. But to cross straight into a consideration of
living and thinking objectivity would be to break the developmental pattern of the logic because thought about such a complex form of objective
existence will presuppose thought about simpler forms. And so the starting point for the consideration of objectivity will again be that of the simple
object as *immediately* grasped by thought. But this object can now be
"developed" with that elaborate conceptual apparatus that has emerged in
the preceding section. Progression here will be from a naive and immediate concept of an object as a simple, self-sufficient thing with its identity
centered on itself, through the more complex idea of an object as grasped
from within the interstices of scientific thought, to the models of teleological and living systems.[24]

Thus here the *Logic* repeats the general patterns of the Schellingian
potences of Hegel's early writings. In "Mechanism" Hegel reconstructs a
movement in thought from a primitive cosmology in which all objects are
conceived in relation to a central object (the sun) which exemplifies object-
hood per se, to a system of objects within which any such self-sufficient
"center" has been eliminated. In this Newtonian world, that which gives
order to the whole now has the ideality of "law," but this is *itself* thought of
as "external" to the system of objects: that is, Newtonian physics has as its
complement a transcendentalist theology in which the "law" is conceived
as originating from the ideal space of God's mind.

For Hegel the rejection of such transcendentalism will progress by finding an immanent ground for the unity of the physical system. Thus in
contrast to mechanism, "chemism" grasps as its objects those "tensed"
particles which in virtue of "affinities" (*Verwandtschaften*) unite with their
opposites to form neutral products. But this form of thought has contradictions analogous to those of mechanism. Chemical processes are thought of
either in terms of this natural uniting of affinitive particles or the complementary splitting of neutral products by the mechanical action of free
particles on such products. But the three "syllogistic" processes involved
(the initial formal unity of the tensed particles, their productive coming
together, the splitting of the product) "fall apart," that is, the starting

24 We can look at this in another way, glancing backward through the text rather than
forward. The immediate concept of an object stands essentially as the first, abstract, negation
of the immediate concept. Its dialectical development will be the working out of the "second"
negation and so we can expect a return of the subjective and conceptual in such a way that its
abstract opposition to the objective becomes reconciled by the opening up of a realm that
serves to ground a type of "objective subjectivity." So on these grounds too we might expect to
move from a type of physicalistic thought to one which in a hermeneutic way appeals to
conceptions of "subjective objects"—beings that we think of and describe as having intentional and subjective characteristics, beings who manifest purpose.

points of any of the component processes do not in all places coincide with the products of either of the other two—they do not form a circular whole. Any process so conceived will come to a halt unless some *externally* posited conditions apply countering the essential direction of the process, the unification of tensed particles into neutral products. That is, in the developed system of chemism, the conditions of the starting points are not produced from within the system itself, and this is what would be needed if chemism were to have the form of being adequate to the structure of objectivity *in general*. This makes the chemistic system the objective equivalent of the circular formal syllogism: it does not "posit" its own "presuppositions,"[25] and the truly absolute "object" would have to be one with no "presuppositions" that were not "posited" by the system itself.

To explore such a model of objectivity, one that can "posit its own pre-suppositions," Hegel turns to the idea of a teleological system containing some intentional subject able to posit in its intentions and produce in its actions some desired outcome for the system. Initially, this unity between the subjective (positing) and the objective (produced) domains articulated within teleology will be "external" in the sense that objectivity enters here not only as the external material in which, or as the means *by* which, subjective purpose is to be achieved but also as that positive state of affairs that is to be changed. The dialectical development of these structures, however, leads to the *internal* teleology of *living* systems in which this externality between subjectivity and objectivity has been overcome.

It is in the course of the discussions of external and living teleology that we once again encounter those mediators or "middles" of recognition from the Jena writings, the tool and the offspring. The analysis of the role of the tool in external teleology shows for Hegel that the effective unity of subjectivity and objectivity sought for in the practical intention is not to be found in any realization of some purely subjectively conceived goal, but rather in the assimilation of a subject to shareable patterns of tool-using activity itself. It is from this insight that the analysis of internal teleology proceeds. Here, the organism, which is the starting point for the logical analysis of life, has its *own members* as its tools for dealing with external objectivity. Furthermore, that it *is* the unity of its corporeal members means that it is itself both tool *and* end.

This gives the organism an essentially *circular* structure. The unity of means and end implies that it is a self-producing and self-positing thing. We can thus see how the system of the living organism promises to go beyond those limitations of the chemistic system deriving from the re-

---

[25] "The process does not spontaneously re-kindle itself, for it had the difference only for its *presupposition* and did not itself *posit* it" (*SL,* 730; *W,* 6:432).

liance on non-posited "presuppositions." But as long as we are examining here the process of the *individual* finite organism, such self-positing will be limited. Just as the constituent processes of chemism came to quiescent rest, the process of the organism will eventually come to a similar resting point when, at its death, it lapses back into the merely mechanistic and chemistic processes of the objectivity external to it. But in its self-positing, the organism is not *simply* a singular thing: it also exists *as* an instance of a living *genus,* and it is in the context of those interactions relevant to *that* aspect of its existence that we find the syllogism of life truly "concluding" itself.

In its singular "living" process, the organism faced an external objectivity whose difference it overcame in appropriation. In the activities of its "genus process," those of sexual reproduction, it faces not just an indifferent objectivity but *another particular* member of its own genus. In the unity with this other achieved in this process it again produces a living singularity, but this is no longer *itself:* it is rather its *offspring.*[26]

As self-producing and re-producing, the organism has achieved external existence as concrete universal—genus. But "though the individual is indeed *in itself* genus, it is not *explicitly* or *for itself* the genus." It is only when it seeks satisfaction *in another* particular being that this explication can take place. But "what is *for* it is as yet only another living individual; the concept distinguished from itself has for object, with which it is identical, not itself as concept but a concept that as a living being has at the same time external objectivity for it, a form that is therefore immediately reciprocal [*unmittelbar gegenseitig*]" (*SL,* 773; *W,* 6:485). The other is not yet that in which the universal, the genus, can exist *for* the organism. Sexual union allows the organism to become in fact part of the species process. Singular and universal are united at the level of the "in itself," but this union is not yet reflected in the ideation of the organism.[27]

---

[26] Hegel understands reproduction in general on the model of *sexual* reproduction—a bias which clearly serves his logic of inverted opposites.

[27] Unlike the structure of human love, mutual sexual desire between two *merely* living beings does not involve each's recognition of themselves *in* the desire of the other: "In the separateness of the two sexes, the extremes constitute totalities of sentience, and in its sex-drive, the animal produces itself as a sentience, as a totality. . . . This case bears a resemblance to the process of assimilation however, for both sides are now independent individuals. The difference is that they are not related to each other as organic and inorganic beings however, for they are both organic beings belonging to the genus, and they therefore exist only as a single kind. . . . The nature of each permeates both, and both find themselves within the sphere of this universality. . . . At this juncture, the Idea of nature is actual in the male and female couple; up till now their identity and their being-for-self merely had being for us in our reflection, but they are now experienced by the sexes themselves in their infinite reflection into each other. This feeling of universality is the supreme moment of the animal's capabilities, but within it, its concrete universality never occurs for it as a theoretical object of

We can see something of the syllogistic structure clearly standing out here. In life, it has taken the interposition of *another particular living subject* to allow the singular organism to unite with its genus: the mediation of a particular has "concluded" the singular and universal. But this does not make life a syllogism, because something more is needed. In this realm "positing" can mean only the type of practical intentionality we recognize as embedded at the dumb level of feeling. The overall articulated living system itself cannot be such that its "presuppositions" are internally *posited* from within. It still requires an external "positing" subject; it does not exist as such "for" itself; it only exists as such "for us," and the system is not yet rich enough to include us *in* our capacity as thinkers. The instantiation of the syllogistic structure is only achieved in spirit, and it would seem that this is precisely the direction in which the evolving model of objectivity is heading.

It is not surprising that the analysis will now proceed to the realm of spirit, to that which we might call the "life of cognition"; and Hegel now examines the dynamics of theoretical and practical reason, yet again returning to a critical analysis of Kant. This section of the *Logic* is too long and complex to be considered here, but two points might nevertheless be made. First, Hegel's approach to Kant continues the earlier focus on the tool, a focus that allows him to thematize critically the implicit *instrumentalism* of the Kantian conception of reason in which the process of coming to know will have its significance entirely in the achievement of the end point aimed at—the possession of knowledge. But we have seen from the earlier sections something of the wrong and right ways to conceive of the relation between subjective intention, tool, and objective achievement. The true significance of the tool lies not so much in its status as *means* for the realization of some plan that is initially subjective, but rather in that it can induce a subject into shareable goal-directed patterns of activity. It is the *middle* between a private subject and objective processes within which the subject can recognize shareable "public" intentions and make them its own. This must have implications for any "instrumental" approach to inquiry such as that of Kant's.

Second, as is his common practice, Hegel picks up on a circularity plaguing Kant's thought and reinterprets it in a positive way by focusing on what Kant takes to be the crucial epistemological "inconvenience" obstructing the I's attempts to know itself. If the I takes itself as an object in knowing itself, it surely must, qua knowing subject, constitute its own form *as* known object. That is, its own spontaneous object-constituting

---

intuition. If it did, it would be thought or consciousness, in which alone the genus attains to free existence" (*EPN*, §368 addition).

activity gets in the way of its knowing its "real" self: it is trapped in a conceptual circle of its own making. But Hegel thinks it ridiculous to label as an "*inconvenience* and, as though there were a fallacy in it, a *circle*" this basic characteristic of the I that it "thinks itself [and] . . . cannot be thought without its being the 'I' that thinks" (*SL*, 777; *W*, 6:490). It is ridiculous because

> [it] is this relationship through which, in immediate self-consciousness, the absolute, eternal nature of self-consciousness and the concept itself manifests itself, and manifests itself for this reason, that self-consciousness is just the *existent* [*daseiende*] pure *concept*, and therefore *empirically perceptible*, the absolute relation-to-self that, as a separating judgment, makes itself its own object and is solely this process whereby it makes itself a circle. A stone does not have this *inconvenience*. (*SL*, 777–78; *W*, 6:490)

The belief that the I *gets in the way* of its own self-knowledge betrays Kant's ultimate recourse to a "substantialist" and hence precritical assumption about the thinking I itself. For Kant it is as if there is a thinking substrate underlying the activity itself and hidden by the activity. Hegel's reference here to self-consciousness as the "*daseiende*" pure concept, that is, the pure concept instantiated within the categorial form of "*Dasein*" within the Logic of Being of book 1, is crucial. "*Daseienden*" come in opposed pairs, and within such pairs "each is equally an other. It is immaterial which is first named" (*SL*, 117; *W*, 5:125). What else could this circle of symmetrically opposed finite and perceptible self-consciousnesses be referring to than the circle within which a finite self-consciousness recognizes itself within the recognition of another whom it recognizes as recognizing it—the circle of reciprocal recognition?

The Absolute Idea

The life of thought as philosophical method is the topic of the final chapter of the *Logic*. At the commencement of the third paragraph of this chapter Hegel clearly suggests that method will here receive a significance different from that which it had within transcendental idealism: "*Method* may appear at first as the mere *manner* peculiar to the process of cognition, and as a matter of fact it has the nature of such. But the peculiar manner, as method . . . is a modality of cognition, and as such is posited as determined by the *concept* and as form" (*SL*, 825; *W*, 6:550–51). Conceived instrumentally as it is in Kant, method will be thought of as applied to an indifferent and given content and so applied as a merely "external" form. But, Hegel tells us, the course of the logic itself has demonstrated the instability of conceptual forms as well as the impossibility that "a given object . . . be the foundation to which the absolute form stood in a merely external and contingent relationship." This means that "method has emerged as the *self-knowing concept that has itself,* as the absolute, both subjective and objective, *for its subject matter,* consequently as the pure correspondence of the concept and its reality, as a concrete existence that is the notion itself" (*SL,* 826; *W,* 6:551). If we are not to think of method instrumentally, then how *are* we to think of it? Here Hegel directs us to language: it is "only as the original *word*" he says, that "logic exhibits the self-movement of the absolute Idea" (*SL,* 825; *W,* 6:550). Like the tool, the word precipitates and codifies a certain pattern of use—here the use of words that constitutes the philosophical method. And by his placing in the position of third to tool and offspring that "tool of reason and the child of intelligent beings" of his early work[28]—the word—Hegel surely intends it to be taken as the mediator of recognition, the means by which one intelligence recognizes and in turn acknowledges another.

Indeed, at the end of the very first paragraph of "The Absolute Idea" Hegel gives what surely is an unambiguous affirmation of the fact that the process of recognition is that infinite form which is the concept. First of all, "the absolute Idea, as the rational concept" is "the return to *life*" but in such a way that "it has no less sublated this form of its immediacy, and contains within itself the highest degree of opposition" (*SL,* 824; *W,* 6:549). We will remember that while life approached the status of a self-positing system, the living individual was only "in itself" the genus and could not recognize itself as such within another particular. Seeking sexual satisfaction in another is what allowed it to achieve *an sich* universality, but it did not find itself in the other's recognition: "what is *for* it is as yet only another living individual" (*SL,* 773; *W,* 6:485).

The concept must become "for itself." It must be *intentional* but "not merely *soul* [*Seele*]," for it needs an objective form so as to be for itself. It must "possess *personality*—the practical, objective concept determined in and for itself which, as person, is impenetrable atomic subjectivity—but which, none the less, is not exclusive singularity, but explicitly *universality* and *cognition* [*erkennen*]" (*SL,* 824; *W,* 6:549). Singularity is, as we have seen, united with universality syllogistically only by the mediation of particularity: according to Hegel's syllogistic logic, this is the *only* way these opposites can be unified. It is the recognitive relation between particulars that here too allows the singular intentional being to achieve the *fürsichsein*

[28] *SEL,* 114; *SS,* 429.

unavailable to the merely living being. It has another similar being over against it within which it can find itself as object: "and in its other has *its own* objectivity for its object [und in seinem Anderen *seine eigene* Objektivität zum Gegenstande hat]. All else is error, confusion, opinion, endeavour, caprice and transitoriness" (*SL,* 824; *W,* 6:549).

If the discourse of the *Logic* itself is an exemplification or presentation of "the word," and if the word is necessarily a recognitive word addressed to another which recognizes the other as a recognizing and cognizing subject, then our relation to this text is certainly not simply that of external beholders of a representation. It is mistaken, I believe, to think of Hegel's discourse as *fundamentally* representational here. We might focus on this by considering the peculiarity of the word "word" *as* a word. Most words *are not* what they signify: "pipe," to take a popular example, is not a pipe. But, of course, "word" *is* a word: it has a directly self-referential moment lost to just about all other words. And much the same applies to Hegel's discussion "of" philosophical method. A philosophical discussion about method cannot be *simply* "about" method: if it *is* philosophical, then it is simultaneously an *exemplification of method.* As both a performance or presentation (*Darstellung*) *of* thought and a reflection or representation (*Vorstellung*) *on* thought, it is "thought thinking itself." But this does not signify that some thinking subject has achieved a narcissistic and exclusive form of self-presence—quite the opposite. Rather, these referential oddities would appear to signal that with the transition to the absolute idea there has occurred a transformation of the relation of the subjectivity of reader to the words of the text itself. We might suspect here that we are meant to understand the words of philosophical method not as a reference to something beyond themselves but as a manifestation of method as such: that we are not confronted with a representation of an ideal philosophical method but with that method. That is, rather than reading *about* reason, we are participants *in* reason because we are the addressees of a speech act directed to us by Hegel—and as such we are being acknowledged as intentional and rational beings for whom that act can be meaningful. We are being invited into the practice of philosophical thought. In the recognitive act in which we are being posited as rational beings and as beings with an *interest* in reason (the topic of the discourse), reason is "positing its own presuppositions."

CHAPTER 8

Right and Its Recognition

IN HIS POSTHUMOUSLY PUBLISHED sketches on hermeneutic epistemology, "The Construction of the Historical World in the Human Sciences," Wilhelm Dilthey credited Hegel with having developed, with his notion of objective spirit, the most explicit account of the conception of social reality implicit in the work of the German hermeneutic-historical school.[1] But for Dilthey, the shortcomings of Hegel's approach lay in his attempts to ground this conception in his *Logic*. Rather than start from an a priori philosophical position, he should have adhered, Dilthey thought, to an empirically scientific point of view and used his concept in the service of epistemological reflection.

Similar assessments of Hegel's major work of practical philosophy, the *Philosophy of Right*, have continued to be voiced by those for whom it stands as self-sufficient and isolable from an insupportable metaphysics. For example, within such otherwise sympathetic works as Charles Taylor's *Hegel* and Allen Wood's *Hegel's Ethical Thought*, one finds the attempt to separate the "good" Hegel, the social philosopher, from the "bad," the metaphysician and systematic philosopher.[2] But as part of the philosophy

---

[1] Wilhelm Dilthey, *Selected Writings*, ed. and trans. H. P. Rickman (Cambridge: Cambridge University Press, 1976), 192–95.
[2] In *Hegel's Ethical Thought* (Cambridge: Cambridge University Press, 1990) Allen Wood describes the Hegel who "still lives and speaks to us" as "not a speculative logician and idealist metaphysician but a philosophical historian, a political and social theorist, a philosopher of our ethical concerns and cultural identity crises" (5–6). Wood is well aware that this is not how Hegel saw and assessed his own work, but here, he thinks, Hegel was simply wrong.

of "objective spirit," *Philosophy of Right* is embedded within a system that is founded on the *Logic*.

The Logical Foundations of Social Philosophy

Exactly what it means to give a logical foundation to social philosophy depends, of course, on what is meant by "logic." As we have seen, Hegel's logic is meant to overcome the "formalism" into which the Aristotelian-based logical tradition had fallen with the rise of modern "subjective" philosophy—that is, the restriction of logic to the "form" of representational thought, understood as separable from and indifferent to the "content" to which it was applied.[3] As such, it is meant to recover *something* of the original "objective" sense that the *logos* had for the Greeks.[4] But for Hegel, the *logos* is not something *simply* implicit in the world, independent, as it were, of the finite human subjects existing in it. We have seen earlier how the hermeneutic movement had reintroduced something of the objectivity of conceptual structures with its Herderian notion of the "spirit" characterizing social existence, and it is *this* sense in which the *logos* is "objective" for Hegel as well. Thought determinations are *posited* in the world by those interacting intentional beings (ourselves) who are a parts of it. But we have *also* seen, in the dialectic of the social relation of master and slave, for example, how such categorial structures and dynamics cannot be simply reduced to the immediate understandings that their bearers have

---

For Wood, the revolutionary theorization of logic in the late nineteenth- and early twentieth-centuries have shown Hegel's logical project to be a spectacular failure, "final and unredeemable" (5).

[3] Hegel comments on the disrepute into which the traditional discipline of logic had fallen in his time: "It has indeed been recognized that the forms and rules of the older logic—of definition, classification, and inference—. . . are inadequate for speculative science" (*PR*, preface, p. 10). However, the incompatibility of Aristotelian logic with the modern world had only been responded to negatively, had "not so much been recognized as merely felt." Abandoning the methodical rigor of logical thought, modern politico-legal studies had lapsed back into contingent and subjective undisciplined speculation.

[4] In many respects Hegel's account of the modern formalization of Greek logic is like that made in this century by John Dewey in his *Logic: The Theory of Inquiry* (New York: Henry Holt, 1938). There Dewey points out that the formalization of logic in the modern period accompanied the structural changes implicit in the passage from Aristotelian to post-Copernican science. For Aristotle logic was not "formal" in the post-Copernican sense, that is, it was not primarily concerned with the formal relations among subjective representations of some independent reality. Rather, its formality resided in its concern with the forms of things themselves—that is, "forms of existence in so far as existence is known (as distinct from sensed or discursively thought about)" (81). When science destroyed the background of essences, logic became merely "formalistic." Thus, he asserts, originally a syllogism was not so much a form of inferring or reasoning, but rather an "immediate apprehension or vision of the relations of inclusion and exclusion that belonged to real wholes in nature" (88).

of them. The dynamics of categorial structures cannot be simply reduced to the "subjective" lives of their bearers although they require the existence of such subjective lives.

Considerations such as this are behind the implicit response that we find in Hegel to the type of Diltheyan objection to the relation of logic to social inquiry raised above, and we see such a response in Hegel's objections, in the *Philosophy of Right*, to the approaches to "right" prevalent in his more "hermeneutic" contemporaries. For Hegel, the "positive" historical sciences studied "right" dispersed into its particular *historical* determinations. Abandoning any philosophical approach to the concept of right itself, this discipline studied the "emergence and development of determinations of right *as they appear in time*," grasping these particular legal rights and practices not abstractly but "in the context of all other determinations which constitute the character of a notion and age." Where logic entered such studies, it was situated *internally* to the empirically described systems, reflecting on the "logical consistency of such determinations by comparing them with previously existing legal relations" (*PR*, §3 remark).

Hegel's attitude toward such an approach exemplifies his attitude toward the *Verstand*-based positive sciences in general. The historical study of law is "meritorious and praiseworthy within its own sphere" but should not try to usurp the approach of philosophy. Specifically in this case, the finding of *historical* grounds for law should not be confused with the philosophical task of its *justification* (*Rechtfertigung*). Hegel's point here amounts to a critique of the "genetic fallacy" and of its nihilistic consequences, as the *normativity* of right is lost in such purely external third-person approaches. By looking for the justification of institutions in history (Hegel's example is the monastery), one in fact undermines the possibility of justification at all: "[I]f this is supposed to amount to a general justification of the thing itself, the result is precisely the opposite; for since the original circumstances are no longer present, the institution has thereby lost its meaning and its right" (*PR*, §3 remark).

The purely empirical approach with its coordinate formal understanding of logic is limited to the inadequate conceptual structures of "essence-logic" and its category of "ground." We might, then, expect that the logical shape of Hegel's *Rechtsphilosophie* will conform in some overall way to the logical structure of the subjective logic, and this is indeed largely the case. The text proper starts from the practical subject in its most immediate and implicit (*an sich*) form—the singular will—and this form of practical intentionality is then developmentally unfolded in such a way that it is provided with successively broader contexts within which it can assume a more explicit determination. This development ends in objective "syllogistic" contexts that are themselves essentially structures of recognition, and the telos of this presentation (*Darstellung*) will be that most fully developed "object" which can be thought of as able to "posit its own presuppositions"—the state. Such an approach *preserves* a normative relation to its object because the idea of a system "positing" its own presuppositions simply *means* one whose recognitive contexts are capable of giving existence to fully conscious and self-conscious subjects—the type of free and rational subjects capable of *supporting* such a social existence and able to be supported by it.

Of course, if Hegel's *Logic* is understood, as is commonly the case, as some type of variant of precritical substance metaphysics, then what is meant by the "state" will be crucially skewed. Indeed, much of the secondary literature manifests such a "substantialist" conception of the state with fairly predictable consequences. But once the basically recognitive infrastructure of the "Idea" with which the *Logic* terminates is understood, the interactive and recognitive character of those "substantive" realms articulated within the state becomes easy enough to discern.

The Will and Its Right

In the concept-logic, the most immediate determination with which the presentation commences is that of the singular subject in its most immediate and abstract determination, the subject *an sich*. Similarly, the *Philosophy of Right* starts out from the abstract and immediate subject conceived practically—the singular will grasped immediately from its own first-person point of view. We might expect then that we will be following its developing determination through a sequence that goes from subject to judgment to syllogism and from there into those concrete syllogisms which, as I have argued, are essentially contexts of reciprocal recognition. What might we expect such a passage to look like?

The "judgment" is a determination of the subject as such in terms of an internal division in which (intentional) subject becomes opposed to and determined by an (intentional) object. Early in the introduction to the *Philosophy of Right*, Hegel sketches this sequence. The will contains first of all "the element of *pure indeterminacy* or of the 'I''s pure reflection into itself, in which every limitation, every content . . . is dissolved" (*PR*, §5) and yet "in the same way, 'I' is the transition from undifferentiated indeterminacy to *differentiation, determination,* and the *positing* of a determinacy as a content and object" (*PR*, §6). Logically, that every judgment can be developed syllogistically means that *no* judgment, here, no practical intentional state, can be taken as given or foundational. It can always be shown to be mediated by another judgment and so is always open to reinterpretation or redetermination. It is this capacity of the will to escape fixity by any *particular* determination despite the constant need *for* determination per se that Hegel captures by the idea of the will as the unity of both of these two moments (*PR,* §7), that is, the unity of immediacy and mediation. The will always has to have a content, some determinate desire, but its unique capacity is that it can withdraw itself from this content. This is not done in the service of having no content at all, but rather in that of positing its presupposed content in such a way that that content is redetermined. But this, of course, is not intelligible as an isolated act of a single willing subject (the Fichtean mistake). It is only intelligible within the context within which a particular will stands in some recognitive relation to another particular will. The presentation follows this type of contextualization and recontextualization of the will through successive realms of intersubjectivity, or *Sittlichkeit,* until that realm is arrived at which is adequate to the idea of such a structure as self-positing.

This start with the immediate subject and its "abstract right" gives to the *Rechtsphilosophie* an initially Fichtean look, but only on ignoring the peculiarity of his logical assumptions is one likely to misunderstand Hegel as an advocate of "possessive individualism."[5] Hegel is not, of course, stating some axioms here from which the rest of the structure will be deduced, and it soon becomes obvious that his content of abstract right is to be contextualized within an essentially recognitive theory of property.

As we have seen, Fichte was limited by his abstract and formal conception of the recognition of a right. For Hegel, it is not adequate simply to conceive of others as having "rights" in an abstract sense. To have a right is to have a right to *do* that which one wills. Thus the adequate recognition of another's right must include an understanding of *what* it is that they actually do will. In short, in concrete cases one must be able to recognize hermeneutically the content of the other's will in order that their right be acknowledged.

This is why the will must come to have a determinate content that is expressed in the intersubjective realm. The first sort of expression of the will considered is that which we have seen in the expression of desire in the *Phenomenology*—action. But in order to recognize the will as determinate, the action must be read as directed to a determinate *object,* some object that the willing agent attempts to appropriate or make its own. In Hegel's expression, there must be some object within which the person can put (*legen*) his will. What is meant by this is not that some strange sub-

---

[5] For an account and critique of this reading see K.-H. Ilting, "The Structure of Hegel's *Philosophy of Right*," in *Hegel's Political Philosophy: Problems and Perspectives,* ed. Z. A. Pelczynski (Cambridge: Cambridge University Press, 1971).

stance leaves the willing subject and lodges in the thing, but simply that typically we can read or interpret some particular person's will in terms of the "object" or state of affairs toward which it is directed. It is *recognition* that forms the link. Thus Hegel notes:

> The concept of property requires that a person should place his will in a thing, and the next stage is precisely the realization of this concept. My inner act of will which says that something is mine must also become recognizable [*erkennen werden*] by others. If I make a thing mine, I give it this predicate which must appear in it in an external form, and must not simply remain in my inner will. It often happens that children emphasize their prior volition when they oppose the appropriation of something by others; but for adults, this volition is not sufficient, for the form of subjectivity must be removed and must work its way out to objectivity. (*PR*, §51 addition)

Thus in writing about willing, Hegel is writing about more than mere desire, the natural desire attributable to living beings per se.[6] To will is to adopt and to express a particular intentional relation to particular objects in the world. Hegel is interested in the type of action with which the distinctively intentional or spiritual will takes up occupancy in objects in the world and so can be recognized by others. In the context of abstract right, we can think of the ensemble of those objects as "property" and the actions relevant as "taking possession," "using," and "alienating."

The first and most immediate form of property is the thing possessed. Hegel has a threefold analysis of this process. First, will can be recognized here in the very action of taking possession of some singular thing in its "physical seizure."[7] But the immediacy of such direct physical connection between the body and the thing is also its shortcoming: "[T]his mode in general is merely subjective, temporary, and extremely limited in scope, as well as by the qualitative nature of the objects" (*PR*, §55).

---

6 As we have seen, Hegel considers the sort of uniperspectival desiring that simply falls on an object in the world and consumes it as the most primitive and nonhuman form of willing. This does not mean that we humans do not do it. Every minute of the day we are appropriating or consuming air in the process of breathing, for example. But this is a type of willing which we share with all living beings; it's not distinctive to us qua humans. As such, it is a type of willing or desiring which does not get beyond the cognitive state of pure nonarticulate feeling: think of the sensation you experience when, on holding your breath, you experience the *desire* for air.

7 Wittgenstein expresses a similar idea that the action of taking possession is a type of immediate natural analogue for the expression of intention: "What is the natural expression of an intention?—Look at a cat when it stalks a bird." Ludwig Wittgenstein, *Philosophical Investigations*, trans. G. E. M. Anscombe (Oxford: Blackwell, 1953), ¶647.

Here we might think of an army taking possession of a hill in a battle or a team gaining possession of the ball in a game. In cases like this the connection between the possessor and the object is merely *external*, a bond of connection which is "neither life nor the concept," and impermanent—fortunes change and this hill or ball is lost. This can hardly be a very useful concept of possession for human life beyond those primitive forms of interaction such as battles or the sorts of games based on them. But it does have a role in organized social life as is reflected in the dictum "possession is nine points of the law."

The next more developed form of the phenomenon of taking possession involves the imposition of *form*. Here the connection between willing agent and thing becomes more complicated (and only graspable by a more developed form of cognition, that of "perception" rather than sense-certainty) and allows for their physical separation. "When I *give form* to something, its determinate character as mine receives *an independently existing* externality and ceases to be limited to my presence in *this* time and space and to my present knowledge and volition" (*PR*, §56). Thus farming imposes a form on the land farmed, and cultivating game and taming animals can be considered a way of forming them. When we recognize some bit of nature as formed in such a way, we recognize in it a *trace* of someone's will. We see the will as being lodged in the thing, even though there might be no longer any physical contact between the actor and the thing.[8]

With the third and most explicit mode of taking possession of a thing, that of *marking* it (*PR*, §58), the constitutive role of others' recognition of my will becomes more apparent.

> Taking possession by designation is the most complete mode of all, for the effect of the *sign* is more or less implicit [*an sich*] in the other ways of

---

[8] Such an idea of the occupancy of the will captures the belief that one *owns* what one has produced, a belief found, for example, in John Locke. But Locke can only conceptualize this form of possession by the quasi-naturalistic idea that in labor one *mixes* the activity of one's body with the thing. (The presupposition that one owns one's body and its labor is itself based on the idea that one must immediately possess one's body.) But whereas Locke explains ownership of the thing as flowing from one's prior ownership of one's body (an idea based on one's physical "possession" of one's body), Hegel thinks that one becomes the owner of aspects of one's body in the same way and as a part of the same process in which one becomes owner of any external thing: "[I]t is only through the *development* of his own body and spirit, *essentially* by means of *his self-consciousness comprehending itself as free*, that he takes possession of himself and becomes his own property" (*PR*, §57). In this Hegel refers to that phenomenon that we have already seen in the slave. In one's natural state, it is because one's impulses are directly given that one is not in wilful possession of oneself. As we have seen, however, it is a characteristic of self-consciousness to resist determination by anything given from outside itself. We can retranslate our desiring relation to objects into other relations like the work relation, and in this we are overcoming the givenness of our own bodies and becoming *proprietors* of ourselves.

taking possession, too. If I seize a thing or give form to it, the ultimate significance is likewise a sign, a sign given to others in order to exclude them and to show that I have placed my will in the thing. For the concept of the sign is that the thing does not count as [gilt als] what it is, but as what it is meant to signify. A cockade, for example, signifies citizenship within a state, although the colour has no connection with the nation and represents not itself but the nation. It is precisely through the ability to make a sign and by so doing to acquire things that humans display their mastery over the latter. (PR, §58 addition)

What the arbitrary sign does is demonstrate the non-naturalness of the relationship of fully human forms of possession and demonstrate that, here, possession exists only in virtue of its being recognized by another: a sign is a sign of something only in virtue of the fact that it is recognized and acknowledged as such.

There are several important things to take note of here in Hegel's discussion of the sign. First of all, Hegel's idea here seems very close to the Searlean (and Chladenean) idea of the central role of the *constitutive rule* in the processes of human life, a role that marks off the human from the natural realm. For Searle, institutions are "systems of constitutive rules . . . of the form 'X counts as Y in context C'." For Hegel as well, it is what the sign *counts as* that is important; and for X to count as Y it must no longer count as the thing that it is—X.

Such an idea of a sign that does not count for what it is but rather "counts for" something else, something that it is not, is, of course, at the very foundation of our human capacity for language. The word is a "signifier" that stands in a non-natural or arbitrary relation for something else, its "signified." The relation, as arbitrary, holds *only* because it is recognized as holding. We might also see Hegel here as anticipating the Wittgensteinian case against any notion of a radically *private* language. That something "counts as" something else is a relation that exists only in that it is recognized. Such recognition can *never* be one-sided or private; it must always be mediated by the recognition of another. Its role as "middle term" between two consciousnesses is fundamental.

"Marking" is the most developed form of taking possession, and thus the property relation is established squarely within the mechanisms of recognition. Property and the system of its dynamics, the economy, will only be able to be considered internally to the structure of spirit.

To some extent, in establishing recognition as the infrastructure of property rights Hegel has built on an analysis of the notion of right found in Kant and Fichte. In *The Metaphysical Elements of Justice*, Kant establishes the idealist principle that property is an *intentional* rather than, like simple possession, a natural relation. I continue to be as much the owner of what is mine regardless of any physical proximity to it. Furthermore, there is a dimension of reciprocal recognition built into Kant's concept of property: "When I declare (by word or deed), 'I will that an external thing shall be mine,' I thereby declare it obligatory for everyone else to refrain from using the object of my will. . . . Included in this claim, however, is an acknowledgment [or avowal—*Bekenntnis*] of being reciprocally bound to everyone else to exercise a similar and equal restraint with respect to what is theirs. The obligation involved here comes from a universal rule of the external juridical relationship (that is, the civil society)."[9]

Hegel's advance here, as elsewhere, is to show that an intentional relation holds only in that it can be recognized from an external point of view. For Kant the property relation involves the acknowledging of the proprietor as a freely willing subject. But this recognition is itself *based on* the moral act of regarding the other as an "end in itself" rather than naturalistically or instrumentally as something to be used for *my* ends. Qua legal institution, property was thus treated as having a universal moral foundation.

Given his criticisms of Kantian morality with its dichotomy of the natural realm and the realm of ideal duty, however, such an approach could not be the *starting point* of any institutional analysis for Hegel. But without a moral foundation the recognition of another's rights needs some mechanism for bringing the wills of individual "persons" into mutuality. Hegel's move here is to look for a form of interaction within the social world which instantiates this form of recognition in a way that does not stand in contradiction to the efforts of willing subjects to pursue their own ends. Hegel finds such a mechanism in the contractual interactions of the marketplace. In fact his move here is similar to that in the *Phenomenology* where he looked to the context of struggle as one that allowed a rudimentary form of recognition to supervene. The way this develops in the *Philosophy of Right* is for the analysis of the notion of property to develop from possession through "use" to *contract:* as the political economists had observed, full ownership involves not just the right to *use* a thing but the right to *sell* it.

Contract

The contract presents the structure of recognition which Hegel requires at this stage of his analysis. On the one hand, the act of *paying for* those goods one is acquiring in a contractual exchange is an act of acknowledgment of the other as their rightful proprietor. Similarly, from the point of view of

---

[9] Immanuel Kant, *The Metaphysical Elements of Justice*, trans. John Ladd (Indianapolis: Bobbs-Merrill, 1965), §8. "*Bekenntnis*" has a performative aspect, as its central senses are those of a *confession* of sin or a *profession* of faith.

the other, the other's actions acknowledge *me* as the rightful owner of that for which I am willing to pay. But this "acknowledgment," as Adam Smith had observed, is not based on any moral regard for the other but rather on self-interest. Hegel's explicit account of the contract in terms of recognition occurs at section 71 of the *Philosophy of Right*.

> Property, in view of is existence as an external thing, exists for other external things. . . . But as the existence of the *will*, its existence for another can only be *for the will* of another person. This relation of will to will is the true distinctive ground in which freedom has its *existence*. This mediation whereby I no longer own property merely by means of a thing and my subjective will, but also by means of another will, and hence within the context of a common will, constitutes the sphere of *contract*.
>   . . . Contract presupposes that the contracting parties *recognize* each other as persons and owners of property [*dass die darein Tretenden sich als Personen und Eigentümer* anerkennen]; and since it is a relationship of objective spirit, the moment of recognition [*Anerkennung*] is already contained and presupposed within it. (*PR*, §71 and remark).

The idea of participation in a common will seems to situate Hegel here on an organicist or communitarian terrain. But as the *zusatz* makes clear, Hegel's "common will" is to be analyzed in terms of the idea of spirit as a system of recognition between finite consciousnesses. There is certainly no substantive supraindividual entity involved here with a will of its own. The participants of an exchange want the same thing, are "like-minded": their wills have a common object—the exchange itself. In this sense, the movement of the commodities in exchange is the objectification of a "common will," a common intention, which they both share. At the same time, however, it is clear that this common intention supervenes upon two different and indexically opposed intentions. When viewed from the singular point of view of each participant, the common will "falls apart" into two different "moments." Here "my will as externalized, is at the same time *another* will. Hence this moment, in which this necessity of the concept is real, is *the unity* of different wills, which therefore relinquish their difference and distinctiveness. Yet it is also implicit (at this stage) in this identity of different wills that each of them is and remains a will distinctive for itself and *not identical* with the other" (*PR*, §73). The common will of the contract is to be explained in terms of a relation between two wills that share a common intention but retain their own indexically *opposed* points of view.[10] Thus the terms we use for the movement of goods—

---

10 It is the indexical *opposition* between the particular wills here which is crucial as it brings

appropriation/alienation, buying/selling, and so on—form indexically complementary pairs.[11] What each contractor primarily wills is the *ego-centric* movement of the object desired, and as a *means* to this, the *allocentric* movement of that which is exchanged is only willed in a secondary or derivative way. That is, each one's recognition of the will of the other, by providing that will with its object, is in truth an instrumental act used *for* the purpose of satisfying its *own* desire.

So, considered as a single event, the exchange itself is the common object (or objective) of the participants; the contract itself qua mutual recognition of rights *is* the substance of the interaction. Indeed, we can see the S P U structure of the syllogism emerging here. A singular subject's willing of some singular thing becomes directed at something more "universal," the exchange that is the object of the "common will," and this is achieved via his recognition of the will of some particular other. But each subject's will is not yet *explicitly* directed to that which is common, as the other's will is as yet still only the *means* for getting what he or she wants. Beyond this it does not "count." The singular and universal aspects of consciousness have not been united *for* the consciousness. Conceptually the contract is only *implicitly* recognitive or syllogistic, and Hegel must pursue the question of how unification can come to exist *for* the members of the interaction.

From Right to Wrong

In treating the economic contract as a structure of mutual recognition in which opposing wills can find a common content, Hegel often seems to approximate to such liberal approaches to politics and society which construe the contract as its *basic* structuring principle. The similarity here is superficial, however. In contrast to such approaches Hegel is far from following the essentialist course of treating the contract as a mode of association which is the essence or foundation of all social relations. Neither is he really interested in the contract in terms of its significance as a mechanism in which individual desires can be fulfilled. He is interested in it *as* a structure of spirit, and so his procedure here is to examine it in terms of its adequacy to that complex "syllogistic" structure. What this leads to is the demonstration that the contract stands in need of a richer framework of

---

out the way that individual points of view are not fully absorbed within the shared intention. There are other ways in which intentions can be shared in which this difference is *not* brought out—as when, say, the members of a family are "at one" in the decision to purchase a new car. But, as we will see, this latter type of "will formation" belongs to a different type of *Sittlichkeit*.
[11] Cf. *Encyclopaedia Logic*, §119 addition: "Thus, for example, debts and assets are not two particular, self-subsisting species of property. What is negative to the debtor is positive to the creditor."

intersubjectivity, which in turn cannot be reduced to contractual arrangements.

Although the contractors' wills are determined thus, as we know, it is the essence of a willing subject to be re-determining. In the section on external teleology in the concept-logic, Hegel tries to demonstrate how the very action of realizing an immediately and subjectively held end can lead to the process of reinterpretation of that very end. Here, too, it is the element of difference that exists between the contracting wills that can lead to an outcome from which the initially instrumental desire can be reinterpreted.

Under "normal" contractual conditions the subjective intention and the recognition of the other as a bearer of rights can coincide. There may be conditions, however, in which this is not the case—for example, any individual opportunity for the theft rather than purchase of something desired. So in this way is opened up the possibility of a new realm, the realm of "wrong" and, from there, a further one, that of justice and punishment. It is in these forms of interaction existing, as it were, symbiotically alongside that of the economy, that the necessary viewpoint grasping the general content of the contract can be found.

It is important that Hegel's analysis of "wrong," essentially crime, is a systematic or speculative one, not an empirical one, for example, a psychological, sociological, or historical one. Neither is it a moral approach to crime—the structure of morality has not yet been introduced into the analysis. Rather, Hegel is interested in the sort of recognitive structure instantiated by crime, the dynamics of the categories of wrong.

So far we have seen the contractual relationship described as a structure in which two opposed wills are at the same time united into a common will embodied in the contract itself. From a *reflected* point of view, both participants will the same thing, but in such a way that each is the inversion of the other. However, the possibility of various forms of wrong instantiates another form of interaction concerning property—here an individual subjective will fails to coincide with the "substance" of the interaction—the legitimate contract.

Again, Hegel sketches a series of three different types of wrong where the particular will diverges from the common will. First, in civil cases, where there is a dispute over ownership, there is a *sense* in which each participant wills the same thing. They will that the property belongs to its rightful owner; they simply disagree over which one of them *is* the rightful owner.

In the second case, fraud, the structure is more complicated. In the fraudulent contract, there is again a sense in which both parties will the same exchange. A person agreeing to buy goods which turn out to be defective, nevertheless did agree to buy *those* actual goods exchanged: there was agreement at the level of the goods *qua singular things*. What there was not agreement about was the exchange of respective *values*. (We might say that there is agreement over the things as sensed singularities but not as universally *perceivable* things with an essential *value*.)[12]

The third form of wrong is criminal wrong, for example, robbery or murder. Here the interaction involves a much stronger negation of right. Whereas in fraud there is at least a description of the transaction in which the victim's will is in accordance with the will of the perpetrator, crime "does not involve the mediation of my opinion . . . but runs counter to it." In crime: "not only the particular—i.e. the subsumption of the thing under my will—is negated, but also the universal and infinite element in the predicate 'mine'—i.e. my *capacity for rights*" (PR, §95). That is, crime, is a violation of another's right *per se*, not just a violation of that person's right but of the principle of right itself.

The equilibration of objects in a contractual exchange demonstrates that the structure of the properties owned by each of the contractants includes a universal element—this element is the *value* of the thing (PR, §§63, 77). This means that there is something illusory about the idea that one person can injure or infringe another's will *simply* by the theft of that person's *particular* possessions. (All the thief can take are particular "beings," and a "being" does not have the appropriate categorial structure for an object of right.) Thus, Hegel says that "when an infringement of right as right occurs, it does have a *positive* external *existence*, but this existence *within itself* is null and void" (PR, §97). What shows that the criminal act is itself *nichtig* is that it will lead to its own annihilation in the act of punishment which the system of right itself brings to bear on the criminal.[13] It is only then that it is brought *into* the system of right as a negative moment.

Again we must not misconstrue what is being put forward here. Hegel is interested in these connections from the point of view of the systematic

---

[12] Although the fraudulent contract presents only an illusory appearance of right, it is still an appearance of it nevertheless. That is, in it right is manifest in a way that it can be recognized, albeit, in a negative form. For Hegel it is a "*Schein*" of right, a concept which, like the English "appearance" can be used both in contrast to reality and as a manifestation or "show" of reality. Thus a fraudulent contract still affirms the rightness of that which it is mimicking, just as, say, a lie makes an implicit acknowledgment or affirmation of truth telling. In both these cases, the rightness of contract *in general*, or the rightness of truth telling *in general* must be an element of the general background against which the fraud or the lie is perpetrated, because without this background those acts would be unintelligible. A fraudulent contract still *acknowledges* right although it does so in a fraudulent way.

[13] So, qua spiritual structure, the institution of property rights itself produces the logical need of its negation—wrong (because of the need of subjectivity, the single "I," to be fully represented), and the existence of wrong itself produces the logical need for its negation, punishment (because of the need for universality, the common "we," to be fully represented).

connections of the categories, that is, the relationships of their use within various institutionalized recognitive contexts; he is not interested in the actual causes of any particular case of punishment.[14] Philosophically, punishment must be looked at from the point of view of the role it plays as a recognitive structure with respect to those systems of interactions, such as economic exchange and crime, with which it interacts. As such, it belongs broadly to the "retributivist" approach to punishment;[15] rival philosophical accounts of the meaning of punishment—as deterrent, as intended to reform, etc.—are regarded by Hegel as superficial because they confuse empirical questions of this sort with those of *institutional logic* (PR, §99).

The idea that crime brings about its own punishment reflects something about the self-contradictory nature of crime, that is, the criminal intention. The criminal is motivated by the same sorts of desires that motivate other economic agents—from his own point of view, he is expressing his own subjectively felt "right" to property. But although others may not primarily will the common content of the contract, neither are their wills in contradiction with it. They do not *negate* the general principle of right. Yet that is exactly what the criminal will does; and so while affirming his own rights, he is denying rights in general.

In its crime the criminal has refused to recognize as subjects of right those with which it interacts and so has cut itself off from the only source within which it could adequately recognize *itself*: their recognition of him; he is cut off from the source of the necessary double structure of intentionality. But it is not as if the criminal thereby simply *ceases* to be recognized by others. Rather, by its act he becomes recognized as the opposite of a person with rights, that is, as a criminal whose rights can be negated. And, as punishment *is* the negation of the criminal's rights, the criminal thus brings about his own punishment. Crime negates right; punishment negates crime; and in this second negation the punishment manifests a new point of view—that which represents the system as a working whole.

What punishment affirms and makes manifest to the participants of the economy is that the recognition of rights implicitly involved in the contract must have a deeper meaning than that of being something of merely instumental value, and it does this by bringing forth a social category that introduces into the system a point of view, that of the *Richter*, or judge, representing the system per se. This is because the system of justice needs some sort of agency not only to do the punishing, but more importantly, *to pronounce the judgment and the punishment*, because it is this verbal act, a

---

[14] In fact he seems to suggest that both historically and psychologically revenge is the motivating force behind punishment (PR, §102 and addition).
[15] Cf. Wood, *Hegel's Ethical Thought*, 108–10.

Richterspruch (*PR,* §228) that acknowledges the criminal *as* a criminal. The criminal's first attitude toward apprehension and punishment may have been to see these as thwarting his satisfaction, but he is now able to find in the punishment the "satisfaction of justice" itself and the "enactment of what is his" (*die That des Seinigen*), his recognition as a legal agent.

Thus, the role of the judge in the system of justice with respect to the criminal may, for example, be seen as analogous to that played by the priest with respect to the unhappy consciousness in the *Phenomenology*. There the priest gave embodiment to a point of view which represented a universal—"God's law"—within whose pronouncements the "sinner" could recognize himself as such. So here the judge instantiates a point of view for recognitive acts within which the criminal can recognize himself as a criminal, see his own crime no longer from the singular first person point of view but from that of the needs of the community as a whole. The contract with its identity in difference between the contracting wills brought a "common will" into implicit existence but it was not recognized as such by the contractants. But the institutions of justice bring into play another particular middle, the judge, who can give direct expression to this general will and who can act as a vehicle within which economic agents recognize themselves as subjects of that which is expressed in the judge's pronouncements, the law itself.

Law and the Moral Law

In the case of the unhappy consciousness the opportunity for that consciousness to recognize itself in the recognition of another person who expressed the religious law, the priest, opened up the way for the complication of consciousness's internal structure. On the one hand, it could, like the slave, continue to regard the universal (here God) as beyond itself. On the other, it could redetermine its concept of itself between those two points of view now available to it and see the universal as its *own essence*. That is, the pathway was opened up for the transition to *moral consciousness*.

An analogous set of links is established in the *Philosophy of Right* from the category of the criminal. Following the discussion of crime and punishment, Hegel moves on to an investigation of the same style of Kantian morality explored in the *Phenomenology*. But again the focus is on the categorial structure, the "logic" of those recognitive processes being explored. Within the context of the mechanisms of the law a subject was able to achieve a view of his or her own actions from the point of view of an agency, the judge, who expressed and applied the law. This opens up the possibility of the economic subject moving its concept of itself from the first person point of view of its immediate desire to that more general point of view now available. As *desiring* subject, it recognized itself in the objects it desired; as moral subject it recognizes itself in those of its *actions,* which it judges to be determined by its "essence," the internalized moral law. But as in the *Phenomenology,* problems loom for the moral self because it is still an essentially univocal conception of the self. For the moral subject, one aspect of itself, the given "in-itself" aspect of its desire, is deemed inessential and as counting for nothing. As a form of *spirit,* the economy, or what we had seen of it, had not been capable of producing an adequately structured intentional subject, and although the required internalized general point of view has been acquired by morality, moral subjectivity had been essentially reflected out of those object-mediated interactions in which it expressed in its desire, its particularity.

We might say here that, in tracing the contract through wrong and punishment to morality, Hegel has explored the economy and its consequences from its "subjective" side. It remains to be explored from its "substantial" side, allowing, for example, its connections with other forms of recognitive intersubjectivity to become apparent. Furthermore, in touching on "morality," we have seen how a particular ethical style can have systematic links with a particular context of recognition, the economy and its attendant institutions. In the next chapter besides seeing something more of the economy considered as a particular form of "ethical substance," or "*Sittlichkeit,*" we will see how those aspects of subjectivity formed within such forms of substance have their own distinctive epistemic and ethical styles.

CHAPTER 9

Sittlichkeit and Its Spheres

THE INTRODUCTORY PARAGRAPHS to part 3 of the *Philosophy of Right,* "*Sittlichkeit,*" are often taken as representative of Hegel's metaphysical conception of social life and, in particular, of his commitment to some form of organicist, anti-individualist, or "communitarian" conception of the relation of individual to community or state. On such a reading Hegel takes the organicist social ontology found within the hermeneutic historicist tradition and gives to it a metaphysical necessity by attempting to derive it from logic. And does the text not bear this out? Does he not describe individuals as "accidents" of some ethical substance that is their "absolute authority and power"? Here the lecture comments recorded by the student Hotho seem to leave little room to contest this common view:

> Since the determinations of ethics constitute the concept of freedom, they are the substantiality or universal essence of individuals, who are related to them merely as accidents. Whether the individual exists or not is a matter of indifference to objective ethical life, which alone has permanence and is the power by which the lives of individuals are governed. Ethical life has therefore been represented to nations as eternal justice, or as gods who have being in and for themselves, and in relation to whom the vain pursuits of individuals are merely a play of the waves. (*PR*, §145 addition)

But readings which uncritically accept notions such as "substance," "essence," "accident," and so on, and which assume that Hegel is advocating an ideal of social life in which individuals somehow dissolve their individuality in the sea of the "ethical substance" of their community, proceed as if Hegel's *Logic* stopped at the end of book 2, the "Doctrine of Essence." But we do not have to appeal to the complete text of the *Logic* to question such an interpretation of Hegel's conception of the relation of individual to society. In the same passages we find the familiar formulae of the *Phenomenology*: subjectivity itself is the "infinite form" (*PR*, §144) and "absolute form" (*PR*, §152) of substance, and the "right of individuals to their particularity" (*PR*, §154) is *guaranteed* by the true nature of substance. Furthermore, while for Hegel the *habitual* adoption of customary behavior is a necessary part of ethical life, the *total* habitualization of behavior is seen as having dire consequences for an agent: "Human beings even die as a result of habit—that is, if they have become totally habituated to life and mentally [*geistig*] and physically blunted, and the opposition between subjective consciousness and mental activity has disappeared" (*PR*, §151 addition). All this should raise some doubt as to whether the "metaphysical communitarian" picture fits these few pages even when isolated from that which precedes and follows them.

Hegel's broaching of the idea of "substance" here must send us back to his reflections in the *Logic* on Spinoza's concept of substance—for Hegel the most advanced attempt to conceive of the whole as some type of self-expressing essence. Articulated within the fixed conceptual framework of essence-logic, Spinoza's concept of substance was self-contradictory. A determinate conception (a "clear and distinct idea") of substance required a distinction, that between the attributes of thought and extension, which was itself *grounded* in the perspective of a finite mode. In order to be redeemed, this one-way *dependence* of "accidental" finite mode on "essential" substance must be overcome. Rather than being conceived as a negation of substance qua essential being, the finite subject (mode) must be understood as the negation or reflection of a fundamental "nothing" or "abyss." That is, "substance" itself is in no sense "substantial," but rather is *essentially* self-negating. It exists *only* inasmuch as there are intentional beings to "carry" it, and it is an essential aspect of these beings that they can abstract themselves from it, and negate or transform it. (That Spinoza cannot demonstrate the *necessity* that substance is particularized into "finite modes" is one of Hegel's constantly repeated objections to his philosophy.)

It is clearly this "nonsubstantial" concept of ethical "substance" that is being appealed to as the logical model for *Sittlichkeit*, a model unable to be cashed out within the categories of the essence-logic itself but demanding the framework of concept-logic. It is a substance within which the "right of individuals to their particularity" is assured because its own determinate existence depends *logically* on the existence of those individuals *in* their particularity. Of course neither are these individuals themselves "substantive," and so neither is society simply an abstraction, a name for what really is a collection or aggregation *of* individuals (*PR*, §156 addition). This is why being given over to socially defined duty which opposes natural desire can be a step toward freedom for individuals. But this freedom could never itself be conceived as self-less immersion within the normative substance of community, even though such a "substance" is that within which one necessarily exists as an individual. If the idea of "immersion" is in any way applicable here, it is an immersion in an abyss or circle of nothingness, that is, in that condition of having one's immediate determination (or "nature") always open to further reinterpretation.

Ethical life must not be thought in terms of the "substance" of the essence-logic. It has the syllogistic determination of the concept-logic; in other words, it is a structure of recognition. I have suggested earlier that it is in the "syllogism of necessity" that we find Hegel's logical account of such objective structures realized in social life.[1] In the *Logic* Hegel deals with this syllogism as that in which the universal plays the role of middle. He describes it as having three forms: the first, in which that universal is immediate and objective; the second, in which it is a "negative unity"; and the third, in which it is the "totality of its particularizations" (*EL*, §191). In the analysis of *Sittlichkeit* we find these structures in their more concrete determinations. These are the three spheres of social life in its developed modern form, spheres whose necessary supportive subjects are themselves formed and supported within processes of recognition: they are the recognitive structures of the family, the economically based "civil society," and the state.

Love and Family

According to Hegel, the family "as the *immediate substantiality* of spirit, is specifically characterized by love, which is spirit's feeling of its own unity" (*PR*, §158).[2] As a form of spirit, the family cannot be grasped naturalistically, for example, in terms of the biological reproduction of the species or in the fulfillment of natural psychological needs. But we must also guard against abstractly opposing spirit and life here. Spirit is neces-

---

[1] Henry S. Richardson, "The Logical Structure of *Sittlichkeit*: A Reading of Hegel's *Philosophy of Right*," *Idealistic Studies* 19 (1989): 62–78, also makes the connection of *Sittlichkeit* with the syllogism of necessity.

[2] "Thus, the disposition [appropriate to the family] is to have self-consciousness of one's individuality *within this unity* as essentiality which has being in and for itself, so that one is present in it not as an independent person [*eine Person für sich*] but as a *member*" (*PR*, §158).

sarily embodied in living beings who need to reproduce themselves and who are subject to a variety of naturally originating desires. We might say that as a *geistig*, or spiritual, institution, the family is significant in terms of the roles it plays, not only in the perpetuation and development of the life of the species per se but also crucially in that of certain modes of human life, in which certain human rational and ethical capacities find their objective supports. Thus both its biologically reproductive role and its educative role in the development of new community members are essential.

As a form of spirit, the family needs some structure of recognition to mediate its relationships, and this is provided by *love*, a form of *Anerkennung* that Hegel had discussed in his Jena writings. But the characteristics of love as a form of recognition mean that as such the family is limited or one-sided: it is spirit in its immediate and undeveloped, quasi-natural form. Love as a form of feeling does not have the adequate internal complexity to instantiate the "'I' that is 'We' and the 'We' that is 'I'" in a way that avoids making one side of the relation between "I" and "We" dominant. This is reflected in the fact that in love the particularity of those involved tends to be absorbed into the unity of the community that comes into being: "Love means in general terms the consciousness of my unity with another, so that I am not in selfish isolation" (*PR*, §158 addition).

Somewhat like natural desire, love is a form of cognitive relation to another in which the dimension of difference cannot be adequately expressed: self and other coalesce into a felt unity.[3] But this cannot be all there is to the issue, because then it would cease altogether to be a spiritual relation and actually be a natural one. It must be the case that the love between family members has a double significance; and, indeed, love does have the necessary "two moments."

The first moment of love is the desire itself, a desire which when compared to a desire like hunger seems to work in the reverse direction. Rather than being a desire to incorporate something *into* the self, love is a desire to *lose* the self in something else. Here: "I do not wish to be an independent person. . . . [I]f I were I would feel deficient and incomplete" (*PR*, §158 addition).

But love is not *just* this desire (otherwise it would be *simply* "chemical"). In its second moment "I attain myself in another person, in them I count for that which they count for in me [*ich in ihr gelte, was sie in mir wiederum erreicht*]" (*PR*, §158 addition; translation modified). Here the word "*gelten*" locates us centrally within the orbit of the concept of *Anerkennung*. Like the

---

3 Thus there is a certain "chemistic" character to this relation as is brought out in the title of Goethe's *Elective Affinities*. In the *Science of Logic* Hegel notes that: "In the animate world, the sex relation comes under this schema [of chemism] and it also constitutes the *formal* basis for the spiritual relations of love, friendship, and the like" (*SL*, 727; *W*, 6:429).

English "counts" it can carry ontological connotations of *significant existence*—that it "counts"—and connotations concerning the particular identity of that which counts—what it "counts as." It is in the other's loving recognitions of me that I recognize that I count and that I count as the singular person that I am.

We might see how quasi-natural desire and act of recognition fit together here by looking at one specific kind of love belonging to this realm: the erotic love between spouses. As a mere natural feeling, sexual desire can be simply a state aimed at a "sexual object" which serves instrumentally as the occasion for the gratification of that feeling. But to serve as the "second moment" of love, it has to be directed at and recognize another (desiring) self-consciousness. A desire could only count as an expression of love when it implicitly contained the acknowledgment that the desired other was himself or herself a desiring subject, not just an object. And the expressions of that first desire would have to be understood by the desired other in that way, as acknowledgments of the other as loved.[4] But what could instantiate this structure?

Perhaps we could here move along a path parallel to that running through the earlier sections on possession and property and say that love becomes explicitly recognitive when its expressions attain a *symbolic* medium and thus become something which, as *mere* expressions of desire, they are not. Such an idea is supported by the emphasis placed on the linguistic ceremony of marriage in which the use of language, "the most spiritual determinate existence of spirit," has brought the marriage bond to completion (*PR*, §164; translation modified).

And yet this should not be taken as affirming any Platonic essence behind a transcendable sensuous appearance of erotic love. Within the spiritual framework the physical passion "is reduced to the modality of a moment of nature" (*PR*, §163), but this does not mean that it sinks from sight. Rather, now it too gains a symbolic significance, counting as an expression of love and not mere univocal desire.[5]

---

[4] But this would seem to mean that one could only love another who loved in return, that is another in whose recognitions one could recognize oneself as anything other than merely desiring subject. Does this mean that for Hegel, unrequited *love* was not just "a bore" but self-contradictory?

[5] Because the *meaning* a biologically originating feeling has for a consciousness existing within the recognitive relation of love cannot itself be something given by nature, love cannot be thought of as *grounded* in nature. Hegel hints at a critique of the modern romanticizing of love found in Romantic thinkers such as Friedrich Schlegel and Friedrich Schleiermacher (*PR*, §164, addition), which is *parallel* to what we will see as his critique of the modern political economists' treatment of the economy. The modern romanticizing of love tries to ground a cultural institution such as marriage in natural love in the same way that the political economists try to ground the cultural institution of the market in natural desires for things.

Both as feeling and family bond, love clearly moves within the circle of spirit in the direction of the collapse of the "I" into the "We." In discussing in the *Logic* the first of the syllogisms of necessity, the *categorial syllogism*, Hegel describes the identity established between singular and universal there as "the substantial identity or *content*" which is "still not at the same time *identity of form*" (*SL*, 697; *W*, 6:394). Thus it would seem that as an objectification of spirit, the family cannot be all there is. In the modern state, those entering into the family do so from the different sphere of *civil society*, just as those leaving the family, the children who have outgrown it, enter into it (*PR*, §§162, 177).[6] It is not surprising then that the type of identity with the universal achieved by singulars in this second sphere will be not one of content but rather one of *form* without content, a type of unity Hegel describes as the "negative unity" characteristic of the *hypothetical syllogism*.[7] The recognitive structure of this economically based civil realm will be, as we might expect, in many ways the inverse or mirror image of that of the family, and in many respects, these two worlds face each other as *inverted* worlds.

Civil Society

As we have seen, Hegel had explicitly signaled his treatment of the economic interaction in terms of spirit in the section on "Right."

Property, in view of its existence as an external thing [*Sache*], exists for other external things. . . . But as the existence of the *will*, its existence for another can only be *for the will* of another person. . . . This mediation . . . constitutes the sphere of *contract*. (*PR*, §71)

Contract presupposes that the contracting parties *recognize* [*anerkennen*] each other as persons and owners of property; and since it is a relationship of objective spirit, the moment of recognition [*Anerkennung*] is already contained and presupposed within it. (*PR*, §71 remark)

---

[6] Hegel now seems to undermine his theoretical presuppositions immediately, however, as the sentence continues: "the sons as heads of new families, the daughters as wives." By this move women are denied direct representation within the sphere of civil society. The family is the woman's realm; the civil sphere the man's. But in doing this Hegel is violating his own principles and making a differentiation of objective spirit, depend on a natural basis, the natural distinction between the sexes.

[7] "The hypothetical syllogism in the first instance exhibits *necessary relation* as connection through the *form* or *negative unity*, just as the categorial syllogism exhibits through the positive unity, substantial *content*, objective universality" (*SL*, 700; *W*, 6:397).

But the nature of recognition operative here is quite the reverse of that found in the family. In that interactive mode at the heart of civil society, the contract exchange, the other person is certainly not the *object* of my desire, this place is taken by something that that person *has*. Here there is no felt unity with a singular, unique other.[8]

As an oppositional form of recognition mediated by the movement of desired objects, there is something of the formal structure of the master/ slave relation. There too there was something exchanged—life itself for the provision of its goods. There are, of course, important differences. Crucially, in the master/slave relation, each identified with and recognized the other in terms of *opposing* roles or categories whereas here the recognition is reciprocal and in terms of an identical category: "proprietor." Nevertheless, elements of the structure of master and slave are still visible. The economic contract involves each participant both as recognized by the other as a *will*, that is, as a proprietor, and as treated instrumentally as a *means* for securing the other's own gratification. Each is both master and slave to the other.

And so, again the double significance of the action of each is apparent to reflection (but not immediately to the participants themselves). In recognizing the other as a proprietor, one recognizes him as a completely *general* will, as he demonstrates himself to be by withdrawing from his object, showing himself to be free from its particular determination. Thus by their actions they show themselves to be the owners of something entirely general—an abstract value. And yet, each can release his particular object from the grasp of his own will only because that place is to be taken by *another* particular object—that which will be gained in the exchange.

This all means that each must recognize himself in the other's recognition in this same dual way. First, the abstract quality of the category "proprietor" allows each to recognize himself and the other as mere instances of a common abstract genus; it is thus the historical emergence of civil society which gives rise to the idea of a common human essence and the generic category "man" (*PR*, §§190 remark and 209). And so we might think of each as recognizing himself qua proprietor in the other's recognition in such a way that each person sees a replication of himself in a mirror. Looked at in this way, this form of recognition *itself* seems to instantiate the Fichtean structure of the " 'I' = 'I'."

But equally each must see himself as the *mere* particular desire used by the other in the satisfaction of *his* desire, and so, as something merely

---

[8] Another way of putting this is that here neither sees himself or herself as related to *specific* others in the way, say, that a daughter may see herself as the daughter of her particular mother or even as a master may see himself as the master of his particular slave. Here there is no recognition of being *tied into* a particular social grouping with the other.

objective or nature-like. That is, in terms of recognizing himself in otherness, each will be posed with the problem of the unresolved and unresolvable duality typically seen in Kantianism. We can therefore appreciate what Hegel means with the idea that civil society is the system of *Sittlichkeit*, "lost in its extremes" (*PR*, §184), with universal and particular having fallen apart. Here the individual no longer sees himself as linked to others in some *common* project.

This should not, of course, lead us to think that civil society is *not* a structure of spirit but a structure of something else, nature for example. It is a mode of spirit but can, no more than the realm of the family, be considered a self-sufficient one. Whereas the realm of the family was unable to give adequate expression to the separability of the "I"s in a "We," in civil society the other extreme is encountered: here the "We" appears as a mere plurality of separate "I"s.[9]

The family and civil society are the extremes into which *Sittlichkeit* falls. They will eventually find their mediation in the state, but as might be expected, there are various levels of mediation within this overarching structure. The first mediation of the abstract dichotomy between family and civil society can be observed when one considers the distinct "masses" into which the ensemble of production and exchange differentiates within the economy. What emerge here are the various "estates" (*Stände*) within which individuals work and attain their public identity:

> The individual attains actuality only by entering into *existence* [*Dasein*] in general, and hence into *determinate particularity*; he must accordingly limit himself *exclusively* to one of the *particular* spheres of need. . . . [O]nly through this mediation with the universal does he simultaneously provide for himself and gain recognition for himself and from others [*so wie dadurch in seiner Vorstellung und der Vorstellung Anderer anerkennt zu sein*]. (*PR*, §207; translation modified)

> When we say that a human being must be *someone* [*etwas*], we mean that he must belong to a particular estate; for being somebody means that he has substantial being. A human being with no estate [*ohne Stand*] is merely a private person and is not situated [*steht nicht*] in actual universality. (*PR*, §207 remark; translation modified)

The estates are differentiated "in accordance with the concept" into the agricultural estate (substantial because it "has its resources in the natural

---

[9] As befits a hypothetical syllogism, the "universal" here has no substantial content, but rather has "formal" or "negative" unity.

products of the *soil* which it cultivates"; the estate of trade and industry (*Stand des Gewerbes*), which gives form to the natural products produced by the first estate; and the "universal estate" essentially made up of civil servants who, in working for the state, work for "the universal" (*PR*, §§202–5). The first and second estates show different relations between the opposed principles of family and civil society working *within* civil society. The agricultural estate, bound as it is to nature, has a disposition that "in general is that of an immediate ethical life based on the family relationship and on trust."[10] As for the second estate, it in turn is composed of *corporations*, associations based on common occupation, which, in protecting and educating members essentially assume the role of "*second* family" for their members (*PR*, §252).

The estates, captured here from the point of view of civil society, that is, in terms of the ways they bear on the needs and interests of individuals, also have important *political* functions that we will consider further on. For the moment, however, it is important to reflect further on the significance for Hegel of the commonly observed difference in *disposition* found between the subjects of the two major estates. As we have noted, the member of the agricultural *Stand* typically has a disposition "based on the family relationship." Here "[t]he human being reacts . . . with immediate feeling as he accepts what he receives; he thanks God for it and lives in faith and confidence that this goodness will continue. What he receives is enough for him; he uses it up, for it will be replenished. . . . In this estate, the main part is played by nature, and human industry is subordinate to it" (*PR*, §203 addition). In contrast, the member of the second estate approaches nature not as a given but as something to be cognitively and practically transformed. Here the individual "relies for its livelihood on its *work*, on *reflection* and the understanding, and essentially on its mediation of the needs and work of others" (*PR*, §204).[11] The self-reliance bred by the work characteristic of the second estate means that "this feeling of selfhood is intimately connected with the demand for a condition in which right is upheld. The sense of freedom and order has therefore arisen mainly in towns." While the first estate is "more inclined to subservience," the second is more inclined to freedom. In short, these two realms breed subjects of different cognitive dispositions.

---

[10] In the addition to this paragraph Hegel concedes that in his time the agricultural economy tended to be run like a factory and "takes on a character like that of the second estate." It will, however, "always retain the patriarchal way of life and the substantial disposition associated with it" (*PR*, §203 addition).

[11] "In the second estate . . . it is the understanding itself which is essential, and the products of nature can be regarded only as raw materials" (*PR*, §203 addition).

Spheres of Sittlichkeit as Cognitive Contexts:
(i) The Familial and the Familiar

What distinguishes the life-forms of *Sittlichkeit* from those of mere nature is that the objective structures and processes in the former are themselves "reflected" within the subjective intentional lives, the consciousnesses, of its particular living members. But such consciousness must be stamped by the particular point of view from which the members reflect on the world to which they belong. Hegel rejects the Spinozist understanding of the relation of these perspectives to the whole onto which they open: there can be no "truth" about *Sittlichkeit* which is the goal of a one-sided overcoming of perspectivity. His understanding of this is more Leibnizian. What is grasped perspectivally is not a first negation, a slice cut out of the whole; rather, it is the whole itself reflected from or into that point of view. To understand the whole is to understand how those points of view can harmonize in such a way that the particularity of each view does not simply drop out.

And so *Sittlichkeit* must be conceived not "substantially" (in the Spinozist sense) and as thinkable in abstraction from all perspective (that is, considered *sub speciae aeternitatis*); rather, that it *is* reflected into distinct subjective ways of being considered is necessary for its existence *as Sittlichkeit*. Furthermore, just as how in our immediate consideration of *Sittlichkeit* as objective spheres of social life we found it divided into distinct masses of interactive forms—familial and civil—when we understand how social life is reflected within the intentionality of the members of these masses, we find its reflected form so divided as well.

One consequence of treating family and civil society as structures of spirit becomes the thematization of their roles as contexts for the *education* of individuals—their "elevation" out of immediately singular existence into some more "universal" frame of mind. This is obvious, of course, in the case of the family where induction of a new, initially biological, being into an existing social reality first takes place. But it applies equally to the realm of civil society. Just as in the context of the family the child must learn to acknowledge the existence of others, in civil society as well, the economic subject is required to continue to come to terms with others as intentional subjects in its economic dealings with them. Indeed, within Hegel's state, the corporations of civil society are formally given the role of the education in those skills involved in the form of work they represent.

But the differences in recognitive structure between family and civil society would seem to ensure that there are *qualitative differences* in these educative processes and in their products—the types of knowing and acting subjects shaped. We might say that the different realms of *Sittlichkeit* have their own distinct epistemic and moral styles. Hegel's suggestions here, although brief, are consistent with his systematic approach to cognitive function in both the *Phenomenology* and the *Logic*.

Within the context of the family, education is seen as a raising up from the singularity or parochialism of an individual's immediately given— here natural—state into an immediately given and concrete realm of spirit. Just as in the context of the family in general, substantial unity prevails over subjective differences: here, Hegel suggests, the educative process is focused on the transmission via discipline of an immediate and substantial content. Parents constitute (*ausmachen*) the universal and essential elements of things for their children (*PR*, §174 addition) for whom the ethical is to be given "in the form of feeling" and "without opposition" (*PR*, §175). By being born into a family, the child becomes the inheritor of certain common ways of making sense of and living in the world—some set of criteria, transmitted by the parents, for the comprehension and evaluation of things and for governing the child's behavior toward those things. Given Hegel's emphasis on the fundamental role of language in the categorial articulation of the discernible things of the world, it is surely warranted to see the learning of language as an essential part of this process of transmission. And while few would deny the simple *empirical* fact that it is normal for children to learn language in some kind of intersubjective context, typically the family, Hegel is not interested simply in reporting or analyzing empirical "psychological" facts. When we attempt to think of them from within the structure of the Hegelian theory of spirit, these rather mundane facts take on a new significance.

I have argued that it is a basic insight of the *Phenomenology* that an individual subject necessarily exists within a structure of intersubjective recognitions and that these recognitions presuppose some sort of conceptual *langue*. Interpreted along these lines and as more than a merely psychological point, Hegel's idea that the intentional subject must *first* come to exist within the concretely substantive context of the family would seem to have much in common with the early hermeneutic idea put forward by Hamann in the eighteenth century and repeated by Heidegger and Gadamer in the twentieth: this is the idea that a knowing subject always exists within or against a background of presuppositions and interpretations historically transmitted by the conventions of the "mother tongue." Heidegger's well-known descriptions of human *Dasein* might serve as an adequate initial expansion of Hegel's suggested idea of a familially constituted self-consciousness. Such a self-consciousness would be one which "has grown up both into and in a traditional way of interpreting itself" and which "understands itself proximally and, within a certain range, constantly" in terms of that interpretation.[12] The experience and thought of such a subject would move within a "hermeneutic circle," the "as-structure" of which was articulated by those traditionally transmitted interpretations determining the identity, meaning, and value of things.[13] Like Hegel, Heidegger thinks of the subject's normal existence as within a world of things that are already bathed in the intentional constructions of others. But against this now not uncommon view of the necessary conditions of subjectivity, we might tease out more of the details of Hegel's view on the basis of his brief comments in the *Philosophy of Right*.

The idea that the very first of the recognitive systems that a subject comes to exist within will itself have a definite categorial structure is linked to a point that has been insisted on throughout this work: in contrast to Fichte's use of the notion, Hegel gives to recognition a definite *epistemological* moment. To the extent that a child is born into a spiritual realm of recognitive interaction with the parents, it will be born into a structure of categories which will determine what that which is recognized will be recognized *as*. We might then broach the question of a *distinctive* epistemology of family life by looking at Hegel's characterization of the type of recognition operative there. Clues on how to proceed can be found in Hegel's insistence on the role of *feeling* as the medium of recognition here and the determinacy of the way in which the other is construed qua intentional object "within" these feelings.

In discussing "feeling" as that which mediates the relations within the family, Hegel clearly does not mean this to be taken as a mere psychological state. Rather, feeling is dealt with as a type of "intentionality": it is a subject's orientation *toward* some other in which that subject relates itself toward the other in a particular way.[14] Such an intentional analysis of feeling brings out the element of conceptuality involved in the determination *of* that intentional content—one loves one's father *as* a father, one's sister *as* a sister, and so on. And such categories are clearly not simply descriptive. They are "action-guiding": there are definite ways to treat fathers, sisters, and so on, and to understand what it is for some other to be a father or sister involves an understanding of how one behaves toward them *as such*.[15]

---

[12] Martin Heidegger, *Being and Time*, trans. John Macquarrie and Edward Robinson (Oxford: Blackwell, 1967), 41.
[13] See especially Heidegger's discussion of "the they" (*das Man*) and the phenomenon of "falling" in *Being and Time*, 164–68, 219–24.
[14] Emotions are then not, as they are for Locke for example, mere "modes of pleasure or pain." Cf. *An Essay concerning Human Understanding* (New York: Dover, 1959), book 2, chap. 20, "Of Modes of Pleasure and Pain."
[15] In chapter 8 of *Ethics and the Limits of Philosophy* (London: Fontana, 1985) Bernard Williams discusses the evaluatively laden "thick" predicates of ethical discourse in this way. But the

Linked to this action-guiding aspect of these categories is their *perspectivity* or *indexicality*. My father exists for me as *my* father—he is not simply *a* father who also *happens* to be mine. This notion of indexicality captures what Hegel says about the way in which these categories capture their objects: "Love means in general the consciousness of *my unity with another*" (*PR*, §158 addition; emphasis added). And the explicit indexicality here is linked to another obvious aspect of this form of intentionality—its strong (Nagelian) *subjectivity*. To place the accent on *feeling* here is to say that there is a definite "what it is like" to intend an object in this way.

As an act within which a conceptual determination takes place, we might think of a recognitive act as containing or involving an implicit form of categorization or *judgment:* to acknowledge is always to acknowledge "as."[16] The use of the term "judgment" here may seem odd until it is remembered that for Hegel a "judgment" (*Urteil*) is not primarily a subjective act of comprehension but, as he puzzlingly puts it, the positing of the determinations of the concept "in" or "by" the concept itself: "Judging is thus *another* function than comprehension, or rather it is *the other* function of the concept as the *determining* of the concept by itself" (*SL*, 623; *W*, 6:301–2). But this accords with our everyday experience. It is not so much that when in addressing my father as "father" *I* am making a judgment, rather, it is more that I am giving voice to a conventional way of talking which is part of a necessary background practice that allows there to *be* persons called "fathers." In this sense such a judgment is not simply *my* act; if it is an "act" at all, one might ascribe it to the impersonal background practices themselves. Herder seems to have had this type of thing in mind when he described speakers as being, besides the *creators* of language, its *creatures*. From a certain point of view we can think of the *language itself* as providing that categorial structure of the world which is presupposed by each of its speakers. In our century, Heidegger has also spoken of the "speaking" of language behind the speaking of individual speakers; and we might hear an anticipation of this in Hegel's idea of the "concept" determining itself in its judgments or divisions: whenever I utter a word such as "father" in my recognitive interactions, "language" itself ("the concept") "speaks" ("judges") through me and fashions the world such that fathers have a place in it.

---

same term can be applied to what other authors have called "basic concepts" (see below, n. 17).

[16] Cf. Heidegger's idea that in the context of a practice such as carpentry, the interpretation "The hammer is too heavy" need not only be expressed verbally. The very activity of exchanging the hammer for a lighter one is *itself* such a conceptually articulated interpretation of the hammer as "heavy" (*Being and Time*, 196–97).

What might we now say about the type of "judgment" involved when, for example, I address my father with "father"? Although clearly there is an element of conceptuality involved (my father is determined *as* a father), it is not dominant; the concept does not "subsume" the intuited particular thing—*my* father *for me* is not simply an instance of the class of fathers. Hegel can capture the categorial structure of such a type of object with the idea that here universal (the universal category "father") and singular (*this* actual person) are in an *immediate* unity: a universal has the form of "being" by being directly instantiated in a "this," a "*Dasein*," of the being-logic. Rather than being for me merely a member of the set (a "species of the genus") "fathers," my father, in at least in some initial, immediate sense, might be more accurately described as an *exemplar* or even "*prototype*" of fatherhood. It is via him that I first learn what a father is, or what being a father "amounts to" or "counts as."

I have interpreted Hegel's idea that parents *constitute* the universal and essential elements of things for their children (*PR*, § 174 addition) in terms of the idea that the child learns to see the world within the categorizations exemplified in the parents' namings and interpretations of the world. It would then seem that the *immediacy* of the descriptive aspect of the constitutive acknowledgments in this sphere would spill over into the way the world was learned about. The world of the child would quickly become furnished with "prototypes," instances of kinds of things which exemplified what it was to be that kind of thing.[17] For the child, such exemplifications presented by the parents in their namings, descriptions, and interpretations would carry the criteria not only for individuating and accounting for what exists but also for evaluating it. This is because exemplification and subsequent identification here must always operate via sensible qualities and because the language of everyday life available for this description is redolent with qualitatively "thick" categories in which evaluative and descriptive elements are fused.[18]

The English vocabulary provides us with a ready-made concept with which the epistemological peculiarity of the intentional realm opened up for the subject within the context of the family might be captured: the *familiar*, the realm of things with which, according to the *Oxford English*

---

[17] Such a notion of a "prototype" is developed in the work of Elinor Rosch. For an overview of empirical work in categorization including the theory of "prototypes" and "basic categories" see George Lakoff, *Women, Fire, and Dangerous Things: What Categories Reveal about the Mind* (Chicago: University of Chicago Press, 1987).

[18] See Williams, *Ethics and the Limits of Philosophy*, chap. 8. Furthermore, it is only inasmuch as elements of the world—objects, actions—are construed as good or bad that the child can learn which of its desires are good or bad and so learn what behavior is appropriate, that is, learn what sort of life it has to lead as bearer of its social role.

Dictionary, a subject is "well or habitually acquainted."[19] And, as I suggested earlier, when we ask as to the *form* of epistemic consciousness which will result from this induction of the emerging subject into the social and linguistic realm of the family, it would seem that the obvious answer here is *perception.*[20]

Indeed, empirical work on the structure of categorization seems to bear out the suggestion that there is something categorically peculiar about the names children learn first. Psychologists claim that the first lexical items to be learned and subsequently most frequently used are those that represent what have come to be called "basic categories."[21] Things categorized by basic categories—for example, cats and dogs but not animals as such; tables and chairs but not pieces of furniture—are things that have a recognizable overall shape and can be easily pictured. Being "human-sized" and, as it were, cut to the fabric of our unmediated senses and practices, they are highly perspectival.[22]

We might use Heidegger's analyses of the phenomenological peculiarities of such an immediate realm of everyday life to bring out something further about it which, if not fully explicit, is quite close to the surface in Hegel's account. In *Being and Time* Heidegger points to a peculiarity of the ontology of this realm: it is structured by what he calls the "hermeneutic as-structure," a structure not reducible to an "apophantic" as-

---

[19] Among the meanings of this adjective the *OED* lists "well or habitually acquainted." Here the use of "acquainted" rather than the more general "known" puts the stress on the immediacy and closeness of an epistemological relation based in immediate experience. It was this immediacy that Russell wished to capture in his contrast of "knowledge by acquaintance" with that more secondhand form of "knowledge by description." It is the same immediacy that is registered in the French "*connaitre*" and the German "*kennen*" contrasting respectively with their epistemic others, "*savoir*" and "*wissen.*"

[20] Perception, it will be remembered, is for Hegel that form of everyday apprehension of the world of discrete things with qualities. In the categories of *Logic*, objects of perception coincide with the "existents" belonging to the everyday realm of existence (*Existenz*), the most immediate form of unity of essence and being. It is this participation of the universal or essence which makes perception, as we have seen in the *Phenomenology*, much more than the raw reception of any immediate sense-content. In perception the perceiver has had to *collapse* his or her own experience into that which is "universally" affirmed such that immediate experience and common affirmation are bonded in an immediate unity. Here, where it diverges, the idiosyncratic and singular is dealt with as *error.* For the child, of course, the correcting "universal" is embodied in the interpretations of the parents.

[21] See, for example, Lakoff, *Women, Fire, and Dangerous Things.*

[22] Lakoff says of the basic categories: "They depend not on objects themselves, independent of people, but on the way people interact with objects: the way they perceive them, image them, organize information about them, and behave toward them with their bodies. The relevant properties clustering together to define such categories are not inherent to the objects, but are interactional properties, having to do with the way people interact with objects." Lakoff, *Women, Fire, and Dangerous Things,* 51.

structure.[23] Heidegger essentially means that phenomenologically it is not the case that a thing of the everyday world *counts as* being what it is on the basis of some explicit criterion or defining property. There is a certain "groundlessness" here if identity is thought of as needing grounding in a particular attribute or set of attributes. Roughly speaking, a thing has a "hermeneutic" rather than an "apophantic" as-structure if its identity accrues from the role it plays within an intentional practice. The "hermeneutic as" is the categorial structure that an object has in virtue of its being grasped from the viewpoint of a practically rather than a theoretically intentional subject.

Indeed, Heidegger's idea of the categorial structure of the "hermeneutic as" and the idea of the "basic category" both fit neatly with what we would expect of this form of categorization applicable to the immediate "existing" (*existerende*) things of Hegel's *Logic*.[24] With their peculiar categorial structure, such things would not enter into the types of processes of abstraction and generalization which constitute what we typically think of as "reasoning." Where there is an immediate identity of universal and singular, the universal could not be appealed to in any critical reflection on the thing. For example, I cannot reflect on, evaluate, or judge the behavior of my father *as* a father if he is, for me, the living exemplar of what it is to be a father.[25]

It is the predominance of unification over individuation which imparts to the family its overall conservative character as domain of epistemic and ethical education. We might think here of how the relations between intimates, close friends, or family members require a background of relatively unquestioned shared beliefs and evaluations. To subject these to critical scrutiny can result in a type of distancing which is here out of place; much "goes without saying." And it is fairly clear how conservative societies with a concrete "we" analogous to that of the family might reproduce this epistemological structure.[26] From this point of view one might appreciate the link between such an epistemology and the structure of a social world in which familial structures were dominant. This was, of course, the type

---

[23] Heidegger, *Being and Time*, 200–201.
[24] See *Hegel's Science of Logic*, bk. 2, sec. 2, chap. 1.
[25] Nevertheless even "being-logic" has its own implicit processes of reasoning which typically take the form of analogical comparison and contrast. What this logic might allow, then, is the analogical comparison of the way my father behaves to me with the way that some other father behaves toward his son. On the role of analogy in being-logic, see my "Hegel's Logic of Being and the Polarities of Presocratic Thought," *The Monist* 74 (1991): 438–56.
[26] Hegel likens peoples under patriarchal governments to children in that they are "fed out of central depots and . . . not regarded as self-sufficient adults" (*PR*, §174 addition). Perhaps we could read this idea of "feeding" as applying at the epistemic level as well.

of society and culture appealed to by Burke and Hamann in their criticisms of the radically questioning "enlightened" culture coming into existence in the eighteenth century, and echoes of this appeal to substantive community are heard in our century in the hermeneutic thought of Heidegger.

From the distinctively *modern* point of view, however, knowledge is *not* typically seen as a repository of wisdom transmitted down through generations as it tends to be seen in premodern societies. In modernity, traditional wisdom becomes irrational "prejudice," and the "grounds" for knowledge are decentered from the shared conventions of a substantive "we" to the sort of abstract "I" which we have seen as characteristic of the marketplace. Descartes's attempt to doubt all socially condoned belief and to look for the foundations of knowledge in the knowing "I" itself is characteristically taken by hermeneutic thinkers as emblematic of a fundamental restructuring of knowledge in modernity. And as we have seen, a type of radical and reflective challenge to socially condoned "appearances" is itself a central feature of modern science.

But even Descartes could not construe the isolated *finite* "I" as the locus of certain knowledge: the ego had to exist within a relation to an infinite all-knowing subject. In turn, Kant's Copernican interpretation of knowledge opened up a communicative reading of the individual finite I's relation to others in a communicative community. But this communicative community must be structured in radically different ways from that of the family. Here the individual subject does not just *submit* to the interpretations of others but demands to be *rationally* convinced. It is obvious that if we were to look to a particular form of *Sittlichkeit* as providing the infrastructure for this Copernican type of thought which goes beyond perception by assuming a radically negative orientation toward the given, a type of thought bound up with the structures of *Verstand* (the "understanding" of chapter 3 of the *Phenomenology*), our attention should be directed not to the family but to civil society.

Spheres of Sittlichkeit as Cognitive Contexts:
(ii) The Epistemology and Logic of the Bürger

Civil society is a realm of *external teleology*, that is, it is characterized by the pursuit by individuals of their own particular ends in which all things and others take on the significance of *means* (or barriers) to the attainment of those ends. And because the use of others presupposes some kind of knowledge of them, this realm also forms a context of the *Bildung*, education or formation of individuals out of their "immediacy and singularity" or "natural simplicity" (*PR*, §187 remark). But it cannot be any truly "natural" being that is the candidate for this realm of *Bildung;* given the *logical* necessity that all subjects are born into the substantive *Sittlichkeit* of familial relations, it must be from the "immediacy and singularity" of the familial context that the subject is elevated on passing into civil society. Essentially this form of *Bildung* means that the subject's theoretical and practical intentionality is developed in the direction of an "objective" movement away from the local and perspectival culture and thought of the family. Because agents here have to take into consideration a range of others who do *not* share their perspectives, satisfaction of their own ends will be achieved "only in so far as they themselves determine their knowledge, volition, and action in a universal way and make themselves *links* in the chain of this *continuum* [*Zusammenhang*]" (*PR*, §187). Hegel is specific as to the form of rationality that these individuals are educated (*gebildete*) into: it is *der Verstand*—the "understanding."

And so along with many subsequent thinkers, Hegel thinks of the abstract understanding as tied to a type of "means-ends" reasoning or "instrumental reason." But Hegel's account of the links of the understanding to the context of civil society is more specific than this. We can see how the shift into the structures of *Verstand* is bound up with the categorial form of the type of recognition characteristic of this realm. Whereas the form of recognition in the family had the structure of determination of the perceptually immediate judgment, the judgment of immediate existence (*Dasein*) (*SL*, 630 ff.; *W*, 6:311 ff.), it is the *judgment of reflection* (*SL*, 643 ff.; *W*, 6.326 ff.) which characterizes the form determination implicit in the recognitive acts typical of the civil sphere and which ties it in with its peculiarly abstract form of reasoning.

Perception grasps the singular thing as an immediate instantiation of some universal category. In the case of reflective judgment, however, the object is determined in terms of some "underlying" and initially nonapparent universal. Such properties are *dispositional* ones, such as is found, for example, in the judgment "this plant is curative" (*EL*, §174), and require the mediation of a third object for their manifestation. Thus the property "curative," predicated of a plant, is (typically) not one I perceive directly; what *is* perceived is the effect of the plant on some third mediating thing, for example, the animal that ingests it. Similarly, to use an example given by Hegel in the *Philosophy of Right,* the arable character of land is expressed only in the context of our planting of crops.[27] This same appeal to some mediating third object likewise characterizes the structure of the sorts of

---

[27] "The relation of use to property is the same as that of substance to accident, inner to outer, or force to its manifestation. A force exists only in so far as it manifests itself; the field is a field only in so far as it produces a crop" (*PR*, §61 addition).

recognitive interactions at the heart of the realm of civil society, the exchange relation.

Within the exchange relation one does *not*, as in the context of the family, recognize the other person in his or her *singularity*. I am not affirming a relation to *this* specific person but doing business with "whoever" will serve my specific interests. Here I *do* recognize the person as a mere instance of a general category: I recognize him or her *as* a proprietor.[28] Furthermore, what singles out *that* person has nothing to do with the question of who the person is; it has to do only with *what that person has*. In each *particular* exchange relation, the other is recognized as proprietor of some *particular thing*—that which is exchanged in the contract. It is precisely *by* exchanging something for that thing, and not simply taking it, for example, that I acknowledge the other's rights of ownership over it. And when we ask the question of how that thing of which the proprietor is the proprietor is conceptually determined, the answer must be precisely *as the equivalent* of that which I exchange for it in return.

Thus the act of recognition contains a mediating third term, analogous to the mediating third term involved in the reflective judgment. Just as in the case of the "curative" plant the interposition of the third body was able to bring out and make apparent the underlying property (or capacity or "force") of being curative, so here the interposition of the object I alienate in my recognition of the other brings out some basic determination of what it is that he or she has: its underlying "value." It is thus that in the exchange relation what I affirm the other as the proprietor *of* is not so much any *particular* object but the *value* of that thing. And of course the same applies exactly from the opposite point of view. What the other is willing to exchange for what I have brings out the value of it, making the notion of value inherently relational. The exchange of A for B determines the value of A as B and the value of B as A. But of course there is a further complication of the determination effected in this relationship. The fact that my contracting partner is not fixed but is just "any" proprietor who happens to suit my interests means that he or she is comparable to all other members of the "genus" of proprietors with their offerings. Thus, it is not simply whatever the other *has* that determines whom I deal with, it is this "whatever" standing in relation to what all other proprietors have. The value of A is not simply B but B *or whatever else* I may exchange A for. What happens on the market, of course, is that something appears whose sole purpose it is to signify this abstract value that results from the equilibra-

---

[28] Of course in the first instance this recognition of the other's rights is, in keeping with the nature of the economic sphere, entirely instrumental. We have seen in the sections on crime and morality, however, how the "cunning of reason" can result in a reinterpretation of what motivates the act of recognizing such a right.

tion of all goods across these exchange relations: money. What this all means is that the particular thing, initially desired because of its particular properties, comes to have a "reflected" structure: behind or underneath those particular properties is an "essence," an exchange value that is no longer conceived as on the same level as its sensuous properties.[29]

This same abstraction characterizes the agent of this realm qua desiring and knowing subject. We might say that whereas perception was directly rooted in given and substantial desires and values, which were shaped in the first instance by the familial context, *understanding* is rooted in a subject, the specificity of whose perspective has been whittled away by being mediated by others and who has thus come to grasp things in terms of some underlying and abstract significance or value. In such a world, this divestment of substantive "content" is of instrumental value. Caught up in the economic fabric of market exchanges, a subject has to be able to provide for the desires of others, different from his or her own. Each must learn to recognize the desires of others, learn to see how something might be "desirable" from a point of view that is not necessarily one's own. This means that one's conception of desire must start to be detached from the particularity of one's own specific desires, just as in the understanding one's concept of a thing has to be detached from the particularity of its appearance. The successful economic agent must, as it were, learn to see desire from a type of "third person" or quasi-naturalistic point of view. As value becomes more abstract, it by necessity becomes relative.[30]

And so the economically rational producer here will be in a situation something like that of the slave. Each producer will have to replace his or her particular will with another will, here the will of a generalized other, a will with no fixed characteristics but which is always subject to unpredictable fluctuation and change. We might say that here *the market* is master.

We can see then how this change in the categorial structure implicit in the recognitive act must result in a change in the world as experienced, desired, and known. From the point of view of this subject the world will cease to be grasped in terms of those perspectivally rooted discrete qualitative things of perception, the sorts of qualities that will be relevant for the

[29] And this in turn is tied up with the abstractness of the determination of the proprietor himself. From this point of view, proprietors no longer are the owners of particular "things" within which we might read their actual substantive desires. They are abstract proprietors of abstract values with abstract desires for "value"—"persons"—rather than concrete humans with particular lives needing particular things and driven by particular desires. They have ceased to be "Italians, Jews, Germans," etc.

[30] But it might be argued that the truth is that this can never escape from being *ultimately* linked to the fact that one *has* desires. Understanding others as desiring beings must ultimately always have a hermeneutic component in which one recognizes *something* of oneself in them.

satisfaction of *immediate* desires. The world will still be grasped "instrumentally" and so in terms of categories construing it as relevant for the
satisfaction of desire, but this desire is now understood as a universal,
impersonal, and fluid desire manifested by the market. Furthermore, it is
not only an object's value to a human desire that is now relevant. Goods
will come to be valued in terms of their instrumental value within the
production process itself—the "desires" of the system need to be taken
into account.[31]

Expressed in the categorial structures of Hegel's logic of essence, this
change represents a passage from the determinations of existence (*Existenz*) to that of appearance (*Erscheinung*).[32] As singular and universal
come apart, all elements of the economic system—commodities, proprietors, desires—lose the substantiality of the "existing thing" of perception
and come to be grasped as elements of the realm of "appearance," as
elements whose significance lies in their capacity to express an underlying
reality, a "play of forces" of impersonal desire manifest in the mechanisms
of the market. And the syllogistic structure within which such abstraction
takes place is the hypothetical syllogism in which "the being of A is to be
taken *not as a mere immediacy*, but essentially as the *middle term of the
syllogism*" (*SL*, 699; *W*, 6:395). But we must remember that the intentional
agents for whom such transformations occur *are themselves* the participants
of this "syllogism" of civil society, and so this process of abstraction will
also characterize the way that the world is reasoned about by them.

In contrast to the analogical thought characteristic of the familiar realm,
structured as it is with its exemplifications and prototypes, now, after the
"reflective" separation of universal and singular has supervened upon the
immediate object of perception, giving it an "internally reflected" structure, the "object" can enter into formally logical inference patterns. Now
the object is an *instance* of a universal rather than a prototype of it; "subsumed" under the universal, it is now on the same level as other things of
the same type with which it shares its determinate properties. It is no
longer centered on a concrete subject for whom the world is familiar; it is
rather centered on a subject who has to grasp himself or herself abstractly

---

[31] Understanding salt as a white, crystalline substance with various manifest qualities will
allow one to utilize it for particular purposes linked immediately to those qualities: one uses it
for its taste, for example. When we start to mediate our perceptual relation to it with other
substances, we make manifest other "underlying" qualities, we might discover its preserva-
tive properties, for example. Finally, understanding it as a molecule of *sodium chloride* (a
nonperceivable "inner") is cognate with an understanding of its place within an unlimited
number of diverse contexts—chemical relations and reactions, electrical processes, metabolic
pathways, and so on. We have now essentially removed all limitations on those purposes to
which it could be put.

[32] See *Hegel's Science of Logic*, bk. 2, sec. 2, chap. 2.

as one of many for whom the world might appear differently than it does for others. "Appearance" then will get a negative connotation—it is not the truth of things but only a surface covering up a nonperceivable essence.

We might express this separation of universal and singular within the known object by saying that it has become fully "propositionalized." While we are "familiar" with "things," what we "understand" in the sense of *Verstand* are not things themselves so much as *facts* about them, and it is these facts that stand within the inferential relations of formal logic, not things.[33]

With this, another dimension of Hegel's critical orientation toward the formal "logic" of the philosophical tradition emerges. Despite the fact that formal logic is thought of as applicable to all and any content, it is far from being ontologically neutral. As a part of a particular epistemological orientation to the world, it presupposes that the world has the "reflective" structure of essence. But being and essence logics mutually presuppose each other, as do the ontologies of things and facts, the epistemologies of perception and understanding, and the "inferences" of the categorial and hypothetical syllogisms. Thinking of knowledge *only* in terms of the understanding and thinking of logic *only* in terms of formal logic is akin to thinking of human subjects *only* as traders on a market. But of course, this is *exactly* how human subjects come to be thought of within certain strains of modern culture.

[33] This is conveyed in the *Logic* by what Hegel says about the form of the judgment—the singular is the universal. There must be two ways of understanding the copula. First, according to the determinations of being-logic, singular and universal will be understood as immediately identical. But understood *reflectively* in terms of essence-categories the proposition will be read as the singular *has* the universal (*EL*, §166).

CHAPTER 10

The Celebration and Criticism of Civil Society: Hegel, Adam Smith, and Jean-Jacques Rousseau

A GLIMPSE OF Hegel's complex vision of the interrelations of *Verstand* and the economic heart of civil society is provided by his comments on the modern science of political economy. In the remark to section 189 of *Philosophy of Right* Hegel comments on this science which has originated in the modern age. It would seem that for Hegel the political economist is indeed a Copernican thinker: in the addition to this paragraph the economic system is likened to the system of the planets! It is the task of thought to lay out its "mass relationships and mass movements in their qualitative and quantitative determinacy and complexity" (*PR*, §189 remark). But this order is not directly perceivable: as in the case of the planetary system it "presents only irregular movements to the eye," since economic activity, governed so much by the contingencies of circumstance, is "apparently scattered and thoughtless." "To discover the necessity at work here is the object of political economy, a science which does credit to thought because it finds the laws underlying a mass of contingent occurrences" (*PR*, §189 addition).

In astronomy it is the locatedness of the viewer within this system that makes its true dynamics not immediately apparent to the eye. Similarly, in the case of political economy our understanding *commences* from the viewpoints (*Gesichtspunkten*) implicit within the economic system itself. From this locatedness it then *goes on* to its explanations. And yet there must be a different order of intimacy between the science of political economy and its object domain from that which holds in the case of modern astronomy. This is because what political economy, itself a form abstract understanding, recognizes (*herausfinden*) as active within the economic system and responsible for its order, *are the operations of the understanding itself*. That is, it is not only the economist who, in order to get a sense of the regularities of its mass movements, must abstract away from his or her own contingent location within the system; the actual agent within the system must do something like this as well. And, indeed, as we have already seen, this is exactly what the economic agent must do in order to function within the system. Not only the scientist but the economic agent as well is a "Copernican."

We have seen in the *Phenomenology* how the abstraction from perception into the understanding gives rise to a counter movement. In the search for comprehensiveness, the understanding gives rise to an abstractly unified world, but this world brings into focus an "inverted world," which contains all those features of experience which the world of the understanding leaves out. The production of an inverted world here too seems to be a consequence of the fashioning of perception into understanding. Hegel claims that the recognition of the operations of the understanding within the economic sphere brings about a conciliatory effect, and yet, conversely, "this is also the field in which the understanding, with its subjective ends and moral opinions, gives vent to its discontent and moral irritation" (*PR*, §189 remark).

There are various interpretations we might tease out from this. One could be the idea that both the celebration of the modern economic system and its moral denunciation are two inverted views that result from the initial standpoint of that very sort of subjectivity which the modern economy has helped to shape. On the one hand, by viewing the system as rational, an Adam Smith, for example, will find "reconciliation" within the system despite the existence of suffering that can be attributed to it.[1] On the other, from a similar starting point (that human goodness is ultimately founded on a type of fundamental self-interest, or *amour de soi*) a Jean-Jacques Rousseau can be led to a moralistic denunciation of the system, a denunciation that is bound up with the inability of the system to satisfy those very interests. And such antithetical views would presumably flow over into the assessment that each position would have of the rationality of *Verstand* itself. In Hegelian terms, while Smith (who appropriately regards humans as basically marketeers) would regard *Verstand* as the essence of human reason, Rousseau would regard it as an immediate negation of a more fundamental form of cognitive life.

---

[1] And the religious connotations of "reconciliation" might well be held onto here; the providential imagery of the "hidden hand" is hard to ignore in Smith.

We might suspect that the inverted view onto itself to which *Verstand* seems to lead will be crucial for understanding Hegel's own conception of the relation between *Verstand* and reason itself, *Vernunft*, and, connected with this, the relation of economy to the overarching spiritual context, the state. Indeed, we might see Hegel's view of modernity and its characteristic epistemology and logic as involving something like grasping the "identity of identity and difference" at work in the views of Smith and Rousseau.

Hegel, Smith, and the Rationality of Civil Society

For Hegel, an economic exchange is an interaction within which two wills find concord without losing their particularity: "[M]y will, as externalized, is at the same time *another* will. . . . Yet it is also implicit (at this stage) in this identity of different wills that each of them is and remains a will distinctive for itself and *not identical* with the other" (*PR*, §73). For Adam Smith, the idea that a free economic exchange allows both subjects to get what they separately want was the key to the rationality of the modern economy. Individuals in their exchanges could indirectly promote the interests of one another by pursuing their own self-interest simply because in an exchange one satisfied one's own interest precisely *by means of* satisfying the interest of the other. In Smith's well-known words: "It is not from the benevolence of the butcher, the brewer, or the baker that we expect our dinner, but from their regard to their own interest. We address ourselves, not to their humanity but to their self-love, and never talk to them of our own necessities but of their advantages."[2] Generalized, such exchange would lead to the situation in which the interests of all would be satisfied to the maximum degree.

> It is the great multiplication of the productions of all the different arts, in consequence of the division of labour, which occasions, in a well-governed society, that universal opulence which extends itself to the lowest ranks of the people. Every workman has a great quantity of his own work to dispose of beyond what he himself has occasion for; and every other workman being exactly in the same situation, he is enabled to exchange a great quantity of his own goods for a great quantity, or, what comes to the same thing, for the price of a great quantity of theirs. He supplies them abundantly with what they have occasion for, and they

[2] Adam Smith, *The Wealth of Nations* (Harmondsworth: Penguin Books, 1970), 119.

accommodate him as amply with what he has occasion for, and a general plenty diffuses itself through all the different ranks of the society.[3]

At a certain level of the analysis Hegel agrees: "The end of subjective need is the satisfaction of subjective *particularity,* but in the relation between this and the needs and free arbitrary will of others, *universality* asserts itself" (*PR,* §189).

That this reconciliation is brought about demonstrates that understanding is more than a subjective principle with which individual members of civil society operate. It is embodied *within* the system itself. For Smith it is *as if* the system had been designed by a rational will so that a good general outcome, something which was for the good of all, resulted from the situation despite the fact that none of the individuals had actually willed it. It is as if each within this system were "led by an invisible hand to promote an end which was no part of his intention." It is this capacity for a general good to flow from the individual pursuit of self-satisfaction that Hegel comments on when he says, more or less following Smith, that

In this dependence and reciprocity of work and the satisfaction of needs, *subjective selfishness* turns into a *contribution towards the satisfaction of the needs of everyone else.* By a dialectical movement, the particular is mediated by the universal so that each individual, in earning, producing, and enjoying on his own account, thereby earns and produces for the enjoyment of others. This necessity which is inherent in the interlinked dependence of each on all now appears to each individual in the form of *universal and permanent resources* in which, through his education and skill, he has an opportunity to share; he is thereby assured of his livelihood, just as the universal resources are maintained and augmented by the income which he earns through his work. (*PR,* §199)

Here each member of civil society has his actions guided by the principles of the understanding, that epistemological position or perspective attained within the sphere of civil society itself, with the result that the system *is* rational in this sense. As such it can *itself* be recognized as a rationally working whole and studied *by* the understanding.

Let us reflect for a moment, however, on the difference between the starting points of Smith and Hegel. Philosophically, Smith is in a somewhat Leibnizian position in terms of his inability to account for the harmonizing of different practical intentions within the market: the "hidden hand" may be a metaphor, but it appeals to the idea of some transcendent intelligence responsible for harmonizing the self-seeking activities of the individual

---

[3] Smith, *The Wealth of Nations,* 115.

beings. In fact, in the earlier *The Theory of Moral Sentiments* Smith is more overt in his appeal to an intelligence that confers order on nature: "Thus self-preservation, and the propagation of the species, are the great ends which Nature seems to have proposed in the formation of all animals. . . . Nature has directed us to the greater part of these by original and immediate instincts. Hunger, thirst, the passion which unites the two sexes, the love of pleasure, the dread of pain, prompt us to apply those means for their own sakes, and without any consideration of their tendency to those beneficent ends which the great Director of nature intended to produce by them."[4]

For Hegel, as we have seen, such a comprehensive conception of what is cannot be an adequate one because of the incoherence of its appeal to a transcendent and indeterminate intelligence "outside" the system from which the whole is posited. Thus in the *Logic* Hegel notes that the harmony of the Leibnizian monads "falls outside them and is likewise pre-established by another being or *in-itself*" (*SL*, 539; *W*, 6:199). A philosophically comprehensive conception of reality must understand reality such that it is *self-determining* and indeed must itself be part of this process of self-determination. Put otherwise, it must understand reality in terms of the recognitive or syllogistic structure of "spirit." Smith's account must ultimately rely on a variety of dogmatically accepted presuppositions about the world and the beings in it: humans are naturally driven by determinate drives that can be generalized as "self-interest"; in their dealings with the world they naturally employ the sort of instrumental reasoning of means and ends which we see at work in the market; because of their self-interest and reasoning they will naturally enter into market relationships with each other, and so on. But on Hegel's reinterpretation of Smithian economics, there is no *linear* explanation from accepted presuppositions here: it is not simply *because* humans are self-interested and rational in this way that they enter into market relations; rather, it can equally be put that they become self-interested and rational in this way because they enter into the recognitive structures of market relations. How then does one break out of the viciousness of this circle and philosophically explain the existence of both this type of society and these types of subjects? The answer here is that one explains them by showing how they are possible and determinate configurations of *Anerkennung* relations, the relations that are the necessary conditions for the existence of society and subjectivity as such. But in fact, Hegel's recognitive reinterpretation of the market brings out an implicit hermeneutic perspective that exists already in Smith.

---

[4] Adam Smith, *The Theory of Moral Sentiments* (Oxford: Oxford University Press, 1976), 77–78.

Smith's conception of the psychological capacity required to enter into market relations already has built into it a hermeneutic epistemological capacity. In order to "address ourselves" to another's self-love and "talk to them . . . of their own advantages" we must be able to understand in what another's self-interest consists. For the hermeneutic psychology necessary to his economic theory here Smith was able to call upon his own earlier moral psychology of *The Theory of Moral Sentiments* in which he had appropriated the quasi-hermeneutic idea of the "sympathetic" recognition of others, an idea found in eighteenth-century Scottish moral-sense theory and which had originated largely in the writings of Anthony Ashley Cooper, the third earl of Shaftesbury. Smith does not use the term "sympathy" in *The Wealth of Nations*, but, as a number of commentators have pointed out, it operates as an essential epistemological capacity for the economic theory contained there. As Patricia Werhane expresses it, for Smith, it is sympathy that enables us "to understand the passions and interests of another even if we felt resentment or even abhorrence towards those passions or towards that person."[5]

Shaftesbury's Stoic-derived holistic and somewhat pantheistic framework had provided a place for actions to be motivated by the non-egoistic "social" affections of sympathy. But such a notion of sympathy as a non-egoistic sentiment was essentially at variance with the modern and individualistic Cartesian point of view from which all apparently non-egoistic motivations were to be explained in terms of egoistic ones. It was in terms of such a deflationary egoistic approach that in the seventeenth century the sympathetic motivation of "pity" could be described by Hobbes as the "imagination or fiction of future calamity to *ourselves* proceeding from the sense of *another* man's calamity" and by Rochefoucauld as "feeling our own suffering in those of others" and as a "shrewd precaution against misfortunes that may befall us."[6] This idea was repeated in the eighteenth century by Mandeville in his influential critique of Shaftesbury; and although the relationships between Smith's moral psychology of *The Theory of Moral Sentiments* and the economic theory of *The Wealth of Nations* is far from clear, something like this egoistic and instrumental reinterpretation of the Shaftesburian idea of sympathy seems to be going on in the work of Smith.

As David Marshall has pointed out, for Smith moral sentiments are

---

[5] Patricia H. Werhane, *Adam Smith and His Legacy for Modern Capitalism* (Oxford: Oxford University Press, 1991), 34. On the implicit hermeneutic dimension of the Scottish tradition here see Donald W. Livingstone, *Hume's Philosophy of Common Life* (Chicago: University of Chicago Press, 1984).
[6] Thomas Hobbes, *English Works*, Molesworth ed., 4:44. Duc de la Rochefoucauld, *Maxims*, trans. Leonard Tancock (Harmondsworth: Penguin Books, 1959), Maxim 264.

explained by the fact that the other serves not in his genuine "otherness" but rather as a type of screen onto which is projected imagined states of the self. Social life is thus conceived of as an ensemble of "theatricalized" relations, within which each regards the other much as a spectator regards an actor on stage and in turn imagines himself or herself as regarded by the other in the same way. It is on the basis of this latter move that, taking into account how the other will perceive and respond to his or her actions, each learns to constrain his or her own immediately egoistic behavior. In this way, sympathy, rather than being any self-less moral concern for the suffering of another, becomes an instrument of intelligent self-interest.

This is something like Hegel's recognitive approach to the economy, except, of course, that for Hegel, recognition is not simply an *epistemological capacity,* an attribute of determinate and substantial subjects, which allows them to *represent* to themselves the states of others. Rather it is the necessarily reciprocal performative act within which subjects and their intentional states *are determined* as such. The peculiarity of recognition in the theater is that it is the very *suspension* of interaction and recognition in the performative sense between audience and actors which is the condition of its existence. It is the nonacknowledgment of the actor in any immediate sense as the particular person he or she is which allows the appearance of the recognizable fictive *character.*

But theater supervenes on everyday life: it is only by virtue of belonging to substantial social relations outside the theater that one can meaningfully exist as a spectator within it. To put this in terms of the interpretation of Hegel pursued in this book, it is the background processes of recognitive interaction within which the categorial structures of life and thought are produced, reproduced, and transformed—the processes within which "the concept" determines itself "within" itself—that are logically presupposed by the purely epistemological capacities that allow a subject to read a "representation." In its reduction of social life to the theater, Smith's analysis was located on the pre-Kantian plane of assuming the existence of a recognizable reality prior to and independent of the knowing subject's interaction with that reality. To correct this, Hegel reinterprets that which Smith thinks of epistemologically and instrumentally as *"Mittel,"* or *means,* as the *"Mitte,"* the recognitive *middle* joining subjects in their relations of identity and difference.[7]

---

[7] For Hegel, of course, there is no possibility of this whole explanatory framework being consistent because of the one-sidedness of its approach. The Smithian approach starts off wanting to explain the sorts of activities in the world with which we are familiar, activities such as apparently non-egoistic ones, but in the course of explanation this familiar world to be explained is gradually explained away. The world of everyday behavior is a mere appearance covering up the underlying reality made up of vectors of self-interested action. We might

Of course, Hegel must not simply dogmatically impose his reading of the market in the place of Smith's, as this would repeat the dichotomizing action of that form of negation of the *Nichts eines Seins*. The thinking through of the Smithian approach to civil society, an approach grounded in the understanding, will lead to its own reinterpretative overcoming. Smithian optimism must be followed through until it results in its inverted form, in which "the understanding with its subjective ends and moral opinions gives vent to its discontent and moral irritation" (*PR*, §189 remark). The view of modernity and the emergence of civil society which inverts Smith's is that of Rousseau.

Hegel, Rousseau, and the Madness of Civil Society

Civil society is a contradictory phenomenon because of the deep penetration of its relations by the mediating activity of *Verstand*. Smith had to abstract from the singular agent with its singular capacities and desires, singular histories and locations in the world, and conceive of economic agents abstractly and uniformly, like bodies in Newtonian space. Singular agents no longer have desires for this or for that, they are motivated by a generic "self-interest." They no longer have this or that degree of development of this or that cognitive capacity; they have the common understanding general to the species. Everything that is singular gets left out of Smithian economics only to be taken into consideration and reasserted by a critic of modernity such as Jean-Jacques Rousseau. Such a critic, by focusing on the singular and nongeneralizable can show the operations of a contrary tendency within the social and psychological effects of the modern market.

For Smith the distancing from immediate desire and feeling achieved through the mediation of the views of others is a function of human natural reason per se. For Rousseau, in contrast, it is a corruption. Similarly, while for Smith the gradual emergence of the free market from the family-like relations of feudalism is the liberation of human nature from the

---

think of the paradox here as parallel to that in which one wants to learn more about colors by studying physics. One will certainly learn something here, but it becomes increasingly harder to see how what one is learning about is *color*. The color that one was initially interested in is something that belongs to the world of familiar things, but the world that one arrives at as one's physical studies are pursued is very different. In the passage from the realm of *Existenz* to *Erscheinung*, from the "manifest image" to the "scientific image," the original *explanans* has somehow disappeared. But *as* a God's-eye view, the "scientific image" is meant to be *comprehensive* and so against the background of this requirement an "inverted" view comes into being representing all those items of the manifest world left out by the scientific view.

trammels of something less than human, for Rousseau it represents a loss of humanity, a decline from the natural human state.

What is significant for us in the opposing views of Smith and Rousseau is that both start from more or less similar premises—the "modern" view that sees self-interest as the underlying force driving human life, even its moral dimension. For Smith self-interest leads us to satisfy the interests of others as the most efficient way of getting what we want whereas for Rousseau: "The source of our passions, the origin and principle of all the others, the only one born with man and which never leaves him so long as he lives, is self-love [amour de soi]—a primitive, innate passion, which is anterior to every other and of which all others are in a sense only modifications."[8] Significantly, for Rousseau, it is the infant's love of its mother, a love which forms the infrastructure of all later moral relations, which is the love that most immediately stems from the infant's own self-love. This is because self-love, a love that is "always good and always in conformity with order," naturally extends from the self to that on which its well-being depends: "[W]e have to love ourselves to preserve ourselves; and it follows immediately from the same sentiment that we love what preserves us."[9] Rousseau does then accept the mediation of others into one's self-relations as an important element of the self's natural maturation. What he fears is the opening up of this mediation to those beyond the intimate reach of the close, "natural" relations that are found in the *family*.

In accepting the family as the natural setting for the development of the morally relevant sentiments, Rousseau's thought aligns with that of the pre-Smithians Schaftesbury and Hutcheson. But in modernity social relations are taken beyond this natural range by the market. Generalized in this way, intersubjective relations now provide the conditions for the degeneration of natural self-interest, *amour de soi*, into the factitious *amour-propre*. While the psychology of amour-propre had been discussed by such earlier "moralists" as La Rochefoucauld, Rousseau's great insight in *Discourse on the Origin of Inequality* was to link it precisely to that kind of reading of the desires of others encouraged by the modern market. Importantly, for Rousseau, it was exactly the type of *theatricalized* recognitive relations to others celebrated by Smith that are at fault here.

In the state of nature, a felt desire would be an immediate reflection of some underlying somatic need. Here no "sympathetic" understanding of desires of others could mediate this relation between need and felt desire. Thus, in the state of nature: "[A]s each man regarded himself as the only

8 Jean-Jacques Rousseau, *Emile; or, On Education,* trans. Allan Bloom (New York: Basic Books, 1979), 212–13.
9 Rousseau, *Emile,* 213.

observer of his actions, the only being in the universe who took any interest in him, and the sole judge of his deserts, no feeling arising from comparison he could not be led to make could take root in his soul."[10] This
comparative form of self-assessment occurred in any social condition but
became particularly acute in the type of social relations formed within
market society. In conditions of extreme mediation such an abstraction
allowed desire and its gratification to run unchecked and unregulated by
what Rousseau took to be its natural, rhythmically operating, somatic
basis. Thus: "[D]issolute men run into excesses which brings on fevers and
death; because the mind depraves the senses, and the will continues to
speak when nature is silent."[11]

The source of this abstraction of desire from natural substantive need
was bound up psychologically with what Rousseau conceived as the
"imagination." By this faculty he essentially meant that hermeneutic
capacity allowing the recognition of the self in others.[12] For Rousseau, the
proliferation of social relations beyond the family characteristic of modern
city life bred a type of perverted self-interest in individuals, based not on
their natural desires but on a *comparative assessment* of the individual's own
state with that of another. This was *amour-propre*.

For *amour-propre* to arise, we must be able to gain a perspective *on* our
own conditions from an external and alien point of view; we must be able
to see ourselves from the position of another consciousness, see ourselves
as another would see us. Put another way, we must be able to see ourselves
in others, see others' states as ones that we might occupy. That is, that
which is the basis for morality and the rationality of the market for Smith is
the cause of the perversion of morality and the irrationality of the market
for Rousseau.

The "theatricality" of modern forms of civil intersubjectivity implicit in
Smith is denounced in Rousseau as leading to a social existence cloaked in
illusion. Modern economic interdependency has required that one must
mediate one's behavior by the viewpoint of others, a viewpoint for which
one must *represent* one's state to others: "Man must now . . . have been
perpetually employed in getting others to interest themselves in his lot,
and in making them, apparently at least, if not really, find their advantage
in promoting his own."[13] Thus: "It now became the interest of men to

---

[10] Jean-Jacques Rousseau, "A Discourse on the Origin of Inequality," in *The Social Contract and
Discourses*, trans. G. D. H. Cole (London: Dent, 1973), 66 n. 2.
[11] Rousseau, "A Discourse on the Origin of Inequality," 54.
[12] The realm of "nature" is important for Rousseau because it provides an image of self, its
passions and actions, as *unified*—an image opposable to the modern fragmented self, driven
by factitious, socially constructed, and imaginatively shaped passions.
[13] Rousseau, "A Discourse on the Origin of Inequality," 86.

appear what they really were not. To be and to seem became two totally different things."[14] Abstracted by these sorts of mechanisms from their natural somatic basis, desires spiral out of control as fulfillment is now interpreted as having more than the other. Thus: "Insatiable ambition, the thirst of raising their respective fortunes, not so much from real want as from the desire to surpass others, inspired all men with a vile propensity to injure one another."[15]

Thus whereas Smith takes desires as given and regards the relations that the desiring agent enters into purely instrumentally, Rousseau understands how those relations themselves actively play a role in the determination of the desires themselves and thus assesses them as fictitious and artificial. States of satisfaction are now no longer a function of fulfilled natural needs but are assessed comparatively. These forces unleashed by the market will play across those singled out by Smith as leading to the general betterment of all.

Hegel is well aware of this aspect of the market, the degree of truth in Rousseau's "inverted view": "Particularity for itself, on the one hand indulging itself in all directions as it satisfies its needs, contingent arbitrariness, and subjective caprice, destroys itself and its substantial concept in the act of enjoyment; on the other hand, as infinitely agitated and continually dependent on external contingency and arbitrariness and at the same time limited by the power of universality, the satisfaction of both necessary and contingent needs is itself contingent. In these opposites and their complexity, civil society affords a spectacle of extravagance and misery as well as of the physical and ethical corruption common to both" (PR, §185).

The recognitive mediations within which desire exists in the market work not as mere means for the satisfaction of given desires but as actively

---

[14] Ibid.

[15] Ibid., 87. Cf.: "I could prove that, if we have a few rich and powerful men on the pinnacle of fortune and grandeur, while the crowd grovels in want and obscurity, it is because the former prize what they enjoy only in so far as others are destitute of it; and because, without changing their condition, they would cease to be happy the moment the people ceased to be wretched" (101).

Rousseau's critique of the subject of modern social life is an early expression of a view which has become more and more commonly made since then. On the one hand, the idea that modern life creates a group of illusory and unfulfillable desires, out of step with our naturally given needs, is behind the sort of recurrent culturally conservative calls to go back to a more "natural" form of life which has been made persistently since the late eighteenth century. Compared with premodern forms of life in which people are more directly concerned with the essentials of life, food, shelter, and so on, modern life and the pursuits that characterize it are often seen as "artificial." This is often accompanied by a type of nostalgia for earlier modes of living concerned with more "natural" or "essential" aspects of life. This type of critique of modernity is a culturally conservative or anti-modernist critique.

generating and shaping those desires themselves. The homogenization of desire, the effacement of its peculiarities and idiosyncrasies which results from the abstractly equilibrating transactions of the economy, is strikingly conveyed in the addition to section 192: "The fact that I have to fit in with other people brings the form of universality into play at this point. I acquire my means of satisfaction from others and must accordingly accept their opinions. But at the same time, I am compelled to produce means whereby others can be satisfied. Thus one plays into the hands of the other and is connected with it."

Rousseau can focus on phenomena that cannot be captured by Smithian political economy. By concentrating on the singular, Rousseau can demonstrate how the general claims of an advocate of the market such as Smith can fail to show how the market can work against the interests of some. Similarly for Hegel:

> The *possibility of sharing* in the universal resources—i.e. of holding *particular* resources—is, however, *conditional* upon one's own immediate basic assets (i.e. capital) on the one hand, and upon one's skill on the other; the latter in turn is itself conditioned by the former, but also by contingent circumstances whose variety gives rise to *differences* in the *development* of natural and spiritual aptitudes which are already unequal in themselves. In this sphere of particularity, these differences . . . necessarily result in *inequalities in the resources and skills* of individuals. (*PR*, §200)

But contra Rousseau, Hegel will not regard these socially generated desires as corrupted or alienated versions of some essential form of desire belonging to a state of nature, and so he is not abstractly opposed to the socialization of the particular: "[I]n the manner of dress and times of meals, there are certain conventions which one must accept, for in such matters, it is not worth the trouble to seek to display one's own insight, and it is wisest to act as others do" (*PR*, §192 addition). The idea of a free existence in a state of nature is mistaken because "a condition in which natural needs as such were immediately satisfied would merely be one in which spirituality was immersed in nature, and hence a condition of savagery and unfreedom" (*PR*, §194 remark).

Both Smith and Rousseau reveal the shortcomings of thought limited to the operations of the understanding. Both operate with some idea of the substantive nature of humans. Unable to grasp the economy as a form of spirit, the political economist grasps it as a form of nature, and so interprets the desires and capacities of participants as *naturalistically given*. In contrast, the critic of modernity sees the generalized economy only as the immediate negation of the natural—as perversion or monstrosity. But

Hegel's response to the modern economy is to view it as an instantiation of *Geist*, specifically as embodying the hypothetical syllogism which with its "formal" reconciliation between singular and universal is an inversion of the more immediate *Sittlichkeit* of the family. Individual freedom and equality are not features of nature as Rousseau would have it; they are aspects of the form of recognition first found explicitly *in* the economy. But they are present there *only* at a formal level. Far from overcoming the arbitrariness and givenness of nature, which is supposed to be the characteristic feature of *Geist*, the mechanisms of the economy only *amplify* these features, because they fail to allow for any adequate recognition of the singularity of those involved.[16] The free economy, while supposed to work for the good of all, actually produces extremes of wealth and poverty.[17] The social relations of the economy are only appearances of free social relations in the Hegelian sense of the term *Scheinen*. They are appearances *within which* free social relations can be recognized, but recognized only as an abstract idea and not as a concrete actuality. Thus while they are *mere* appearances, negations of free social relations, they are also the first appearance of something that can be made concrete because agents can now consciously act in ways so as to make these free relations actual.

There can be no resolution of the opposition between Smith and Rousseau within their own terms. One must move beyond the sorts of conceptual structures that work with categories such as "being" and "essence" and to that thought articulated by the subjective "concept-logic." In thinking about human capacities and qualities such as desire, one has to take its "being-recognized," its *Anerkenntsein*, as an essential moment of its being

---

[16] "The spirit's objective *right of particularity* . . . does not cancel out the inequality of human beings in civil society—an inequality posited by nature, which is the element of inequality—but in fact produces it out of the spirit itself and raises it to an inequality of skills, resources, and even of intellectual and moral education" (*PR*, §200 remark).

[17] Hegel gives a further account of the mechanisms of the production of poverty within the system of civil society at *PR*, §241: "Not only arbitrariness, however, but also contingent physical factors and circumstances based on external conditions . . . may reduce individuals to *poverty*. In this condition, they are left with the needs of civil society and yet—since society has at the same time taken from them the natural means of acquisition . . . , and also dissolves the bond of the family in its wider sense as a kinship group . . . —they are more or less deprived of all the advantages of society, such as the ability to acquire skills and education in general, as well as of the administration of justice, health care, and often even the consolation of religion."

And at §243: "When the activity of civil society is unrestricted, it is occupied internally with *expanding its population and industry.*—On the one hand, as the association of human beings through their needs is *universalized,* and with it the ways in which means of satisfying these needs are devised and made available, the *accumulation of wealth* increases; for the greatest profit is derived from this twofold universality. But on the other hand, the *specialization* and *limitation* of particular work also increase, as do likewise the *dependence* and *want* of the class which is tied to such work; this in turn leads to an inability to feel and enjoy the wider freedoms, and particularly the spiritual advantages, of civil society."

that which it is.[18] The expression and recognition of desire are not, as in Smith, merely means for the satisfaction of desire; neither are they, as in Rousseau, traps by which desire is alienated from its true and essential being. Expression and recognition of desire constitute a moment of the will which assigns to it a content, that moment which "makes isolated and abstract needs, means, and modes of satisfaction into *concrete, i.e. social* ones" (*PR*, §192).

From Hegel's perspective, Smith and Rousseau will draw on contradictory applications of the categories of the objective logics of "being" and "essence" because they orient their thought from the opposed perspectives of the opposed spheres of modern *Sittlichkeit*, the opposed "syllogisms" of civil society and family. Each will treat that which it finds in its sphere, its social relations, its modes of thought, its typical desires, as constituting the naturally or essentially human and will evaluate what it finds in the opposed sphere as negations of these essences. Thus Smith, for example, will think of economic relations as "natural" for humans while in his analysis of feudalism, for example, will see family relations as a type of obstructing and nonessential matrix from which the natural relations of the market should be freed. Rousseau, in contrast, will see the type of human existence maintained within close intimate relations such as those of the family as what is essential and natural to human life and will see the relations and subjectivity of the market as a type of pathological degeneration of the human.

We have of course by now seen this figure many times before—for example, in the inverted relation between the metaphysics of Fichte and Spinoza. But the whole cannot be grasped from within a single clear and comprehensive view, and the attempt to understand it so will always split into such complementarily inverted views. Early in his career Hegel had characterized such an opposition in terms of the failure of reciprocal recognition between such inverted positions: "Since reciprocal recognition is in this way suspended, what appears is only two subjectivities in opposition; things that have nothing in common with one another come on stage with equal right for that very reason; and in declaring that what is before it to be judged is anything else one likes . . . criticism transposes itself into a subjective situation and its verdict appears as a one-sided decision by violence" (*CJI*, 276).

Apparently what is required is for each thinker to grasp the other *as* grasping the world from a "place" that is the inversion of its own. This would be to effect the transition to *Vernunft* and philosophy. But *from*

[18] Nisbet's rendering of *Anerkenntsein* as "quality of being recognized" does not quite bring out the *ontological* weight of this "recognized-being."

"where" does one get such a view? One is tempted to answer here by invoking the third of the "syllogisms of necessity," the *disjunctive syllogism*, and that social realm that appears to instantiate it, the *state*. This, I think, does essentially coincide with the direction of Hegel's answer. But like so many of Hegel's answers, it is easily misunderstood. It is to this nexus of the state and philosophy that I turn in the next and concluding chapters.

CHAPTER 11

The Recognitive Logic
of the Rational State

AS WE HAVE SEEN, the common charge laid against Hegel has been that his philosophy is ultimately contextualized within a model of an infinite mind's knowledge of itself, a relation to self that excludes the existence of anything beyond that mind, anything "other." Even as sympathetic a reader as Hans-Georg Gadamer, for whom Hegel's work is both rich in hermeneutic insight and deeply engaged with the issue of intersubjectivity, thinks of Hegel's philosophy as ultimately defeated by this lapse into a dogmatic pre-Kantian metaphysical framework. My contention has been that such a view is based on a misunderstanding of Hegel's work and that his combination of Kant's Copernicanism on the one hand and hermeneutic thought on the other allowed him to at least point the way beyond the achievements of both these streams of modern philosophy. And this is as clear in his political thought as elsewhere.

As has been noted earlier, Gadamer believes that the pantheistic orientation characteristic of late eighteenth-century German culture continued as the hidden framework of the hermeneutic thought up to Dilthey. Speaking of Schleiermacher and Humboldt, Gadamer notes that despite their professed Kantianism and regardless of however much "they emphasize the individuality, the barrier of alienness, that our understanding has to overcome, understanding ultimately finds its fulfilment only in an infinite consciousness, just as the idea of individuality finds its ground there as well."[1] For the hermeneutic-historical tradition this infinite consciousness

---

[1] Hans-Georg Gadamer, *Truth and Method*, 2d rev. ed., translation revised by Joel Weinsheimer and Donald G. Marshall (New York: Crossroad, 1992), 342.

is historical knowledge, which has its telos in the contemplation of the totality of possible forms of life and thought, a totality containing the instance of the historian's own initial horizon. "The fact that all individuality is pantheistically embraced within the absolute is what makes possible the miracle of understanding. Thus here too being and knowledge interpenetrate each other in the absolute."[2] In this context Gadamer makes a revealing comment that sheds light on his understanding of Hegel. Despite their antagonism to Hegel, the romantic hermeneuts' concept of knowledge "ultimately finds its justification in Hegel" and "neither Schleiermacher's nor Humboldt's Kantianism, then, affirms an independent system distinct from the consummation of speculative idealism in the absolute dialectic of Hegel."[3] It would seem then that Gadamer believes that the essential difference between the nineteenth-century hermeneuts and Hegel is that Hegel is self-consciously aware of his metaphysically pantheist conception of the relation of mind and being. But Hegel is no metaphysical pantheist, and when we look at Hegel's political philosophy we find him opposing his position to one that seems distinctly pantheist in exactly this sort of way—that of Rousseau. To see this let us look at the respective approaches of each to two central concepts of Rousseau's political thought, the "social contract" and the "general will."

Hegel and Rousseau on the Social Contract and the Common Will

In standard Hobbesian social contract theories, individuals enter into the "social contract" for the same sorts of reasons that they enter into particular economic contracts: it is a move dictated by rational self-interest. From such a point of view the state stands as an instrument created to secure the boundary conditions of the constitutive practices of the realm of civil society.

For Rousseau, however, the social contract is not a device for the satisfaction of individual interests but rather one for the formation and expression of the *general will*, a unified "will" that expresses the interest of the substantially conceived community taken as a whole. The task of political theory is thus to find a form of contract which institutes social relations that are more like the relations between the parts of a single self-interested corporate entity than relations between opposing self-interested individuals. From his point of view, the *distortions* of desire under conditions of

---

2 Ibid.
3 Ibid.

social existence and social dependence show what is wrong with the Hobbesian model. It is only when the individual is conceived as contextualized within the *totality* of the social relations to which it belongs that these individual distortions can be factored out. In Rousseau's abstract terms:

> 'The problem is to find a form of association which will defend and protect with the whole common force the person and goods of each associate, and in which each, while uniting himself with all, may still obey himself alone, and remain as free as before.' This is the fundamental problem of which the social contract provides the solution.[4]

What such a contract demands is "the total alienation of each associate, together with all his rights, to the whole community; for, in the first place, as each gives himself absolutely, the conditions are the same for all." Total alienation of individual rights is required because each individual "in giving himself to all, gives himself to nobody."[5] That is, by making each equi-dependent on the whole, the evil of dependency of individuals on particular others, a dependency that generates the distortions of *amour-propre*, is overcome.

For Hegel, the Rousseauian conception of the state as based on the principle of the *will* marks an important step forward. Rousseau recognizes the principle of the will as at the center of the state not only in terms of *content*—the general will manifesting the *interest* of the social body as a whole—but also as *form;* that is, it is the general interest *as* willed. We might say that with his concept of general participation within legislative deliberations Rousseau grasps that it is not simply the general interest per se but its willed and thoughtful *positing* that is crucial. However: "Rousseau considered the will only in the determinate form of the *singular* [einzelnen] will (as Fichte subsequently also did)" (*PR*, §258 remark). That is, Rousseau, restricted as he was to a unitary conception of the will, could conceive of the social whole and its willing only on the model of a single act of a willing subject writ large.

This inability to think beyond the idea of the will in its singularity draws Rousseau's thought into a general pattern with which we are now well familiar—the problem of making the substantial (the social interest) subjective (willed). In his account of desire in the *Discourse on the Origin of Inequality*, Rousseau's naturalistic conception of individual self-interest, *amour de soi*, finds its natural expression only in the solitary state. It is precisely the passage from solitary to intersubjective existence that leads to

---

[4] Jean-Jacques Rousseau, "The Social Contract," in *The Social Contract and Discourses*, 174.
[5] Ibid.

the distortions of *amour-propre*. In *The Social Contract* this model of the natural expression of the solitary will was then applied at the collective level to the social body. It is the well-constituted society that now exists as a type of solitary "asocial" individual. Its will, the general will, is the natural expression of this collective *amour de soi*. Of course, the society is not a single organism: a "social body" can only have and act on a "will" in virtue of the fact that its members can communicatively come to share it. But to bring in the theme of communication here is to return precisely to the theme of the distorting effects of intersubjectivity. Language and intersubjectivity are both the conditions for the formation of that which represents the collective natural interest *and* the very sort of factors which distort the expression of natural interest into its perverse forms.

We can then start to see how, in trying to get an undistorted representation of its real interests within the naturalistically modeled social totality, the individual willing subject is threatened. The *conditions* of the subject's cognition—in Rousseau's case, its existence as a particular being within communicative relations to others—have to be negated in the very act of fulfilling the aims of that cognition. Like Spinoza, Rousseau can consider the *particularity* of a subjective view in a negative light only, as that which distorts a true theoretical or practical cognition.

And so we can see how from Hegel's point of view the danger here is once again the total eclipse of the singular subject within some all-encompassing "substance": Rousseau too is prone to the "Spinozist" problem of abstract self-negation, the intolerance to any perspectival aspect of the self which hinders the total coincidence between the self and its universal substance, here, the legitimate state. Perceiving particularity, especially dependence on other *particular* individuals, as a threat to individual freedom, Rousseau attempts to unify the singular and the universal in the general will by the abolition of all intermediate social relations, that is, abolition of the mediating structures that according to Hegel's concept-logic *allow* the unification of singular and universal. Thus in the Rousseauian state an attempt is made to eliminate all mediating social bodies between the government and the individual so that that individual's "true" interests can find direct expression in the common will. In the Hegelian state, it will be precisely such mediating bodies, properly constituted, that allow for the articulation of the singular views of individuals with the general view formulated from the position of the government.

The willing subject in Rousseau's well-constituted state faces a dilemma akin to that faced by the Spinozist finite mode qua knowing subject: both are hampered by the particularity of their perspectival relation to the whole of which they are a part and which they aim to comprehend. And for Rousseau as for Spinoza, the inadequacies of all perspectival immediate understandings—in Rousseau's case one's immediate understanding of one's self-interest—are measured against the objectivity that can be achieved when one thinks from the point of view of the whole itself. Apparent self-interest is a negation of a real, essential one; it is the negation of a "being."[6]

When understood from within the movements of Hegel's concept-logic, however, this whole cannot be thought of as univocally positive or substantial. The illusions of individual self-interest can indeed be reflectively revealed from some more general viewpoint: as a member of a corporation within which one is linked to others occupying a similar place within the social whole, one is likely to perceive one's interests differently than one would as a simple individual within civil society. But it could be further grasped that one's corporation itself was only a particular totality within a greater whole to which one also belonged, and so one's understanding of one's interests from *its* perspective might in turn come to be reflected upon as *itself* one-sided and correctable. In short, the correcting view itself could always come to be seen as correctable: as something positive that negated the initial view, it could itself succumb to further negation. The immediate image that presents itself here is that of a type of ladder leading all the way up to "the state" from which one achieves one's real, "objective" interest. But this is not Hegel's view. The state may be the "circle" constituted of those more local *particular* circles, the family, the corporation, and so on, but *it* must not be thought of as that final "essential" being which simply negates the localness of all smaller circles.

To think in this way would be to remain within the categorial structure of essence-logic, the logic of that form of thought most developed in Spin-

---

6 In "Freedom, Dependence, and the General Will" (*Philosophical Review,* 102 [1993]: 363–95), Frederick Neuhouser perspicuously reconstructs the two ways in which Rousseau takes the general will to secure the freedom of individual citizens. On the one hand, membership of the well-formed state is a precondition of *civil* freedom in which the universality of law mediates dependence relations among individuals; on the other, such membership, with its dimension of self-legislation, embodies *moral* freedom. Neuhouser separates the two aspects of freedom involved by calling on the Hegelian distinction between "objective" and "subjective" freedom, noting the tension that develops in Rousseau's account around his infamous conception of the individual's being *forced to be free.* Here, the objective concept of freedom wins out over the subjective because it is a sense of freedom "in which the general will's being the will of each individual does not depend upon the individual's recognition of it as such" ("Freedom, Dependence, and the General Will," 370).

Such an antithesis for Hegel would be an indication that despite the fact that the principle of the will is recognized as being at the center of the state in Rousseau's account, ultimately the moments of form and content within that will remain abstractly opposed. Here, as in the *Phenomenology,* we can see the "right" of the individual as based on the fact that he remains conscious of that moment of his "absolute independence," the dimension of immediate self-certainty, an awareness related to the fact that qua individual he *is* the "absolute form" (*PS,* §26; *W,* 3:37).

oza's philosophy. In Hegel's puzzling logical shorthand, it would be to think of the contrast between the interest understood from the more general point of view and that understood from the more particular as a contrast between a "being" and a "not-being," a *Sein* and a *Nichtsein*. But that which is negated is properly thought not as the "not-being of a being," but rather as the *Nichts eines Nichts*, the "nothing of a nothing"! (*SL*, 400; *W*, 6:25; translation modified).[7]

This all will sound paradoxical if one wants to find at the center of "the state" some type of "thing" with either an immediately given or a mediately discoverable *nature*. Rousseau's idea of the common interest expressed in the general will typifies such an essential "thing" or "being." Thought of as the expression of a natural collective *amour de soi*, the will is conceived such that a way must be found for the community to form an explicit intention that comes to coincide perfectly with this naturally determined interest. This will mean that for Rousseau the collective communication and deliberation that make up the processes for the determination of the *volonté générale* will be thought of in an essentially instrumental manner as a way of bringing this already existent interest to consciousness.

In contrast, the state has to be thought of not as an immediate "being" or its reflected equivalent, the "essence" underlying a given appearance, but *syllogistically*, and specifically, as I have earlier suggested, in terms of the structure of the third of the syllogisms of necessity, the "disjunctive syllogism." In this syllogism, the concrete universal is, says Hegel, "the *universal* sphere of its particularizations and is determined as a singularity" (*SL*, 702; *W*, 6:339).[8]

We will return to the second aspect of the Hegelian state referred to here, its determination "as a singularity." Let us for the moment consider the idea of the state as the "universal sphere of its particularizations"—we might say, the sphere within which all the particular social bodies constituting the state are related. Thus the state is not a being but a set of relations between beings. We might describe it not so much as an "inter-

---

[7] "*[D]as Andere . . . ist nicht das Nichtsein eines Seins, sondern das Nichts eines Nichts.*" This formula is from the beginning of book 2, the "doctrine of essence"; however, it is clear that Hegel thinks that such an idea cannot be understood *within* that logic. Thus in *The Encyclopedia Logic* he notes that within essence-logic the categories of science and metaphysics are contained "as products of the reflecting understanding, which both assumes the distinctions as *independent* and at the same time posits their relationality *as well*." But it only links these assumptions together with an "also": "it does not bring these thoughts together; it does not unite them into the Concept" (*EL*, §114 remark). We might think of the meaningless phrase "the nothing of a nothing" as the essence-logic's attempt to say something that can *only* be said within the framework of concept-logic.

[8] Cf.: "The mediating *universal* is also posited as the totality of its *particularizations* and as a *singular* particular [or] excluding singularity [*ein einzelnes Besonderes, ausschliessende Einzelheit*]" (*EL*, §191).

subjective" sphere as an "inter-institutional" one, that is, not as relating subjects per se but as relating different institutionalized spheres of intersubjectivity—a "circle of circles." And construed *politically*, the specific types of relations involved are, as we will see, *communicative* and hence *recognitive* ones.

The Estates as Representative and Deliberative Bodies

Hegel's idea of representation is both like and unlike the conventional liberal view. The key to understanding it is to orient it against the background of his reinterpretation of the instrumental "means" into the mediating "middle."

Within the context of civil society the *Stände* (estates) are those "masses" into which the economic realm of production, consumption, and exchange is differentiated. But Hegel also makes the estates the *channels of political representation*. Individuals are not represented *as such* in the legislature, but rather as members of some corporation or estate. We might say that it is the objective *interests* that are primarily represented and that individuals are represented in virtue of having those interests. Thus the legislature is composed of two houses: one represents the "substantial" agricultural estate and is the house of a hereditary nobility; the other is composed of deputies who represent the corporations (*PR*, §§308, 311).[9]

That the individual is not immediately represented in the legislature contrasts with the conventional liberal approach and highlights the distinctness of Hegel's own concept of representation. Hegel shares Rousseau's skepticism concerning an individual's spontaneous ability to understand his or her own interests. Representation by estates thus provides a mechanism for a more "objective" representation of an individual's interests. Of course from the liberal point of view this is likely to be seen as a sacrifice of the individual to the group. Indeed, it is the individual who is typically regarded as the best judge of his or her own interests.

It is this last fact which brings out the basically empiricist or "subjectivist" orientation of liberalism on the question of the determination of interests—"preference" or "wants" typically performing this task. But this is exactly the type of immediate determination that the Copernican singles out for reflective interpretation and criticism. From the Copernican point of view, the idea that an individual is seen as the best judge of his or her interests would be yet another instantiation of the noncritical foundationalism of Aristotelian thought. The Copernican would want to intro-

---

[9] The participation of the third "universal estate" is secured via its role in the executive.

duce some idea of the role of reflective redetermination here, a reflection that could be secured only by bringing into consideration an account of the subject and its wants which was to be had from a viewpoint other than the subjects own. But any such criticism would, of course, have to be rationally persuasive—it would have to be able to be communicated to the first subject in such a way as to produce conviction (*Überzeugung*) and not mere persuasion (*Überredung*). That is, the subject would have to be able to come to recognize epistemically his or her own interest in this new representation even though he or she might not have spontaneously expressed this interest in that way. In short, a Copernican account of a subject's perception of his or her own interests would have to allow for the reflective reinterpretation of those interests achievable within some communicative context.

We can clearly see this Copernican element in Hegel's approach to political representation. Neither an individual's local and perspectival view of what is in the subject's own interest nor the interest of any concrete "circle" could be in any way foundational. Thus Hegel emphasizes that the representatives not be considered as "commissioned or mandated agents" (*PR*, §309); that is, they are not the simple channels for the transmission of their constituents' interests as those interests are understood by their constituents; they are not simply mouthpieces for the "opinions" of their constituents. But also clearly such "opinion" is far from irrelevant for determining what is in a circle's interest. The first person "subjective" view is unavoidable; what has to be effected is a dialogue with other local views, on the one hand, and some more "universal" view, on the other.[10] The state, qua process of the determination of the general will, is that dialogue: "[D]eputies are elected to deliberate and decide on matters of *universal* concern. . . . The determination [*Bestimmung*] of their assemblies is to provide a forum for live exchanges and collective deliberations in which the participants instruct [*unterrichten*] and convince [*überzeugen*] one another" (§309; translation modified).

That is, the play of interests as represented in the legislature is not like a system of forces which resolve into some single force within which the components forces are expressed as vectors—an image implicit in the instrumental understanding of representation. There the resolution is, as it were, purely quantitative. Rationally, each participant hopes and strives for a result in which his own interest is *maximized*. But while each might view the question of his political representation instrumentally in this way, the system will itself be open to that "cunning of reason" operative in

---

[10] See here Hegel's account of the role of public opinion, *PR*, §§316–18. For an assessment see Harry Brod, *Hegel's Philosophy of Politics* (Boulder, Colo.: Westview Press, 1992), chap. 6.

external teleology.[11] The very process of representing those interests within a communicative and deliberative context opens those interests up to the processes of reinterpretation. Thus Hegel notes that "[v]iewed as a *mediating* organ, the Estates stand between the government at large on the one hand and the people in their division into particular spheres and individuals [*Individuen*] on the other. Their determination requires that they should embody in equal measure both the *sense* and *disposition* of the *state* and *government* and the *interests* of *particular* circles and *individuals in their singularity* [*Einzelnen*]" (*PR*, §302 translation modified).[12] Although the representing bodies had initially been conceived of as *Mittel*, or "means," their true significance can be understood only when they are viewed as *Mitte*—"middle" or "mean." In the accompanying remark Hegel notes that it is "one of the most important insights of logic that a specific moment which, when it stands in opposition, has the position of an extreme, loses this quality and becomes an *organic* moment by being simultaneously a *mean* [*Mitte*]." The estates and corporations are the mediating particulars that stand between the singular individual and the universal, the state, and only against the background of such an understanding can the representational role of the estates and corporations in the legislative process of the state be properly appreciated.

In effect, the state is an instantiation of that self-positing circle of recognition. That which is posited, "the general will," cannot be thought of as some determinate content that pre-exists the positing. If this is how it is viewed, as it is with Rousseauian political theory, then the general will can be no more than a merely negative force that, when the particularity implicit in any resolution is perceived, will destroy that resolution in the name of the purely abstract notion of a truly universal will. This, of course, was Hegel's assessment of the fate of the French Revolution. But the action brought into play in the very attempt to realize the general will results in the creation of the "middle" that is *itself* the manifestation of "the will," not the mere means of its manifestation. The content of this will produced at any particular time is never the expression of some pure universal interest. But this is not a failure so much as a demonstration that the idea of an *an sich* "pure universal interest" is an incoherent one, entrapped in the framework of an inadequate logic.

Viewed logically, the difficulties with the individualistic Hobbesian liberal state and the holistic Rousseauian one include the central difficulty of reconciling singular with the universal. The difficulty with the standard

---

[11] Cf. *Hegel's Science of Logic*, 746.

[12] Cf. "The proper significance of the Estates is that it is through them that the state enters into the subjective consciousness of the people, and that the people begins to participate in the state" (*PR*, §301 addition).

contractarian state concerns the "abstract" nature of its universality. Viewed as an instrument for the satisfaction of needs, the state is "external" to the individual, and so the individual is unable to mediate its own subjective point of view with one that can be taken as that of the society as a whole. The difficulty posed for the Rousseauian state is in many senses the reverse of this. Here it is the *difference* between the viewpoints of individual and society which is threatened. In contrast to the reflective civil forms of recognition structuring the liberal state, the Rousseauian state bases itself on complementary and unifying familial forms.

As in the case with his relation to Spinoza, Hegel's divergence from Rousseau's thought is subtle but crucial: it involves a reversal in perspective onto the relationship between the deliberative process for the formation *of* a common intentionality and the common interest that is meant to be expressed *in* that intentionality. For Rousseau communication and deliberation are the means to an end already determined by nature; for Hegel they are the *element,* or *aether,* within which the collective interest is posited. The adequacy of this determination cannot be judged in terms of its ability to bring some presupposed thing-like substance, the collective interest, to the level of representation and expression in legislation. Such an idea is not just practically but *logically* flawed. That is, the general will conceived in this way is not just difficult or impossible for the society to discover; its very concept is incoherent because it is prey to the contradictions of the "objective" logic within which it is formulated. Rather, the communicative and deliberative processes of the state must themselves be regarded as primary and not secondary to the instrumental task they are meant to serve. They are to be regarded as instantiations of the recognitive circle of spirit and assessed according to the adequacy to the structure of the "idea."

When we keep this in mind, it starts to become clear that of the two thinkers Rousseau is the one whose thinking is governed by the schema of a self-relation in which being and thought come to coincide in the way of a single self-consciousness, and Hegel's distance from Rousseau is a measure of his departure from this schema. But we can also approach this from another angle, that of the fate of the singularity of conscious subjects within the political realm. And here the second aspect of the universal characteristic of the "disjunctive syllogism" becomes relevant, the universal's "determination as a singularity," the category that is instantiated here in the role Hegel attributes to *the monarch.*

The Monarch

In considering the structure of the representative institutions, we have seen how Hegel attempts to conceive of a recognitive structure that can reconcile the individual qua member of a *particular* estate with his role as member of the *universal,* the community as a whole. But in contrast to the liberal state with its concept of the representation of *individuals* and not interest groups, the Hegelian solution is faced with the difficulty of finding a place for the recognition of each individual in his *singularity.*

As has been stressed, the constitution of the state is to be understood in terms of the logic of the concept, the internal recognitive architecture of "the idea." But as in other parts of *Realphilosophie,* philosophical thought here will consist of a redetermination within this framework of the results of investigations of the world undertaken from the standpoint of the understanding. It is not surprising then that Hegel starts from Montesquieu's doctrine of the (conveniently tripartite) separation of powers. But this conceptual redetermination results in important transformations of the doctrine at different levels.

To start with, in Montesquieu's articulation the different state powers are seen as simply *limiting* each other.[13] But to conceive of these powers as *an sich* beings that relate to each other only in the sense of providing limits or checks for the exercise of each others' powers is to stay at the level of objective logic. Presumably this concept of a limiting negation must be raised to the more adequate form of the "nothing of a nothing" for the relations among these powers to be grasped philosophically, and this is something that can be adequately understood only from within the dynamics of concept-logic.[14]

When conceived of from within concept-logic, the triparticity of the distinction will be thought in terms of the syllogistic relation of singular, particular, and universal within the political self-legislating will. Of these, the legislative function of the formulation of *universally applying laws* will occupy the position of the universal, while the executive in its function of *carrying out* the laws in the realm of particularity will stand in the place of the particular. In Montesquieu's schema the third power is, of course, the judiciary; but for Hegel the judiciary is actually located within the realm of civil society and does not belong to the political state. The third state "power" within Hegel's system is that of the *monarch,* and it is the monarch who instantiates the category of singularity (*PR,* §§272–73).

Hegel's monarch is a constitutional monarch, whose function in the well-constituted state is essentially *formal,* as the substantive roles of creating and executing laws are given over to the other two powers. The king is "bound by the concrete content of the advice he receives, and if the constitution is firmly established, he often has nothing more to do than to sign

---

[13] Montesquieu, *The Spirit of the Laws,* trans. T. Nugent (New York: Hafner, 1962).
[14] "Here . . . the other is not *being with a negation,* or limit, but *negation with the negation*" (*SL,* 399; *W,* 6:24).

his name" (*PR*, §279 addition), to "say 'yes' and to dot the 'i'" (*PR*, §280 addition). Nevertheless, despite its formality, this role is an essential one. "But this *name* is important: it is the ultimate instance and *non plus ultra*" (*PR*, §279 addition).

To that which had been decided on and advised by his officers the king has to add the "I will it." That is, he must supply that element of singular subjectivity that "the will" needs in its full articulation as idea. Without it, that which is willed will not escape the determination of coming to be seen as some *an sich* being, the almost mechanical or natural result of the interested reasonings of the legislative representatives, rather than as something whose existence is *posited*. In willing *what* he has been advized by his officers, the king is "positing" the "presuppositions" of his own institutional identity and action. It is in this act that the state becomes a self-positing system, an instantiation of the idea itself.

Any view that regarded the formality of the monarch's role as a mark of its redundancy would, from Hegel's point of view, betray its instrumentalist understanding of the state. The subjective position of the king is required for the very conceptual coherence of the state qua act of collective self-positing constituted by the play of reciprocal recognitions adequate to the idea. For Hegel, as for Burke, that a singular and irreplaceable human being embodies these institutions is crucial. But while for Burke this was required for affective reasons, which stood in some sort of dichotomous opposition to modern rational ones, for Hegel they are equally affective and rational: they are rooted in the logic of the concept itself. Grasping this in terms of the purely *affective* dimension of its functioning is to see these recognitive relations on the model of the family and to assume as normative the patriarchal state. But Hegel agrees with Rousseau's insight that the principle of the state is the *universal* will. However, an act can only be *recognized* as an act of willing if it is enacted through a singular subject. The king's "I will" is a singular act within which citizens can recognize a human intention as such. It gives singular form to the universality of the content and provides an address within which each citizen can recognize himself as that singular being who is addressed.

The king occupies a place in the political sphere analogous to that occupied by the judge within the civil sphere (and the priest within the religious sphere): each becomes a mouthpiece of the law. The judge (*Richter*) in that judgment which acknowledges the act of some criminal subject as a crime (the *Richterspruch*) speaks from a point of view which gives voice to the universal law itself (*PR*, §§99–102, 219–28). For Hegel this is meant to do no less than redetermine the criminal's own intentional relation to his crime. Whereas the criminal may have hitherto construed his act solely from the perspective of his own particular needs, the judge characterizes the act from the perspective of the transgressed law itself. The criminal now has access to a different interpretation of his act because he can recognize himself and his act in the judge's own act of addressing and recognizing him. That is, recognizing himself in the utterance of the judge, he recognizes himself within an interpretation that now brings the act under the universal law.

But the universal element that has now been recognitively incorporated into the criminal's own self-conception is abstract. Judgment and punishment can bring about reconciliation with society, but only such that the criminal now construes himself as a featureless abstract particular bearer of rights on a par with all other legal subjects.

The abstractness of right at the heart of civil society pervades this reconciliatory structure of the court and affects its functionaries, including the judge. As a member of the professional civil service recruited from the middle class, the judge is a replaceable "organ of the law" (*PR*, §226). Qualifications to be a judge depend not on birth but on capacity and knowledge of the law. What is important here is not who one *is* but what particular qualities and capacities one *has:* "[T]he *individuals* who perform and implement [the particular functions and activities of the state] are associated with them not by virtue of their immediate personalities, but only by virtue of their universal and objective qualities. Consequently, the link between these functions and particular personalities as such is external and contingent in character" (*PR*, §277).

This all stands in striking contrast with the situation that obtains in the case of the king, "an *immediate* singularity [*Einzelnheit*] . . . [who] is essentially determined as *this* individual, in abstraction from every other content, and this individual is destined [*bestimmt*] in an immediate and natural way, i.e. by his natural *birth,* to hold the dignity of the monarch" (*PR*, §280). When subjects recognize themselves in the universal laws addressed to them by such a singular agent, they not only grasp themselves from the universal point of view of the law itself; they also simultaneously recognize themselves in the singular form of that address in all their brute singularity. In the pronouncements of *a* judge I recognize myself as a particular bearer of rights on a par with all the others, but in the utterances of *that* person, the monarch, I recognize myself in my peculiar determination as *this* person who *I* alone am. Here, the sheer contingency and groundless character of the monarch's identity, which is such an outrage to the republican, is a plus. The answerless question "Why should the king be *that* person?" is perfectly matched by "Why should *I* be *this* person?"[15] The total groundlessness of the monarch's identity is emblematic of my own or

---

[15] Thomas Nagel brings out the sense of puzzlement that can accompany the apprehension of the self under such different categorial forms in *The View from Nowhere* (Oxford: Oxford University Press, 1986), chap. 4.

that of any other subject taken in the aspect of its singularity. But at the same time, the monarch gives embodiment to the institutional structure of the society itself and so personifies the coexistence of the universal law uniting all citizens with the irreducible singularity marking each of them.

The materials that Hegel is attempting to think through philosophically are, of course, historically contingent ones. Constitutional monarchy may (or may not) have provided a realistic way of addressing this logical problem in the context of early nineteenth-century European politics. It is unlikely, however, to be so regarded in the late twentieth century, let alone for "all time." But to think that Hegel is here offering institutional solutions *for* all time is again to misunderstand the basic nature of the framework of his reasoning, the logic of the concept. It is a type of reasoning meant to provide for the non-enduring nature of *any* content, and a properly Hegelian appraisal of his theory of the monarch would have to be open to the very collapse of the institution of monarchy as a historical solution to the problem of the unity of the rational state.

Speculative Logic and Practical Philosophy: Allen Wood's Reconstruction of an Autonomous Hegelian Ethical Theory

The account presented here of the interconnectedness of Hegel's political philosophy with his more general systematic thought agrees with the traditional view that Hegel's philosophy stands or falls as a whole, but differs as to which of these two outcomes it affirms. But, of course, there are intermediary views, for which aspects or areas of Hegel's philosophy can be isolated from the whole and saved, and it has been in the area of political philosophy especially, that this has been a popular strategy for those wanting to hold onto Hegel's insights in that area but wary of his broader system. One common move here has been to reconstruct Hegel's approach in terms of an "anthropological" understanding of the notion of spirit. Allen Wood has followed such a strategy in his *Hegel's Ethical Thought*, in which he interprets and defends Hegel's *Philosophy of Right* as a valuable practical philosophy that can be read and evaluated independently of the framework of speculative logic.[16]

---

[16] Allen W. Wood, *Hegel's Ethical Thought* (Cambridge: Cambridge University Press, 1990). (Henceforth, references will be included in the text as *HET*, followed by the page number.) Wood's reconstruction is based on the orthodox view that Hegel's metaphysics was a failure (for Wood, a "spectacular" and "unredeemable" one [5]). In contrast, however, Wood regards Hegel's moral philosophy as representing "an attempt, in many ways strikingly successful, to remodel classical ethical theory, exhibiting its fundamental soundness by investing it with the style, and adapting it to the content, of a modern self-understanding" (7). This soundness, he

For Wood, Hegel's theory is a theory of "self-actualization," which is based on "a complex conception of human nature."[17] This makes Hegel's ethical theory a species of *naturalism* or *realism*, comparable to the classical naturalism of Plato and Aristotle, but differing from those accounts in its *historical* dimension: "It views the human nature to be actualized as a historical product, the result of a dialectical process of experience involving the acquisition of self-knowledge, the struggle to actualize the self, and an interaction between these activities, which modifies the self that is known and actualized" (*HET*, 33). Although he does draw attention to the importance of the notion of recognition found in the *Phenomenology*, for Wood recognition gains its significance in terms of the role it plays in the process of self-actualization. Although Kojève is not referred to, Wood's analyses share some of the salient features of the "classic" earlier account. In Wood's anthropological reconstruction of spirit we start with a fundamental human desire, the desire for "self-worth" or "self-certainty,"[18] and then move through a progressive series of historical attempts by human agents to achieve such self-certainty. Although this desire is satisfied "only through something external . . . an objectivity whose independence is done away with or 'negated'," the "attempt to achieve self-certainty through the appropriation of things proves inadequate" (*HET*, 84–85). As it turns out, this desire can be satisfied only by the recognition provided by another human subject, and so the desire for self-certainty leads to the desire for recognition.[19]

Thus the *Phenomenology* presents a "rational reconstruction of the process through which the mutual recognition of persons might have

argues, rests on philosophical foundations that are quite different from those speculative ones that Hegel put forward, and it is this autonomous Hegelian practical philosophy that Wood attempts to reconstruct in this work. Wood's work is itself strikingly successful in rendering Hegel's practical philosophy intelligible and defensible, but not so, I suggest, in its attempt to reconstruct this philosophy on grounds other than Hegel's own. As we shall see, Wood's analyses lead us back to issues at the heart of Hegel's logic of recognition.

[17] In fact, Wood identifies the notion of self-actualization as at the heart of any successful ethical theory: "If there is any hope for ethics as a branch of rational inquiry, it lies in showing how ethical conceptions and a theory of the human good can be grounded in human self-understanding. Ethics must be grounded in a knowledge of human beings that enables us to say that some forms of life are suited to our nature, whereas others are not. In that sense, ethical theories generally may be regarded as theories of human self-actualization" (*HET*, 17).

[18] "Hegel follows Fichte in regarding the human self as *fundamentally* a striving of the 'I' against the 'not-I,' of self against otherness, an impulse to overcome all otherness. . . . Hegel expresses this by saying that self consciousness is 'desire'" (*HET*, 84; emphasis added).

"Hegel's argument *begins* with his view of human beings as spiritual beings, whose *fundamental* desires include the desire to establish their self-worth through self-positing and self-interpretation" (*HET*, 90; emphases added).

[19] Wood however, avoids the contradiction at the heart of Kòjeve's account by denying that for Hegel recognition is a "transcendental condition" for self-consciousness as it is for Fichte.

developed out of simple forms of self-consciousness" (*HET*, 84). And while Hegel's account "may look more like an abstract fable than a philosophical argument," it is a reconstruction grounded in five "main theses"—namely: that "selfhood involves the desire for self-certainty"; that "self-certainty requires recognition"; that "one-sided recognition cannot succeed"; that "mutual recognition requires universal self-consciousness"; and that "recognition through universal self-consciousness requires a community of persons, standing in mutual relations of abstract right" (*HET*, 90–91).[20] These theses form, as it were, the philosophical skeleton structuring the intelligibility of the *Phenomenology*'s quasi-historical narrative, a narrative analogous to that found in traditional social contract theory.[21]

The Paradoxical Logic of Absolute Freedom

The self to be "actualized," in Wood's reconstruction of Hegel's practical philosophy, is *free*, but Wood is well aware that the Hegelian conception of freedom cannot be reduced to that concept of individual freedom which is most at home in liberal political theory: "negative freedom" or freedom *from* external constraint.[22] It is not that Hegel has no place for such a "subjective" concept, quite the reverse. Against any anti-liberal understanding of Hegel, Wood brings out the essential role that subjective freedom plays within Hegel's theory of the modern state. It is this which allows Wood to show how Hegel's political philosophy approximates the conclusions of liberalism even if it does not share its starting point. Nevertheless, the place that is given to such freedom is assigned to it by way of another, larger concept of freedom, which Hegel describes as "absolute freedom."

[20] Such an idea of a group of "fundamental theses" at the base of a philosophical position looks very much like the Fichtean understanding of philosophical system that Hegel had criticized in the *Difference* essay.

[21] We can see then how this might start to fill out the "meta-ethical" conception of Hegel's ethical theory as a type of "historicized naturalism." At the heart of the theory is a set of "anthropological" theses concerning a fundamental human drive and the conditions of its development and satisfaction. This drive is the drive for self-certainty, which plays an analogous role to that played by the drive for survival within Hobbesean political theory. (Wood himself draws the analogy to Hobbes's historical reconstruction. [*HET*, 91]). This drive can only be satisfied within the context of intersubjective recognitive relations, and it is this combination that allows Hegel's theory to be historically and culturally sensitive in ways traditional forms of ethical naturalism are not. But such sensitivity is not purchased at the expense of relativism as the social relations of different times and cultures satisfy the human drive for self-certainty to a greater or lesser extent.

[22] That is "negative freedom" in the terms of Isaiah Berlin. As Wood points out, Hegel's use of this term is somewhat different.

It is indeed the "paradoxical" notion of absolute freedom that would normally direct us to those notions at the heart of Hegel's speculative logic. Hegel discusses absolute freedom in terms of the idea of "being with oneself in another," a phrase redolent with that "coincidence of opposites" at the heart of his logic. But for Wood, such a paradox need not scandalize us "once its point is properly understood," and understanding it does not require any "new system of 'dialectical logic'" (*HET*, 46). However, this attempt to save Hegel from either scandal or dialectical logic in explicating the point of this paradoxical phrase does not succeed.

Concerned with avoiding the metaphysical labyrinths surrounding the notion of spirit, Wood models spirit on the Fichtean absolute ego, understood as "not some metaphysical entity distinct from your self and mine, but a transcendental structure or type necessarily exemplified by any particular self" (*HET*, 18). Here too, he understands the type of freedom that Hegel attributes to spirit—absolute freedom—on the analogy of the type of freedom available to an individual self-actualizing subject. "Freedom for Hegel is a relational property. It involves a self, an object (in the widest sense of that term), and a rational project of the self. Any object, simply as object, is an 'other' to the self whose object it is" (*HET*, 47).

From this formulation, it would appear that freedom is a characteristic of a type of intentional relation between a subject and its object, a relationship structured in terms of the subject's *project*. (This is, after all, simply what we mean when we standardly attribute freedom to a *will*.) But a level of complexity is added with Hegel's Fichtean idea that the "essence of selfhood is the tendency to absolute self-activity or self-sufficiency," that is, the self's tendency to free itself from dependency on all that is *other* than itself. Thus "the rational project of the self" within which self and other are intentionally linked must be conceived of as one that involves the *overcoming* of the "otherness" of the object. For Wood's Hegel: "True independence in relation to another is achieved . . . by struggling with otherness, overcoming it, and making it our own" (*HET*, 48). And so: "[B]ecause a self is actual by identifying itself with a set of rational projects involving objects, the otherness of an object can be overcome when the object is integrated into the self's rational projects" (*HET*, 47).

The *Philosophy of Right*, according to Wood, presents us with four types of "object" that provide candidates for the self's project of "making its own": the will's own *given* determinations (for example, natural desires); external objects (for example, things owned); the subject's own actions and their consequences (equivalent to the moral attitude of taking responsibility for one's actions); and social institutions. The sorts of normative considerations determining which among the objects belonging to these different ranges would be appropriate for one's identification have to do with which can be *rationally* integrated into those existing projects and relations to objects which make up one's existing identity.

It is presumably the simple schema of freedom as a "relational property" that is behind Wood's hope that such paradoxical formulae as "being with oneself in another" can be rendered intelligible in the range of structures available to a *nondialectical* logic. However, such a schema is not adequate to the attempt to render intelligible the relation between individual selves and those "objects" listed above. As we have seen, for Hegel a subject's relation to "objects" such as its property or its own actions can be only superficially considered in terms of the schema of a simple relation *to an object.* In all such cases it turns out that such a relation holds only because simultaneously other subjects recognize it as holding. That is, while the property relation, for example, *looks like* a relation between the owner and the thing owned, it is in fact, dependent on a relation *between* owners: the "relation of will to will is the true distinctive ground in which freedom has its *existence*" (*PR,* §71). Furthermore, we have learned from chapter 4 of the *Phenomenology* what fate awaits us when we approach another subject with the idea that "true independence" in relation to it was to be achieved "by struggling with (its) otherness, overcoming it, and making it our own."

As Robert Williams has pointed out, for Hegel the action of recognition necessarily involves an "action" that runs counter to that of "making one's own,"—an action of *releasing* (*Entlassen*) that other, "granting the other the freedom to recognize or withhold recognition" because "the recognition that really counts is the recognition from the other that is not at the disposal of the self."[23] That is, starting with his individual concept of the will and its freedom, Wood has been led into an arena of "objects" and "relations" which cannot be understood with the conceptual tools at hand (which belong to what Hegel calls the "logic of the understanding"). Such tools have a coherent application only *within* the framework of a single "fixed" perspective, but Wood has been led into the realm of "spirit" as that complex of recognitive relations existing *between* opposed perspectives, a realm for which Hegel felt the need for a new conceptual architecture, a new logic.

By collapsing the Hegelian notion of spirit into the more Fichtean thought of the generic ego, Wood has interpreted an idea at the heart of Hegel's approach to freedom—"self-sufficiency"—along lines dictated by the meaning such a term takes on in the context of its application to an

[23] Robert R. Williams, *Recognition: Fichte and Hegel on the Other* (Albany: State University of New York Press, 1992), 155.

individual.[24] Self-sufficiency thus comes to be understood as autonomy and independence from others: aspiring to this state, one would be driven to release oneself from the influence of others by struggling with such influence, overcoming it, appropriating it. But for Hegel, the "self-sufficiency" of spirit (or its capacity to "stand alone"—its *Selbstständigkeit*) means more the capacity of a spiritual *system* to "posit" its own "presuppositions."

In this context, to grasp human political existence in terms of the notion of self-sufficient spirit is to grasp it in terms of its ability to sustain subjects with rich enough theoretical and practical intentionality to make them capable of leading free and rational lives. And while the drive for self-sufficiency will play a *role* in those lives—a role provided by the modern institutions of civil society—this will not be at the expense of opposed contexts where this sort of autonomy is *relinquished*—typically, in the close relationships of the family.[25] These latter forms of individual relation to self and others are not just unfortunate limitations or inconveniences resulting from the fact that our rational subjectivity is mired in resistant nature. Rather, they are part of the whole infrastructure of our intentional lives, and they play positive roles. We might see Hegel as concerned in a Leibnizian way with the "harmonization" of these opposed perspectives from which individuals understand and act in the world, but for him such harmonization is something to be created rather than discovered. There can be no appeal, as in Leibniz, to an external harmonizer who determined or "posited" the system as having some determinate harmonious architecture: *it* must be self-positing and self-sufficient, and so the "positing" must come from within. Wood clearly grasps this latter point with the emphasis he places on the notion of "self-actualization," but his tendency to conceive of spirit on the analogy of the individual ego obscures this insight. Again, it would seem that because of a reluctance to venture beyond the "logic of the understanding" with its implicit semantic and ontological commitments, Wood is unable to do justice to the full richness of Hegel's social and ethical thought.

[24] The tension in Wood's Fichtean reading of Hegel's concept of freedom is apparent when Wood describes Hegel as "simultaneously a proponent and a critic of the radical Fichtean idea of freedom as 'absolute self-activity'" (*HET,* 44).

[25] In marriage, individuals "give up" (*aufgeben*) their natural and individual personalities (*PR,* §162); each partner "surrenders or sacrifices" (*hingebt*) his or her "personality or immediate exclusive singularity [*Einzelheit*]" (*PR,* §167).

CONCLUSION

The Nature of Hegelian Philosophy

I HAVE SUGGESTED that the structures of family and civil society are adequate to the development of perceiving and understanding forms of subjectivity respectively. Could it be then that analogously the state as circle of these particular circles will be for Hegel the recognitive context adequate to *reason* and, hence, philosophy itself? Indeed it would seem that for Hegel there *is* a systematic connection between philosophy and the state. Thus he notes in the preface to the *Philosophy of Right* that "philosophy with us is not in any case practised as a private art, as it was with the Greeks, for example, but has a public existence [*Existenz*], impinging upon the public, especially—or solely—in the service of the state" (*PR*, p. 17). Perhaps this nexus will allow us to understand further Hegel's thought about both.

Kant and Hegel on Philosophy and Politics

The deep and systematic significance of the monarch's addition of the singularity of form to a universal content, the "I will" added to the universal law expressing the common interest, is brought out by Hegel in the remark to paragraph 280 of the *Philosophy of Right*, where he notes that the transition to the singularity of the monarch "is of a purely speculative nature, and its cognition accordingly belongs to logical philosophy," and in which he refers us to his discussion of the nature of the will in the introduction to that work. There the conception of the will's *form* being added to an

238

empirical content is perhaps most clearly demonstrated in the idea of the difference between the human will and the merely natural desire of the animal. The addition to paragraph 11 notes that the animal has "drives, desires, and inclinations, but . . . no will." Whereas, as had been earlier learned, an essential aspect of the will is its ability to extract itself from any content, the animal "must obey its drive if nothing external prevents it." This means that we cannot think of the human will as something like animal desire even when it has a natural content. If the will has a natural content, then the willing agent must have given this to itself: "The drive is part of nature, but to posit it in this 'I' depends upon my will" (PR, §11 addition). That is, in order for a natural desire to become a part of the intentional economy of the human agent it has to have added to its content the form "I will."[1] In fact, what is being expressed here in the context of a discussion of practical reason seems nothing less than Hegel's version of the Kantian "I think" able to accompany all mental representation—the Kantian "transcendental unity of self-consciousness."[2]

Hegel was of course critical of the pure formality of the Kantian transcendental subject with its abstract opposition to the empirical self: here was yet another case of abstract opposition between singular and universal needing the mediation of another self-consciousness for its resolution. Might we not learn something about Hegel's conception of philosophy by taking seriously his insistence on the monarch in an otherwise basically "republican" polity?

We might recall Kant's republicanism here. In the pamphlet *Perpetual Peace* a gesture is made toward deriving republicanism from the fundamental principles of logic itself, the rationality of the republican constitution being demonstrated with an analogy to the structure of the syllogism: "Every form of government which is not representative is, properly speaking, without form. The legislator can unite in one and the same person his function as legislative and as executor of his will just as little as the universal of the major premise in a syllogism can also be the subsumption of the particular under the universal in the minor."[3] To understand Kant's reasoning here we must first understand that for Kant the relevant political

---

[1] On the analogy to the monarch's utterance we might suppose that properly willing an otherwise natural desire involves giving it a description so that the sentence "I will . . . " can be completed. For Hegel the act of "positing" (*Setzen*) does not produce a content from nowhere; it has presuppositions (*Voraussetzungen*). We might think of positing one's presuppositions as an act that involves raising something natural and given to the level of representation by giving it an interpretation.

[2] Kant, *Critique of Pure Reason*, trans. Norman Kemp Smith (New York: Macmillan, 1929), B131–32.

[3] Immanuel Kant, "Perpetual Peace," trans. Lewis White Beck, in *Kant on History* (Indianapolis: Bobbs-Merrill, 1963), 96.

contrast to be made is between republicanism and despotism and that the difference between these two political forms hangs on the relationship that exists between the legislative and executive functions in each. A republican constitution is one that subordinates the actions of a particular executive to a representative legislature that can give expression to the public will—essentially, the Rousseauian *volonté générale*. In contrast, despotism exists where the executive itself legislates, that is, where "the public will is administered by the ruler as his own will."[4]

If we now extend the idea of Kant's republicanism backwards from his politics to his epistemology, we can discern something of the Copernicanism present in Kant himself and developed by later post-Kantian epistemologists such as Peirce, Popper, Habermas, and Bernard Williams.[5] From this position, what characterizes science's rationality is not any access to certain contents but its self-correcting mode of development within a freely communicating and deliberating body of scientists: objectivity is conceived as what scientific opinion converges toward when mutual criticism within a community of inquirers can free the experience feeding into that opinion of the particular and idiosyncratic. That is, the more the members of the scientific community can, like Rousseau's *citoyens*, free their cognition from the determinations they received as particularized *hommes*, the more they can approach objectivity—*pensée générale*. We have seen what for Hegel is missing from Kant's republican polity. Might not such "republican" epistemologies suffer from the same logical flaw?

As we have seen, republicanism, according to Hegel, provides no mechanism within which subjects can recognize themselves *in their singularity* within that legislation that is meant to manifest the common will. For Hegel, this negative relation between a singular subject and a legislative content was evident in the course of the French Revolution. The Rousseauian revolutionary subject could grasp itself as universal, as *citoyen*, only in bracketing all that which constituted its own singular determinacy

---

[4] Ibid. Kant's argument here is reminiscent of Wittgenstein's well-known arguments against the idea of a private rule or a private language. For Wittgenstein, where there exists no *external* criterion against which any application of a rule could be judged—that is, where legislation and execution are one—there can be no sense in which that which is being applied *is* a rule. Kant's basic idea here seems to be the same: "To conform to the *concept* of law," he claims, "government must have a representative form, and in this system only a republican mode of government is possible; without it, government is despotic and arbitrary" (ibid., 97; emphasis added). The act of the nonrepublican form of government would be arbitrary rather than lawful because there would be no external standard against which the act could ever be judged. There could be no fact of the matter as to whether the act was an *application* of an existing law or a further *determination* of that law.

[5] Onora O'Neill has brought out the political dimension of Kant's epistemology in "Vindicating Reason" in *The Cambridge Companion to Kant*, ed. Paul Guyer (Cambridge: Cambridge University Press, 1992).

and difference, its status as *homme*. But no political structure could survive the fanatical purism of such a critical subject—all attempts to establish political institutions would be seen as expressing factional, that is, particular, rather than general interests. For Hegel this process was acted out in the Revolutionary Terror—"a time of trembling and quaking and of intolerance towards everything particular. For fanaticism wills only what is abstract, not what is articulated, so that whenever differences emerge, it finds them incompatible with its own indeterminacy and cancels them. This is why the people, during the French Revolution, destroyed once more the institutions they had themselves created, because all institutions are incompatible with the abstract self-consciousness of equality" (*PR*, §5 addition). And as we have seen from chapter 3 of Hegel's *Phenomenology of Spirit*, such a mode of progress within the sciences must inevitably be at the expense of all that is *singular* in experience. The inverse side of the process of the "deepening" of a subject's knowledge of the world will issue in the paradoxical result that the "world" as known will become ever further distant from the world originally inquired into—the world the inquirer otherwise lives "within." The perspectivism and subjectivity built into these latter notions is precisely what has been given up in the course of making one's knowledge more objective.

The objectivity of the world of *Verstand* had been purchased at the cost of the loss of truth to the experienced world of each singular subject. We might say, then, that from the point of view of the fate of singularity, republican politics and the abstract understanding of the positive sciences present the same problem: their products cannot be recognized as expressions of the experience of *subjects* at all. The positive sciences produce knowledge "without a [singular] knowing subject" just as republican politics produce the lawful principles for anonymous intentional action, a "general will" without *a* willing subject.

All this has important effects for the very nature of the knowledge produced. First, it bears on issues to do with the practical applicability of knowledge. Cognitively depriving the singular subject of its "manifest world" (or "life-world"), the objectivizing sciences deprive that subject of a world to act *in* and leave it only with a world of objects to act *on*. As Heidegger has emphasized in this century, practical knowledge thus becomes purely technical or instrumental.[6]

These are problems of modern *scientistic culture* commonly pointed to by its critics. For Hegel, they all follow from the logic of republican thought, the logic that cannot assign a place to singularity. But rather than abandon

---

[6] Cf., for example, Martin Heidegger, *The Question concerning Technology and Other Essays*, trans. William Lovitt (New York: Harper and Row, 1977).

reason itself, Hegel contrasts the impersonality of *Verstand* with the *vernünftig* thought of philosophy, which operates with the conceptual structures of "concept-logic," structures within which it is possible to find a place for universality, particularity, *and* singularity.

We might hazard then that just as the monarch is required for the insertion of singularity into the general will, so too will some analogous *philosophical* subject need to be inserted into the dynamics of philosophical reason. But here it must be remembered that for Hegel the will of the monarch receives the entirety of its *content* from the impersonal rational procedures of a universal legislature: the monarch's task is to add the form of the "I will it." And so in terms of its *content*, the thinking activity of the philosopher must be in something of the same situation. Hegel's *vernünftig* philosophical thought, cannot, as it were, generate a content independently of the results of the *Verstand*-based sciences: the philosopher, in a position analogous to that of the king, adds an "I think" to thought contents that have been produced in such a way that they achieved the status of universality but with the cost of impersonality and anonymity. And like the monarchical "I," the philosophical "I" must be an irreducibly singular and finite one, located in a particular time and place, subject to local, idiosyncratic, and groundless conditions. Thus philosophy is "its own time comprehended in thoughts" (*PR*, preface, p. 21).

With this necessity placed on the distinctness of the philosopher from the scientist in that he or she speaks from a position that includes the singularity of his or her own experience of the world, we have reached a position that is complementary to that which was reached at the conclusion of the *Science of Logic*. I have earlier stressed that the discussion of philosophical method with which that work concludes be understood equally as representation and exemplification *of* method. As representation, it has the reflexivity of science—it reflects on the general categories involved in thought itself and the relations and processes these enter into. But as method, it *is* that which it is also the general concept *of*. Functioning at this pragmatic level of exemplification, Hegel's act is a vehicle, the "middle," of an act directed toward the reader who is thereby posited as rational. It is a recognitive/performative "word." And as a word in which a reader can recognize himself or herself qua singularity, this word must come from another who can also be recognized as singular. That philosophical knowledge acquires its own unity and coherence, it must be because the philosopher is, qua philosopher, a singular and naturally grounded subject for whom theoretical and practical aspects of cognitive functioning cannot be simply severed from each other as they are for the scientist.

Regarded in the light of this latter aspect, philosophy might be seen as having cultural features more commonly associated with art and religion than with science. It would share with art a resistance to that sort of generalizing in which singular and immediate aspects of thought and experience were factored out, and with religion, a performative dimension involving the *institution* of a some type of relation between self and other and world.[7] Furthermore, just as we tend to think of the public and professional lives of artists and priests as not so neatly divided from their more naturally rooted personal existence as in contrast to the professional and personal lives of scientists, so too, presumably, might we consider the activity of the philosopher in such a way. Finally, the enduring element of singularity within the realm of philosophy would seem to mean that philosophical knowledge could never be completed in any sense of having achieved some final or absolute view of the world, a view in which the singularity of the knower were totally eclipsed. Philosophical knowledge would have to be remade over again for each particular age, indeed, for each single subject, aspiring to it, because the intersubjective recognitive relations adequate to it could not suppress the difference or newness of each age or interlocutor that came to it.

Hegel and the Limits of Philosophy

Since the late eighteenth century, the type of debate about the nature of value of modern life and thought which we have seen exemplified in the opposition between the views of Adam Smith and Jean-Jacques Rousseau has never really abated. In the following century, the hermeneutic-historicist outlook was itself linked with a nostalgic romantic movement that considered modernity more as a threat than a promise. And in our century, Heidegger, possibly more than any other single thinker, was able to give a philosophical voice to widely shared and deeply felt concerns about the spirit of the modern world. (Here, Heidegger's influence has been all the more remarkable given the appalling political paths he followed, apparently guided by such concerns.)

Given the emblematic role played by the new science in the birth of the modern world, it is not surprising that the stakes of reason itself have been bound up with that of modernity. The hermeneutic approach was able to adopt its own culturalist approach to reason and its role in modernity, comparing the value of organizing personal or collective life in such a way

---

[7] Philosophy's relation to religious thought is somewhat parallel to that of science in that philosophy and religion share the same *content*. In the former, however, this content is in the form of *Vorstellungen* (representations) while in the latter it is in the form of *der Begriff* (the concept).

with that of other ways, which are based, for example, on the unquestioning acceptance of tradition. And naturally, the stakes of philosophy itself have risen and fallen with those of reason. Thus it is not surprising that philosophy has commonly come to have a generally "deflationary" tone, as was commented on in the introductory chapter. Perhaps this tone is best summed up in the "ironism" advocated by a prominent apostate from scientific philosophy and advocate of "hermeneutics," Richard Rorty.[8]

Under these sorts of cultural conditions Hegel tends to get regarded in contradictory ways. For Rorty, for example, Hegel is the thinker who introduced a historicist, hermeneutic dimension to philosophy, which would break through and rid intellectual and cultural life of the anachronistic and discardable Greek framework that Hegel himself had inherited from his philosophical forebears.[9] Earlier we saw something of the same attitude toward Hegel in Gadamer's picture of the richly hermeneutic thinker who was nevertheless defeated by the lure of dogmatic metaphysics. Others, however, focusing on Hegel's pretensions to a complete philosophical system and to the standpoint of "absolute knowledge" have seen him as the representative of all that is evil in the advocacy of an imperialistic and totalizing reason—the last of the pre-modern metaphysicans.[10]

Many of these assessments of Hegel are, of course, made on the basis of a general understanding of his work as a whole which I have attempted to dispel throughout this book. It would seem, however, that many of Hegel's critics tend to have an even more *general* objection lying beyond this—an objection to the "hubris" of the commitment to "reason" found within the philosophical tradition as a whole, and within Hegel's philosophy, given his own situating of his thought as at the culmination of this tradition. In a sense *this* critique of philosophy *is* just an extension of Hegel's own objection to the imperialistic *Verstand,* but Hegel thought he had freed philosophy from the equation of rationality with *Verstand* with his own conception of *Vernunft.* The deeper question here is whether or not *any* reinterpretation of the nature of rationality (and so the nature of philosophical thought) would be acceptable to these critics. And this question bears on no less an issue than the nature of that which one advocates as providing a framework for the conscious reflection on and guiding of individual and collective life. Hegel had enough in common with the earlier Enlightenment to think that "reason," and hence philosophy, could aspire to such a

[8] Cf. Richard Rorty, *Contingency, Irony, and Solidarity* (Cambridge: Cambridge University Press, 1989).

[9] See, for example, Richard Rorty, *Consequences of Pragmatism* (Minneapolis: University of Minnesota Press, 1982), chaps. 1 and 8.

[10] This seems to be the approach of Emmanuel Levinas in *Totality and Infinity: An Essay on Exteriority,* trans. Alphonso Lingis (The Hague: Nijhoff, 1969).

goal. At the end of the twentieth century, such a view is contested just as widely, if not more widely, than it has been at any other time in the last few hundred years of European intellectual life. But perhaps here the crucial question being begged is: *reason in contrast to what?* Are we meant to deflate our expectations about reason to the extent that our choices are meant to be articulated in some other way?

We might take the views of Gadamer as representative here. For Gadamer, it would seem that there are insights that would be ultimately *denied* to philosophy regardless of how it were to be conceived—insights such as the Aeschylean tragic wisdom, which is "ultimately a *religious* insight" (*TM*, 356–57; emphasis added). Given that Greek tragedy was, from our viewpoint, simultaneously a religious and an artistic product, we could expand on Gadamer's statement here and refer to "religious" and/ or "aesthetic" insights that he conceives as somehow denied to philosophy.

Hegel thought of *Vernunft* as rich enough to incorporate such insights, but Gadamer's idea that these lie *beyond* philosophy complements a position that is, in contrast, more skeptical and more *Kantian*. Thus in his foreword to the second edition of *Truth and Method*, commenting on his own phenomenological-hermeneutic methodology—a "fundamental methodical approach [which] avoids implying any metaphysical conclusions"—Gadamer goes on to acknowledge his "acceptance of Kant's conclusions in the *Critique of Pure Reason:* I regard statements that proceed by wholly dialectical means from the finite to the infinite, from human experience to what exists in itself, from the temporal to the eternal, as doing no more than setting limits, and am convinced that philosophy can derive no actual knowledge from them" (*TM*, xxxvi).

Here Gadamer implies that even the dialectic of Hegel be considered as a process that proceeds from "statements" and aspires to "actual knowledge" or "metaphysical conclusions"—an assumption that seems to run in the face of all that Hegel says of the philosophical method from his earliest critique of Fichte to his critique of formal logic in the *Science of Logic*. Furthermore, rather than have it that philosophical thought is *incapable* of the type of "insights" that can be conveyed in religion or art, Hegel's claim is more that philosophical thought or reason itself is already based on or presupposes such insights. This is meant, of course, not in the sense that philosophical statements can be shown to presuppose "statements" of that type logically, but rather in the sense that philosophical thought or reason pragmatically presupposes a certain kind of "community" based on orientations toward the world and others more typically dealt with in artistic or religious ways.[11]

---

[11] Indeed, Gadamer's apparent dichotomizing of reason and "insight" (philosophy and

The two centuries that have passed since Hegel first started to work on that body of writing which was to become his philosophical legacy have, of course, seen changes within global life unimaginable to a person of his place and time. But if there is one idea that European culture has been disabused of during this time of transformation, it is that such changes can be intelligibly ordered according to the simple, unitary idea of "progress." Indeed, the problematization of this idea is often expressed in terms of a rejection of Hegel, who is regarded as exemplifying such a naïve and flawed approach to history, indeed, as having raised it to the level of metaphysical necessity. But such a view of Hegel is centered on an understanding of his philosophy which I have contested throughout this book. (Moreover, such a rejection is often premissed on the idea that this is a view that we have simply *progressed* beyond.) As we have seen, Hegel's approach to progress is not that exemplified by Adam Smith; it rightly contains a rejection of such a one-sided view as well of that of its inversion, exemplified by Rousseau. We might say, that for Hegel, history with its positive and negative evaluations was something that was not to be simply *presupposed*; it was something that was to be *posited*. That means, it was something that had to be raised to the level of interpretation and recognition, or, as Gadamer puts it, "integrated" into the present: "Hegel states a definite truth, inasmuch as the essential nature of the historical spirit consists not in the restoration of the past but in thoughtful mediation with contemporary life" (*TM*, 168–69).

My argument has been that, because of fundamental misunderstandings of his philosophy, such an approach to Hegel himself has yet to be even tried. But the need for some coherent philosophical approach to the complex world we have inherited, an approach that has learned from the failures of those one-sided forms of philosophy diagnosed by Hegel, is as pressing as ever. Up until now, the resurgence of interest in Hegelian thought characteristic of the last few decades has been largely concerned with working a way out of the labyrinth of those traditional interpretations which have dominated the reception of Hegel but which are now being increasingly recognized as inadequate to his thought. Here I have tried to do no more than take a few tentative steps in such a direction. What remains to be seen is what a real attempt at a "thoughtful mediation" of Hegelian philosophy into the present would look like and what its results might be.

---

religion/art) seems to imply that reason is possible *without* insight. But Hegel's attempts were, as we have seen, constantly directed to showing how all cognitive activity presupposed complex recognitive activities and relations with their accompanying "insights." And this applied especially to the "formal" type of reasoning elaborated within "*Verstand*," the "*Verstandeslogik*" at the heart of the entire post-Aristotelian philosophical tradition.

Bibliography

Allison, Henry E. *Benedict de Spinoza: An Introduction.* New Haven: Yale University Press, 1987.
——. *Kant's Transcendental Idealism: An Interpretation and Defense.* New Haven: Yale University Press, 1983.
Aristotle. *The Complete Works of Aristotle: The Revised Oxford Translation.* Princeton: Princeton University Press, 1984.
Beiser, Frederick C. *The Fate of Reason: German Philosophy from Kant to Fichte.* Cambridge, Mass.: Harvard University Press, 1987.
Bell, David. *Spinoza in Germany from 1670 to the Age of Goethe.* London: Institute of Germanic Studies, University of London, 1984.
Bencivenga, Ermanno. *Kant's Copernican Revolution.* Oxford: Oxford University Press, 1987.
Bernstein, J. M. "From Self-Consciousness to Community: Act and Recognition in the Master-Slave Relationship." In *The State and Civil Society: Studies in Hegel's Political Philosophy,* edited by Z. A. Pelczynski. Cambridge: Cambridge University Press, 1984.
Blumenberg, Hans. *The Genesis of the Copernican World.* Translated by Robert M. Wallace. Cambridge, Mass.: M.I.T. Press, 1987.
Breazeale, Daniel, and Tom Rockmore, eds. *Fichte: Historical Contexts/Contemporary Controversies.* Atlantic Highlands: Humanities Press, 1994.
Brod, Harry. *Hegel's Philosophy of Politics.* Boulder, Colo.: Westview Press, 1992.
Burke, Edmund. *Reflections on the Revolution in France.* Harmondsworth: Penguin, 1969.
Cavell, Stanley. "The Avoidance of Love." In *Must We Mean What We Say? A Book of Essays.* Cambridge: Cambridge University Press, 1976.
——. *The World Viewed.* Enlarged edition. Cambridge, Mass.: Harvard University Press, 1979.
Chladenius, Johann. *Introduction to the Correct Interpretation of Reasonable Discourses and*

Writings. Translated by Carrie Asman-Schneider in *The Hermeneutics Reader*, edited by Kurt Mueller-Vollmer. Oxford: Blackwell, 1986.

Cloeren, Hermann J. *Language and Thought: German Approaches to Analytic Philosophy in the Eighteenth and Nineteenth Centuries*. Berlin: de Gruyter, 1988.

Craig, Edward. *The Mind of God and the Works of Man*. Oxford: Clarendon Press, 1987.

Descartes, René. *The Philosophical Writings of Descartes*. Translated by John Cottingham, Robert Stoothoff, and Dugald Murdoch. 2 vols. Cambridge: Cambridge University Press, 1984.

deVries, Willem A. *Hegel's Theory of Mental Activity: An Introduction to Theoretical Spirit*. Ithaca: Cornell University Press, 1988.

Dilthey, Wilhelm. *Gesammelte Schriften*. Göttingen-Stuttgart: Vandenhoeck and Ruprecht, 1914–1977.

——. *Selected Writings*. Edited and translated by H. P. Rickman. Cambridge: Cambridge University Press, 1976.

Dove, Kenley. "Hegel's Phenomenological Method." In *New Studies in Hegel's Philosophy*, edited by W. Steinkraus. New York: Holt, Rinehart & Winston, 1971.

Droysen, Johann Gustav. *Historik: Vorlesungen über Enzyklopädie und Methodologie der Geschichte*. Edited by R. Hübner. Munich: R. Oldenbourg, 1977.

Düsing, Edith. "Genesis des Selbstbewusstseins durch Anerkennung and Liebe." In *Hegels Theorie des subjectiven Geistes*, edited by Lothar Eley. Stuttgart-Bad Cannstatt: Frommann-Holzboog, 1990.

——. *Intersubjectivität und Selbstbewusstsein*. Köln: Dinter Verlag, 1986.

Düsing, Klaus. "Absolute Identität und Formen der Endlichkeit: Interpretationen zu Schellings und Hegels erster absoluter Metaphysik." In *Schellings und Hegels erste absolute Metaphysik (1801–1802)* edited by Klaus Düsing. Köln: Jürgen Dinter, 1988.

Elliston, Frederick, and Peter McCormick, eds. *Husserl: Shorter Works*. Notre Dame: University of Notre Dame Press, 1981.

Engel, S. Morris. "Kant's Copernican Analogy: A Re-examination." *Kant-Studien* 59 (1963): 243–51.

Ermarth, Michael. *Wilhelm Dilthey: The Critique of Historical Reason*. Chicago: University of Chicago Press, 1978.

Ewing, A. C. *A Short Commentary on Kant's "Critique of Pure Reason."* Chicago: University of Chicago Press, 1938.

Ferry, Luc. *Political Philosophy 1: Rights—The New Quarrel between the Ancients and the Moderns*. Translated by Franklin Philip. Chicago: University of Chicago Press, 1990.

Fichte, J. G. *Early Philosophical Writings*. Translated and edited by Daniel Breazeale. Ithaca: Cornell University Press, 1988.

——. *Gesamtausgabe der Bayerischen Academie der Wissenschaften*. Stuttgart Bad-Cannstadt: Friedrich Frommann, 1964–.

——. *The Science of Knowledge*. Edited by Peter Heath and John Lachs. Cambridge: Cambridge University Press, 1982.

——. *The Science of Rights*. Translated by A. E. Kroeger. Philadelphia: Lippincott, 1869.

Flay, Joseph. *Hegel's Quest for Certainty*. Albany: State University of New York Press, 1984.

Forster, Michael N. *Hegel and Skepticism*. Cambridge Mass.: Harvard University Press, 1989.

Fukuyama, Francis. "The End of History?" *The National Interest* 16 (Summer 1989): 3–18.

——. *The End of History and the Last Man*. New York: Free Press, 1992.

Gadamer, Hans-Georg. *Hegel's Dialectic: Five Hermeneutical Studies*. Translated by P. Christopher Smith. New Haven: Yale University Press, 1976.

——. *Truth and Method*. 2d rev. ed. Translation revised by Joel Weinsheimer and Donald G. Marshall. New York: Crossroad, 1992.

Galilei, Galileo. "The Assayer." Reprinted in *Philosophy of Science*, edited by Arthur Danto and Sidney Morgenbesser. Cleveland: Meridian Books, 1960.

——. *Dialogue concerning the Two Chief World Systems*. Translated by Stillman Drake. Berkeley: University of California Press, 1967.

Habermas, Jürgen. "Labor and Interaction: Remarks on Hegel's Jena *Philosophy of Mind*." In *Theory and Practice*, trans. John Viertel. Boston: Beacon Press, 1974.

Hamann, J. G. "Metacritique of the Purism of Reason." Translated in *J. G. Hamann, 1730–1788: A Study in Christian Existence, with Selections from His Writings*, by R. G. Smith. London: Collins, 1960.

Hanson, Norwood Russell. "Copernicus' Role in Kant's Revolution." *Journal of the History of Ideas* 20 (1959): 274–81.

Harries, Karsten. "Descartes, Perspective, and the Angelic Eye." *Yale French Studies* 49 (1973): 28–42.

Harris, H. S. *Hegel's Development: Toward the Sunlight, 1770–1801*. Oxford: Clarendon Press, 1972.

——. "Hegel's System of Ethical Life: An Interpretation." In *Hegel's System of Ethical Life and First Philosophy of Spirit*, edited and translated by T. M. Knox and H. S. Harris. Albany: State University of New York Press, 1979.

——. "Skepticism, Dogmatism, and Speculation in the Critical Journal." In *Between Kant and Hegel*, edited by George di Giovanni and H. S. Harris. Albany: State University of New York Press, 1985.

Hartmann, Klaus. "Hegel: A Non-Metaphysical View." In *Hegel: A Collection of Critical Essays*, edited by Alasdair MacIntyre. Notre Dame: University of Notre Dame Press, 1976.

——. "On Taking the Transcendental Turn." *Review of Metaphysics* 20 (1966): 223–49.

Heidegger, Martin. *Being and Time*. Translated by John Macquarrie and Edward Robinson. Oxford: Blackwell, 1967.

——. *Hegel's Concept of Experience*. Translated by K. R. Dove. New York: Harper and Row, 1971.

——. *The Question concerning Technology and Other Essays*. Translated by William Lovitt. New York: Harper and Row, 1977.

Heine, Heinrich. *Religion and Philosophy in Germany*. Translated by John Snodgrass. Boston: Beacon Press, 1959.

Henrich, Dieter. "Fichte's Original Insight." Translated by David R. Lachterman in *Contemporary German Philosophy*, Vol. 1, 1982, edited by Darrel E. Christensen et al. University Park: Pennsylvania State University Press, 1982.

——. "Logische Form und Reale Totalität: Über die Begriffsform von Hegels eigentlichem Staatsbegriff." In *Hegels Philosophie des Rechts: Die Theorie der Rechtsformen und ihre Logik*, edited by D. Henrich and R.-P. Horstmann, 428–50. Stuttgart: Klett-Cotta, 1982.

Hösle, Vittorio. *Hegels System*. 2 vols. Hamburg: Meiner Verlag, 1987.

Houlgate, Stephen. *Freedom, Truth, and History: An Introduction to Hegel's Philosophy*. London: Routledge, 1991.

Humboldt, Wilhelm von. *Werke in Fünf Bänden*. Stuttgart: Cotta, 1960–1981.

Husserl, Edmund. *Phenomenology and the Crisis of Philosophy*. New York: Harper and Row, 1965.

Iggers, G. G. *The German Conception of History*. New York: Columbia University Press, 1968.

Ilting, K.-H. "The Structure of Hegel's *Philosophy of Right.*" In *Hegel's Political Philosophy: Problems and Perspectives,* edited by Z. A. Pelczynski. Cambridge: Cambridge University Press, 1971.

Jacob, Margaret C. *The Radical Enlightenment: Pantheists, Freemasons, and Republicans.* London: Allan and Unwin, 1981.

Jacobi, F. H. *Werke.* Edited by Friedrich Roth and Friedrich Kloppen. Darmstadt: Wissenschaftliche Buchgesellschaft, 1968.

Jurist, Elliot L. "Hegel's Concept of Recognition." *The Owl of Minerva* 19 (1987): 5–22.

Kant, Immanuel. *Critique of Judgment.* Translated by Werner S. Pulhar. Indianapolis: Hackett, 1987.

——. *Critique of Pure Reason.* Translated by Norman Kemp Smith. New York: Macmillan, 1929.

——. *The Metaphysical Elements of Justice.* Translated by John Ladd. Indianapolis: Bobbs-Merrill, 1965.

——. "Perpetual Peace." Translated by Lewis White Beck, in *Kant on History.* Indianapolis: Bobbs-Merrill, 1963.

——. *Prolegomena to Any Future Metaphysics.* Translated by Lewis White Beck. Indianapolis: Bobbs-Merrill, 1950.

Kierkegaard, Søren. *Concluding Unscientific Postscript.* Translated by David F. Swenson and Walter Lowrie. Princeton: Princeton University Press, 1941.

Kirk, G. S., J. E. Raven, and M. Schofield, eds. *The Presocratic Philosophers : A Critical History with a Selection of Texts.* 2d ed. Cambridge: Cambridge University Press, 1983.

Kojève, Alexandre. *Introduction to the Reading of Hegel.* Edited by Allan Bloom. Translated by J. H. Nichols, Jr. New York: Basic Books, 1969.

Kolb, David. *The Critique of Pure Modernity.* Chicago: University of Chicago Press, 1986.

Koyré, Alexandre. *From the Closed World to the Infinite Universe.* New York: Harper, 1958.

Kuhn, Thomas. *The Copernican Revolution.* Cambridge, Mass.: Harvard University Press, 1957.

——. *The Structure of Scientific Revolutions.* Chicago: University of Chicago Press, 1962.

Lacan, Jacques. "The Mirror Phase." In *Écrits: A Selection.* London: Tavistock, 1977.

Lakoff, George. *Women, Fire, and Dangerous Things: What Categories Reveal about the Mind.* Chicago: University of Chicago Press, 1987.

Leibniz, Gottfried. *Discourse on Metaphysics / Correspondence with Arnauld / Monadology.* Translated by George R. Montgomery. La Salle: Open Court, 1973.

Levinas, Emmanuel. *Totality and Infinity: An Essay on Exteriority.* Translated by Alphonso Lingis. The Hague: Nijhoff, 1969.

Livingstone, Donald W. *Hume's Philosophy of Common Life.* Chicago: University of Chicago Press, 1984.

Makkreel, Rudolf A. *Imagination and Interpretation in Kant: The Hermeneutical Import of the "Critique of Judgment."* Chicago: University of Chicago Press, 1990.

Marcuse, Herbert. *Reason and Revolution: Hegel and the Rise of Social Theory.* Boston: Beacon Press, 1960.

Matthews, H. E. "Strawson on Transcendental Idealism." *Philosophical Quarterly* 19 (1969): 204–20.

Montesquieu. *The Spirit of the Laws.* Translated by T. Nugent. New York: Hafner, 1962.

Mueller-Vollmer, Kurt, ed. *The Hermeneutics Reader.* Oxford: Blackwell, 1986.

Nagel, Thomas. *The View from Nowhere.* New York: Oxford University Press, 1986.

———. "What Is It Like to Be a Bat?" In *Mortal Questions*. Cambridge: Cambridge University Press, 1979.

Neuhouser, Frederick. *Fichte's Theory of Subjectivity*. Cambridge: Cambridge University Press, 1990.

———. "Freedom, Dependence, and the General Will." *Philosophical Review* 102 (1993): 363–95.

Nicholas of Cusa. *Of Learned Ignorance*. Translated by Fr. Germain Heron. London: Routledge and Kegan Paul, 1954.

O'Neill, Onora. "Vindicating Reason." In *The Cambridge Companion to Kant*, edited by Paul Guyer. Cambridge: Cambridge University Press, 1992.

Pelczynski, Z. A., ed. *Hegel's Political Philosophy: Problems and Perspectives*. Cambridge: Cambridge University Press, 1971.

———. *The State and Civil Society: Studies in Hegel's Political Philosophy*. Cambridge: Cambridge University Press, 1984.

Philonenko, Alexis. *La liberté humaine dans la philosophie de Fichte*. Paris: Vrin, 1966.

———. *L'ouevre de Fichte*. Paris: Vrin, 1984.

Pinkard, Terry. *Hegel's Dialectic: The Explanation of Possibility*. Philadelphia: Temple University Press, 1988.

———. *Hegel's "Phenomenology": The Sociality of Reason*. Cambridge: Cambridge University Press, 1994.

Pippin, Robert B. *Hegel's Idealism: The Satisfactions of Self-Consciousness*. New York: Cambridge University Press, 1989.

———. *Modernism as a Philosophical Problem: On the Dissatisfactions of European High Culture*. Cambridge, Mass.: Blackwell, 1991.

———. "You Can't Get There from Here: Transition Problems in Hegel's *Phenomenology of Spirit*." In *The Cambridge Companion to Hegel*, edited by Frederick C. Beiser. Cambridge: Cambridge University Press, 1993.

Prauss, Gerhold. *Kant und das Problem der Dinge an sich*. Bonn: Bouvier Verlag Herbert Grundman, 1974.

Putnam, Hilary. *Reason, Truth, and History*. Cambridge: Cambridge University Press, 1981.

Redding, Paul. "Hegel's Logic of Being and the Polarities of Presocratic Thought." *The Monist* 74 (1991): 438–56.

———. "Hermeneutic or Metaphysical Hegelianism? Kojève's Dilemma." *The Owl of Minerva* 22 (1991): 175–89.

Renaut, Alain. *Le Systèm du droit: Philosophie et droit dans la pensée de Fichte*. Paris: Presses Universitaires de France, 1986.

Richardson, Henry S. "The Logical Structure of *Sittlichkeit*: A Reading of Hegel's *Philosophy of Right*." *Idealistic Studies* 19 (1989): 62–78.

Riley, Patrick. "Introduction to the Reading of Kojève." *Political Theory* 9 (1981).

Rockmore, Thomas. "Fichtean Epistemology and Contemporary Philosophy." *Idealistic Studies* 19 (1988): 156–68.

———. *Hegel's Circular Epistemology*. Bloomington: Indiana University Press, 1986.

Rorty, Richard. *Consequences of Pragmatism*. Minneapolis: University of Minnesota Press, 1982.

———. *Contingency, Irony, and Solidarity*. Cambridge: Cambridge University Press, 1989.

———. *Philosophy and the Mirror of Nature*. Princeton: Princeton University Press, 1979.

Rosen, Stanley. *G. W. F. Hegel: An Introduction to the Science of Wisdom*. New Haven: Yale University Press, 1974.

Rousseau, Jean-Jacques. *Emile; or, On Education*. Translated by Allan Bloom. New York: Basic Books, 1979.

——. *The Social Contract and Discourses*. Translated by G. D. H. Cole. London: Dent, 1973.

Russell, Bertrand. *Human Knowledge*. New York: Simon and Schuster, 1948.

Schelling, F. W. J. *Ausgewahlte Schriften*. Frankfurt am Main: Suhrkamp, 1985.

——. *Bruno; or, On the Natural and the Divine Principle of Things*. Translated by Michael G. Vater. Albany: State University of New York Press, 1984.

——. *Ideas for a Philosophy of Nature as Introduction to the Study of This Science*. Translated by Errol E. Harris and Peter Heath, with an introduction by Robert Stern. Cambridge: Cambridge University Press, 1988.

——. *System of Transcendental Idealism*. Translated by Peter Heath. Introduction by Michael Vater. Charlottesville: University Press of Virginia, 1993.

——. *The Philosophy of Art*. Edited and translated by Douglas W. Stott. Minneapolis: University of Minnesota Press, 1989.

Schiller, Friedrich. *On the Aesthetic Education of Man*. Translated by E. M. Wilkinson and L. A. Willoughby. Oxford: Clarendon Press, 1967.

Schleiermacher, F. D. E. *Hermeneutics: The Handwritten Manuscripts*. Translated by James Duke and Jack Forstman. Missoula, Mont.: Scholars Press, 1977.

Schnädelbach, Hans. *Philosophy in Germany, 1831–1933*. Translated by E. Matthews. Cambridge: Cambridge University Press, 1984.

Searle, John. *Speech Acts*. Cambridge: Cambridge University Press, 1969.

Sellars, Wilfrid. "Philosophy and the Scientific Image of Man." In *Science, Perception, and Reality*. London: Routledge and Kegan Paul, 1963.

Siep, Ludwig. *Anerkennung als Prinzip der praktischen Philosophie: Untersuchungen zu Hegels Jenaer Philosophie des Geistes*. Freiburg: Alber Verlag, 1979.

Smith, Adam. *The Theory of Moral Sentiments*. Oxford: Oxford University Press, 1976.

——. *The Wealth of Nations*. Harmondsworth: Penguin Books, 1970.

Spinoza, Benedict de. *A Spinoza Reader: The "Ethics" and Other Works*. Edited and translated by Edwin Curley. Princeton: Princeton University Press, 1994.

Stekeler-Weithofer, Pirmin. *Hegels analytische Philosophie: Die Wissenschaft der Logik als kritische Theorie der Bedeutung*. Paderborn: Ferdinand Schöningh, 1992.

Taylor, Charles. *Hegel*. Cambridge: Cambridge University Press, 1975.

Theunissen, Michael. *Sein und Schein: Die kritische Funktion der Hegelschen Logik*. Frankfurt am Main: Suhrkamp Verlag, 1980.

Toulmin, Stephen. *Cosmopolis*. New York: Free Press, 1990.

Weeks, Andrew. *German Mysticism: From Hildegard of Bingen to Ludwig Wittgenstein*. Albany: State University of New York Press, 1993.

Werhane, Patricia H. *Adam Smith and His Legacy for Modern Capitalism*. Oxford: Oxford University Press, 1991.

White, Alan. *Absolute Knowledge: Hegel and the Problem of Metaphysics*. Athens: Ohio University Press, 1983.

Williams, Bernard. *Descartes: The Project of Pure Inquiry*. Harmondsworth: Penguin, 1978.

——. *Ethics and the Limits of Philosophy*. London: Fontana, 1985.

Williams, Robert R. *Recognition: Fichte and Hegel on the Other*. Albany: State University of New York Press, 1992.

Wittgenstein, Ludwig. *On Certainty*. Oxford: Blackwell, 1969.

——. *Philosophical Investigations*. Translated by G. E. M. Anscombe. Oxford: Blackwell, 1953.

Wood, Allen W. *Hegel's Ethical Thought*. Cambridge: Cambridge University Press, 1990.

Yovel, Yirmiyahu. *Spinoza and Other Heretics: The Adventures of Immanence*. Princeton: Princeton University Press, 1989.

Index

Circularity (*cont.*)
See also Hermeneutic circle
Civil society, 17, 174, 184, 187–91, 198–
217, 220, 223–25, 229–31, 237–38
Cloeren, Hermann J., 40n22
Coincidentia oppositorium. See Opposites,
coincidence, indifference, or unity of
Common sense (*sensus communis*), 10–11,
74–75, 87–88, 94, 95n36, 115
Common will. *See* Will, common
Communication, 16, 76, 79–81, 85–87,
114–18, 125, 130–32, 136, 141, 146,
164–65
role in Gadamer's hermeneutic philosophy, 44–46
role in Kant and post-Kantian philosophy, 8–12, 23, 24n10, n11, 39–40, 240
within the institutions of the state,
222–28
See also Reason and reasoning, communicative and linguistic grounds of
Communitarianism, 175, 182–83
Concept, the (*das Begriff*), 77n11, 145, 148,
156, 161–64, 194, 210, 224, 229–32,
243n7
Concepts and intuitions, 10, 65–70, 84,
91, 113, 126
Confession and forgiveness, 122, 131–32,
139, 174n9
Conscientiousness, the moral stance of,
130–31
Consciousness, 67–69, 72–89, 94, 97–99,
105n8, n9, 106–7, 111–13, 121–31,
176
common, everyday, or ordinary, 74–75,
124
doubleness of, 77–79
facts of, 75
forms or shapes of, 80–84, 98, 124, 136,
145–46, 191
in general, 8, 40, 77, 98
moral, 129–31, 139, 180
natural consciousness as protagonist of
the *Phenomenology*, 78–83
religious, 127, 132–42
representationalist conception of, 30,
53, 75
various senses of, 76–78
See also Intentionality; Subjectivity; Unhappy consciousness
Constitution, 229, 232, 239–40
Contract, 174–81, 187–88, 200, 220–21,
228, 234
See also Property
Contradiction, 111, 118n25, 244
within categories of thought, 146–47

within consciousness, 80, 86–87, 110–
11, 130
within processes of life or spirit, 108,
179, 183, 214–17, 228
within scientistic worldview, 91, 95–97
See also Opposites, coincidence, indifference, or unity of
Conviction versus persuasion, 9, 85, 226
Copernican:
cosmology, 1, 4–6, 24–25, 204
critique of immediacy, 4–7, 8–11, 97,
116, 150, 153, 225–26
move or turn, 3, 5–6, 13–15, 20n4, 29,
45, 89
revolution in philosophy, 1, 4–17, 51,
116, 198, 219, 240
science, 1, 4–7, 20n4, 88–89, 147, 204–5
Copernicanism, 4–7, 22–24, 39, 49–51,
219, 240
Copernicus, 6n7, 25
Corporations, 190–91, 220, 223–27
Cosmology, 1, 4–5, 25–27, 159
Counting as, 36–37, 81, 103–6, 173, 176,
185–86, 195–97
See also Hermeneutic as-structure
Craig, Edward, 19n1
Crime, 177–80, 200n28, 230–31
The Critical Journal of Philosophy, 63–64,
74, 94
Critique of Pure Reason, 4, 9–10, 40, 45, 67,
237, 245
contradictions within, 10n19, 51–52,
101

Death, 107, 111, 128, 131, 144, 161, 213
Demonstratives, logic of, 84–86
Dennett, Daniel, 108n13
Descartes, René, 11–12, 18–22, 26, 29–30,
75, 83, 87–88, 198
Desire, 67, 69, 99–100, 104–7, 109–12,
125–26, 181, 184–86, 212
in the context of the market, 188–89,
201–2, 211–17
desire for recognition, 120–21
in relation to the will, 170–71, 195n18,
220–21, 234–35, 239–40
sexual, 69, 161n27, 186
Determination, 87, 92, 102–6, 114n20,
176–77
Determinations:
of ethical life and the state, 183–85,
189–90, 224–31
ideal or thought determinations, 61–
62, 65–69, 146–48, 155, 158, 167,
193–94, 199–202
of right and will, 168–70, 188, 214, 235